D0935085

BLACK JACKS

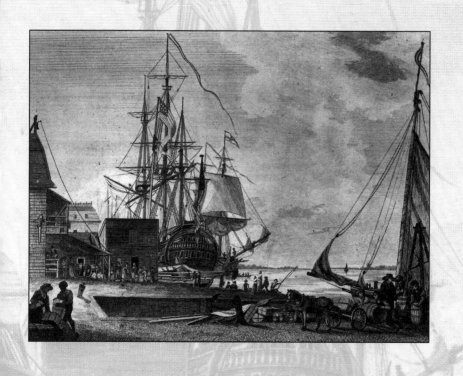

BLACK JACKS

African American Seamen in the Age of Sail

W. JEFFREY BOLSTER

HARVARD UNIVERSITY PRESS

CAMBRIDGE, MASSACHUSETTS

LONDON, ENGLAND

1997

Copyright © 1997 by the President and Fellows of Harvard College
All rights reserved
Printed in the United States of America

Designed by Marianne Perlak

Bob Marley and Peter Tosh, "Get Up, Stand Up,"
© 1974 Fifty-six Hope Road Music, Ltd., Odnil Music, Ltd., and Stuck on Music.
Reprinted by permission of PolyGram Music Publishing.
Langston Hughes, "The Negro Speaks of Rivers," from *Selected Poems*
by Langston Hughes, © 1926 by Alfred A. Knopf, Inc., and renewed 1954
by Langston Hughes. Reprinted by permission of Alfred A. Knopf, Inc.,
and Harold Ober Associates Incorporated.

Library of Congress Cataloging-in-Publication Data

Bolster, W. Jeffrey.
Black jacks : African American seamen in the age of sail /
W. Jeffrey Bolster.   p.   cm.
Includes bibliographical references (p.   ) and index.
ISBN 0-674-07624-9 (alk. paper)
1. Afro-American merchant mariners—History. 2. Sailing ships—
United States—History. I. Title.
VK221.B65   1997   387.5′08996073—dc20   96-44928

For Molly,
in remembrance and expectation
of all our voyages

PREFACE

HISTORIANS once strove for objectivity, veiling themselves in books whose sources alone were meant to tell the tale. Fashions change. Today, as scholars openly mediate among themselves, their readers, and their subjects (and strive to comprehend their own biases), confessionals seem more appropriate. It may be germane that I am not black; again, possibly germane that I am a seaman of sailing ships.

For ten years I followed the sea to many of the places explored here. Along the way I listened to stories told by veteran skippers and seamen, many of them black West Indians recounting with the longing of old men their youthful exploits—carrying cattle under sail from the eastern Caribbean to Santo Domingo; careening their schooners at Grenada; jamming a sloop hard on the wind from Virgin Gorda to St. Martin; and steering by the stars long before those islands had looming electric lights, and longer still before they had ever graced a souvenir t-shirt. One night in the 1970s, as we were rolling before the northeasterly trades on a passage to Cape Haitian, a shipmate aboard the schooner *Harvey Gamage* lent me the remarkable eighteenth-century autobiography of an accomplished slave sailor named Olaudah Equiano, who himself had once sailed that route. Where, I asked, was the bridge between historic slave sailors and the old black schoonermen I knew? How could one understand early black America without recognizing that plantations were connected to a larger world of black people, as well as to world markets, by black seamen? And given seaports' historic function as crossroads for people and ideas, what roles had sailors played in the formation of black America?

When I left the sea I returned to those questions about African Americans' maritime history. This book is my answer.

CONTENTS

Introduction: To Tell the Tale   *1*

1. The Emergence of Black Sailors in Plantation America   *7*

2. African Roots of Black Seafaring   *44*

3. The Way of a Ship   *68*

4. The Boundaries of Race in Maritime Culture   *102*

5. Possibilities for Freedom   *131*

6. Precarious Pillar of the Black Community   *158*

7. Free Sailors and the Struggle with Slavery   *190*

8. Toward Jim Crow at Sea   *215*

Tables   *233*

Notes   *241*

Acknowledgments   *297*

Index   *301*

ILLUSTRATIONS

Frontispiece
Arch Street Ferry, Philadelphia, 1800. Historical Society of Pennsylvania.

Following page 112

Cantino World Map, c. 1502. Biblioteca Estense Universitaria, Modena, Italy.
Negro's cannoes, carrying Slaves, on Board of Ships att Manfroe, engraving by J. Kip, c. 1700. From Awnsham Churchill's *A Collection of Voyages and Travels* (London, 1732), Boston Athenaeum.
Carrying Slaves to a Portuguese Brig in the River Bonny, by T. F. Birch, 1837. National Maritime Museum, London.
Eén der plantages van Jonas Witsen, by Dirck Valkenberg, c. 1707. Amsterdams Historisch Museum.
Ten Views in the Island of Antigua, by William Clark, 1823. Beinecke Lesser Antilles Collection, Hamilton College Library.
Sketch of a pettiauger in Georgia, by Philip Georg Freidrich van Reck, 1739. Det Kongelige Bibliotek, Copenhagen, Denmark.
Speightstown boat, by George Tobin, 1800. Mystic Seaport Museum, Mystic, Connecticut.
Sailors with cabin boy, by Rowlandson, 1785. Mary Evans Picture Library, London.
Cooking, by W. Heath. National Maritime Museum, London.
Lord George Graham in His Cabin, by William Hogarth, 1745. National Maritime Museum, London.
Joseph Johnson with the ship *Nelson* on his head, by John Thomas Smith, 1815. From *Vagabondiana, or Anecdotes of Mendicant Wanderers through the Streets of London* (London, 1817), Guildhall Library, Corporation of London.
Watson and the Shark, by John Singleton Copley, 1778. Gift of Mrs. George von Lengerke Meyer, courtesy of Museum of Fine Arts, Boston.
Portrait of a black sailor, anonymous, c. 1790. Private collection.
The Ship "Abula," Capt. John Dillingham, Entering the Port of Marseille, by Nicolay Cammilliere, 1806. Mystic Seaport Museum, Mystic, Connecticut.
Portrait of Olaudah Equiano, anonymous. Royal Albert Memorial Museum, Exeter, U.K.
John Jea, African Preacher of the Gospel, c. 1800. Frontispiece engraving from *The Life, history and unparalleled sufferings of John Jea, the African Preacher,* Bodleian Library, Oxford.
Detail of *John Updike's Marine Society Certificate, View of the Providence, Rhode Island, Waterfront,* anonymous, c. 1800. Courtesy of the Rhode Island Historical Society.
The Harbour of Charles Town, by Joseph F. W. DesBarres, late eighteenth century. From the Atlantic Neptune, National Maritime Museum, London.

Cudgelling Match between English and French Negroes, by Augustin Brunias, 1779. Courtauld Institute of Art, London.

Head-butting in a Venezuelan village. *Harper's Weekly*, August 15, 1874.

Portrait of a black sailor during the revolutionary war, anonymous. Courtesy of Dr. Alexander A. McBurney.

Drawing of Captain Paul Cuffe, by John Pole, engraving by Mason and Mass, c. 1812. Old Dartmouth Historical Society, New Bedford Whaling Museum, New Bedford, Massachusetts.

African Episcopal Church of St. Thomas, in Philadelphia, by Breton, Kennedy, and Lucas. Historical Society of Pennsylvania.

The Young Brutus, by Frederic Roux, c. 1830. Courtesy of Childs Gallery, Ltd., Boston, Massachusetts.

Massacre of the American Prisoners of War at Dartmoor, engraving by George C. Smith, 1815. Massachusetts Historical Society.

Richard Seaver, known in Dartmoor Prison as "King Dick." From Alexander Laing, *American Sail: A Pictorial History* (New York: E. P. Dutton and Company, 1961), p. 288.

Japanese watercolor scroll, 1845. Old Dartmouth Historical Society, New Bedford Whaling Museum, New Bedford, Massachusetts.

Stove Boat, watercolor by unknown whaleman. Old Dartmouth Historical Society, New Bedford Whaling Museum, New Bedford, Massachusetts.

Oil portrait of Captain Absalom Boston. Nantucket Historical Association, Nantucket, Massachusetts.

George Henry. From George Henry, *Life of George Henry, Together with a Brief History of the Colored People in America* (1894; reprint: New York, 1971), inset within detail of Fielding Lucas, Jr.'s, chart of Chesapeake Bay, 1832. Maryland State Archives.

Robert Smalls, the pilot of the gunboat *Planter*. Engraving from *Harper's Weekly*, 1862, courtesy of U.S. Naval Historical Center.

The Gunboat "Planter." Engraving from *Harper's Weekly*, 1862, courtesy of U.S. Naval Historical Center.

Farragut in the "Hartford" at Mobile Bay, August 5, 1864. Beverly R. Robinson Collection, U.S. Naval Academy, Annapolis, Maryland.

Lithograph of the clipper ship *Contest*. Peabody Essex Museum, Salem, Massachusetts.

Crew of a Union navy ship. Lothrop Papers Photo Album, Massachusetts Historical Society.

Negro Boys on the Quayside, David Norslup, c. 1865, oil on panel. In the Collection of the Corcoran Gallery of Art, Museum Purchase, Gallery Fund and William A. Clark Fund, 1960.

Maps

The Atlantic world in the age of sail   *xii-xiii*
The Caribbean   *8*
Coastal West Africa in the eighteenth century   *46*

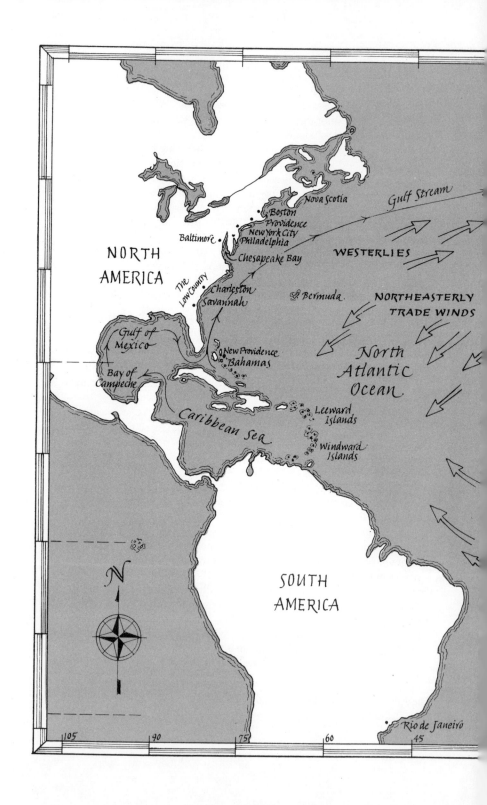

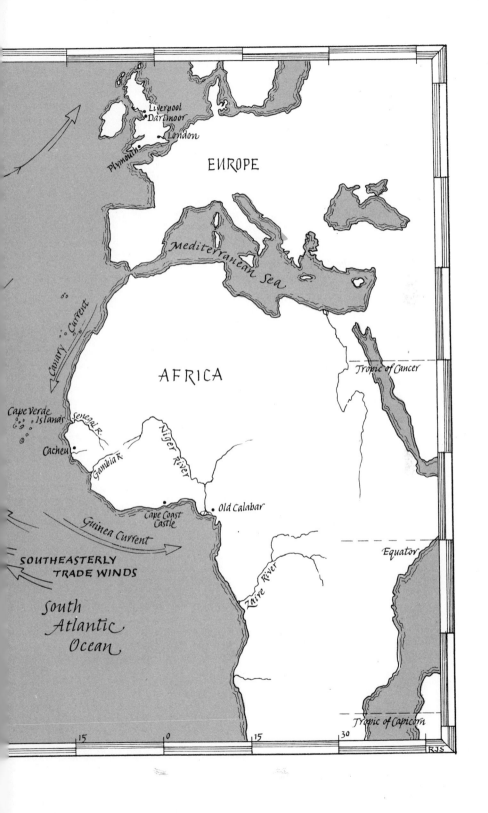

Liverpool
Dartmoor
London
Plymouth

EUROPE

Mediterranean Sea

Canary Current

AFRICA

Tropic of Cancer

Cape Verde
Islands
Senegal R.
Cacheu

Niger River

Gambia R.

Old Calabar

Cape Coast
Castle

Guinea Current

SOUTHEASTERLY
TRADE WINDS

South
Atlantic
Ocean

Equator

Zaire River

Tropic of Capricorn

15   0   15   30

RJS

INTRODUCTION:
TO TELL THE TALE

Half the story has never been told.

BOB MARLEY AND PETER TOSH,
"Get Up Stand Up" (1974)

"THOSE BEAUTIFUL VESSELS, robed in white, and so delightful to the eyes of freemen," wrote Frederick Douglass of the sailing ships he saw daily during his boyhood slavery along the Chesapeake Bay, "were to me so many shrouded ghosts." Douglass contrasted the ships, "loosed from [their] moorings, and free," with his own condition— "fast in my chains, and . . . a slave!" And he swore, "This very bay shall yet bear me into freedom." As a skilled but still-enslaved ship caulker in Baltimore, Douglass worked shoulder to shoulder with black and white sailors and, in his own words, "knew a ship from stem to stern, and from keelson to crosstrees, and could talk sailor like an 'old salt.'" No stranger to waterfront tales of hardship, brutality, and deprivation at sea, he nonetheless persisted in his metaphorical view of ships as "freedom's swift-winged angels," because, unlike the white men who spoke movingly of the "slavery" aboard ship, he knew real slavery firsthand.[1]

As it turned out, Douglass employed a seafaring subterfuge instead of a ship to escape his chains. Rigging himself out in "a red shirt and tarpaulin hat and black cravat, tied in sailor fashion, carelessly and loosely about [the] neck," he borrowed a Seaman's Protection Certificate from a liberty-loving black sailor and brazenly struck out for Philadelphia by train. He succeeded that September day in 1838 because free black seamen were then so common as to draw few second looks.[2]

As American shipping expanded during the early nineteenth century, employing more than 100,000 men per year, black men like Douglass's benefactor filled about one-fifth of sailors' berths. Black Jacks had long been prominent on quays around the Atlantic. Eighteenth-century black leaders frequently rolled out of the forecastle, a worldly origin eclipsed by the subsequent dominance of the pulpit as the wellspring of black organization. Yet no meaningful African American maritime history has linked prominent mariners like Captain Paul Cuffe, the driving force behind the first black-led back-to-Africa movement, and Denmark Vesey, the mastermind of the largest slave conspiracy in South Carolina's history. More anonymous black sailors have simply sunk from sight, like the slave aboard the Virginian sloop *Jean* in 1779, ritually scarified with "Guinea marks on each of his temples"—reminders of having come of age in Africa—and the free man who told a slave in Savannah during the 1830s "that his home was in New York; that he had a wife and several children there, but that he followed the sea for a livelihood and knew no other mode of life."[3]

In lieu of these politically astute and worldly black sailors, an image of manacled ancestors crammed together aboard slave ships has triumphed as the association of African Americans with the sea. It reinforces whites' belief that blacks were acted on, rather than acting; that blacks aboard ship sailed as commodities rather than seamen. Yet until the Civil War black sailors were central to African Americans' collective sense of self, economic survival, and freedom struggle—indeed central to the very creation of black America.

In 1850 the black abolitionist William Wells Brown grasped the ambiguities of ships within the collective African American imagination, painting several into his *Original Panoramic Views of the Scenes in the Life of an American Slave*. The fifth of his twenty-four-scene traveling canvas depicted the brig *Creole* and the schooners *Pearl* and *Franklin*—slave ships aboard which triumphant slaves mutinied successfully for freedom, or on which other slaves repeated the shackled passage of their ancestors as they were shipped to markets in the expanding cotton kingdom. If vessels have long represented the union of opposites to all human beings—slavery and freedom, exploitation and exhilaration, separation and reunion—these antipodes have been amplified notoriously for black Americans. Brown honored that. But he neglected black sailors.[4]

Relatively fortunate for black men of the time, seamen of African descent nevertheless navigated a tortuous channel through the North Atlantic. Beset by the deeply felt oppression of race and slavery, by commercial capitalism's sustained exploitation of maritime workers, and by the dangers of the deep during an era of frail wooden ships and uncertain navigational reckoning, black seamen struggled valiantly to free themselves and the race. A black veteran sea-cook remembered facing "the most dreadful whirlwinds and hurricanes," enduring forty-two thirsty days adrift on an unnavigable hulk, and suffering "ill treatment" at the hands of white seamen. "They used to flog, beat, and kick me about the same as if I had been a dog; . . . and sometimes they would call me a Jonah." Yet he persisted for years at seafaring, one of the few occupations open to a free man of color in 1806, because it allowed him to spread the "Methodist evangelicalism, revolutionary egalitarianism, and . . . nascent black nationalism" through which he defined himself and the black diaspora.[5]

Individual slaves routinely drew on maritime work to take charge of their lives and to communicate with distant blacks. Born on Maryland's eastern shore and "well known there and in Baltimore," Samuel Johnson matured in the heady days of the American Revolution, when Virginia's royal governor, Lord Dunmore, extended the promise of freedom to slaves who deserted to the British. Johnson capitalized on wartime turmoil, making several voyages to the West Indies as a free sailor before his re-enslavement in Philadelphia. The wily Johnson ran away again in 1785. The last his master knew, the strolling sailor was telling some people "that he is free, and others that he has a master in Baltimore, and is going home to inform him of his being wrecked down the bay, carrying him a parcel of goods." Undoubtedly, the freedom-loving Johnson talked with blacks in Virginia, Philadelphia, and the West Indies about more weighty matters during that revolutionary age ablaze with "liberty."[6]

Whether looking for a ship in Philadelphia, loading hogsheads of sugar into moses boats on Jamaica's north coast, sheeting home the mainsail aboard a rice-laden pettiauger on the Waccamaw River, or stewing salt beef in the smokey caboose of a London-bound tobacco ship, free and enslaved black sailors established a visible presence in every North Atlantic seaport and plantation roadstead between 1740 and 1865. As winds and currents kept the ocean itself from stasis, so seafaring men of color stirred black society and shaped Atlantic maritime culture.

Black seafaring thus had social and psychological ramifications far beyond the workplace. In the universe of southern and Caribbean plantation slaves, ships and boats were a pipeline to freedom and a refuge for slaves on the lam. Worldly and often multilingual slave sailors regularly subverted plantation discipline. Among northern free blacks, struggling during the critical first two generations after the American Revolution to create a footprint for freedom, seafaring became one of the most common male occupations. Maritime slaves bought before the Revolution to enhance captains' status and reduce their payrolls had established that precedent, as had those slaves who negotiated with masters the right to hire themselves for voyages. A postwar shipping boom that stretched into the early nineteenth century had created the jobs free blacks so desperately needed. Maritime wages provided crucial support for black families and underwrote organizations such as churches and benevolent societies through which black America established an institutional presence and a voice. Rakes and renegades certainly roamed the waterfront, but many sailors of African descent were prominent figures in free black communities then angling for respectability. The keeper of a boardinghouse for black sailors referred to "one of the Sons of *Neptune*" as "every inch a *man*."[7]

If seafaring in the age of sail remained a contemptible occupation for white men, characterized by a lack of personal independence and reliance on paltry wages, it became an occupation of opportunity for slaves and recent freedmen. Seamen wrote the first six autobiographies of blacks published in English before 1800. Finding their voices in the swirling currents of international maritime labor, seafaring men fired the opening salvo of the black abolitionist attack and fostered creation of a corporate black identity. Blacks joined white seamen in a common effort to balk the captains and merchants who abused them—although black sailors knew full well that race rarely disappeared, even among shipmates. Actively contributing to the Atlantic maritime culture shared by all seamen, African Americans were at times outsiders within it. That culture created an ambiguous world in which black men simultaneously could assert themselves within their occupation and find with white sailors common ground transcending race, while also being subject to vicious racist acts.

Opportunities or not, shipping-out posed unavoidable problems for men of color. In 1780 seven African Americans from Bristol County, Massachusetts, petitioned the revolutionary legislature of that state, claiming that "we have not an equal chance with white people neither by Sea nur Land." Eight years later another group of Massachusetts blacks protested the dangers free black men faced of being kidnapped into slavery from shipboard jobs: "Hence it is that maney of us who are good seamen are oblidge to stay at home thru fear."[8] Yet discrimination and kidnapping, as blacks painfully knew, were also hazards of shore life. Neither social threats like these nor the violence of the ocean itself kept African American men from following the sea until well into the nineteenth century.

Maritime work not only provided wages and allowed widely dispersed black people a means of communication, but also affected the process through which free people of color shaped their identities. Seafaring addressed squarely the duality of being black and American. Beginning in 1796, the federal government issued Seamen's Protection Certificates to merchant mariners, defining them as "citizens" of the United States, a nicety to which African American leaders pointedly referred during debates on blacks' citizenship status. Black sailors interacted regularly with customs collectors at home and consuls abroad on the basis of their citizenship, and carried papers in their deep sailors' pockets incontrovertibly demonstrating it to wives, sweethearts, and friends. Many expressed a radical African American patriotism, demanding black inclusion (not assimilation) in the United States. Seafaring left other marks. Characterized by long male absences and female-headed households, maritime rhythms became inextricably entwined in the family life, community structure, and sense of self of northern blacks in the early republic.

In 1740, when this tale begins, deep-sea maritime labor in the

Anglo-American world was largely white, and virtually all seafaring blacks were slaves. By 1803 black men (mostly free) filled about 18 percent of American seamen's jobs. The tide then turned at mid-century. With American Emancipation, when this tale ends, a new and distinct constellation of forces relegated maritime work to a bit part in black life. Freedmen in 1865 could not turn to an expanding maritime industry with a history of color toleration, as had northern black males following the Revolution, because the American merchant marine was in decline. White southerners, moreover, were determined to keep blacks on the land to make a crop. And mid-century changes in waterfront hiring practices already had begun to squeeze African Americans out of the maritime labor force.

Racist exclusion did not keep all blacks from the sea after Reconstruction. There were explorers like Matthew Henson, who shipped out during the 1880s and sought the North Pole with Commodore Robert Peary in 1909; visionaries like Marcus Garvey, who founded the Black Star Steamship Line in 1919; and writers like Langston Hughes, who voyaged to Africa in 1923 and called his autobiography *The Big Sea*. But shipboard work became less significant to black America as a whole after Emancipation. Before 1865 seafaring had been crucial to blacks' economic survival, liberation strategies, and collective identity-formation. Sailors linked far-flung black communities and united plantations with urban centers. Although black sailors' tale has never been told, the rise and fall of African American seafaring in the age of sail was central to the creation of black America.

1. THE EMERGENCE OF
BLACK SAILORS
IN PLANTATION
AMERICA

I am not a ward of America; I am one of the
first Americans to arrive on these shores.

JAMES BALDWIN,
The Fire Next Time (1963)

ON A DECEMBER DAY IN 1747 Briton Hammon, a slave to
Major John Winslow of Marshfield, Massachusetts, walked out of town
with, as he put it, "an Intention to go a voyage to sea." Tucked into
the sandy bight of Cape Cod Bay, some thirty miles south of Boston,
and reeking of tidal flats and Stockholm tar, Marshfield was a minor
star in the galaxy of Britain's commercial empire, and only a short
walk from Plymouth, where Hammon shipped himself the next day
"on board of a Sloop, Capt. John Howland, Master, bound to Jamaica
and the Bay" of Campeche for logwood. Experienced at shipboard
work, as were approximately 25 percent of the male slaves in coastal
Massachusetts during the 1740s, Hammon had not run away. But like
all black people in early America who wrought freedom where they
could, nurtured it warily, and understood it as partial and ambiguous
at best, Hammon seized the moment. Prompted by memories of
luxuriant Jamaican alternatives to sleety nor'easters, he negotiated the

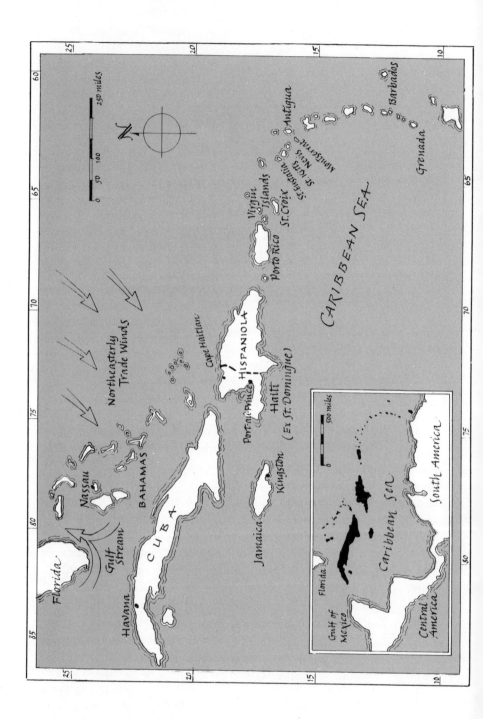

Florida

Havana

Gulf Stream

CUBA

Nassau

BAHAMAS

Northeasterly Trade Winds

Cape Haittian

HISPANIOLA

Port au Prince

Haïti (Ex St. Domingue)

Kingston

Jamaica

Porto Rico

Virgin Islands

St. Croix

St. Kitts
Nevis
Montserrat

Antigua

Barbados

Grenada

CARIBBEAN SEA

250 miles

0   50   100

Gulf of Mexico

Florida

Caribbean Sea

Central America

South America

0   500 miles

right for a voyage when his master Winslow's frozen fields were untillable, and earned a brief sojourn in the black tropics—the productive heartland of the Anglo-American plantation system. Winslow, of course, pocketed most of the wages.[1]

Hammon's *Narrative of the Uncommon Sufferings, and Surprising Deliverance of Briton Hammon, a Negro Man*, the first voyage account published by a black American, indicates the extent to which enslaved sailors and nominally free men of African descent rode economic and military currents to every corner of the eighteenth-century Atlantic world. Hammon's voyage launched him on a twelve-year odyssey embracing shipwreck, Indian captivity in Florida, imprisonment and enslavement in Cuba (where he toted the Catholic bishop's canopied sedan chair and "endeavour'd three times to make my escape"), Royal Navy service under fire against the French during the Seven Years War, hospitalization in Greenwich, dockwork in London, and a near voyage to Africa as cook aboard a slaver. Hammon, his black shipmates, and those with whom they conversed were citizens of the world.

Men of African descent had sailed the Atlantic from the time Europeans began their piratical forays and plantation settlements, mustering in the ranks of Columbus, Balboa, and Cortez at the birth of the Atlantic system. Other Africans, including mariners, had traveled to Europe even earlier, both as slaves and as free men. A Venetian oil painting of black waterfront workers in 1495 suggests that no fifteenth-century Mediterranean seaman would have been startled by Africans on the quayside. By 1624, the year British planters settled Barbados, a black seafaring tradition had taken root within the embryonic Anglo-American world. "John Phillip, a negro Christened in England 12 yeers since," told the Council of Virginia in 1624 "that beinge in a ship with Sir Henry Maneringe, they tooke A spanish shipp aboute Cape Sct Mary." In 1625 a "negro caled by the name of brase" helped Captain Jones work his ship from the West Indies to Virginia. The historian Ira Berlin has labeled men like Phillip and Brase "Atlantic creoles"—people of African descent who originated neither in the heart of Africa nor in colonial America, but in the expanding commercial world linking the two, black men who often arrived in America not in chains, but as sailors or linguists on commercial ships. "Atlantic creoles" were as accustomed to the foredeck as to the field.

They faced fewer liabilities because of color than would their black descendants in the New World slave societies that developed later, and in which race became even more cramping.[2]

During the middle of the seventeenth century, western European governments stepped up state-sponsored support of private enterprise, creating a highly profitable Atlantic plantation system built on "European capital, American land, African slave labor," and maritime transportation. Unwilling plantation laborers in Virginia, Barbados, and elsewhere produced commodities such as sugar, tobacco, coffee, and rum for which the wealthy, and later the workers, of Europe developed insatiable cravings. Plantations and ships were peas in the pod of commercial capitalism, separate yet dependent on each other. No other part of the global economy relied as heavily as New World plantations on maritime transportation to import supplies, people, and food, and to export the crop. Colonial plantations transformed the palates of European consumers, redefining as staples the sweetness and smoke that once had been luxuries. Plantations were also central to the "Commercial Revolution" that eroded England's customary agricultural economy, and set into motion wrenching new forms of labor organization on both sides of the Atlantic—dominated by slavery on an unprecedented scale.[3]

European statesmen then assumed that the natural order of things was a world in which nation-states competed for what Sir Josiah Child called "profit and power," not only with force of arms, but through overseas production and trade. As feudalism gave way to capitalism in Europe, privatization of various means of production, notably land, allowed entrepreneurs to accumulate capital. That spurred commercial growth. Legal justifications for the appropriation of producers' surpluses conditioned merchants to think less of that capital's human cost than of its investment potential, often in the plantations in which slaves, sailors, and slave-sailors played such important roles.[4]

The sanction of profit, the severance of mutual obligations between employer and employee, the international influence of racial thought, and the availability of slaves in African markets all seemed to condone the immoral practice whereby certain white individuals in England (along with those in the colonizing states of France, Holland, Portugal, Denmark, and Spain) could attain property rights to other individuals—specifically blacks who worked in plantation colonies. This presence of slavery within capitalism, explains Sidney Mintz, "gave to the New World situation its special, unusual, and ruthless character." Saluted by coldly admiring eighteenth-century Englishmen as "the mainspring of the machine which sets every wheel in motion," the trans-Atlantic slave trade peaked from about 1760 to 1780, when a torrent of approximately 65,500 Africans arrived annually in the Americas, a fraction of the approximately 10,000,000 who arrived in chains. The nefarious traffic did not cease until the final smuggler made landfall during the late nineteenth century, long after African Americans had forged themselves into a new people.[5]

Heroic in proportion and tragic in its human particulars, the Commercial Revolution's plantation system was a pan-Atlantic phenomenon. Ships and sailors not only followed the setting sun in a linear track from the Old World to the New, bringing capitalism and captive Africans to the Americas, but continuously cross-pollinated an emerging Atlantic world of new ecological, social, and racial relationships. Black sailors emerged from the confluence of forced black labor and maritime transportation that defined the plantation system. As conduits between the new centers of black population on the western rim of the ocean, sailors helped define and connect a new black Atlantic world.

Seamen recognized a daunting kinship between vessels and plantations. Both manifested harshly exploitative elements of feudalism and capitalism, combining in one workplace the virtually unchecked personal authority of the feudal lord and the impersonal appropriation of workers' labor so fundamental to capitalism. One captain, white sailors complained in 1726, treated them as if they were "bought Servants"; another "refused to Supply them with a Necessary quantity of Provisions," reducing them "to the Utmost Extreamity." Beatings to enforce discipline aboard the sloop *William* in 1729 "did Occassion Great Effusion of Blood." Yet seafaring nevertheless appeared desirable to black males whose alternative in the European-dominated Atlantic world remained debilitating field labor with heavy hoes or billhooks and the substantially more savage discipline of laws designed to regulate slaves. Freedom beckoned—inconsistent and illusory though it became aboard the tempestuous ships of an expanding commercial economy.[6]

By the late seventeenth century, enslaved seamen worked in even predominantly white provinces like Massachusetts. In Boston in 1690, "a Negro man, Sambo by name (being young, strong, & able & of very good health)," was shipped by his owners on board a ketch bound for Barbados at "thirty shillings by the month certain, & more if any higher wages were given to any foremastman that should after be shipped." Clearly Sambo could dexterously "hand, reef, and steer," the essence of the seaman's craft. Skill, moreover, allowed a black sailor to hold his own among fellow tars, even while facing peremptory challenges. Strolling upon Boston's Fort Hill in 1694, a self-confident black man who belonged "to the Sorlings Frigat" struck up a conversation with two white youths, and offered to buy one's earring for a piece of eight. With "two pieces of eight and a piece of gold abt the bigness of an English Crown" that he said he "got . . . privateering," the sailor ashore with "ready money" epitomized seafaring liberality and affronted whites' image of black subservience. "Sirrah come along with me," crowed a white man in pursuit, before subjecting the privateersman to the indignity of a search.[7]

Nevertheless, paternalistic New England masters allowed maritime slaves certain leeway. Although John Mico carefully instructed the captain to whom he hired his slave Jeffrey for a voyage to Barbados and London in 1703 to "restrain and keep him . . . as if he were your owne," he also explained that Jeffrey "may have a mind to see my father and Brother [in London], if he should hint so much to You, let Ye Black Gentleman have his Desire." Despite white constraints, the small community of seventeenth- and early-eighteenth-century black seafaring men found a degree of personal freedom in the regimented milieu of the ship alien to most plantation slaves, and a cosmopolitanism denied even to many urban blacks. If any slaves still wore the mantle of quasi-autonomy once characteristic of "Atlantic creoles," it was sailors.[8]

Resentful slaves ashore hungered for that mite of liberty. Pompey, a slave who fled his New England master in 1724, successfully hid in the firewood aboard Captain Moffatt's *Morehampton*. Although Moffatt swore that "sd Negro was altogether useless aboard ship," Pompey sailed to Oporto, Portugal, where he again outfoxed the exasperated Moffatt "and secretly conveyed himself to Spain," before coming home to New England with Captain Gilley. The choice to return may well

have been his own. Moreover, with two trans-Atlantic passages under his belt, Pompey had acquired skills useful for future voyages—
authorized or not.[9]

One higher-stakes alternative to such limited freedom-seeking
within the commercial system then existed. Bold black seamen joined
disgruntled white soldiers, sailors, and servants confederating as pirates along sun-drenched Caribbean sea-lanes. Contemptuous of the
authority that had always repressed them, truculent as game cocks,
and unencumbered by attachments except to like-minded comrades,
these "desperate Rogues" created an egalitarian, if ephemeral, social
order that rejected imperial society's hierarchy and forced labor. Buccaneering tempted black seamen with visions of invincibility, with
dreams of easy money and the idleness such freedom promised, and
with the promise of a life unfettered by the racial and social ideology
central to the plantation system. Unattached black men operating in
the virtually all-male world of the "Brotherhood of the Coast" realized
those yearnings to a degree, but also found abuse and exploitation, as
well as mortal combat and pursuit.[10]

By 1716 the Bahama Islands were referred to, with cause, as a "nest
of Pirates." New Providence became their headquarters, much to the
dismay of local planters, who lamented that the pirates passed time
"plundering the Inhabitants, burning their Houses, and Ravishing
their Wives." The few slaves on New Providence capitalized on this
destabilization, becoming "very impudent and insulting." Some fled
to the buccaneers. From 1716 to 1726, the heyday of large-scale Euro-
pean-directed piracy, some five thousand buccaneers sailed "under the
banner of King Death." From a theater of operations rooted in unin-
habited Caribbean harbors, the sea robbers "dispers't into severall
parts of the World." Most were white, and most turned pirate when
other pirates captured the merchant ships on which they sailed. No
accurate numbers of black buccaneers exist, although the impression
is that they were more numerous than the proportion of black sailors
in commercial or naval service at that time.[11]

Few blacks in the early-eighteenth-century Atlantic world had any
choice but slavery, and little room within slavery for the sheet anchor
of family. Partially socialized to the ways of Europeans, more so, at
least, than many plantation slaves, black sailors welcomed the oppor-

tunity to give up slavery in legitimate commerce for a share of spoils as pirates. When Edward Teach, better known as Blackbeard, fought to his death at Ocracoke Inlet in 1718, five of his eighteen-man crew were men of color. According to the Governor's Council of Virginia, the five blacks were "equally concerned with the rest of the Crew in the same Acts of Piracy." One of Teach's men was remembered as "a resolute Fellow, a Negroe, whom he had bred up" and trusted. A few years earlier, the pirate captain Lewis had recruited a crew in the West Indies ultimately numbering eighty men. "He took out of his Prizes what he had occasion for, 40 able Negroe Sailors, and a white Carpenter," wrote Daniel Defoe. Some men volunteered; others were forced. Lewis began his depredations with a canoe and six comrades near Havana. They seized a Spanish pettiauger (a modified dugout), and with that captured a turtling sloop, and kept leap-frogging from one vessel to another yet larger until they took "a large pink-built ship bound from Jamaica to the Bay of Campeachy."[12]

No first-hand testimony exists to document blacks' attraction to piracy. But pirate captains like Bellamy spoke straight to the oppressed. "Damn ye, you are a sneaking Puppy," he is reputed to have snarled at a captured merchant captain in 1717, "and so are all those who will submit to be governed by Laws which rich men have made for their own Security, for the cowardly Whelps have not the Courage otherwise to defend what they get by their Knavery . . . They vilify us, the Scoundrels do, when there is only this Difference, they rob the Poor under the Cover of Law, forsooth, and we plunder the Rich under the protection of our own Courage." Reinforcing this ideological appeal was pure pragmatism. "In an honest Service," quipped Captain Bartholomew Roberts, "there is thin Commons, low Wages, and hard Labour; in this, Plenty and Satiety, Pleasure and Ease, Liberty and Power . . . when all the Hazard that is run for it, at worst, is only a sower Look or two at choking. No, *a merry Life and a short one,* shall be my motto." Piracy substantially multiplied a black sailor's immediate freedoms. The promise of "Pleasure and Ease," even if passing, appealed to bold men degraded by extortion and race.[13]

Pirates also elected skilled seamen of color to positions of authority. "There is a principal Officer among the Pyrates, called the Quarter-Master, of the Men's own choosing," explained Defoe. Acting as a "civil

Magistrate," the quartermaster ensured that necessaries were distributed equally, and that no man—including the captain—got more than his share. In keeping with their high post, quartermasters often led boarding parties or took charge of captured vessels. When Captain William Kidd anchored off Gardners' Island, New York, in 1699, two sloops spent several days lying near to him, one of whose "Mate was a little black man . . . who, as it was said, had been formerly Captain Kidd's Quarter Master." In 1696 a runaway West Indian slave named Abraham Samuel sailed as quartermaster on the pirate ship *John and Rebecca* during a voyage from the Caribbean to the Indian Ocean. Later, in an odd twist of fate, he became "king" of Fort Dauphin on Madagascar, with slaves, wives, and trading profits at his disposal. In "Honest service" a skilled black sailor had little authority, but among freebooters a man like Abraham Samuel could be popularly elected to a position of honor contingent upon his strength, charisma, and wits.[14]

Yet most still lacked the stomach "to go upon the Account." "A Negro man named Francisco" charged with piracy was acquitted by a special Court of Admiralty held in Boston in 1724, "it appearing to Said Court he was taken out of a Vessell on the high seas from one Capt. Lupton & was a forced man." Francisco had reason to pause. For all their equality and fraternalism, pirates played a high-stakes game in which violent death—their own and their victims'—loomed large. Between 1716 and 1726 some four hundred to six hundred pirates were "pushed off" on gallows erected by imperial officials and vengeful colonists intent on responding to terror with terror. But Francisco may have held back for other reasons.[15]

As welcoming as most white pirates were to skilled black sailors, in part because they "entertain'd so contemptible a Notion of Landsmen," sea robbers were not race-blind. None of the renowned pirate captains at the turn of the eighteenth century was a black man, and pirates generally sold captured slaves with the rest of their plunder. Many kept slaves aboard ship for pumping and other heavy work disdained by sailors who wished to impersonate "gentlemen." Captain Edward Low reputedly extended no welcome to black sailors at all, duplicitously enslaving those who attempted to join. Pirates, moreover, often forced themselves on slave women, leaving "prudent" women alone. In 1683 one crew traded a ship for a slaver with sixty African women, departing on what they hoped would be a saturnalia aboard the renamed *Batchelor's Delight.* To many white pirates the majority of blacks were pawns, workers, objects of lust, or a source of ready cash. If "able Negro sailors" like Abraham Samuel or Kidd's quartermaster were welcome in the Brotherhood of the Coast, it was with the understanding that black and white pirates preyed on black and white victims. Their response to the plantation system's degradation was at once considered and impetuous, political and opportunistic.[16]

Survivors kept alive memories of that era well into the eighteenth century, igniting in young black men a desire to get to sea. William Williams, an Englishman who spent at least five years at sea during the 1740s (and who, according to the well-known painter Benjamin West, "spoke the Negro and Carrib tongue"), recollected in his autobiographical novel, *Mr. Penrose: The Journal of Penrose, Seaman,* "frequent converse with an Old Negro man, a native of the Island of Jamaica, who in his younger days had been well acquainted with many of the Buckneers, sail'd with them, and knew many of their haunts." The "White headed old fellow," who "had come in by the Queens Act of Grace and then followed Piloting or went out to hunt after wrecks about the coast," conversed readily about his youth, as old men are wont to do.[17]

Organized piracy was a spent force by 1726, although individual black seamen gravitated to maritime marauding for years. A mulatto named Stewart and three white shipmates seized the schooner *Amity* off Virginia in 1785 and, with a flourish indicating awareness of an earlier era, signed an oath to "Perform on a Cruce In Defense of Our Selves and Against all Other Nation and Nations." The conspirators collectively agreed that any individual who broke their covenant "shall Be Put to Death or any Punishment that the Rest Shal think they Justley Deserv." Within a month they had recruited two black men for their cruise, though it came to naught when they were apprehended in Massachusetts.[18]

Piracy shaped the lives of far fewer mariners of color than did more prosaic forms of slavery. Maritime slavery played an indispensable role in the plantation complex, notably in coastal boats, but increasingly in deep-sea work as well as the eighteenth century wore on. It constituted one aspect of the New World slave system that scholars now recognize as having been diversified well beyond agricultural work. Indeed, once established, slavery insinuated itself into virtually every occupation in plantation societies, and into many occupations elsewhere, even in far-flung corners of the empire like Marshfield, Massachusetts. But whether they worked in agriculture, domestic service, or seafaring, slaves collectively shaped evolving African American belief systems and behaviors in tension with the labor they performed. As the plantation complex became established, black sailors worked in virtually every aspect of the colonial maritime trades, and their lives and labors became central to the formation of Afro-America.

Caribbean economies and demography dictated that maritime slavery exist there in more diverse forms than anywhere else in the Atlantic world. Vital to the transportation of sugar and to naval protection of the plantation system, ships and boats provided one of Caribbean slave societies' most porous boundaries. Across it flowed goods, ideas, individuals, and aesthetics, contributing to the hybridity of Afro–West Indian culture. "Divers Felonies and Frauds have been committed," read an Antiguan statute in 1773 attempting to seal that boundary, "by Means of Boats, commonly called Bum Boats, being permitted to trade with the Ships and Vessels in the Harbour and Road of St. John." But try as they might, legislators could not stop enslaved boatmen from interacting with black and white seamen.[19]

Most planters envisioned an ideally ordered society as one in which blacks would be kept not only out of skilled trades and retailing but out of boats. Boat work made slaves "insolent" and "independent," introduced them to seamen, and kept them aware of shipping news. For the bold, it provided a conduit out of the colony. As early as 1700, Antigua's assembly noted that "Taverns, victualling-houses, Punch-houses, Sloops, Shallops, and Boats [that] belong to this Island, are for the most part managed by Negro Slaves, to the great Discouragement of White Men who want Employment." The Jamaican legislature's "Deficiency Laws" required a specific number of hired or indentured white servants to be kept proportionally to the number of blacks in certain trades. One white man "for every boat, wherry, and canoe; and three-fourths of the crews on board of droguers or coasting-vessels . . . to be white men," is how Edward Long described the requirement, though he noted simultaneously that by the 1760s planters had given up all pretense of complying. Slaves virtually monopolized many maritime trades, and white Jamaicans simply paid their fines, turning what had been a measure for social control into a revenue act. According to the Leeward Islands' Governor Ralph Payne in 1774, coastal shipping (touted by mercantilist theoreticians as the "nursery of seamen") was dominated there by slaves. In every island colony, ship-dependent economies and predominantly black populations combined to provide certain slaves with constant access to the surrounding sea.[20]

Fragmentary sources preclude exact knowledge of what percentage of the male slave population in eighteenth-century Caribbean colonies followed the sea. Edward Long estimated in 1773 that about 15 percent of Jamaica's 170,000 slaves were "tradesmen, sailors, fishermen &c. in domestic employments." Of these it seems likely that several thousand were mariners, wharf workers, and fishermen—roughly 3 to 4 percent of the male slaves in what was then a mature sugar economy. Clearly, most of these men worked along the busy Jamaican coast, although some rode the Gulf Stream to North America or bucked the Atlantic to Europe. A tally on Nevis in 1765 counted 500 slaves in fishing and other trades, and a rough approximation suggests that fishermen, boatmen, and sailors constituted about 3 percent of Nevis's total slave population that year. These enslaved West Indian mariners worked within an occupational structure encompassing regular deep-sea sailors, occasional deep-sea sailors, boatmen, fishermen, and "wharf Negroes." Mixing with them were black runaways aboard ship, whether with or without prior seafaring skills. Some were hired, others were paying for or working their passage, yet others had been inveigled aboard by captains intent on selling them elsewhere. Like the foam rising to the top of a boiled pot, this small percentage of the male West Indian slave population provided island slaves with a crucial point of contact with black and white worlds beyond their shores.[21]

The degree to which slaves worked in maritime pursuits varied dramatically from colony to colony, as suggested by slave registrations in 1834, at the very end of the British West Indian slave era. In agricultural Jamaica, only 1.5 percent of male slaves worked on wharves or at shipping in 1834; in the Bahamas archipelago, almost 16 percent of male slaves did. Barbados, like Jamaica, had a mature sugar economy, and less than 3 percent of male slaves were mariners, but on tiny

Nevis (inhabited by only 8,837 slaves and already relegated to the margins of world sugar production), almost 14 percent of the men followed the sea. Although in the Caribbean as a whole maritime slavery shared certain characteristics relative to those of the rest of the Atlantic world, each Caribbean colony extended special possibilities and limitations to enslaved maritime workers. One of the most significant social distinctions for slave mariners remained the fault line between coastal and deep-sea work.[22]

Most slave boatmen worked with other slaves aboard droghers, lighters, and canoes. Droghers were decked sloops or schooners of thirty to seventy tons operated by two to five slaves, both with and without the troublesome presence of a white man. Depending on size, they were capable of extensive coastal or inter-island voyages. Droghers connected outports or remote plantations with capital towns; Nathaniel Millberry remembered a drogher in 1762 "Carrying Sugars from Distant parts of the Island of Granada to Basseterre." Boatmen's daily life differed substantially from that of slave seamen like the man born on St. Kitts who "served some time to the cooper's trade" and made "several voyages to sea" in the 1770s. Boatmen slept ashore, ate local foods in season, had more regular contact with relatives, and avoided the clock-time regimentation of seafaring watches. As slaves in a slave society rather than in a detached shipborne fragment, they felt both comfort and circumscription.[23]

Other Caribbean slaves crisscrossed the Atlantic—often in all-black crews—because entrepreneurs in Bermuda, the Bahamas, and Caribbean capital towns systematically organized deep-sea labor through slavery. Captured by a privateer in 1776 as he commanded the brigantine *Betsy* en route from Grenada to Virginia, Captain John Bynoe lamented the loss of "five Negro Man Slaves . . . which were all the men he had to Navigate his Vessel." This made black West Indian seafaring unique: elsewhere slaves were assigned to ships' crews more sporadically, and interspersed among white sailors.[24]

Enslaved Caribbean mariners who voyaged to metropolitan centers like London not only frequently liberated themselves but connected island communities to a wider world. More blacks from distant regions congregated in London than anywhere else, making it the hub of the black Atlantic. Among other attractions, London remained the clearinghouse for news about efforts to meliorate the hemispheric plight of black people, such as the Somersett decision in 1772 that led slaves who had once set foot in England to regard themselves as legally free. By 1766 a Jamaican named Charles, "as compleat a seaman as any Negro can be," had made two voyages to England. For "most of the last war a french-horn man," Charles was sure to have found company and musical camaraderie among London's blacks. When the snow *Fanny* departed St. Vincent for London in 1776, her complement of eight included four black seamen and a black boy. In London, West Indian blacks met other men of African descent, seamen like themselves, or runaways-turned-seamen like "old man Cuffee," who triumphantly wrote to his master in Antigua from the Downs, "telling him he had hired himself on board of Capt. Johnston for Jamaica at 25/ pr. month as Cook." By setting blacks in motion, maritime slavery not only provided them with perspectives denied to island-bound slaves, but contributed to the embryonic antislavery movement in London itself. Slavery increasingly appeared as a concrete problem for white Londoners with the growing visibility of blacks on London streets.[25]

London's black society helped lucky West Indian seamen learn the ropes of systems far more complicated than full-rigged ships, giving them the confidence to negotiate for freedom. The case of a sailor named Williams makes the point. After fleeing Grenada aboard ship, Williams got homesick. So in 1797 he "entered at London on board the *Holderness* bound for Grenada, as an ordinary seaman out and home." In Grenada, however, his former master claimed him, and Williams began to negotiate. The agreement reached between them, and Captain Brown of the *Holderness*, stipulated that Williams would be manumitted once Brown paid his master "30 joes," "which was accordingly done by a regular instrument of manumission," provided that Williams agreed to work for Brown as a seaman for three years at wages lower than the current rate. Recrossing the Atlantic to London, however, Williams argued that his agreement to serve for substandard wages had been made under false circumstances. He had been in England, and that, he claimed, made him a free man. The court disagreed, decreeing Williams "as free as any of us while in England," but "a runaway slave in Grenada," where he signed the indenture. Although the sassy sailor did not get the raise he wanted, he bargained himself to legal freedom, and in the interim undoubtedly gave Grenadian slaves both an earful about London and the inspiration of his example. His freedom, of course, came at the price of estrangement from Grenada.[26]

The extent of West Indian slave seafaring challenges conventional images of late-eighteenth-century maritime commerce and its implications. Imagine a graphic rendition in black of the volcanic Caribbean archipelago. From each island radiate short spokes that dead-end, like antennae: the out-and-back daily voyages of slave fishermen. Each island, too, is encircled by loops from point to point along its shore: the coastal trips of slave boatmen. Bold lines connect virtually every island to others: the inter-island voyages of black and white crews and runaway slaves. Finally, even more prominent lines arrive at most islands from (and depart to) African, American, and European ports: international voyages on which blacks sailed. Instead of charting an exchange of commodities, we have mapped currents of black people in motion carrying and exchanging ideas, information, and style. If mercantilists' cartographic vision of the "triangular trade" speaks to one aspect of eighteenth-century maritime activity, this dynamic graphic of black seafaring speaks to the evolution of diasporic consciousness and blacks' cultural hybridity, and to the spread of blacks' news—subversive and otherwise.

As in the Caribbean, coastal boatmen in the Carolina low-country and the Chesapeake tidewater harbored fugitives, transported runaways visiting relatives, and accelerated the pilferage with which slaves tried to compensate for masters' constant appropriation of their labor. Indeed, had whites ever been able to seal black access to vessels in those waters, black society would have suffered inordinately. Seamen's tales fueled blacks' expectations, and their travels exemplified the flight for which slaves yearned. Mariners constituted about 9 percent of South Carolina's skilled slaves in the eighteenth century, and a full 25 percent of skilled runaways. In fact, Philip D. Morgan's detailed reconstruction of South Carolinian slaves' occupational structure in the eighteenth century, based on probate inventories, reveals that maritime work was the third largest occupation among males, after agriculture and woodworking. As South Carolina's mercantile community was small and financially weak until the 1740s, locally owned small

craft manned by slaves and overseas ships from Britain manned by
white sailors initially defined the low-country seascape. During the
1740s and 1750s, however, merchant vessel construction and ownership
rose in Charleston. "At its peak in the 1770s," writes one economic
historian, "shipping absorbed the energies of more people and more
money than any other commercial activity in South Carolina save
planting." Slaves like Peter, described in 1771 as "a good Fisherman,
and very handy on board of Ships or Coasters," enjoyed extensive
mobility within the confinement of slavery.[27]

Many slaveholders remained ambivalent about, if not hostile to, the
relative worldliness and freedom that ocean voyaging bestowed on
bondsmen, even though they willingly employed slaves coastwise.
Robert Pringle, a merchant in South Carolina, experienced frequent
business delays due to shortages of seamen between 1740 and 1744.
One of his vessels "was Detain'd sometime (as most Ships are) for
want of hands," in 1743. A year and a half later, he again complained,
"Seamen are so very Scarce & Difficult to be Procured here." Henry
Laurens, another South Carolina merchant, made similar complaints
in 1747 and 1755. Each of these men owned slaves, hired slaves, and
employed them aboard coasters. Pringle wrote to one of his captains
in 1742, "I have also hired & sent by Mr. Comeur's Boat Four Stout
Negro Men to assist you on board & who are us'd to be upon the
Water & Understand to Work on Ship board." These merchants, and
others like them, could have obviated their chronic shortage of seamen
by employing slave sailors. Yet many southern merchants regularly
chose not to send slaves to sea.[28]

This decision had more to do with slaveholders' concern about
losing prime hands, whom they could not regularly control in ports
of call, than it did with mercantilist policy. Nevertheless, merchants
hiring white seamen kept in line with official preferences about the allocation of labor. Political economists and royal officials believed enslaved sailors subverted Britain's mercantilist system. Governor Parry
of Barbados wrote to the Colonial Office in 1786, "The Numbers of
Negro Slaves employed in Navigating the Trading Vessels in these Seas
(particularly from Bermudas) seems to me to increase so much as to
require the attention of the British Legislature, as it throws so many
English Seamen out of Employment." Despite certain slaveholders'

misgivings and officials' foreboding about the employment of enslaved sailors on deep-sea routes, unceasing demands for maritime labor pulled numerous Africans and African Americans aboard not only coasters but ships.[29]

Forty-six percent of slave mariners in South Carolina between 1732 and 1782 were "sailors" as opposed to "boatmen" or "fishermen"— men who either crossed oceans or sailed extensively coastwise and could connect low-country slaves with blacks throughout the hemisphere. Three enslaved seamen who arrived together at Charleston in 1784 from St. Croix, via Jamaica, exemplified the international connections and personal uprootedness of slave-sailors in the Atlantic world, many of whom were sold more often than agricultural slaves. John, raised by a pilot, had a sister living in Charleston, and he was "American born," although he had recently been sold to Jamaica. One of his shipmates, James, had been born on St. Eustatius, Dutch West Indies. His other shipmate, Cato, hailed from Port Antonio, Jamaica. They swapped stories of life and labor in those places, and came to recognize a commonality of black interests transcending regional distinctions. After deserting the brigantine *Friendship*, the three "stole the canoe that crosses the river Ashley" and headed toward Savannah.[30]

Most maritime slaves worked closer to home. As coxswains of rowing craft and captains of sloops and schooners, elite maritime slaves used their considerable responsibility to subvert slavery. In the low-country these captains were known as patroons; both there and in the Chesapeake they also served as pilots for ocean-going vessels. Like drivers in the fields, they had to balance competing interests between masters and other slaves to secure their positions, although it is clear that many used their positions to convey unauthorized slaves from place to place and to nourish slaves' illicit market in stolen goods. This workaday resistance flared into open rebellion during the chaos of the American Revolution, when maritime slaves piloted British invasionary forces intent on destroying their masters.

Revolutionary unrest may have contributed to the desertion of a "stout Negro" named Shadwell from John Alleyne Walters's schooner at a landing near Lamboll's Bridge, South Carolina, on November 21, 1775. He had "been a long time a patroon of a schooner," Walters claimed, "and [was] well acquainted with all the rivers and inlets to the southward of Charleston." Slaves like Shadwell, along with the slaves under his command, had considerable amounts of time without white supervision, substantial freedom of movement, and independent income from petty trading. Larger coasting vessels like Henry Laurens's schooner *Brother's Endeavor* often sailed with a white captain and a crew consisting of slaves and white sailors. Referring to "2 negro seamen," Laurens made clear to his captain that "the Negroes are entitled to no wages being my property as slaves, except clothing & provisions from me & good usage from you." Although the exposure of black deckhands to different places facilitated information-gathering and temporary escapes, they could do considerably less for slave society than could patroons.[31]

Capitalizing on their employability and knowledge of white ways, enslaved Chesapeake sailors worked at the border of slavery and freedom. The historian Gerald Mullin calculated that nearly one quarter of skilled runaway slaves in Virginia between 1736 and 1801 were mariners. Maritime slavery grew at mid-century. The small sloops conducting Chesapeake Bay's internal commerce, according to Virginia's Governor William Gooch in 1730, relied on "planters with negroes." These slaves, wrote the governor, "can't properly be termed seamen." A patronizing remark that refused to associate blackness with mobility and skill, it contained a kernel of truth: many of the Bay's slave-sailors had never been beyond Cape Charles and Cape Henry to the sea. In 1730 maritime slavery had yet to develop as a significant institution in the Chesapeake economy. Slave watermen's horizons expanded after tobacco regulation began in Virginia in 1730, and in Maryland in 1747. New laws established public warehouses and required planters to transport every hogshead of tobacco for inspection. Hogsheads formerly hauled short distances from plantation to landing and then lightered to ships in the stream were now moved greater distances in bay craft manned by slaves.[32]

Gooch's comment also obscured how readily slave boatmen could get to sea, and how the navigation of sloops provided rudimentary training in fundamental seafaring skills, especially as the century progressed. As in the lower South, enslaved men of color in the Chesapeake took charge of vessels, managing their crews, their navigation, and their lading. By 1770 it was common to refer to runaway slaves' considerable experience as watermen; one such slave had "gone Skipper of the Sloop for some Years past, and is well acquainted with the Bay and most of the Rivers in Virginia and Maryland."[33]

The rise of an indigenously owned Chesapeake merchant fleet in the middle of the eighteenth century pushed more slaves seaward. As London merchants lost their grip on the Chesapeake tobacco trade in the middle of the century, Bay shipping increasingly became controlled by merchants in ports such as Annapolis, Chestertown, and Norfolk, as well as by planters investing in shipping. In 1742 Virginians owned and operated only about 25 ocean-going vessels, ranging from sloops to ships. Twenty years later Virginians owned 102 vessels, of 6,168 registered tons, manned by 827 sailors. Shipowning in Maryland grew in a parallel fashion. As the preeminent maritime historian of the Chesapeake explains, "Men like Robert Carter of Nomini Hall, who owned interests in iron mines, forges, mills, and farms, constantly employed schooners and sloops for transporting goods from one river to another, for collecting cargoes, lightering large ships anchored in the channels of rivers, and for the exchange of grain and lumber for West India products and south European wines."[34]

By 1783, 56 percent of the sea captains in Annapolis owned slaves, and eight of nine slaveowning captains (including those with the most slaves) owned no land. Apparently they employed slaves aboard ship. Carter himself owned at least two schooners regularly engaged between Richmond and Norfolk: a mulatto man named William Lawrence sailed as master of the *Harriot* in 1774; "negro Cesar" skippered the other. The life of a slave called Ishmael, who fled in 1778, suggests how maritime slavery grew with the rise of an urban mercantile class. Ishmael "had been bred to the sea by Mr. Cornelius Calvert of Norfolk."[35]

Chesapeake politicians nevertheless recognized seafaring's pipeline to freedom. In 1753 the House of Delegates in Annapolis passed "An Act to prevent masters of ships and vessels from clandestinely carrying servants and slaves. . . out of this province." Legislators tried to halt the black runaways who gravitated to chronically shorthanded ships in hopes of replacing white deserters. White seamen felt that the tobacco colonies were "one of the worst countries in the Universe for Sailors." European seamen in the Chesapeake were prone to "Fluxes,

Fevers, and the Belly-Ache," according to a local in 1746 who blamed them for indulging too much in fresh fruits and fresh water; "and then," he fumed, "they in their Tarpawlin Language, cry, God D——the Country." Seamen also feared impressment by Royal Navy squadrons in Hampton Roads and Norfolk throughout much of the war-torn eighteenth century. With mariners' wages frequently better in Philadelphia, tobacco ship crews routinely lit out for Pennsylvania. Shorthanded captains chose not to inquire about the background of willing hands. A slave named John, who "has been used to going by Water," according to his master, probably "made off in some vessel." A mulatto fellow named Jason, who ran from near Patapsco Neck in Baltimore County in 1763, "will endeavor to pass for a Sailor, as he has been for some Time by Water." On the Bay, as in other parts of the Atlantic world, the distinction between enslaved boatman and quasi-free seaman could easily blur.[36]

Voyaging between the West Indies, Europe, and the American mainland enabled enslaved seamen to observe the Atlantic political economy from a variety of vantage points, to subvert their masters' discipline, and to open plantation society to outside influences. Thus maritime slavery came at no small cost to slaveholders. It came at no small cost to slaves, either: the deep-sea trades in the middle of the eighteenth century were still manned primarily by white men, who, though they accommodated blacks in their midst, also forced them to cope with a largely white world. Even as the maritime labor force became more racially diverse by the end of the century, seafaring slaves had no choice but to straddle black and white worlds.

Slaves were drawn increasingly into the maritime labor market of the northern colonies during the middle of the war-torn eighteenth century, when seamen often were in short supply. When Pennsylvania's lieutenant governor dispatched several ships from Philadelphia for Hispaniola to exchange French prisoners during the Seven Years War, half the seamen were "Negro Mariners." Ten percent of the slaveowners in Philadelphia in 1767 were mariners, men who frequently owned a slave before they owned a home. And two of the ten-man crew aboard Briton Hammon's sloop were of African descent on his voyage in 1747, although the population around Boston was nowhere near 20 percent black.[37]

In the estimation of many white northerners, sailors and slaves were cut from similar cloth: following one of the worst anti-impressment riots in Boston's history, the Knowles riot of 1747 (just weeks before Hammon sailed), Boston's Town Meeting claimed "that the said Riotous Assembly consisted of Foreign Seamen Servants Negroes and other Persons of Mean and Vile Condition." More than wartime disruption and hierarchical ideology pushed slaves seaward, however. Northern masters frequently did not have regular work for bondsmen, especially once the harvest was stored. Some male slaves alternated between farm and forecastle. But the greatest difference between northern maritime slavery and its plantation variant was that a higher proportion of northern maritime slaves were seamen as opposed to coastal boatmen. Working in largely white crews, and often under the watchful gaze of their masters, they sailed regularly to Europe, the West Indies, and Africa.[38]

Slaves constituted only 2 or 3 percent of the mid- to late-eighteenth-century population in Connecticut, New Hampshire, and Massachusetts, but they frequently lived clustered in maritime towns such as New London, Portsmouth, and Boston. Maritime slavery shaped local black society until the American Revolution; free black seafaring shaped it thereafter. In Rhode Island, the undisputed leader of the American slave trade and the blackest province in the region, enslaved sailors and stevedores were common. A Rhode Island newspaper advertiser sought "5 Negro Men," specifying three sailors and two coopers. Quam Briggs, a slave mariner from Newport, left "on a Whaling Voige in the Ship george" in September 1775, having been hired by his master to Captain Aaron Sheffield. For New England masters, slaves were productive workers as well as status symbols. In their own estimation, as the founders of Newport's Free African Union Society put it in 1780, slaves and recent freedmen were "strangers and outcastes in a strange land, attended with many disadvantages and evils . . . which are like to continue on us and on our children while we and they live in this country."[39]

New England slaves labored not only for ostentatious merchants such as Boston's Peter Fanueil and Rhode Island's Godfrey Malbone, but also for distillers, ropemakers, shopkeepers, yeomen, coopers, innkeepers, tanners, and victualers—ambitious men who wished to

emulate their betters. Twenty percent of the male slaves in Massachusetts's Suffolk County during the 1740s were owned by mariners,
shipwrights, and fishermen; many others were held by shipowning
merchants or by nonmariners who nevertheless hired out their slaves
as seamen. And the eighteenth-century Nantucket whale fishery long
relied on black and Indian labor.[40]

Men of color like Briton Hammon and Moses Newmock (his mulatto shipmate) were thus pushed by masters and pulled by personal
predilection into an Atlantic labor market of "renegades, castaways,
and mariners." Although New England seafaring attracted sons of
established farmers who would someday inherit land, but who in the
meantime sought wages as a supplement to family income, it also en-
snared penniless locals, along with men that Hammon called "strangers." They were white men without connections near Cape Cod or
Plymouth, and quite likely without attachments to land elsewhere,
who worked for wages as North Atlantic capitalism reorganized traditional labor arrangements. White sailors sometimes feared that a
black shipmate might be worth more simply because he could be sold.
They were not far from the mark. When Hammon's sloop was "cast
away on Cape Florida," murderous Indian wreckers spared only him
as they plundered the vessel.[41]

ATTRIBUTING THE EXISTENCE of maritime slavery simply to a
demand for labor, to the rapid succession of wars that drained white
manpower from merchant vessels, or to the demographics of slave
societies is to miss the dialectical nature of slavery itself. Blacks affected
their own destiny. Obviously, many slaves found themselves at sea
through their owners' decisions, like the New York bondsman advertised in 1761 as "brought up from his Infancy to the sea." But slaves
like Briton Hammon negotiated with their masters to allow them the
privilege of a sea voyage. Slaves like Samuel Johnson, a Chesapeake
runaway during the American Revolution, ran *to* the relatively anonymous wharves and ships of the eighteenth-century Atlantic world.
Slaves like Cudjoe, the patroon of a schooner in South Carolina,
expressed a preference for maritime work over agricultural labor; such
men derived status from their travel, trading, skill, and identity as
mariners.[42]

Seafaring lured black men with certain psychological profiles. Embarking upon a voyage below the distant horizon literally meant striking out anew. Aesthetically, a well-navigated ship in the midst of the primal sea conveyed a powerful image of stability in flux—an image profoundly appealing to those with little control over their lives. Unconscious yearnings and subliminal images did not keep ships from being potentially hellish workplaces, much less keep worms from the hardtack. Those yearnings and images, however, dovetailing as they did with certain aspects of the social psychology of African American people, cast seafaring in a fundamentally appealing way for slaves— complemented, perhaps, by the ancestral African reverence for water spirits. Joshua Blue, a New York slave who ran away in 1800, had, according to his owner, probably gone to sea, as he had often mentioned that "if free, he should prefer that mode of life."[43]

Slaves like Blue recognized their limited choices and chose to ignore much of contemporary whites' folk wisdom about seafaring hazards. "Those who would go to sea for pleasure would go to hell for a pastime," ran one proverb. Gear failures aloft sent men plunging to their deaths, while common navigational errors—and plain bad luck—stranded ships and drowned sailors. Mariners who cheated death faced other aggravations. Ships bred vermin and forecastles stank of fetid bilgewater. Sailors were debilitated by vitamin-deficient food, blazing sun, and wet accommodations; threatened by their own ship's equipment and the sea's perils; and answerable to tyrannical captains backed by harsh admiralty laws. Yet ships nonetheless became both a means to escape and an end in themselves for black men on the lam, as well as an appealing workplace for maritime slaves. The terrible cycle of degradation that most slaves faced ashore dulled the jagged edges of life before the mast, as Johnson and Cudjoe well knew.

Eighteenth-century seafarers of color lived with ironic contradictions. Moment to moment, all sailors endured confinement. Five brisk paces would span the length of most colonial merchantmen's quarterdecks from the taffrail to the break of the deck; another six or seven steps would carry a resolute man to the very eyes of the vessel, where the windlass and knightheads checked his stride. If a sailor was not hemmed in by the bulwarks and the sea itself there was always the law: desertion remained a crime for sailors who had not completed their stipulated voyage. Slavery compounded seafaring's confinement.

Joseph, a cook on the *Dragon* and the sole black aboard for more than a year voyaging between London, Jamaica, and Boston, felt the isolation of being the only black, the only slave, and the only cook. Moreover, slaveholders hiring out a mariner like Joseph or Caesar, "an Artful Fellow" and "a very good Seaman," routinely cautioned captains to "keep him on Board, for if he gets on Shore am afraid of his running away." By contrast, sailors' workplaces encompassed virtually limitless horizons compared with those of their enslaved brothers and sisters toiling ankle-deep in field muck, or scouring a white woman's floor. The political consequences of black seafaring originated to no small degree from the comparative lessons in political economy internalized by veteran slave voyagers who managed to get ashore or talk with lightermen in ports of call.[44]

Royal Navy press gangs worked in concert with maritime slavery, and blacks' own predispositions, to solidify a black seafaring tradition. During the interminable wars of the eighteenth century, sailors throughout the Atlantic world watched warily for the aggressive rush of the press. Black sailors shared "the same fate as the free-born white man," according to Admiral Lord Colvill in 1762, and were commonly impressed.[45] This forcible conscription of seafaring men to work the king or queen's ships had long been considered a prerogative of the crown. At the end of each war the Admiralty shortsightedly reduced the navy to a skeleton force. New hostilities always renewed the need for sailors and grossly overtaxed the chronically inefficient recruitment systems. In 1755 Henry Laurens observed from Charleston that a man-of-war was "pressing men for a whole Week, during which the *Orrels* Men [merchant sailors] lay hid in the Country." Sailors desperately tried to dodge the press during the War of the Spanish Succession (Queen Anne's War), the War of Jenkins's Ear, the War of the Austrian Succession (King George's War), the Seven Years War, the American Revolution, and the Wars of the French Revolution, or Napoleonic Wars. But for 65 of the 115 years between 1700 and 1815 war raged at sea. Naval ships (like sugar plantations) consumed men at a voracious rate, and Britain's much-vaunted fleet could be manned only at the expense of sailors' liberty.[46]

Black and white sailors regarded impressment and naval service from their own distinct vantage points. Black men had every reason to fear the press: it was quite colorblind. But free black sailors circulating around the Atlantic faced the constant and greater fear of enslavement. After Peter van Trump shipped in a brigantine from St. Thomas, bound, he thought, for Europe in the summer of 1725, he discovered that Captain Mackie's actual destination was North Carolina. A white man there corralled him as a slave, despite van Trump's protest that it was "against all right." Blacks were invariably assumed to be slaves unless they could prove otherwise. Thus "One Negro Named Henry Who pretends to be free" was given "three years to prove his freedom" by a Rhode Island Admiralty Court judge after being seized from the sloop *Postilion* in 1746, "during wch time he remain in the Captors hands."[47]

White sailors faced no such threats, and many opted for work in the West Indies, where fewer press gangs prowled. "The [white] Seamen in Jamaica, being chiefly employed in Sloops, either in Privateering or Trading on the Coast of [New] Spain," wrote Captain Nathaniel Uring, "are unwilling to sail in Ships, because there is more Work, and loath to go to Europe, for fear of being imprest into the Publick Service." Black sailors like Olaudah Equiano, by contrast, loathed the West Indies for its slavery. Equiano had served years in the Royal Navy and knew about impressment firsthand. He had even worked with a press gang when "we wanted some hands to complete our complement." Once free and working as a mariner in the merchant service, he preferred to take his chances on the coast of Europe, fearing impressment into "Publick Service" substantially less than re-enslavement in the Caribbean.[48]

Blacks often found the navy a refuge from the myriad oppressions arrayed against them, even as white sailors (especially impressed ones) rhetorically described naval service as slavery. Black sailors' definition of freedom accommodated that rigid hierarchical structure. As a rule, naval ships had easier work and better food than vessels operated by parsimonious merchants, who scrimped on victuals and on the number of men they hired to work a ship. Naval service also held out the promise of prize money, pensions, and hospitalization for aged or injured seamen. Although free-born white English seamen raged against the despotism of impressment, many actually preferred service on the king's ships to merchant seafaring for these concrete reasons, especially in peacetime.

Most important for blacks was that the navy protected them from man-stealers and slavemasters. When in 1758 a Maryland slaveowner claimed a black naval sailor named William Stephens as his slave, the Admiralty refused to surrender him. Stephens had volunteered for the king's service; he was also a skilled seaman too valuable to lose in time of war. The lords of the Admiralty intervened that same year on behalf of William Castillo, who as a slave-sailor had worked for his owner and captain on a Boston merchant ship during the early 1750s. Running from his master, Castillo joined the navy, as had Stephens. But in 1758 his master met him on an English street. He had Castillo arrested, and secured him with an iron collar aboard ship, threatening to sell him in Barbados. When the collared Castillo wrote to the Admiralty for protection, their lordships responded that "the laws of this country admit of no badges of slavery, therefore the Lords hope and expect that whenever he [Admiral Holburne] discovers any attempt of this kind, he should prevent it; and that the Lords desire to be informed how Castillo is rated on the ship's books." By no means could every runaway slave find safety or liberty aboard naval ships, but skilled seamen often did, especially in wartime.[49]

Throughout much of the eighteenth century, when most mariners of color were slaves, racial stereotyping defined black men's roles aboard ship. Blacks frequently filled special billets as cooks, officers' servants, or musicians, reinforcing their distinction from the seamen proper. In fact, the emergence of black sailors in the Atlantic plantation system hinged to some degree on whites' belief that blacks should fill certain service positions—ashore or at sea. Of some forty-five men mustered aboard the Rhode Island privateer *Revenge* in 1741, four were black: James Jennings, a free seaman, and three slaves—the cook's mate Daniel Waller, the first mate's servant Samuel Kerby, and the "Captain's Negro and Drummer," Richard Norton, also called "Negro Dick."

There is little evidence of the meaning African American men on the *Revenge* attached to their service aboard ship, or of how Jennings's experiences differed from those of the enslaved black men. We know that Jennings received small arms along with white sailors who shipped with him in the Bahamas, for both blacks and whites were fighting men. Richard Norton probably benefited from some perquisites of the cabin in his role as the captain's servant. The slave Olaudah Equiano remembered being "very happy" while serving as the captain's personal steward aboard H.M.S. *Aetna,* "for I was extremely well-treated by all on board; and had leisure to improve myself in reading and writing." Slaves aboard ship as officers' servants were rarely mustered as sailors, and though possibly lonely, their position allowed some autonomy in the relative privacy of the cabin.[50]

Sharing much of the work but separated from the rest of the men by responsibility for food, and often by race, cooks and cooks' mates like Daniel Waller frequently bore the brunt of sailors' deviltry. No statistics are available for the eighteenth century, but at Baltimore in 1806, 16 percent of the African American mariners were recorded as cooks or stewards in the crew lists, as were 24 percent at Philadelphia in 1803, and 51 percent at Providence, Rhode Island, in 1810. Most telling is that at those ports, and at turn-of-the-century Salem, Massachusetts, almost no white men filled the cooks' or stewards' berths— roles reserved for blacks. Aboard a man-of-war the cook had charge of a real galley below decks, with a substantial brick hearth and sizable kettles. Most cooks, however, sweated and swayed aboard tiny merchantmen, sloops or schooners from forty to sixty feet long manned by only eight or ten men. There the cook's domain was the caboose, a sort of stunted sentry box lashed to the deck and sheltering a crude hearth on which he "dressed the Victuals" by boiling or roasting. Hunched in the swirling woodsmoke and braced against the relentless motion of the ship, a merchantman's grimy cook coped with few utensils, monotonous salted provisions, and more abuse than glory at mealtime.[51]

Black musicians savored more of the limelight. As the drummer aboard *Revenge,* Richard Norton constantly drew attention to himself on deck and ashore. Privateersmen drilled at great guns and small arms and repaired to battle stations when the drummer "beat to quarters." Norton may have enjoyed the satisfaction of watching crowds gather round him in ports of call, too. Privateering captains recruited sailors by establishing a rendezvous (called a "rondy") at a tavern, where men would be encouraged to sign ship's articles (the contract between sailors and captains) and receive credit for an outfit. Captains "drummed up" men for the rondy by sending drummers and fifers to march through the streets.

Although black men did not hold a monopoly on musicians' berths, prescribing such roles for men of color remained common. A "Negro Drummer" named Diamond sailed aboard the sloop *Albany* on a trading venture down east from Massachusetts in 1732, and "a negro boy named Abraham, about 16 years of age," who "beats the drum" probably had little trouble finding a berth in Charleston in 1779. The master from whom Abraham fled believed him to be "lurking about the wharfs, or on board of some vessel, as he is fond of the sea." Black Sam, "a good drummer and fifer," deserted from the *Comet* brigantine of war at Charleston in 1777. Equiano's first master, Captain Pascal, wanted him to learn the French horn; and John Marrant, a free black man in South Carolina during the American Revolution, asserted that he "was pressed on board the *Scorpion,* sloop of war, as their musician, as they were told I could play on music." Marrant was, by his own admission, "master both of the violin and of the French horn." A tavern near St. Katherine's Stairs in London regularly used for enlistment rendezvous suggested this association between black sailors and music: the proprietor called it "The Black Boy and Trumpet." As late as 1808 a U.S. naval surgeon wrote, "There will be no difficulty in procuring a 'fiddler,' *especially* among the coloured men, in every American frigate, who can play most of the common dancing tunes."[52]

Enslaved musicians brought status to their masters—especially aboard privateers and naval vessels, where black boys with trumpets were considered showpieces. Being assigned as musicians, a niche of notoriety if not honor, was not necessarily a liability for blacks provided that they had talent. Stereotypical roles like this often have provided maneuvering room for African Americans, even though such roles pandered to the caste system in which blacks were expected to serve whites. But seatime as musicians, much less as servants, did not introduce black men to the mysteries of the sailors' art, nor initiate them fully into the fraternity of seafaring men. And it accentuated racial division aboard ship.

The case of seafaring black servants and musicians suggests that slavery, maritime or otherwise, meant much more than the exploitation of labor. Moral complacency and the desire for privilege led whites to incorporate race into the social structure of the early modern Atlantic world. White colonial culture superimposed racial meanings on a form of labor organization that need not have been racial. Long after maritime slavery had become virtually extinct in the deep-sea trades, cooks' and stewards' berths were frequently assigned by race; captains' and mates' berths inevitably were.

Seamen of color became part of the process by which black people forged a complex, though not homogenous, racial identity—a process that spoke to the constantly changing cultural distinctiveness of black Americans. Although marvelous histories exist revealing complex relationships between American slaves, free blacks, masters, and other whites, there is nonetheless a tendency in much African American social history to narrow the range of possibilities open to black people throughout history. Insufficient attention is generally paid to the tensions and contradictions among blacks. Too many histories assume implicitly that black people were restricted by their culture, or that their culture assured their distinctiveness. Culture, however, can be imagined as a river—picking up contributions from contacts alongshore and feeder streams, relegating parts of itself to back-eddies, losing yet others to silent evaporation or stranding, and constantly mixing its elements, even while it moves inexorably along a course that it continually redefines. A static sense of culture, by contrast, almost invariably leads to the impression that culture confines—that it is more like the channel than the river itself.

Sailors constantly crossed cultural and geographic boundaries as they maneuvered between white and black societies ashore and maritime society afloat. Through interactions in the maritime workplace, African American sailors combined and recombined their various identities (racial, regional, gender, class, occupational) in different ways. Among a ship's crew of black and white sailors, for instance, Briton Hammon defined himself as one of "the people" collectively chiding the captain; in Spanish Cuba, as an Englishman and slave desperate to escape; in Indian camps, a civilized man; in New England, "a Negro Man"; and aboard the slaver on which he enlisted, a free seaman on wages or a Briton—not a captive African. Strikingly absent from Hammon's account of seafaring during the 1740s and 1750s is any sense of a unified identity among people of color, something to which black seamen contributed as the century wore on.[53]

Hammon's multiple identities and his equanimity with the harness of benevolent slavery were counterpointed by the rage of blacks like

Cyrus, "a lusty young Negroe Man" who fled a Virginia master in 1751 after he "formerly belong'd to the Estate of Merchant Bell, of London, and follow'd the Sea." Seeking freedom pell-mell, Cyrus had already "been a great Run-away, tried for his Life and burnt in the hand" when he headed for the York River "to endeavour to get on board some Vessel." Hammon's and Cyrus's varied actions, and the cosmopolitanism of black sailors in general, substantiate James Clifford's notion that identity can be "conceived not as a boundary to be maintained, but as a nexus of relations and transactions actively engaging a subject." Through such encounters roaming black sailors nurtured the creation of a black America that, though embodied in various communities and riven by various identities, would come to understand itself during the late eighteenth century as "African"—of a piece with, yet separate from, Africa.[54]

Situated on vessels connecting all corners of the Atlantic world, black seafaring men were newsmongers central to the formation of black America and a multidimensional racial identity. They broadcast accounts from blacks' perspectives regarding the Haitian Revolution, the movements to abolish the slave trade and emancipate slaves, and the debate over colonization that centered on the question of whether people of color would remain in the United States. Outside the pale of these debates and events, the mundane ebb and flow of black sailors' daily lives substantiated the unity of the black Atlantic, even as it brought into focus differences among diasporic blacks. A slave named Jim fled down Virginia's James River in 1802 to City Point, or Norfolk, and then went "to Philadelphia and New York on board of a vessel," which, his master said, "I am inclined to think . . . he makes a practice of." Seamen like Jim compared the lives of blacks on plantations with those in seaports; and, drawing on storytelling traditions prominent among sub-Saharan Africans and Atlantic seafarers, they talked. Seamen also achieved distinction as leaders within eighteenth-century Afro-America. The list is long, and includes Prince Hall, James Forten, Denmark Vesey, Paul Cuffe, and Olaudah Equiano.[55]

Seafaring thus conveyed dramatically different status and perquisites for black and white workers. Whereas white seamen were among the most marginalized men in white society, black seamen found access to privileges, worldliness, and wealth denied to most slaves.

Nothing conveys this more strikingly than the fact that sailors wrote the first six autobiographies of blacks published in English before 1800. Not only did their pens bridge oral black culture with what had been an exclusively white world of letters, but theirs was the opening salvo in what would become a barrage of antislavery literature by black authors dedicated to liberation. Seafaring men were in the vanguard of defining a new black ethnicity for the many African peoples dispersed by Atlantic slavery.[56]

Pioneering black men of letters did not rely on the sea as a literary device, nor on their own seafaring as a metaphor in the vein of white authors like William Falconer or Richard Henry Dana. They chose to identify themselves not primarily as seamen, but as Christians and Africans—roles that served their antislavery cause and the creation of a diasporic consciousness. Relatively privileged compared with their brethren toiling in the fields, they nevertheless understood seafaring as yet another form of compulsory and unpaid labor. Their wide-ranging maritime work informed their writing, however, as it honed their perspectives on variations in race and slavery throughout the Atlantic.

Early black seafaring autobiographers did not root their personal narratives in American or European locales. As citizens of the world, they were detached from place in a way that the authors of many later slave narratives were not, and in ways that few whites wished to be. Olaudah Equiano (in 1789) and James Albert Ukawsaw Gronniosaw (circa 1770) paid substantial attention to their African cultural and geographic origins, defining themselves in opposition to the societies in which they currently lived. But with little chance of repatriation to a now strange Africa, these black intellectuals envisioned themselves as members of an international black community.

Blacks had to reconcile their potential for personal attachment to a region and its black community with their legal exclusion from its polity and their moral objection to its laws. Nevertheless, some African-born slaves created such bonds in Barbados, Jamaica, and South Carolina. This became easier for subsequent generations who were born in a colony or whose ancestors (or fictive kin) were interred there. White Barbadians proudly regarded their island as the "most ancient" British West Indian colony, and according to the British traveler George Pinckard, exhibited "a sense of distinction" that was

"strongly manifested in the sentiment conveyed by the vulgar expression so common to the island—'neither Charib, nor Creole, but true
Barbadian.'" Pinckard reported that the sentiment was shared "even
by the slaves, who proudly arrogate a superiority above the negroes
of the other islands! Ask one of them if he was imported, or is a
Creole, and he immediately replies—'*Me neder Chrab, nor Creole,
Massa!—me troo Barbadian born.*'" Pinckard may have taken slaves'
ready response too much at face value: parodying whites was a favorite
form of expression among slaves. But less controversial evidence un-
earthed by Philip Morgan in eighteenth-century advertisements for
runaway South Carolinian slaves suggests "some extraordinary instances of attachment to a particular locale." Compare that with a
sample of fifty black sailors shipping out of Philadelphia in 1798. Only
five were native Philadelphians. Repeatedly removed from place in a
way that most slaves were not, traveling sailors cultivated an identity
with the Atlantic community of color.[57]

African-born seafarers like Olaudah Equiano and John Jea recognized the ability of Africans in America to redefine the term "African"
in a characteristically creole way. Jea's consistent description of himself
as an "African" illuminates the creation of "Africa" itself in the identities of late-eighteenth-century black people, and refers to much more
than his birthplace on the continent. Born at Old Calabar on the Niger
Delta in 1773, Jea could have been born an Ibo, an Efik, an Ibibio, or
into any other ethnicity common there. His family probably had not
long considered themselves "Africans." Nondiscerning Europeans imposed "African" as a general label on blacks native to a host of
ethnicities and polities. Ibo, Mandingo, and Ashanti people, among
others, then refashioned the term into a diasporic black identity in
the ports and plantations of the New World. For individual blacks
this did not happen immediately; few eighteenth-century black slaves
born in Africa readily discarded their birth ethnicity and assumed an
"African" identity. An intermediate stage of acculturation to Euro-
American practices, and reassessment of the role of blacks in the New
World, almost invariably intervened. Equiano's autobiography makes
this clear. He declines to label himself an "African" in early chapters,
referring to himself instead as an Eboe or as a man from Benin. After
three years of slavery he had become substantially acculturated to

English ways, in a few particulars "almost an Englishman," he wrote, largely because he had spent so much time aboard ship in the company of Englishmen. As his political consciousness developed, however, he began to refer to himself as "the African," or "the oppressed Ethiopian."[58]

The African identity cultivated by worldly diasporic blacks emphasized racial and political realities, and was by no means synchronous with that of indigenous peoples of the continent. Nothing reveals this more clearly than the resounding refusal of most free African Americans to embrace their own deportation to Africa as part of the colonization movement. As the sailmaker James Forten wrote from Philadelphia to Captain Paul Cuffe in 1817, "We had a large meeting of males at the Rev. R. Allen's church the other evening. Three thousand at least attended, and there was not one soul that was in favor of going to Africa." Many African Americans' new African identity, like that of Equiano, was heavily laced with Christianity, "civilization," and market values. Although less-educated black sailors were not as Europeanized as Equiano, they no longer defined themselves primarily through referents from the continent of Africa (even if they referred to themselves as "African") but through hybridized black American ones.[59]

Through their daily confrontations with whites, seamen straddling black and white worlds became more self-consciously "African" than were many slaves immersed in the black majorities of South Carolina or Jamaica. Cultural norms do not depend on an "other" the way that race (a specific social relationship) does. Ancestral spiritual communications, ring-shouts, and certain funerary practices, for instance, were heartfelt expressions of slaves' cosmology, largely irrelevant to the existence of whites. Many of the slaves' cultural practices were inward-looking, serving to bond people of color to one another in black contexts, but not necessarily to delineate them from whites. The specifically "African" identity espoused by many African American sailors, by contrast, emerged not so much from blacks' cultural separation from whites as from political contact with them.

Sailors thus became for black people in the Atlantic world what newspapers and the royal mail service were for white elites: a mode of communication integrating local communities into the larger community of color, even as they revealed regional and local differences.

In November 1756 a Bermudian-born slave named Thyas, "an extraordinary good Caulker, and a tolerable good Ship Carpenter," fled from the master to whom he had been sold on St. Eustatius. Eight months later he was seen in Bermuda; fourteen months after that his master "heard that he had got to South Carolina," where he was "harboured somewhere with a run away Wench." Thyas capitalized not only on his maritime skill to circulate between those places, but on networks of information about how to proceed and what he might find. Other sailors appropriated ships as conduits for political dissent, as the careers of Equiano, Jea, Denmark Vesey, and Robert Wedderburn clearly testify.[60]

Whites leery of black threats recognized the danger posed by seafaring men of color moving freely along shipping lanes, especially during the Haitian Revolution that began in 1793. But try as they might to stop the flow of blacks' ideas around the Atlantic world, whites could not. "We may expect therefore black crews, and supercargoes and missionaries [from revolutionary St. Domingue] into the southern states," wrote Thomas Jefferson after President John Adams reinstituted trade between the United States and St. Domingue in 1799. "If this combustion can be introduced among us under any veil whatever, we have to fear it."[61]

Seamen like the ones who scared Thomas Jefferson by circulating revolutionary ideas were among the most worldly of all slaves. Many were well traveled and multilingual—a skill useful for fostering links between otherwise discrete black communities. A "Negro man named Luke" ran off from his master in Cainboy, South Carolina, in 1763. He "has been us'd to the seas, speaks English, French, Spanish, and Dutch, and probably may attempt to get off in some vessel." A "mustee man slave, born in Caracoa [that is, Curaçao, Dutch West Indies], about 50 years of age," ran off from the schooner *Hannah* in Charleston, South Carolina, in 1783. He had lived for a while in North Carolina but, more important, had been "employed in the West Indies as a coasting sailor [and] speaks all the languages used there." His frustrated master felt that the man may have headed back to North Carolina or may "have gotten on board some vessel going to sea."[62] Multilingual men like these, with extensive knowledge of the Americas, had better-than-average chances to escape from their masters and, perhaps more significantly, the ability to spin yarns that implicitly or explicitly dramatized commonalities (and differences) among widely dispersed people of color. Throughout the Caribbean, then, legal and clandestine inter-island trade introduced slave-sailors to interstices in the slave system, and to the recognition that whether they spoke English, French Creole, Danish, or papiamento, they had a great deal in common throughout plantation and maritime America.[63]

The constant movement of storytelling black sailors became an integral part of the process through which various blacks created a sense of both connectedness and individuality within their new black ethnicity. Fundamental to diasporic identity was the recognition that all New World blacks, whether in New England, North Carolina, Nevis, or New Spain, inhabited a common ground closed to whites. Divisions certainly existed, creating fear and suspicion. But time after time, in seaport after seaport, vessels arrived with strange black men who led local blacks to the revelation, during lengthy port stays, that those strangers inhabited a definably black cosmos of dance, spirituality, and resistance to slavery; and that the African identity they imported had broad applicability.

MONEY VOSE was one of the ten million Africans transported across the dangerous water stretching westward to the land of the dead, where he became one of the melancholy founding fathers of a new people. Shortly after the American Revolution, Vose eluded his slavery and mysteriously arrived in Essex County, Massachusetts. Essex County ran east-northeast from Boston along the rockbound coast, through Salem's smugly prosperous Georgian streets and the pungent salt-cod ports of Marblehead and Gloucester, past proud Cape Ann jutting seaward and the undulating salt marshes near Ipswich, right to the New Hampshire border. More than oceans separated it from the ancient stretch of tropical West Africa on which young Vose had hawked bamboo baskets and learned pidgin English before the slavers came.[64]

But with few alternatives, he stayed. Buoyed perhaps by a 1783 judicial decision that abolished slavery in Massachusetts, or anchored by his marriage into the county's black population of 880 domestics, farm workers, and seamen, Vose attached himself to the household and patronage of Captain Fitz William Sargent and began to follow the sea, finding a limited freedom before the mast. Like other Essex County men who lived afloat for months each year and stood helm watch in heavy weather, Vose adopted a rolling gait to counter the unceasing motion of lively brigantines and pinkey schooners. "His name may be found on the Custom House books in Gloucester," his step-daughter, Nancy Prince, proudly recollected. "His last voyage was with Captain Elias Davis, in the brig Romulus." Captured at sea by a British warship and "pressed into their service," Vose "died oppressed, in the English dominions" in 1812, leaving a disconsolate widow with eight children. Although a man who strove to provide for his family, he left no estate. No stone marked his grave. But Money Vose left stories.[65]

Raised in Africa until young manhood, resocialized by blacks in New England, and employed for years aboard ship, Vose maneuvered between several continents and cultures. Caught up in circumstances beyond his control, he found his behavior and his beliefs—like his gait—in transition. His stories bespoke an undying connection to Africa; his identity, a new orientation to America. Surrounded by one of the most unbending regional white cultures in the New World, one for which the old Puritan taboos against transgressing social boundaries still resonated eerily, Vose dramatically revealed the instinct of Africans in America (and their black descendants) not to separate, but to envelop; not to emphasize purity, but to embrace diversity. He married a mustee woman by whom he had black American children of African and Indian descent, settled into a Protestant family for whom the old gods echoed faintly in spirit possession and song, and moved to new rhythms, embodying the cultural hybridity that redefined eighteenth-century Africans as black Americans.

It is no surprise that Vose's descendants remembered him best for his stories. Storytellers had been venerated in his ancestral home, and both African American people and Atlantic seafarers had a propensity for constructing elaborate oral tales in which outrageous actions and actual experiences amused and edified their listeners while connecting them with a larger universe. Putting the sea squarely in his version of black history, Vose's tales illuminated special places—the Africa of his boyhood and the Atlantic ports in which he plied his trade—and bestowed a legacy of worldliness on his children. One tale spoke directly of freedom. Coming from a man who in his own words was "stolen from Africa," his freedom tale commanded an audience. While Vose told his eloquent and melodious stories in the dramatic performance style of an African raconteur, accompanied by his listeners' murmured shouts and enthusiastic encouragement, his step-daughter, who had "often heard him tell the tale" of his escape from the slaver with a shipmate, remembered only its essence.

> I have heard my father describe the beautiful moonlight night when they two launched their bodies into the deep, for liberty. When they got upon soundings, their feet were pricked with a sea-plant that grew under water, they had to retreat, and, at last they reached the shore. When day began to break, they laid down under a fence, as naked as they were born.[66]

With a captivating tale, Money Vose linked memories of his youthful manhood with hope for his family. He spoke of symbolic death aboard the white men's slaver, of bold action in the darkness, of struggle and tribulation at sea, and rebirth ashore. In his tale of trial and redemption, Vose rewrote the history of the Middle Passage to end on an affirmative note for the black Yankees who listened—for his father-in-law, also a New Englander stolen from Africa, for his wife (the child of that slave and an American Indian), and for his children, several of whom followed him to sea during the growth of American shipping in the early republic. Like other salt-streaked black storytellers, Vose deftly embroidered a bitter Atlantic maritime sampler with his vision of hard-won, if partial, black freedoms, and diasporic expansion.

Money Vose knew firsthand wormy bread and salt beef, unceasing motion and constant noise, days of monotony and moments of fear. He shared in the distinctions with which sailors—black and white—set themselves apart from other laboring men, and he recognized that however brutal and seamy seafaring was, it offered leeway to men of color. Seafaring also kept him in flux. Plying the Atlantic, he remained eternally suspended between Africa and America. Each rising sun brought with it memories of his youth, and of the beach on which he became such a proficient swimmer. We turn eastward now to the Africa of his ancestors.

2. AFRICAN ROOTS
OF BLACK SEAFARING

▶◆◆◆◆◆◆◆◆◆◆◆◆◆◆◆◆◆◆◆◆◆◆◆◆◆◆◆◀

I bathed in the Euphrates when dawns were young.
I built my hut near the Congo and it lulled me to sleep.
I looked upon the Nile and raised the pyramids above it.
I heard the singing of the Mississippi when Abe Lincoln
went down to New Orleans, and I've seen its muddy
bosom turn all golden in the sunset.

I've known rivers:
Ancient, dusky rivers.

My soul has grown deep like the rivers.

LANGSTON HUGHES,
"The Negro Speaks of Rivers" (1926)

IN 1780 A SLAVE named Caesar, who had "been accustomed to go by water" and who would probably "endeavor to get on board some vessel," gave the slip to his master in Prince George's County, Maryland. Caesar was about twenty-five years old, African-born, but capable of speaking good English. According to his master, he "boasts much of his family in his own country, it being a common saying with him, that he is no common negro." A black sailor named Conner on the Virginian sloop *Jean* in 1779 exhibited connections to Africa of another sort—ritually incised "Guinea marks on each of his temples." Speaking "good English," wearing a European-style "thick blue sea jacket patched with canvass," "appear[ing] much like a sailor," and surrounded by white men, Conner otherwise seemed a very assimilated African in 1779.[1]

Seamen like Conner worked primarily with whites in one of the most racially integrated labor forces in eighteenth-century America. Yet whether braced against the tiller of a merchant sloop under a white man's command or pensively gazing seaward, Conner viewed his maritime work from the perspective of his African heritage. His ritual scars and Caesar's boasts about his "own country" speak of how profoundly different African sailors were from the white seamen with whom they sailed.

Africans who became sailors in the New World arrived from a three-thousand-mile swath of western Africa bounded by Senegambia and Angola. They had been born into societies with substantially different languages, kinship systems, political organizations, religions, and decorative arts. Nevertheless, underlying cultural unities provided a distinctly African foundation from which African American culture would evolve. Africans who came to know one another through New World slavery struggled to forge common bonds out of the African cultural elements and American social realities they shared. Thus the two boatmen who absconded from William Martin's pettiauger at Elliott's Bridge, South Carolina, in 1738—"one an Angola Negro, named Levi . . . the other an Ebo Negro named Kent"—had come to understand the pettiauger itself, the water on which it floated, the talismans on which they relied, and Martin himself in ways that he could not comprehend, and in ways that might have been strange even to them just several years earlier. Their new ways transcended their separate Angolan and Ebo origins but retained a distinctively African character.[2]

African legacies—including tangible skills, historical memories, and spiritual knowledge—contributed to a new black Atlantic seafaring tradition in the Americas. The New World plantation system relied on canoes and pettiaugers to transport supplies and plantation products; and African boating skills kept that plantation system afloat. Yet as African-born slaves handled vessels in Caribbean surf and Carolinian rivers, supernatural associations distinguished their perceptions of water and watercraft from those of white mariners. Africans did not differentiate between categories such as canoe travel and the influence of ancestral spirits. All were intertwined in a sacred worldview. Canoes and ships had their own layered meanings for Africans, as did the cowrie shells used by many West African peoples for money and

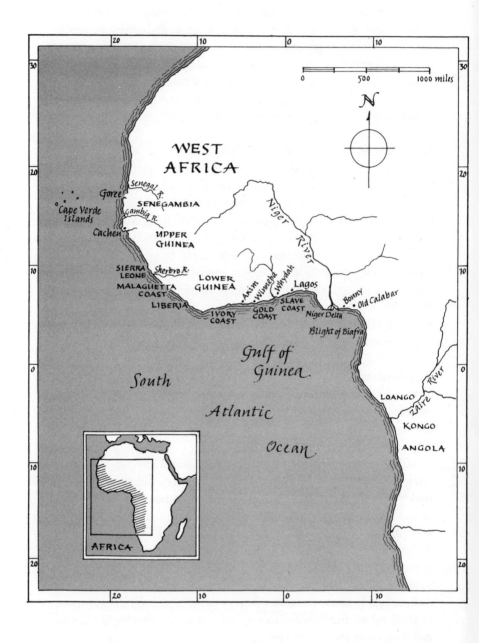

WEST AFRICA

- Goree
- Cape Verde Islands
- Senegal R.
- SENEGAMBIA
- Gambia R.
- Cachen
- UPPER GUINEA
- SIERRA LEONE
- Sherbro R.
- LOWER GUINEA
- MALAGUETTA COAST
- LIBERIA
- IVORY COAST
- GOLD COAST
- Axim
- Ninneba
- Whydah
- SLAVE COAST
- Lagos
- Niger River
- Niger Delta
- Bonny
- Old Calabar
- Blight of Biafra
- Gulf of Guinea
- South Atlantic Ocean
- LOANGO
- Zaire River
- KONGO
- ANGOLA
- AFRICA

N

0   500   1000 miles

decoration and regarded as hallowed because they came from deep water. African sailors' consciousness is only recoverable through a kaleidoscope of African maritime memories, New World maritime slavery, and African spiritual associations with water.[3]

A F R I C A N S did not build or navigate complex ships like the *caravelas redondas* in which Portuguese seamen arrived on the west coast of Africa during the fifteenth century. African canoe mariners rarely voyaged intentionally out of sight of land, and many slaves who ultimately came to America had never seen the sea until forcibly marched to the coast. With the exception of *grumetes*, or Africans from Upper Guinea who worked for Europeans along the coast, few had voyaged in deep-sea vessels. Yet long before Portuguese seamen began their advance down the African coast, sub-Saharan peoples had developed extensive commercial networks by water. "Not only did the Niger-Senegal-Gambia [river] complex unite a considerable portion of West Africa," writes the historian John Thornton, "but the Niger provided a corridor that ultimately added the Hausa kingdoms, the Yoruba states, and the Nupe, Igala, and Benin kingdoms to a hydrographic system that was ultimately connected to the Atlantic." In west central Africa, "riverine commerce was connected with coastal commerce and African craft plied the coastal waters between the Zaire and the Kwanza."[4]

Europeans regarded African watercraft with a curious mixture of intrigue (dugout canoes were exotic); respect (African canoes handled surf better than European boats); and disdain (Africans' maritime technology unquestionably was less sophisticated than that of Europeans). At the mouth of what Portuguese mariners named the Rio Grande River in 1455, Alvise da Mosto and his men encountered dugouts that he called *zopoli*, which, he wrote, "in truth were of a great size; one was almost as long as one of our vessels, but not so high; and in it were thirty Negroes." Fernandez reported "huge canoes carrying 120 warriors" on the Sierra Leone River about 1506. Writing from near the Gold Coast's Elmina Fortress during the late seventeenth century, a Dutch factor named William Bosman provided European readers with more detail regarding "a sort of Boats called *Canoas;* the

largest of which are about thirty foot long and six broad . . . Instead
of Oars [the canoemen] use a sort of Paddles made like a Spade,
having a Handle about the same length; with which paddling they
keep the *Canoa* in a very swift Course." Watching "Five or Six Hundred
Canoes which went a Fishing every Morning," Bosman belittled Africans' navigation with typical European condescension: it "is not very
considerable," he thought. Yet simultaneously he noted how dependent European traders were on Africans and their boats. Canoes were
"capable of carrying a reasonable Merchant-Man's Boat lading," he
wrote. "We generally use them in the transportation of our Goods
from place to place."[5]

In canoes of various lengths and designs, carrying from one person
to more than one hundred paddlers and warriors, coastal Africans
conducted commerce and war before they met Europeans. Thereafter,
canoe-borne trade began to complement that of European deep-sea
ships, securing much of western Africa in the web of Atlantic commercial capitalism. Shallow and maneuverable, canoes could navigate
vast stretches of African waterways impassable to deep-draft vessels.
Propelled by paddlers, they did not rely on the wind. Quicker to
respond to short, rapid-fire paddle strokes than were European boats
(with their full ends and more cumbersome oars), certain canoes
could better negotiate the tumbling surfs that constantly broke over
much of the coast. Canoes were efficient for short-haul trade, too:
Mandinga vessels called *almadias* on the Gambia River carried approximately one ton of cargo.[6]

Canoemen's collective skill, along with European traders' dependence on them, comes across clearly in Captain Nathaniel Uring's
awestruck description of small boat work during a slaving voyage to
Loango in 1701. "We saw the Sea break so high, that we began to be
afraid to venture, and were inclined to return," he wrote, "but the
Canow People encouraged and assured us there was no Danger. The
Canow was large, and had Eight Men to paddle her." Uring neatly
juxtaposed the canoemen's rhythmic teamwork with nature's fury.
"When we came near the Breakers they laid still and watched for a
Smooth, and then push'd Forward with all their Force, paddling the
Canow forward or backward as they saw Occasion, often lying between
the Breakers, which was very terrible to see, roaring both before and

behind us; when they saw a fair Opportunity they paddled with all their Might toward the Shore and got safe thither." Competent to command a ship back and forth across the Atlantic, Uring recognized that he was out of his element in the surf. He willingly entrusted his life to skilled African boatmen.[7]

European observers like Uring understood at best only half of what they saw regarding Africans and their boats. Watching Gold Coast canoe-builders at work on massive tree trunks, larger even than the giant cypress that boat slaves would hollow in South Carolina, an informant of the Dutch geographer Olfert Dapper noted that canoes "of the largest size are made at *Cabo das tres Puntas,* where trees grow which are seventeen or eighteen spans in circumference"—seven to eight feet in diameter.[8] Dapper's informant, like Uring, saw only the physical and the immediate. The huge silk-cotton trees from which Bullom canoe-builders in Upper Guinea hewed boats were considered sacred residences of spirits called *bloms* (a noun derived from the same root as the Bullom's name for themselves); and a local proverb affirmed that "the blood of kings and the tears of the canoe-maker are sacred things which must not touch the ground." More than a century later black Jamaicans still revered silk-cotton trees as sacred. For many Africans, then, canoes embraced a defining unity of the sacred and the secular, a unity transferred to America and sustained in various forms in African American culture. The ex-slave Charles Ball remembered an African in early-nineteenth-century South Carolina decorating the grave of his departed son with "a miniature canoe, about a foot long, and a little paddle, with which he said it would cross the ocean to his own country."[9]

Skilled African boatmen like the Kru understood vessels as both workplaces and connections to the spirit world. The Kru inhabitants of Liberia, a region once called the Malagueta or Pepper Coast and located just south of Sierra Leone, always impressed Europeans as expert boatmen. The Kru were not enslaved as often as peoples from Senegambia, the Gold and Slave Coasts, and Kongo-Angola, in part because slavers worked less frequently on the Kru coast than elsewhere; in part because Europeans valued the Kru as boatmen and interpreters and chose not to antagonize them. But exceptions existed. The preponderance of slave imports to South Carolina during the quarter-century before the American Revolution originated in Sierra Leone and Liberia. Some Carolinian boatmen undoubtedly could trace their spiritual appreciation of canoes and their boat savvy to the Kru coast.[10]

Europeans reserved their highest accolades for Gold Coast canoemen like the ones John Barbot saw fitting out "large canoes in which they make coasting voyages, as far as *Angola*." Barbot believed the Mina to be "the fittest and most experienced men to manage and paddle the canoes over the bars and breakings," but he also praised canoemen from Axim and Winneba who handled gracefully "the worst and most beating seas." Because many Yoruba and other lagoon-fronting peoples on the "Slave Coast"—a four-hundred-mile stretch from the western Ivory Coast to the Niger Delta—avoided the open sea, European traders planning to land at Slave Coast towns such as Whydah, Allada, and Lagos often employed Gold Coast canoemen, carrying them and their canoes aboard ship on coastal runs. Skilled canoemen were indispensable to trading on stretches of beach dominated by the implacable surf.[11]

Mobile, adaptable, and skilled, African mariners mediated between mercantile Africans and Europeans. They served as linguists, pilots, and surfmen from Senegambia to Calabar, although the nature of European-African commercial connections varied from place to place. African boatmen called *grumetes* in the Senegambia and Sierra Leone region known as Upper Guinea became virtual clients of European traders. In the Niger Delta, maritime trade occurred with Africans maintaining considerable autonomy.[12]

American boat slaves recollected not only African maritime traditions but the interaction of Europeans and Africans on the African coast. The American slaves who were most likely to have acquired European seafaring skills in Africa were those who lived and worked in Senegambia and Sierra Leone. Both the Senegal and the Gambia Rivers provided extensive access into the Upper Guinean interior along their considerable watersheds, and overland portages even allowed canoe trade between the mouth of the Senegal and the Niger Rivers far inland in the Bambuhu region. With more than two dozen rivers flowing independently into the sea between the Gambia estuary and Cape Mount, Portuguese traders called that section of the coast "the rivers of the Guinea of Cape Verde." They were quick to merge local seafaring and boatbuilding practices with Portuguese sails and rigging, resulting in a sailing canoe derived from local surfboats.[13]

Portuguese commerce led to the creation of an Afro-Portuguese community of *lancados*, traders whose political and cultural orientation was Portuguese, even though by the late seventeenth century they were physically indistinguishable from other Africans. Besides the *lancados*, another community arose called *grumetes*, comprised of African boatmen, seamen, soldiers, and others (including women) who worked for Europeans and the Afro-Portuguese. John Atkins noted in 1721 that the English private traders in Sierra Leone "all keep Gromettas (Negro Servants) which they hire from Sherbro River, at two Accys or Bars a Month . . . The Men-servants work in the Boats and Periagos, which go a trading." Nicholas Owen and two other white men with a dozen *grumetes* navigated a sloop along the coast from near the river Gambia to the Cape Verde Islands in 1753. According to Owen, "Black saylors, commonly known by the name of gremetoes, volonterely went with us in our expedition for a small demand of wages." [14]

Nurturing a collective identity marginal to both Africans and Europeans, *grumetes* often lived in their own villages and practiced an Africanized Catholicism. Limited land and a predisposition to trade forced them into commercial pursuits, though generally at a less prestigious and profitable level than the *lancados* whom they served. During the seventeenth century, when the port of Cacheu (between the Bijagos archipelago and the Gambia River) was at its peak, the majority of the numerous skilled boatbuilders there were *grumetes* trained by the Portuguese. At the turn of the eighteenth century, when famous French and English buccaneers ranged from the Caribbean to West Africa and on to Madagascar, they recruited sailors among *grumetes*. Forty-five of the 157 men captured or killed by the Royal Navy aboard Captain Bartholomew Roberts's pirate ship off Cape Lopez in 1721 were Africans. These men seem to have been neither slaves nor shareholding members of the pirate crew. They were probably *grumetes* on wages. But *grumetes*' primary business was slaving.[15]

In Upper Guinea, then, groups of Africans somewhat acculturated to European ways worked prominently in maritime trades, especially in slaving. Their complicity did not always spare them from enslavement themselves, and when they came to America they brought their culturally hybrid African maritime skills. "Two Free Negro Men, who had been hired . . . at Senegal as Sailors, & Interpreters" by Captain John Tyrie were carried ashore on Hispaniola in 1777 without distinction from the sixty-eight slaves they had helped manage on the sloop *Amelia.* Tyrie did not betray them: it was the French privateersmen who overpowered *Amelia* during the opening days of the American Revolution. Although Senegalese and other Africans often sailed aboard slavers as deckhands and interpreters, every seaman of color had to be wary boarding a ship bound for slave territory. Canoemen and *grumetes* who fell out of favor could be double-crossed at any time, "like the free native mariner on board our ship Providence . . . who," according to C. B. Wadstrom in 1791, "once in irons lost his spirits irrecoverably" and died by the "sulks." African seamen in the employ of Europeans were also subject to retribution from slaves. Captain Joseph Harrison of the *Rainbow* slaver explained in a letter to his employers from Barbados in 1758 that "the negroes rose on us after we left St. Thomas's [Sao Thome]; they killed my linguister whom I got at Benin."[16] African mariners in the slave trade exhibited the nervous detachment of men simultaneously smug about their own favored position and constantly leery of their European employers' potential duplicity or of other Africans' revenge.

As slave ships plowed westward, captives carried a shadowy knowledge of Euro-American work routines and plantation slavery garnered during months of confinement in African trading compounds. African boatmen knew the barracoons and coastal castles firsthand; they had often been to moored slave ships while ferrying slaves in canoes, and a few had even voyaged to the Americas as linguists and mariners. Many more African seamen who had not crossed the western ocean knew Africans who had, or knew white sailors' stories about the Americas, second- and thirdhand though they might be. That constantly humming human telegraph explains Thomas Phillips's recollection, from his voyage in 1693–1694, of Africans' "having a more dreadful apprehension of Barbadoes than we can have of hell."[17]

The case of a free sailor named Amissa indicates how at least a few Africans learned firsthand about life in the Americas. Amissa signed seaman's articles to make a voyage from the coast of Africa to Jamaica and back, as a sailor on board a Liverpool trading ship about 1776. He probably shipped from the Gold Coast or Bight of Biafra, as approximately 78 percent of the slaves bound for Jamaica between 1776 and 1791 originated there. When they were anchored off Jamaica, his captain assigned him with three other sailors to row a group of slaves ashore, where Amissa learned that he too had been sold. The duplicitous captain informed people upon his return to the African port that Amissa had died on the voyage. But a year or two later another black fortuitously returned from Jamaica with news that Amissa was alive, an announcement that prompted his friends to commission a Jamaican-bound captain to redeem him. This white man kept his word, and after nearly three years of slavery Amissa arrived in London, where, according to the *London Chronicle,* "the matter was laid before the African Committee, who ordered the Defendant [the captain] to be prosecuted, as a means of deterring captains of ships from like practices in the future."[18]

Grumetes like the Senegalese sailors on board the *Amelia,* as well as Africans who talked with Amissa, knew what awaited them in slavery. Two "new Negro men" who recently landed in Maryland from Africa aboard the slave ship *Jane* in 1760 appropriated a sixteen-foot yawl and absconded from their master. "One of them," he claimed, "has liv'd among the English on the Coast of Guiney, and can speak some English." He "denies being a Slave, and is supposed to be gone to dispute it with the Captain." The commissioner for Sierra Leone acknowledged that some maritime slaves destined for the Americas had already become accustomed to Europeans in Africa. Writing of a slave mutiny aboard the French slaver *Deux Soeurs* in 1825, he explained that "the crew were overpowered by the slaves who" wished to land "on some part of the coast near to the Plantain Islands . . . The catastrophe on board may be attributed to several of the slaves who had been employed as labourers and boatmen . . . These men were aware of the consequences of being taken to the coast which no doubt induced them . . . to effect their liberation." The process of cultural adaptation referred to as "creolization," through which Africans transformed themselves into African Americans, began, not on the shores of America, but on those of Africa, and aboard the slavers that bridged the two.[19]

On the African coast the nature of maritime work (and thus the nature of the maritime inheritance brought to America) varied by region.
No distinguishable group like the Senegambian *grumetes* emerged on
the Gold Coast, for instance, where Africans' trade with Europeans
was more structured by companies and localized in castles than was
trade in Upper Guinea. African canoemen, linguists, and sailors in the
employ of Europeans there did not shed their ethnic identity to the
extent that *grumetes* did, but instead remained rooted in their indigenous social and political structures. Gold Coast canoemen's status,
wealth, military obligation, potential for social mobility, and occupational identity were thus largely determined by African social conditions—conditions significantly influenced, however, by the long reach
of European commercial capitalism.[20]

Ephemeral sources make understanding Gold Coast canoemen's
work from their own perspectives difficult. It is not clear if the canoemen organized themselves into a guild or association, how they were
recruited, what constituted a crew, and whether they had their own
headmen, much less how these social relations may have been repro-
duced in a modified form among Caribbean and Carolina boat slaves.
Occasional references to the "headman of the canoemen" suggest that
they obeyed the authority of one of their own, who in turn negotiated
working conditions with Europeans. Ample sources, however, reveal
that European factors regarded Gold Coast canoemen as "seamen" as
early as the fifteenth century. First Portuguese and then English,
French, Dutch, and Danish traders wrote of canoemen who "deserted."
They flogged canoemen whom they suspected of stealing or of breaking other regulations. They haggled over and withheld canoemen's
wages.[21]

As transportation workers in an international system, Gold Coast
canoemen were subject to a host of exploitative and threatening
practices, similar to those faced by free African sailors and some
enslaved African American seamen. Kidnapping, enslavement, and
forced removal from one place to another were foremost among the
threats they shared. In 1704 an African official at Cape Coast Castle
charged that a Captain Hamilin had attempted to sell a canoeman into
West Indian slavery because he had damaged a canoe and deserted.
In 1739 the chief factor of the Royal African Company complained of

canoemen running away and setting fire to stores on the beach. "In the last few months the canoemen have been very obnoxious and have refused to do their common duty," he wrote. "I told them if they still refuse we can do without them and take them as slaves."[22]

The number of canoemen employed by Europeans on the Gold Coast alone rose from about 350 in 1650 to 800 or 1,000 each year by 1790. Canoemen loaded and unloaded the European store ships that arrived off the Gold Coast during the dry season, from September to March. They ferried ashore building materials such as bricks and lime; staples for the garrisons including tobacco and brandy; and trade goods—textiles, metalware, tools, weapons, and miscellaneous items such as beads, mirrors, and hats. Canoemen also conducted an extensive year-round coastal trade, serving Europeans who needed trade goods moved from their central forts or castles to outposts. They likewise served African middlemen such as Captain Quacounoe Abracon of Little Komenda, and acted as couriers and mailmen. Canoemen were a significant presence in the African towns near European forts, and they were often among the rioters in the towns' frequent disturbances.[23]

The vast majority of Gold Coast canoemen were free, although some of the European chartered companies had their own "castle slaves" who worked in boats. In the Niger Delta and ports farther east, enslaved canoemen worked for African slavers. An English seaman named Isaac Parker noted about 1765 that many canoemen transporting slaves from the interior to Calabar (a slaving port in the Bight of Biafra near Bonny, from which Ibo and Ibibio slaves were shipped to the Americas) were themselves slaves of Efik traders.[24]

Africans caught in the tentacles of the international slave trade came to realize that the meaning of slavery in various West African societies differed dramatically from that of the American plantation system. Although most West African slaves were both commodities and workers in an economic system long dependent on bound labor, many became subordinate members of their masters' society; for example, they sometimes formed "a fictitious quasi-kinship relationship to the master's lineage," which served to reduce their marginality and promote assimilation. This often took generations, however, during which slaves' status and standard of living differed substantially from that of their masters. Other Africans lived and labored in the *jonya* system (from the Mande word *jon,* for captive). A *jon* "was not transferable, he owned the bulk of what he produced and, in societies in which the system flourished, he belonged to a socio-political category that was part of the ruling class and thus had a share in the sovereignty of the state and its political apparatus." Most slaves in Africa were workers, but some were military leaders, merchants, and even judicial officers. Some owned slaves of their own. In any case, the chasm of status between master and slave was not so vast in most West African slave societies as in America, nor was the more elastic slave system encumbered with the ideological distortions of race. No African word corresponded to the English "slave" in all its layered meaning and total denigration of person. Canoemen transported to the Americas who had been slaves in Africa discovered a fundamentally different institution across the waters.[25]

European seamen at the boundary of African society presumed their superiority in almost every way. Despite the canoemen's indispensability, Europeans often described them as "rascally," "impudent," "ruffians," "outcast," "vagabonds," "wretched," and "criminal." Yet African canoemen were not the creatures Europeans constructed, but individuals on their own terms. An indication of what canoemen thought of themselves and their work emerges from a few scattered references. In 1695 Edward Barter hired a crew of canoemen to ferry corn through the surf. Their canoe overturned, and Barter later beat one of the men "because he would not help to carry the corn to the croome [a town or village]." As Barter remembered, "He told me he came to paddle not to carry corn at all."[26]

This sense of self survived the Middle Passage. A man named Bonna, who "says he came from a place of that name in the Ibo Country, in Africa, where he served in the Capacity of a Canoe Man," became a slave in tidewater Virginia by 1772. Bonna not only maintained his identity as a canoeman in America but discussed it so much that the Virginia master from whom he fled broadcast it as one of Bonna's distinguishing characteristics.[27]

Fifteen to 22 percent of eighteenth-century black mariners in the American South were African-born; as such, they had opportunities to contribute African legacies to a new black Atlantic seafaring tradition. An African who "cost thirty pounds Sterling out of the ship" in Antigua was later sold by Walter Nugent. Describing him to Abraham Redwood in Rhode Island, where the man had been sent, Nugent wrote in 1731, "The Negroe man is a Peice of a Saylor and a fine Papa Slave." Phill, a "Native of Africa" who had lived some years in the West Indies, fled in Petersburg, Virginia, in 1772. Phill had "been used to the Sea," wrote his frustrated master.[28]

Many mariners bore ritual tribal scars. For Africans, scarification was both decorative and identifying. A man's scars revealed his ethnicity, or village of origin, and the adolescent initiation rites through which he had been ceremonially made one with his village society. African scarification, referred to by white Americans as "country-marks," testified to a communal bond and to a sense of one's place in society and history. A sailor working aboard *Amity's Assistance* in South Carolina in 1761 had "a cross or country mark on the back of each leg, and the same round his waist." But in South Carolina such marks were more a means by which masters could identify men as their property than a reaffirmation of communal ties. When in 1771 "a squat made black African Fellow named Will" who had "been bred a Sailor" fled from his Virginia master, he was described as having been "marked in the Cheeks according to the Custom of his Country."[29]

Most Africans had no maritime background, but every new slave came face to face with European seafaring technology during the ordeal of the Middle Passage. That technology baffled most slaves. Olaudah Equiano remembered asking another captive "how the vessel could go," and being told that cloth was put on the masts, and that "the white men had some spell or magic they put in the water, when they liked, in order to stop the vessel." Equiano also remembered that the crew took precautions "so that we could not see how they managed the vessel," perhaps for fear the slaves would mutiny and change its course.[30]

The officers and crew aboard that ship guarded their maritime knowledge more conscientiously than most slaving crews, who routinely put African slaves to work aboard ship. After one Captain Edmonson arrived in Gambia from Rhode Island in the sloop *Ark* in 1726, he "communicated some pyratical Designs to his Crew," prompting most of the white sailors to desert. Left with "three white Boys," Edmonson supplemented his crew with what an observer called "six ignorant new purchased slaves."[31]

White sailors in the slave trade died at a higher rate than their black captives, leaving shorthanded ships to be worked by slaves. Deadly diseases including malaria, dysentery, and yellow fever felled European and American tars at Cape Coast Castle and Old Calabar. An anonymous sailors' rhyme put mariners on their guard:

> Beware and take care
> Of the Bight of Benin.
> For one that comes out
> There are forty go in.

While the feeble tars who survived tossed their shipmates' bodies over the side, remembered the slaver James F. Stanfield, selected slaves were "freed from their irons, and *they* pulled and hauled as they were directed by the inefficient sailors." Royal Navy press gangs hunting for sailors could decimate a crew just as rapidly as West African fevers. Captain Hugh Crow had to teach slaves how to handle his vessel on more than one occasion after naval officers impressed his white sailors. An Englishman watching slavers arrive in late-eighteenth-century Barbados noted, "So useful do many of the negroes become, during the passage, and the time they are detained on board, that their assistance is of much service in working the vessel." Many slaves who left Africa with no maritime skills thus acquired rudimentary ones on the Middle Passage, along with some knowledge of European work routines and social organization.[32]

Coerced by threats and kicks, if occasionally enticed with the promise of more food or momentary release from irons, Africans aboard ship hauled halyards and manned windlasses. They pumped eternally, the most onerous of sailors' tasks. Africans not only observed but managed European technology—even if they explained it through magic or spiritual power. They noticed the regimented clock time of seafaring watches and the brutal hierarchy with which the white men governed one another. White seamen aboard slave ships learned African practices just as Africans learned theirs, listening, for instance, as slaves working at rhythmic tasks reflexively began the songs that had always lightened and timed collective labor.

White men on slavers capitalized on Africans' skills during the Middle Passage. "The captains of Guineamen often relieve their ship's company from the duty of the boat, by training some of their black cargo to the use of the oar," wrote George Pinckard from Barbados in 1806. "We occasionally see the master of a slave ship rowed ashore by four of his naked Africans, who appear as dextrous in the management of the boat as if they had been for years accustomed to it." Any collegiate rowing coach will attest that Pinckard misinterpreted the immediacy of their training: four inexperienced oarsmen cannot swing together, especially in the ocean swell of a Barbados roadstead. Those Africans probably *had* been accustomed to rowing for years. After the confinement of a slaver, the assignment to row provided liberation of a sort, and it may have been accompanied by perquisites like better food or the opportunity to bathe. Captives imbibed lessons about slavery in the Americas from instances like these, in which whites relied on Africans and took pride in their appearance and dutifulness without understanding much about them. Slaves in the early stages of reading white ways learned that perquisites might be exchanged for skill and a certain demeanor.[33]

Concerted resistance to white oppression also began aboard slavers. At least 155 documented slave mutinies occurred aboard ship, and an equal number of slavers are known to have been interrupted, or "cut off," by Africans. The actual numbers are probably substantially larger. Most slave resistance was disastrous, suppressed in a welter of blood, but inspirational tales of success bobbed to the surface. Seafaring storytellers etched vignettes of Africans' resistance into their listeners' memories, vignettes of the Fante canoemen's strike at Anamabu in 1753, or of the successful mutiny aboard a Danish slaver lying in the Rokel estuary in 1788. The ex-captive heroes from the Danish ship established a free settlement called Deserter's Town in the hills outside Freetown, Sierra Leone, a point not lost on black sailors whose daily work connected corners of the Atlantic world, and whose survival one day might depend on knowing the location of safe territory.[34]

Africans disembarked in the New World with more than memories of resistance and sketchy knowledge of whites' ways. They brought tangible skills to American maritime work—as they did to cattle-rais-ing, rice cultivation, herbal medicine, and basketry. A white seaman named John Willock noted with admiration in 1781 the small-boat handling abilities of slaves on St. Kitts. As on most of the Leeward and Windward islands, good harbors were rare. A continuous surf, like that on much of the West African coast, made it dangerous to land. Willock believed that "the negroes" were "by no means afraid of dying by water," and that this enabled them to perform "what would be very difficult to any other person." "They are very dextrous in the management of their canoes," he decided, both landing them and getting under way. "Each canoe is manned by two negroes, who, in an instant leap on board of her, and proceed to whatever ship they are destined." [35]

Canoes like the ones Willock saw and periaugas, or pettiaugers (also constructed from hollowed logs in a variation of African style), be-came the heart of the local transportation system, including ship-to-shore lightering, from the Chesapeake Bay to the Caribbean. They carried rice, timber, tobacco, and everything else that slaves moved in bulk along the labyrinth of southern waterways. Many were substan-tial. A boat for sale near Charleston in 1764 was "eight feet wide and forty feet long, with a small cabin." Pettiaugers in Georgia "carrying from 25 to 30 Tons" had "two Masts, which they can strike and Sails like Schooners." Delegal's Plantation on Skidaway Island had a six-oared canoe "painted white outside and red inside, with a black bottom, about 27 feet in length." Dugouts like these often were vital to slaves' transportation needs in the Chesapeake and especially in the Carolina low-country. These hybridized craft, with modified dugout hulls and European-style sailing rigs, were similar to the sailing trade canoes built by *grumetes* in Senegambia, and to African *periagos*.[36]

American small boats and the skill necessary to build and handle them were truly creole—an amalgam of West African, European, and Native American technologies. But Africans have rarely been given credit for their contributions. In 1804, for instance, the *Naval Chronicle* referred to a periauga as "a two-mast Boat used by the Charibs"; in 1817 off Jamaica, Edouard de Montule described a "pirogue, or tree trunk hollowed out in the Indian manner." Of course, by 1817 Indians in Jamaica were only a memory. The style of construction and the silk-cotton wood of the Jamaican canoes noticed by Edward Long in 1774 were the same as those in Upper Guinea, where canoe-builders' tears were "sacred things which must not touch the ground." Without knowledge of African canoe-builders, contemporary chroniclers simply assumed that canoes and piraugas were of Indian origin. But Africans clearly had a hand in building the ubiquitous small craft that were such a distinguishing feature of the early-American waterfront.[37]

Euro-American seamen like Willock might marvel at the surfmen's dexterity and learn techniques of boat construction and boat-handling from them, but for the most part Europeans eschewed small-boat work in the Americas, making it the province of slaves. Olaudah Equiano's master owned a fleet of small vessels and droghers in Montserrat to go about the island collecting rum, sugar, and other commodities. Equiano remembered, "I understood pulling and managing those boats very well; and this hard work, which was the first that he set me to, in the sugar seasons used to be my constant employment. I have rowed the boat and slaved at the oars, from one hour to sixteen in the twenty-four." Blacks' handiness with boats was accepted matter-of-factly by whites. One white Carolinian referred to his slave as "a very good Sailor, and used for 5 years to row in Boats." Others were billed as "all fine Fellows in Boats or Pettiau's."[38]

John Willock, who had sailed in Europe, Africa, and the Americas, believed that African canoemen were not "afraid of dying by water." His rationalization of the dangers was one of many that whites constructed to deny the inhumanity of slavery and to make sense of the social division known as race. Equiano knew differently: "My life hung daily in suspense, particularly in the surfs . . . These are extremely violent throughout the West-Indies, and I was ever exposed to their howling rage and devouring fury in all the islands. I have seen them strike and toss a boat right up [on] end, and maim several on board."[39]

Skilled slaves not only facilitated the business of their masters in small boats and canoes but brought with them a bargaining chip to help determine the nature of their work in the New World slave system. Even in places like New England, where the number of slaves relative to the white population was never very great, slaveowners could not completely control their bondsmens' daily work. In the West

Indies or in South Carolina whites had even less immediate control. Although the omnipresent threat of the lash made the ultimate outcome of labor relations weighted heavily in favor of slaveowners, masters also found it in everyone's best interest to suit slaves to their work and to allow them some incentives and autonomy. Oppressive and domineering as it was, slavery worked dialectically, as do all social relations of authority and power. Masters got the lion's share of what they wanted, but they did not escape the influence of their bondsmen.

African boatmen and seamen were introduced to American ways in part by white sailors, in part by their experiences in different ports. Olaudah Equiano learned a great deal about his new world from Richard Baker, a white boy about his age with whom he sailed in the Royal Navy. Africans aboard ship, however, clearly lived among a controlling white majority. Whereas some like Equiano cultivated the art of interacting with whites on white terms, many black seamen found themselves psychologically disabled by their forced assimilation into a predominantly white environment. Denied power, always on guard, and never entirely sure of the cultural meanings of certain signs, words, and situations, African seamen daily confronted their outsider status in a white-defined world. Although seafaring sped the acculturation of many Africans and enabled them to maneuver in the slave system more effectively, seafaring also cast in bold relief the cultural differences between Africans—some still ritually scarred—and white mariners.

African sailors, however, were not simply becoming accustomed to the culture of whites: they were creating a black Atlantic maritime tradition. African-born sailors and some of their descendants in America fashioned a new cultural self-consciousness that linked meaning and experience in ways foreign to whites, and that reflected Africans' fusion of the sacred and the secular. Many Africans, for instance, felt the power of the water in profound and immediate ways. Across West Africa, the surface of the water served variously in myth and ritual as the boundary through which spiritual communications occurred. And intercourse with spirits, both benign and evil, affected the daily life of all Africans.[40]

For the Bambara in Senegambia, many of whom were transported to colonial Louisiana, an androgynous water spirit called Faro maintained an individual's soul or vital life force after death. Refreshed and purified under water, the soul would reappear in the next-born member of the family. Ibo peoples from near the Bight of Benin had similar associations with the transmigration of souls in water: a slave in Georgia testified that Ibos there intent on killing themselves to end their slavery would "mahch right down in duh ribbuh tuh mach back tuh Africa." For historic Kongo peoples a watery barrier called the Kalunga line divided the living from the spirit world. To the Kongolese, Kalunga conveyed powerful associations with the elderly and with those departed who had been exceptionally wise and strong. As Wyatt MacGaffey, a prominent anthropologist of the Kongo, has written concerning twentieth-century Kongolese, "The Atlantic Ocean is only one of a number of waters that may serve to represent the ideal barrier, which is called Kalunga. Boats of various kinds are vehicles for transporting souls or for returning to this shore such exceptional individuals as prophets, who are able to come and go."[41]

Kalunga suggests a deeply held belief in spirits (or "the living dead") who were accessible across a watery interface, and without whom no conception of the self could exist. To Africans water was clearly a potent metaphor for life beyond this world, even if, as examples from Bambara, Ibo, and Kongolese people reveal, it was understood variously by different peoples. Such beliefs survived the estranging Middle Passage, as the actions of a slave named Minc reveal. During the late nineteenth century, a white American southerner named Harry Stillwell Edwards recalled that in boyhood he had watched the African-born Minc catch a terrapin, "and with a bit of wire ground to an exceedingly fine point cut on its shell a number of curious signs or hieroglyphics," before releasing it, a process Minc repeated innumerable times. During the 1980s, an American art historian found "ritual experts called *nganga nkodi* and *nganga nsibi*" in the northern Kongo communicating with ancestors in the same way. "They cut their signs *(bidimbu)* into the shell of a tortoise so that the reptile, diving back into the water, will carry them across the *Kalunga* line into the world beyond." This may explain why African captives aboard a slaver in 1750 refused to eat turtle meat, despite their hunger. The ship's surgeon observed that they understood turtles as "fetishes."[42]

Historic Kongolese beliefs about the relationships between humans, water, and spirits clearly took root in the Caribbean and the Carolinas. It would have been surprising had they not: approximately 25 to 30 percent of the slaves brought to mainland North America alone originated in the Kongo-Angola region. As the anthropologist Melville J. Herskovits noted years ago, "In all those parts of the New World where African religious beliefs have persisted . . . the river cult or, in broader terms, the cult of water spirits, holds an important place. All this testifies to the vitality of this element in African religion."[43]

Slave funerals afford insight into the multilayered appreciation of the sea shared by uprooted Africans, including mariners. Dr. George Pinckard observed a festive late-eighteenth-century interment in Barbados. Grave-diggers told the Englishman that Jenny, the deceased, was an African washerwoman. Slaves at the gravesite, according to Pinckard, professed "full faith in Jenny's transmigration to meet her friends, at her place of nativity; and their persuasion that death was only a removal from their present state to their former home—a mere change from a state of slavery to a state of freedom"—seemed to alleviate their affliction. As the women each threw a handful of earth onto the grave, they cried out: "God bless you, Jenny, good-by! remember me to all friends t'other side of the sea, Jenny! Tell 'em me come soon! Good-by, Jenny, good-by!" Mourners, including five robust fishermen prominent in the funeral procession for their "antick gambols," also expected, as Pinckard relates, "to hear from poor Jenny . . . before morning" regarding the messages she brought to the ancestors for them. Among mariners like these fishermen, boating work was shaped not only by the social relations of production (in this case, by European maritime customs and slave codes) but by African associations with water.[44]

These Africans understood that in death Jenny would undo the transformative Middle Passage. They knew she would simultaneously cross the sea to Africa and the Kalunga line to her ancestors. She would accomplish in death what some "new Negroes" tragically tried to do in life, misunderstanding the immensity of the Atlantic. A "Negro Fellow named Tom . . . imported from Africa about 2 1/2 years ago" to Rock Creek, Maryland, "made an Attempt to get to Sea in an open Boat" in 1761. Home beckoned from across the sea, understood as both a physical and a metaphysical connection to Africa.[45]

Associations with the sea gripped Africans' imaginations. Kongolese people still understand the "meaning of life as a process shared with the dead below the river or the sea—the real sources of earthly power and prestige." In contemporary Kongolese cosmology, "the sea-passage of slaves is not fully distinguished from the passage of souls, the slave-trader from the witch, the geographical America from the land of the dead." Beliefs of this sort endured among eighteenth-century Africans transplanted to South Carolina. Sacred pottery marked with the Kalunga line was ritually thrown into South Carolina's rivers by slaves. The amount of such pottery recently retrieved by archaeologists indicates that Kalunga and other spiritual associations with water long remained a psychic compass for Africans who came to work in a white-dominated world. Indeed, some twentieth-century African American gravesites are still decorated with objects associated with water. Sea shells are prominent. Vessels for holding water and model boats for transmigration of the spirit are common. As the black artist Bessie Jones, of St. Simon's Island, Georgia, said in 1975, "The shells stand for the sea. The sea brought us, the sea shall take us back. So the shells upon our graves stand for water, the means of glory and the land of demise."[46]

Just as slaves forced to work on plantations developed an affinity for the land rooted in African religious, agricultural, and burial practices, so eighteenth-century African mariners brought their own multilayered understanding of the sea to that realm of toil and struggle. The ceremonial "John Canoe," a prominent mummer at Christmas and Easter festivals in the Bahamas, Jamaica, and North Carolina, wore masks that revealed the importance of migration and sea-voyaging (both actual and metaphysical) in slave culture. Anthropologists have noticed Nigerian rituals closely resembling John Canoe in which head-dresses represent ancestors "who had returned to life for the occasion." The Englishman Matthew Lewis observed early-nineteenth-century Jamaicans' John Canoe wearing similar headdresses—"bearing on his head a kind of pasteboard houseboat filled with puppets representing some sailors, others soldiers, others again shown at work on the plantation." The nefarious Middle Passage and other sea voyages made by the living and the dead clearly remained prominent within certain slaves' intellectual and ceremonial lives.[47]

Yemaya, the Yoruba goddess of the sea, is still worshipped in Rio de Janeiro today by macumba religious groups, albeit in a creolized fusion with the Virgin Mary. Yemaya's centuries-long endurance in Brazil suggests that at least some eighteenth-century Yoruba boat slaves, raised to honor the witchcraft of riverine and sea goddesses, approached their workplace knowing they were in the presence of powerful underwater beings. How long Yoruba slaves sailing out of American ports would have retained such beliefs without a supportive religious community like that in Rio is open to speculation. What is clear, however, is that at least for some time African seamen saw and understood the sea in ways distinctly different from those of their white shipmates. Their richly allegorical appreciation of the sea did not mitigate the harsh material conditions of their working lives, but it provided an anchor for the soul safe from their masters' prying eyes.[48]

Creating a black Atlantic seafaring tradition from African maritime practices, New World maritime slavery, and African spiritual associations with water, black sailors fashioned a workplace culture that remained closed to whites in certain ways. The case of Joseph Johnson, a superannuated black merchant sailor in early-nineteenth-century London, is illustrative. Lacking a naval pension, and having no claim to parish relief because of his foreign birth, he had no choice but to entertain for sustenance. A white Londoner suggested that "novelty . . . induced Black Joe to build a model of the ship Nelson; to which, when placed on his cap, he can, by a bow of thanks . . . give the appearance of sea-motion." The aged Johnson tramped the streets with his unique ship model upon his head, gracefully dancing his way to a beggar's livelihood.[49] But neither novelty nor necessity alone inspired Johnson's elaborate headgear. In a classic case of cultural cross-over, Johnson appropriated a European artifact, one that had become meaningful to him through his own years of sea service, and reinvested it with African meanings to create a characteristically black cultural expression. Most white contemporaries looked at Joe Johnson through the distorting glass of race and saw an old black sailor cleverly manipulating a full-rigged ship on his head. London blacks, on the other hand, saw an aged mummer bobbing through the streets, connecting them with his coded ship to West Indian and Carolinian slaves, and to people on the Gold Coast and the Niger Delta. Forced to represent himself with fawning propriety to white almsgivers, Johnson undoubtedly took psychological refuge in their inability to comprehend him fully, even as he shook his creolized African past in their faces.

3. THE WAY
OF A SHIP

There be three things which are too wonderful
for me, yea, four which I know not;
The way of an eagle in the air;
the way of a serpent upon a rock;
the way of a ship in the midst of the sea;
and the way of a man with a maid.

PROVERBS 30: 18–19

"In the time before steamships," remembered a nine-teenth-century tar, "man-of-war's men or merchant sailors in holiday attire, ashore on liberty . . . [sometimes] would flank, or like a body-guard quite surround, some superior figure of their own class . . . In Liverpool, now some half a century ago, I saw under the shadow of the great dingy street-wall of Prince's Dock . . . a common sailor so intensely black that he must needs have been a native African . . . in his ears were big hoops of gold, and a Highland bonnet with a tartan band set off his shapely head . . . In jovial sallies, right and left, his white teeth flashing into view, he rollicked along, the center of a company of his shipmates."[1]

Herman Melville's description of an archetypal "handsome sailor" may have been symbolic fiction, but it represents a great deal about the way of a ship during the late eighteenth and early nineteenth centuries. Relationships between black and white sailors were shaped by the specific circumstances of the seafaring workplace as well as by customary racial stereotypes. At sea black and white sailors faced down the same captains, weathered the same gales, and pumped the same infernally leaking ships. Work pulled them together. An inexperienced white sailor in the Bahamas who lacked the knack for making fishing lines readily admitted his reliance on an "old Negro on board of our schooner" who taught him "to soak the leaves of the Coritoo or the Aloe and work it into fibres." Sailors like these bridged the distance between blacks and whites, ignoring the concerns of planters and merchants that interracial contacts subverted social order.[2]

Race never disappeared aboard ship, of course. Everyone in eighteenth-century America had internalized some of its conventions, and racial burdens fell primarily on blacks, who decided in each situation how much of their guard to let down. Black men understood that among sailors, race worked in an ambiguous and sometimes contradictory fashion. Although certain roles aboard ship reinforced racial stereotypes imported from shore, most seafaring customs worked to black men's advantage. So the way of a ship—the nature of shipboard work, the laws regulating shipboard society, and the attitudes and behaviors that defined Atlantic maritime culture—often provided opportunities for blacks to escape the prevailing racism of other occupations and to improve their condition.

CERTAIN ASPECTS of seafaring changed little between 1740 and 1820. Refinements in rigging were modest, such as the substitution of a gaff-rigged spanker for a lateen mizzen. The average size of ships did not increase substantially either, though they became more efficient because shipowners hired fewer sailors per ton of vessel as the eighteenth century progressed. From sailors' perspective the single greatest improvement was the eradication of scurvy on long voyages, at least aboard ships where masters chose to dispense newly recognized antidotes like lemon juice. With no major technological or navigational changes aboard ship, and with an unchanged watch schedule and virtually unchanged maritime laws, sailors in 1820 experienced working conditions similar to those experienced by sailors in 1740. One of the most significant changes during this period was the increase in black mariners.[3]

Mariners over generations—slave and free, white and black—created an Atlantic maritime culture that reflected their work and status. The cultural heritage of deep-sea mariners reached back to coastal European antecedents that initially bore no trace of black influence. But maritime trades throughout the eighteenth century became integrated by blacks like Jasper, who sported "much the air of a sailor," and Jack, who "walks heavy as a sailor, he being used to the sea." As these slaves made themselves into sailors, they affected their white shipmates. Atlantic maritime culture evolved to reflect the presence of blacks in its music, style, and concern with liberty.[4]

White sailors shared with slaves a reputation as threatening, subversive, and exploitable men. The differences, of course, were that free seamen received wages, voluntarily acquiesced to a temporary bondage (unless impressed into the navy), and did not transfer their status across generations. White seamen surrendering personal liberty for the duration of their voyage suffered a situational "slavery"; most African American slaves endured a real and perpetual one. White sailors, nevertheless, frequently spoke of themselves as "slaves" and empathized with the plight of blacks. William Ray, a New Yorker sailing at the end of the eighteenth century, lamented:

> Some *slaves* might independence hail,
> Or sing of *liberty* in *jail*,
> With more propriety than we,
> For all of *us* were *bound*—to sea.

Sailors like Ray were not fully secure in their identity as independent white men. It is no coincidence that sailors called their leisure time "liberty."[5]

Frequently impressed against their will into the Royal Navy before 1815, sailors realized the fragility of their personal liberty. Mariners were also traded cavalierly like commodities by merchant captains who sometimes separated "troublemakers" from their confederates by discharging them into the British Navy. Having sailed from Philadelphia to Malaga in 1792, Captain Samuel Kelly told the consul that he "had two ill-behaved men on board which I wished to get clear of," and asked to arrange for "the captain of the [British sloop of war] *Zebra* to take them from me." In 1739 Captain John Lush faced a mutiny in

Caribbean waters aboard the New York privateer *Stephen and Elizabeth*. He therefore traded sixty privateersmen for sixty of His Majesty's sailors with an admiral in Jamaica. Cowed by a detachment of royal marines, Lush's men had little say in the swap. Almost sixty years later, when H. M. Frigate *Ambuscade* stopped the brigantine *Lark* near St. Domingue in 1796 and pressed two white men, *Ambuscade*'s officers realized that they had left the brigantine dangerously short of hands. They "sent him in return one Black Man named William More." Disciplined, impressed, and traded like blacks—or even traded for blacks—white sailors could not help seeing analogies between themselves and blacks. A Spanish "seafaring man, about forty or forty-five years of age, tall, very athletic and of a steady determined countenance," articulated the point. He swore that "he disliked everything in Charleston, but the Negroes and the sailors."[6]

Naval discipline became more severe toward the end of the eighteenth century because so many merchant seamen were forcibly recruited into naval service. Floggings increased, as did what J. H. Parry calls "long, indeterminate commissions, and the close incarceration of men on board ship when in harbour, to prevent their running away." Jacob Israel Potter, a black sailor from Delaware, spent at least nine years in unwilling servitude to the Royal Navy after his impressment in 1804. Potter probably rarely had "liberty" ashore during those years, because naval officers knew that impressed sailors would run at the first opportunity. Potter and thousands of other Americans appeared suspect when they refused the opportunity to enlist formally. Such balking irritated British officers and resigned the sailors to working without pay, without bounty, and without prize money. The forcible impressment of mariners by armed agents of the British government, their lengthy compulsory labor, and their subjection to naval officers' "vexatious niggling discipline" distinguished seafaring as labor without liberty. Not without cause was a young white Virginian told that the navy would "cut him and staple him and use him like a Negro, or rather, like a dog."[7]

Although blacks had varied perspectives on the navy, they became more critical of impressment after the American Revolution. Consider the distinct attitudes of William Castillo, who found refuge from slavery in the Royal Navy in 1758, and Jacob Israel Potter. Castillo's choices were limited to the Boston slavery he fled, the man-killing Barbados slavery with which his master threatened him, or the navy. Service in the Royal Navy looked safe and predictable compared with the alternatives. Real freedom for Castillo was not an option: the number of free blacks in North America in 1758 was minuscule. Potter, however, belonged to the first generation of northern American blacks freed from slavery in appreciable numbers, a generation raised after the American Revolution and imbued with its possibilities for liberty. Potter had options and visions, and he did not want to serve in the British Navy. As he wrote, "I was an American and likewise I was a Citizen & besides I had a wife and family."[8]

Outside the navy, maritime labor relations lay under the umbrella of Admiralty law, a specialized English code. Predating English common law and drawing substantially on continental European legal practice, Admiralty law denied to seamen the rights and protection afforded most landbound Englishmen, and later white Americans. Fostering a tractable labor supply through strict obedience, Admiralty law put mariners under the authority of individuals with recourse to corporal punishment. Just as slaves could be maimed or killed by their masters with virtual impunity during much of the slave era, sailors aboard British (and later American) merchant ships could be legally— and at times mortally—flogged by their officers well into the nineteenth century.[9]

No codes matched offenses to punishments aboard merchant ships, or meted out labor discipline in a systematic way. Instead, sailors suffered arbitrary and personal "correction" from officers. "Sampson got a flogging by the captain," wrote the diarist Stephen Reynolds in 1811, "after which he jawed us, called us thieves, country boogars, infernal scoundrels." Captain Nye followed abuse with reward, a classic tyrant's technique, and "let the people have tobacco in the evening." Officers like Nye rarely feared the restraining influence of the law. As he flogged a young sailor on the brigantine *Ocean* in 1803, the mate boasted, "You are not the first one I have beaten & he [the other] could get no recompense." The mate then "measured one fathom of the rope & cut off one half of it & gave it to Jenks, saying take this & carry it to Court with you." Seamen, like slaves, were constantly caught off guard with the arbitrariness of severe punishment for actions they did not even know warranted reprisals.[10]

Black men often suffered disproportionately the capricious nature of shipboard punishments. Aboard the *New Hazard*, the captain and his three mates dominated a crew of twenty, of whom two—the cook and the steward—were black. Listen to the white diarist. March 10, 1811: "We had tainted meat for dinner . . . the mate struck the cook with a large stick of wood." March 31, 1811: "Cook sick; Iverson [the first mate] flogged him severely." April 14, 1811: "Iverson gave the Steward a smart rope's ending." April 22, 1811: "Captain flogged cook for not getting victuals enough." May 11, 1811: "Iverson says the steward imposed on him when the captain was gone, gave him a number of strokes with a two-inch rope. Captain made inquiries and evidence in steward's favor." December 16, 1811: "Cook and Steward tied back to back." During this voyage from Boston to the northwest coast of America, only eight of the twenty men escaped a flogging, and none escaped abuse. But between them, the two black men endured a large number of the floggings—seven of the twenty-eight. The steward even "told Capt. Nye he would give all his wages if he would let him go home" from the Pacific in another vessel. White sailors gave "evidence in the steward's favor," and the white diarist, referring to the black steward's plight, lamented: "Judge how hard we live! Alas, hard and discontented." [11]

Admiralty codes were not the only laws that singled out seamen for special treatment akin to that of slaves. Local laws from Massachusetts to Barbados attempted to ensure a regular and tractable supply of maritime labor and reinforce the subordination of sailors to their captains. Statutes pertaining to seamen conformed remarkably to those aimed at slaves. Early in the eighteenth century, the colony of New Hampshire penalized people who harbored or entertained a sailor without consent from the seaman's master. New York's legislation restricting deserting sailors mirrored similar statutes regarding fugitive slaves. Colonial elites in New Hampshire, Connecticut, New York, and South Carolina forbade innkeepers and other vendors of spirits to extend credit to seafaring men.[12]

Guaranteeing a seafaring labor supply was only one aspect of local control. Freeholders feared transient and masterless seafaring men and attempted to regulate them by force and fear, as they regulated slaves. Laws in colonial New York stipulated that disobedient seamen should be whipped. Laws in Virginia prohibited seamen in port from going ashore after sunset or traveling without a pass. South Carolina lawmakers empowered "every free white person" to catch runaway seamen. And Grenada's "Police Act" of 1789 lumped together male slaves, free people of color, and sailors, who, "to the ruin of their own health and morals, and to the evil example and seduction of others," gambled and frolicked in island gaming houses.[13]

The greatest social division in eighteenth-century British America after race was between individuals who were economically independent and those who worked for others. The meanest white freeholder or tradesman considered himself a significant step above whites who worked at service or for wages, as sailors did. All white men understood that ownership of productive property and wealth conferred respectable independence. Prominent men, moreover, embraced social hierarchy because for them a ranked society meant an orderly one in which lesser men would defer to their authority. Clearly, the extent to which powerful men were successful in achieving their prized personal independence hinged on the number of dependent workers, servants, or slaves whose labor they could claim. White sailors who were subject to captains' authority shared with slaves and indentured servants the stigma of dependency and its characteristic psychology. Racial stratification was just one means by which powerful people perpetuated the dependency of others.

Race relations had their own logic aboard deep-sea ships. Hoary shipboard traditions and a rigid shipboard hierarchy did not have as much place for race as the customs associated with many occupations ashore. Seafaring's punctiliousness provided structure and rules for groups of men confined in exceptionally small spaces, often for long periods of time, and maintaining the rules gave each man a form of personal armor in a world in which he had little privacy. Aboard ship, social relations were not determined primarily by technology, tradition, or the challenges of the marine environment; they were made by men with vested interests in a certain social order that, coincidentally, did not depend on race for its perpetuation.

Sailors by no means succumbed without resistance to the wishes of those in authority, whether captains or shipowners. Should civil authorities in Boston looking to arrest a sailor send "constables to Search Ships," wrote Captain Hector McNeill, "from what I know of Seamen . . . such a man on such an errand would be likely to Loose his life or some of his Limbs, rather than find the person he was in pursuit of." Nonetheless, merchants' demand for obedience, codified in Admiralty law and in local statutes, meant that shipboard life and Atlantic maritime culture evolved around the concept of order—no matter how contested. Today our language retains the image "ship-shape" as one of compulsive orderliness.[14]

The shipboard order in which late-eighteenth- and early-nineteenth-century black and white sailors found themselves was maintained through a precise "distinction of role and status."[15] The ship's articles, or contract, that each man signed indicated his position (mate, second mate, carpenter, cook, seaman, ordinary seaman, "boy," or inexperienced hand, and so on), almost immutably fixing his status on board. Boundary maintenance—between officers and men, larboard and starboard watches, idlers and watchstanders, skilled and greenhands—was the essence of life aboard ship, for boundaries delineated privileges, perquisites, and punishments. Although formal boundaries could flex to accommodate human relationships, they never entirely broke down, and they essentially defined the social combinations and conflicts at the heart of seafaring life. Racial boundaries certainly existed, but they were often secondary to those established by the institution of the ship.

For a black man, then, ships provided a workplace where his color might be less a determinant of his daily life and duties than elsewhere. At Nooaheevah in 1813, four American sailors deserted together from the frigate *Essex*—a black named Isaac Coffin and three of his white shipmates. Coffin was then "a prisoner for attempting the second time to make his escape," according to Captain John M. Gamble, but his shipmates freed him before they absconded together "in a whaleboat." Whether asserting themselves in the spaces allocated to them aboard ship or fleeing oppression, African American men found considerable maneuvering room in maritime society. This is clear from John Wilson's responses in a United States Circuit Court. Wilson had sailed in

1819 with Captain Henry Ford of Baltimore, the commander of a privateer under the flag of the Oriental Republic of La Plata, one of the
breakaway South American colonies then struggling against Spain and
Portugal.

> *Question:* In what capacity did the black men serve on board
> the schooner?
> *Answer:* They fought the same as the rest of the crew when
> they engaged a Portuguese Schooner, and did duty as the
> rest of them.
> *Question:* When any Goods were given to the crew for clothing,
> did not the Black men receive the same as the rest?
> *Answer:* The Black men received the same as the other part
> of the crew.[16]

No less indicative of the fact that a seaman's billet meant more than
his race were the innumerable Yankee ships on which black men before
the mast ranked higher and earned more than their white shipmates.
The best-paid sailor aboard the Rhode Island brig *Mary* sailing to
Cuba in 1819 was Cato Burrill, a black veteran of twenty-five years at
sea. On the brig *John* in 1806, each of the seamen—one black, one
white, one mulatto—earned $18 per month, whereas the white cook
and the white ordinary seaman each earned only $14. The historical
precedent arising from such black men's experiences and their shipmates' respect contributed to Herman Melville's introduction of a
manly black as the archetypal handsome sailor: "the center of a
company of his shipmates," he was "on every suitable occasion always
foremost."[17]

The anonymity of working for wages and the protection available
to blacks from the prevailing shipboard hierarchy provided modest
opportunities for men of color. Late-eighteenth- and early-nineteenth-
century seafaring occupied a transitional position in the evolution of
labor management from traditional and paternalistic forms of bound
labor to newer contractual forms of wage labor. This often worked to
the advantage of black men, especially toward the turn of the century.
As waged workers rather than bound ones, sailors and would-be
sailors were among a constantly changing pool of applicants for
available berths. This allowed free black men (or those claiming to be

free) to come aboard ships on a similar footing with transient and inexperienced white workers.

But the degree of freedom extended to black men within seafaring society had clearly defined limits. Black sailors found, made, and filled specific niches at sea. Some of those niches (like the cook's billet) were defined by race, and some (such as able seamen's billets) were not. As able seamen, black sailors were on a par with white men in the same station. Skilled blacks, however, had virtually no chance to assume responsibility as officers, and unskilled blacks were relegated to sailing as ordinary seamen or "boys," where racial opprobrium was sometimes piled on low shipboard status. Moreover, all newcomers were hazed, and black men often got the worst of it. "I met with many enemies, and much persecution among the sailors," frankly stated James Albert Ukawsaw Gronniosaw, an African who went privateering out of New York. "One of them was very unkind to me, and studied ways to vex and teaze me."[18]

New hands, whether black or white, found themselves perplexed and in the way on sailing day, revealing how much skill and experience mattered in the exclusive world of the ship. "I was quite unacquainted with the sea, and was very much pleased in going on board the vessel," remembered John Jea, an ex-slave from New York who first agreed to a seafaring job about 1806, "but the case was soon altered." The captain and experienced men ridiculed Jea for not bringing more clothes and hazed him as he scoured the unutterably dirty iron kettles in which he was to cook. Seaward of the lighthouse, Jea recollected being "afraid the ship would fall, and I strove to keep her up by pushing, and holding fast by different parts of the ship, and when the waves came dashing against the sides of the ship, I thought they were sea lions, and was afraid they would beat a hole through the ship's side." In his fright and seasickness, he had no satisfactory response when Captain Stovey asked him "how the sailors' suppers got on."[19]

A young white novice named Richard Henry Dana was similarly confused on his first day under way. "In a short time every one was in motion, the sails loosed, the yards braced, and we began to heave up the anchor," he wrote. "I could take but little part in all these preparations. My little knowledge of a vessel was all at fault. Unintelligible orders were so rapidly given and so immediately executed; there was such a hurrying about, and such an intermingling of strange cries and stranger actions, that I was completely bewildered. There is not so helpless and pitiable an object in the world as a landsman beginning a sailor's life."[20]

Jea's and Dana's mutual befuddlement as greenhands makes an important point regarding sailorly skill, one too often lost in studies of seafaring labor in which analogies between ships and factories prevail. Although the social relations of production unquestionably proletarianized seamen, the able seamen whom Dana envied were not skill-less men working by rote. Despite the rigid hierarchy aboard ship, despite the officers' close supervision of sailors, and despite the enforced response of sailors to every command with a deferential "Aye, Aye, Sir," able seamen had a craft skill with important implications in the workplace. They were by no means able to control all aspects of production, or to organize time on their own, but their work provided for initiative, ingenuity, and discretion. They constantly interpreted orders, anticipated problems, and used their knowledge of ropework, steering, and shiphandling to execute the captain's or mate's plan. For many operations, such as sending up or down royal or topgallant yards, setting stun'sails, or reeving peak-halyards, able seamen made their own plan. Getting a one-hundred-ton brig under way would be impossible without skilled men able to interpret orders intelligently. Mastery of a basic repertory of the seaman's craft could provide any man—black or white—with a status defined by skill aboard merchant sailing ships. And once skilled, black sailors were partially insulated by maritime custom and shipboard hierarchy from whites' antagonism.[21]

Sailors developed skills in two fundamental categories. Navigating the vessel constituted their first duty: that is, making and taking-in sail, steering, trimming sails, and performing other related watch-standing tasks. On a full-rigged ship, this demanded knowledge of the names, locations, and functions of hundreds of lines, as well as an in-depth knowledge of tackle, purchases, and anchoring techniques. Experienced sailors like Dick, a slave described in 1788 as "a very good seaman and rigger," instinctively understood shiphandling and had internalized the relationships of wind speed, sail trim, rudder angle, and current. His skill allowed him to manipulate one of the most complicated pieces of machinery known to his society. Enslaved pilots routinely handled ships in dangerous inshore waters.[22]

Maintaining their ship was the sailors' secondary duty. This involved tasks that were both onerous and creative, and constituted much of the day's work. "I never knew, except in bad weather, any man belonging to the watch on deck to spend an idle moment," remembered George Little, "and it may well be said that a sailor's work, like a woman's, is never done." Sailors worked relentlessly to halt nature's assault on their vessels. They scraped and sanded then oiled and painted their ships' wooden planks. They slushed masts and tarred shrouds. They payed pitch into deck seams and filled checks in yards or gaffs. They replaced old rigging with new, which they fabricated on board—stropping blocks, reeving lanyards, and constantly heaving-taut rigging made slack by the ocean's ceaseless swell. Then they disassembled the old cables and ropes into "small stuff" and spun-yarn that would be employed in seizings, servings, and chafe-gear. Even the most mundane coasting sloop or schooner was complicated to a degree; full-rigged merchant ships and great ships of the line were extremely complex.[23]

The way of a ship evolved with great respect for the hierarchy of skill. Individual sailors rated themselves as able seaman, ordinary seaman, or "boys" when they signed the ship's articles, the master having previously indicated how many of each station he desired. This was just one of seafaring's longstanding customs that allocated to sailors, whether individually or collectively, some of the decisions that affected who did which task. Men in each watch—not their officers—usually arranged the helm rotation and lookouts among themselves. Although the mate had the authority to intervene, he rarely did so because to meddle was to invite the men's disrespect and risk having them interfere with the ship's efficient functioning. Likewise, it was "considered a decided imputation upon a man to put him upon inferior work." The most challenging jobs, and those that demanded the neatest work, were usually assigned to the most experienced men. An able seaman could be ordered by the mate to sweep the decks or to pick oakum, but if there were boys around and true seamen's work was going on elsewhere, such a task would be considered punishment.[24]

A full-grown man without sea experience had no choice but to ship as a "boy" on his first voyage—no matter his size, age, or race—and to perform a boy's work. Custom held that "a boy does not ship to know anything," and experienced hands often hazed boys unmercifully. Boys turned the spun-yarn winch. They coiled up rigging, held the log-reel while a superior calculated the ship's speed, and were sent aloft to loose and furl light sails. As part of their initiation, they were taught to make common hitches, bends, and knots, and to learn the names and locations of all the ship's running rigging. Boys might learn the rudiments of steering a ship, especially if she were a small one, but they made little progress in rigging or marlinespike seamanship. That was men's work.[25]

An ordinary seaman had to be able to "hand, reef, and steer," but was not expected to perform all the duties of an able seaman competently. For instance, "if an able seaman should be put in his place at the wheel in very bad weather, or when the ship steered with difficulty, it would be no imputation upon him, provided he could steer his trick creditably under ordinary circumstances." Although an ordinary seaman customarily knew how to splice small ropes, serve a shroud, or clap on a workmanlike seizing, his shipping as "ordinary" meant that he did not profess accomplishment at the finer points of rigging work. But no man would enter as "able" without an adequate knowledge of rigging and ropework. "To put a marlinespike in a man's hand and set him to work upon a piece of rigging, is considered a fair trial of his qualities as an able seaman," wrote Dana. Seamen's caricature of a real tar, "every hair a rope yarn, every finger a marlinespike," turned the sailor himself into the tools and materials of his trade.[26]

The allocation of particular jobs contributed to the way race worked at sea. When it came time to bestow workplace honors in reefing topsails or steering a crank ship in a quartering sea, skill mattered more than race, especially in the small crews of merchant ships. Many shipboard customs reflected a race-blind hierarchy. Seamen's "proper place" when they were on deck but not at work was forward of the after-foreshroud, that is, on the forward third of the deck. "The men do not leave this to go aft or aloft unless ship's duty requires it of them," noted Dana. Status etiquette that lumped together "the people" (black and white) in distinction to the officers overshadowed racial etiquette. The degree to which race was mitigated in the hierarchy of the ship is indicated further by customary nautical language. The "men" were able seamen, often contrasted with "the light hands"—a group that encompassed boys and ordinary seamen. Aboard ship a black "man" had privilege and priority over a white "boy"—even if that boy was older or from a slave society.

The career of a "valuable Mulatto sailor" whose loss Captain Samuel Kelly lamented in 1792 is illustrative. The man had shipped with Kelly in Philadelphia, but on shore in Malaga he enlisted on board a British sloop of war. Kelly generally praised sailors sparingly. "Our ship's company being very lazy and deficient in their duty had given me a great deal of trouble on the passage," he wrote. The man of color compared favorably with these "deficient" sailors. To have acquired the skills of an able seaman on previous voyages the mulatto man would have had to be accepted by white sailors and assigned duties by white mates. "Working upon the rigging is the last thing to which a lad training up to the sea is put," explained a veteran, "and always supposes a competent acquaintance with all those kinds of work that are required of an ordinary seaman or boy." As one of the most skilled men on board, the "valuable Mulatto sailor" expected the respect due his position. He would not have stooped to the menial and unskilled tasks of the white boys.[27]

Cooks and stewards, who were frequently black, inhabited an ambiguous social sphere belonging neither to the officers nor to the men. Ensuring that no supplies were squandered forced them to act on behalf of stingy owners and subjected them to captains' wrath. "This day, for waist of Coffee, by making it without grinding or pounding of it, I seazed up, the Cook & Steward," wrote the captain of the *George*. "Pardoned the former, & flogged the latter." Cooks' ability to bestow delicacies could inspire favoritism among forecastle hands, but stewards—the cabin servants—were often regarded as the captains' flunkies. One sailor flatly stated that "the crew do not consider him as one of their number."[28]

The cook and the steward guarded their territorial autonomy. Although supervision of a space aboard ship could insulate them from racist jabs to a degree, it sometimes reinforced their separateness from the men. The cook "spends his time mostly in the cook-house, which is called the 'galley,' where he cooks both for the cabin and the forecastle . . . Keeping the galley, boilers, pans, kids, &c., clean and in order, occupies him during the day." A seaman aboard a New York-to-Liverpool packet thought the galley "a strange-looking place enough; not more than five feet square, and about as many high; a mere box to hold the stove, the pipe of which stuck out of the roof. Within it was hung round with pots and pans; and on one side was a little looking-glass, where he used to shave; and on a small shelf were his shaving tools, and a comb and a brush."[29]

Sailors constantly accused cooks of being dishonest, filthy, or neglectful of their duty. But only blacks were demonized with fears that they would poison the crew. The nineteenth-century historian William C. Nell memorialized the rubber-stamp trial and execution of a black sea-cook in Charleston in 1817. One of the men aboard his ship died, "apparently in consequence of poison being mixed with the dinner." As Nell wrote, "The evidence . . . was—first, that he was [the] cook, and, therefore, who else could have poisoned the mess? . . . The real proof, no doubt, was written in the color of his skin, and in the harsh and rugged lines of his face." A white passenger on board the brig *Eliza,* which had a black cook in 1827, recollected "making an observation to Capt. Bukup in which he stated that there ought not to be quarrels on board the vessel between the Cook and Captain as the cook might in revenge poison the passengers."[30] If able seamen's skill mitigated racial differences and provided opportunities aboard ship to men of color, jobs as cook or steward reinforced racial stereotypes. Black mariners were both beneficiaries and victims of role assignments in the hidebound world of the ship.

Collective work tended to pull black and white shipmates together. Voyages began with "those peculiar long-drawn sounds," remembered Richard Henry Dana, "which denote that the crew are heaving at the windlass." Capstans and windlasses were hand-powered machines that multiplied human strength. Sailors inserted stout wooden poles called handspikes into the windlass barrel to turn it. It took "some dexterity and address to manage the handspec to the greatest advantage," explained William Falconer in 1769, "and to perform this the sailors must all rise at once upon the windlass, and, fixing their bars therein, give a sudden jerk at the same instant, in which movement they are regulated by a sort of song or howl pronounced by one of their number." Aboard ships fitted with capstans every able-bodied man and boy leaned his weight into bars on its head, and then went dancing round the capstan to the tune of "Off She Goes" or some other capstan shantey. Much of seafaring was collective work, especially heavy tasks such as heaving up the anchor, mastheading the topsails, and getting the tacks of the courses aboard, as Cato Wood and Caeser Lee knew from their stations at the foretopsail and crossjack braces aboard the ship *Boston* in 1777.[31]

Making and taking-in sail was an everyday occurrence for seafaring men, except on languid tropical passages in the trade-winds, where sheets and braces might not be started for several days. More typically, the vagaries of the weather, combined with the captain's desire to maximize ship speed, demanded frequent sail changes. Handling light sails such as royals and staysails would be left to boys and ordinary seamen. But furling, reefing, or setting big sails such as topsails and courses normally took place in unsettled weather, with the ship plunging and the gale intensifying or abating. These tasks demanded all hands.

The true meaning of collective work came home to men furling topsails. The sailors perched on a footrope, fifty or sixty feet above the plunging deck of their ship, looking ahead occasionally as she lurched into a trough or staggered to rise. Mostly they looked at the sail they had been sent to tame. The light hands or boys laid out to the yardarms, furthest from the mast, and fisted the leech (edge) of the sail up to their waists before stretching it tautly along the yard. The two most experienced men would stand in the slings on each side of the mast handling the bulkier clews (corners) and bunt (middle panels) of the sail. Soaked, and stiff from salt or cold, the sailcloth often resisted the kind of neat stow that would keep the wind from insinuating itself later to burst the sail free. So it was teamwork— reaching and fisting in unison, balancing together on the footrope, pausing instinctively as the ship stumbled—that made stowing sail safe and effective. The ex-slave Peter Wheeler remembered that while "taking a double reef" in 1809 he "used to be 'bout as much of a sailor as any on 'em." Human foibles notwithstanding, sailors aloft subordinated petty disputes to working together.[32]

The rhythm of seafaring as a whole also heightened sailors' collective sense that they shared a distinctive calling. No fixed schedule regimented farm workers' lives. The work day ashore lasted as long as there was work to be done, and intense labor alternated with idleness all year. This held for urban day-laborers and coastal fishermen, too, like the black fishermen in Charleston's "Mosquito Fleet." Attentive to the shoaling and migration patterns of fish, dependent on tidal currents, and always aware of the necessity to catch a favoring breeze and to run for shelter in the face of unsettled weather, coastal boatmen worked at their own discretion. But at sea the officer's hour-glass and half-hourly bells regimented the work day with a precision unknown to almost every other early modern worker.

Ships' crews were divided equitably into two groups, the starboard and the larboard watches. The term "watch" was also used to describe the basic unit of work time at sea. Watches (or "shifts," as a landsman might call them) lasted four hours each. From 4 to 8 A.M. was the morning watch; 8 to noon, the forenoon watch, and so on. The evening watch, from 4 to 8 P.M., was always split into two-hour shifts called dog-watches. This staggered the duty schedule, making seven watches instead of six so that neither the starboard nor the larboard watch would have to work the same schedule every day. Instead they alternated so that those who stood two watches on deck the first night would only stand one watch the next night. At best, every man had four hours of duty on deck and four hours "below," day in and day out. But on most vessels all hands were employed on deck during the afternoons; and in the event of unsettled weather or broken gear, all hands were called instantly. The longest uninterrupted sleep a seaman ever got was a little less than four hours, at which he would hear an authoritative thump on the scuttle overhead and the hoarse cry of a shipmate: "All the starboard watch, ahoy! Eight bells; d'ye hear?" Whereas inclement weather released farm workers and outdoor laborers from their tasks, nasty weather simply accentuated work for the sailor, reinforcing how different his work was from that of men ashore.[33]

Confrontations were frequent aboard ship, especially between sailors and officers. Seamen devised strategies of retaliation based on their particular circumstances. Giving captains the slip was a favorite. Originally "to give the slip" was a mariner's expression for an anchored ship hurriedly avoiding trouble by slipping (that is, jettisoning) her anchor cable. As instant mobility saved ships, so it saved sailors. Seamen deserted to escape what they called "grievous" short allowances of victuals, to avoid press gangs or disease, when fed up with cruelty or abuse, or to trifle with authority. Seamen deserted for life-saving reasons or for no reason at all. Most simply melted away, like the "negro man named Patrick Dennis" who ran from the brigantine *Andrew Doria* in Philadelphia in 1777, and who was "supposed to be concealed in town, or gone to Wilmington in hopes of making his escape in some of the vessels there."[34]

Men deserted abroad in search of "higher wages . . . than those they had been engaged at in America for the Voyage," a practice, consuls complained, that "occasioned the most serious inconvenience & loss to the Ship Owners." Sailors like John Brunto, a Rhode Island black who shipped aboard the *Betsy* in 1802, did not even wait to sail. Brunto brazenly absconded with his advance wages. Unlucky deserters like Aaron Gibson, "a Black man and Mariner" picked up by a Boston constable after he agreed to ship from New Bedford in 1802 "on a voyage to the Cape of Good Hope and elsewhere," were lodged in jail until sailing time.[35]

Sailors also antagonized captains and shipowners by capitalizing on laws that required seamen to be citizens. When the crew of the "American Vessel Fanny at Greenock" swore to British officials in 1793 that they were not Americans, *Fanny* legally could not "proceed to Sea," nor, wrote Consul James Maury, could she be permitted to ship any English sailors as replacements. Maury inveighed against the sailors' "swearing and counterswearing," as he later railed against a black man named Samuel Johnson who deserted the American ship *Hull Packet* to enlist in the Royal Navy. "This man was duly admitted an American citizen at this Custom House on oath. He thought proper since to desert . . . under plea of his *saying* that he was born in Halifax. Such a precedent," Maury lamented, has "a tendency to subject our vessels here to endless vexations." That was precisely what the angry sailors wanted.[36]

Like other members of the laboring poor, sailors faced "dead time" or "slack time"; they also confronted joblessness when hurricanes blew and harbors froze, and between voyages. Except when warfare and privateering spurred mariners' pay to "an Extravagant height," as Boston selectmen claimed in 1745, sailors' wages often lagged behind the cost of meat, drink, and lodging ashore.[37] Unscrupulous captains compounded these ills by withholding pay, especially from black men. "When we were unloaded I demanded my wages," wrote Equiano of a voyage that terminated in Jamaica in 1777, "which amounted to eight pounds five shillings sterling; but Captain Baker refused to give me one farthing, although it was the hardest earned money I ever worked for in my life." Blacks did not have recourse to court in the West Indies, but elsewhere they did. After several trans-Atlantic crossings as "cook and Mariner," a free black man named Woolford Oxford sued his captain for wages at Annapolis in 1785. Thomas Gardner, a black man from Virginia who shipped on the sloop *Clarissa* there in March 1798, joined three white shipmates in a successful suit for wages the following June in Rhode Island.[38]

Seeking profit in addition to paltry wages, free and enslaved black sailors often became petty traders. Equiano felt fortunate during the 1760s in voyaging to St. Eustatius because he could parlay his small capital—originally invested in a glass tumbler—into more tumblers and a jug of Geneva gin. He "blessed the Lord" that "in the space of a month or six weeks" he could acquire a dollar's profit. Another seafaring slave with whom he sailed brought "his little all for a venture, which consisted of six bits' worth of limes and oranges in a bag." As slaves ashore in Jamaica and the low-country negotiated for the right to grow truck gardens and market their produce for profit, so enslaved sailors moved along the edges of New World capitalism, striking deals in taverns and on wharves.[39]

By no means, however, were all black sailors of one mind concerning wages. "I never regarded money in the least," remembered James Albert Ukawsaw Gronniosaw, as he related how after one privateering voyage he did not tarry for his prize money, and how after another he had been defrauded of more than one hundred and thirty-five pounds sterling. "If I had but a little meat and drink to supply the present necessaries of life, I never wished for more," he said, "and if I had any, I always gave it if I saw an object in distress." Gronniosaw's attitude may have been conditioned to some degree by the ethic common to many white seafarers and expressed by Jack Cremer: "Sailor-like, [I] was always for a Short life & a merry one." Some white sailors like Cremer simply sought "Ready Money"—cash, but not capital. Eager to live for the moment, and often without a secure base ashore, sailors accumulated only the clothes and trifling possessions they could stash in their sea-chests. "A Rowling Stone never gathers Moss," is how Cremer put it. The African-born John Jea shipped out repeatedly, "not to seek my own interest, but the interest of my Lord and Master Jesus Christ; not for the honour and riches of this world, but the riches and honour of that which is to come." Evangelical Christianity, combined with an African up-bringing, reinforced a spiritual distance from materialism for some African seamen, providing a counterpoint to the accumulative ethic of blacks like Equiano. Alternative attitudes about money created tensions within sailors' collective ethos, but men of both races found themselves in each camp.[40]

Escalating prices in New York prompted seamen to seek a substantial raise in October 1802, from ten dollars to fourteen dollars a month. According to a newspaper, the "black seamen in the port united in the combination, under the direction of two *black commodores*, who acted in concert with the *white*, they in a subordinate capacity." How subordinate the black men were is a matter of conjecture. Two white "commodores" wrote to all the waterfront boardinghouse keepers telling them not to ship men for less than the new fourteen-dollar wage. Then in the fashion of eighteenth-century crowd protests, the striking seamen paraded "with drums beating and colors flying" in the wake of their "commodores," whose hats "were decorated with ribbons and feathers." The protest lasted for several days, during which the strikers demonstrated solidarity by threatening other tars willing to sail for the old wages. When threats did not suffice, they boarded at least one schooner "and with great coolness and order . . . proceeded to dismantle her of her sails and rigging, which they carefully stowed away in the hold." The authorities finally broke the strike, but not before black and white sailors united around mutual interests.[41]

WHEN NOT ASHORE in boardinghouses, or slinging their hammocks on the gun deck of a naval vessel, sailors slept, ate, and relaxed in a cramped forecastle. The forecastle was not a clean and well-lighted place. Forward in the very eyes of the ship, it suffered extremes of motion. Green water cascading over the deck above invariably seeped through the caulking. Forecastles were damp dens whose history remained in the odors of densely packed and unwashed bodies, stale pipe smoke, mildew, and the acid reek of tallow candles. Ventilation, light, and sailors themselves came through the scuttle, a hatch in the deck from which a ladder or steep set of stairs dropped into the compartment. Bunks lined the perimeter, and sea-chests lashed to the deck served as personal storage lockers, seats, and tables. Custom and practice as ancient as the common law reserved the forecastle for the sailors alone, and no officer concerned for the effectiveness of his authority—or his physical well-being—would trespass in the men's domain without fair warning. There, remembered one sailor, "You hear sailors' talk, learn their ways, their peculiarities of feeling as well as speaking and acting; and moreover pick up a great deal of curious and useful information in seamanship, ship's customs, foreign countries, &c., from their long yarns and equally long disputes." August Lemonier, a black man in a racially integrated crew aboard the brig *Hercules,* suggested that the men got along easily in their cramped quarters, and referred to "the general conversation of the hands at their meals" in which black and white sailors second-guessed their captain.[42]

Through their yarns, or sea stories, Lemonier and his shipmates whiled away the boredom of hours, days, and weeks in the same company. Yarning was a sailor's stock-in-trade. A homespun entertainment like singing or dice, yarning also defined workers as seamen and informally introduced them to their shipmates. Based first and foremost on personal experience, yarns were a gauge of experience and authenticity. In the forecastle during the watch below, "the yarns go round and round and you are not counted a sailor if you can't keep your end up," recollected a seaman. Sailors yarned of head-winds, passages, and privations, of infamous shipmates, commanders, whores, and ships. Snatches of individual black sailors' yarns remain. "Baily Negar hath just been here and hath been telling the descriptions of a voige round cape horn which a black man give him," confided the Rhode Islander Lydia Hill Almy to her diary in 1798. Years later one of the owners of the schooner *J.E. du Bignon* remembered: "One time I was loading this *du Bignon* in Savannah when three Negro sailors came by and one exclaimed 'Why there's the old *du Bignon*. I used to sail in her and she *p'ints five p'ints to windward of de' wind!'"[43]

Yarning affirmed men as members of the brotherhood of the sea and educated them in "the way of a ship"—in the signs, institutions, roles, and rights peculiar to sailors. More important, yarning educated sailors about shipboard politics and provided self-defense in the face of exploitation. When four mariners appeared at the Maryland Admiralty Court in 1786, they complained "that the captain with whom they originally signed Articles has left the vessel and that they are now subject to the Command of a Captain they never consented to be governed by, that he does not treat them in such a manner as Sailors ought to be treated, and as the Captain with whom they signed Articles originally covenanted to do." The content and cadence of most yarns evaporated with the wind long ago, but in this deposition traces remain. The men's gripe had been well rehearsed, not as a self-conscious staging for the judge, but in the comparative yarns they swapped in the *New Ceres*'s forecastle.[44]

Slavemasters often accused orally expressive blacks of deceit, and thus put a pejorative twist on the recognition that for slaves—as for sailors—quick wits and a ready tongue constituted one of the few resources at their disposal. Black storytellers moved easily along the waterfront, adding their voices to the yarns of men before the mast. Sam ran from his Maryland master in 1779. He had a "proud bold lofty carriage, with an impudent look" and a knack for stories: "in seaports, he said he was a sea faring Cook, and wanted to take shipping to some of the French islands." According to his irate master, Sam "will tell so many pretty tales, that he will almost make any man believe he is a free man." Billy Ballendine, a slave who was "tolerable proficient at sundry trades" including "going by water," had "as smooth and deceitful a tongue as ever hung in a fellow's head." Ballendine said he was "going to Baltimore, to assist in bringing a vessel belonging to Colonel Robert Howe, of Alexandria, round to Potowmack." A "negro Fellow named Stepney" who "used to go by water" told "many tales and plausible stories," according to the master from whom he absconded in 1781. "I suppose he has hired, or will endeavor to hire himself on board some vessel."[45]

A folk song sung by generations of plantation blacks asserted:

> Got one mind for white folks to see
> 'Nother for what I know is me;
> He don't know, he don't know my mind.

Seafaring imparted a new twist to this code. Aboard many ships, "white folks" in the forecastle were separated from those aft by class and custom. As part of "the people" before the mast, black men discussed their officers' foibles and faults with their white shipmates. "It appeared to him," deposed a black sailor of a voyage in which a mixed-race crew was shipwrecked, "as if the Brig was run on the Reef purposefully . . . It was smooth water—both anchors were on the bows and cables bent . . . and it would have been easy to let go an anchor until they should know where they were—this was the general conversation of the hands at their meals." The politics of class and craft informed this yarn, just as the politics of race and class informed the stories Ballendine and Stepney told pursuers and challengers.[46]

Yarning was an activity during which rules of race could be temporarily suspended. Of course, seamen did not play all their private cards with their shipmates. Surviving in a world with little privacy meant maintaining a private mind "for what I know is me." Even so, the culture and sociology of seafaring often led black and white men to grumble together and confide in one another. Forecastle life provided a middle ground in which black men did not necessarily assimilate "white" norms, nor maintain an autonomous "black" culture, but in which black and white men could afford temporarily to suspend attention to racial division. Most Atlantic seafarers accepted that differences existed between blacks and whites, but found that forecastle life mitigated them. The "total character" of shipboard life and its isolation bound seamen to a society of their own making, which, for all its difficulties, was quite exclusive.[47]

Atlantic maritime culture included strong egalitarian impulses that frequently confounded the strict racial etiquette of slave societies. Three white sailors from the brig *Neptune*, after being befriended in 1787 by a Georgian slave named Charles, "thanked him, [and] shook him by the hand"—a gesture unthinkable to most white Americans. During the War of 1812, the crew of an American warship, invited to a theatrical performance in New York City honoring their bravery in battle, "marched *together* into the pit, and nearly one half of them were negroes."[48]

This rough egalitarianism appealed to black men, as did other maritime traditions. Samuel Taylor Coleridge acknowledged a distinctive maritime culture of sailors

> Crowded in the rank and narrow ship,—
> Housed on the wild sea with wild usages.[49]

Sailors' "wild usages" included "a dialect and manner peculiar to themselves," which for its bluntness and candor earned them the reputation as straight-talking "plain dealers." Seafarers' oath-ridden argot maintained group solidarity and set them apart from landsmen.[50]

Sailors also affected a costume and stance that stamped them indelibly as members of the seafaring fraternity. A "bright Mulatto Man slave" named Sam sailed as a hand in 1771 aboard the sloop *Tryall* in Virginia. His "cloathing is such as is worn by Seamen, and [was] imported from England ready made," claimed an observer. A "short well-set Negro Fellow" manning a schooner on the Chester River wore "a blue Fearnothing Pea Jacket, patch'd with German Serge," whereas a "likely well made negro man, named Mial . . . of a very black complexion" who "used to go by water" sported "cotton trousers made sailor fashion and much tarred." Sailor fashion meant wide and baggy trousers, tight at the waist and cut a few inches above the ankle so as not to get soaked from the seawater frequently running over the decks. Dress pants, by contrast, were purposefully long and flowing. "Fearnought" jackets and pea coats were tailored short; long coat-tails could snag a man as he clambered over the futtock shrouds, or tangle dangerously as he let a halyard coil run free from the deck. But whether a seaman was black or white, whether he was working closer to Annapolis or to London, his clothing was distinctive and characteristic of trade, not race.[51]

Black and white sailors plaited their queues in distinctive fashion and were more likely than white men ashore to wear earrings. Daniel, an enslaved sailor in New York in 1804, sported "his hair tied in a short tight queue," as did "a Mulattoe man, named Jack Jones," who "went on board the *Providence* privateer" commanded by Captain John Paul Jones in 1776. In the middle of the eighteenth century, many black men from Long Island wore queues secured with an eelskin, a style favored by white naval sailors well into the nineteenth century. "A cask of eelskins, well pickled in brine, was kept handy," according to Clifford Ashley. "The queue was tightly worked to a point, and the eelskin, having been carefully rolled wrongside out into the form of a doughnut, was rolled back over the queue and seized." Whether African Americans or white sailors first wore their hair this way is moot; what is significant is the cultural predisposition that led both groups to adopt a unique style. In such instances, an occupational subculture rooted in interracial contact came to transcend race.[52]

Much as sailors marked themselves with a fearnought jacket or a queue, landsmen wore them too. Not so with tattoos, a badge reserved in the eighteenth century almost exclusively for deep-sea tars. "Tattoo" is a Polynesian word, and the practice increased among seamen after Captain James Cook's first voyage in 1769–1770. Those rare seamen who had voyaged to the Pacific, including the unlucky men aboard Captain Bligh's *Bounty*, returned much adorned with Polynesian tattoos. But seamen had been marking themselves in that fashion long before Cook sailed. Ned Ward wrote in 1708 of shipboard artists working "the Jerusalem Cross" and other designs into their shipmates' forearms by "pricking the Skin, and rubbing in a Pigment," usually india ink or gunpowder. Tattooed sailors self-consciously set themselves apart from landsmen and some other seamen. Regulars at the core of the craft, they emphasized their occupational identity. Like many ethnics, they recognized that the more distinctive a group is, the more likely it is to survive. Tattoos attracted attention to sailors' social separation and to their particular ways.[53]

Most tattooed black sailors sported the same designs as their white shipmates, including initials, anchors, mermaids, dolphins, and crucifixes. Michael Jones, an African American born in Louisiana in 1774, eschewed conventional designs: he had a figure representing "Justice" pricked into his skin. Thomas Lane identified himself as American with an eagle and stars adorning his palm. Most white seamen, and an even larger proportion of black sailors, were not tattooed. But in a sample of 846 American seamen who applied for Seamen's Protection Certificates between 1796 and 1803, an impressive 21 percent had designs pricked into their skin. In an era when tattoos were virtually never seen save on the weatherbeaten skin of a seafaring man, they spoke to an occupational identity not dependent on race.[54]

Ships, sea, and sun blazed other marks on seafaring men that spoke mutely to the shantey stanza "It's a damn hard life, full of toil and strife, We whalemen undergo." Thomas Smith of Boston, a black hand on the *London Packet,* had "a very remarkable scar on the right side of the head," an enduring memento of how close to death he had come, and "the little finger of the right hand [was] much deformed, & [he] is pitted with the small pox." A dark mulatto man named Joseph Warner had "a small scar on his left wrist [and] a large scar on his right leg." Scars marked shifting cargos, broken blocks, and hot tempers, except on an individual such as the cook of the *Eliza Vickery* in 1806, whose "sundry marks on his face" had been ritually cut in Africa. White and black tars together bore other imprints of their trade—the furrowed, leathery faces that came with years before the mast, and the calloused palms and toughened fingers that, hand-over-hand, had pulled miles of hemp rope. Marked in notorious fashion, they announced their trade to other tars, to inquisitive constables, and to the king's press gangs as well.[55]

DESPITE COLLECTIVE WORK and similar appearances, and an easy familiarity between many black sailors and their white shipmates, social identities still were conditioned significantly by race. Many white seamen simply did not like blacks. White seamen manned the ships that made the Middle Passage possible; they trafficked in slaves themselves with personal ventures; they raped captive African women; and they mercilessly quashed rebellious slaves' shipboard uprisings, called, like the insurrections of seamen themselves, "mutinies." Should a vessel transporting slaves come to grief by fire, stranding, or leaking, white sailors readily nailed down the hatches to prevent black captives from escaping to the deck, or from vying with seamen for the boats.

The white quartermaster Peter Vezian of the privateer *Revenge* mustered all his eloquence in 1742 to persuade a judge in the New Providence Vice-Admiralty Court that black sailors taken prisoner were slaves. "It does not stand to Reason," began Vezian's tirade, "that Slaves who are in hopes of Getting their freedom wou'd own they are so. Does not their Complextion and features tell all the world that they are of the blood of Negroes and have suckt Slavery and Cruelty from their Infancy?" Taking aim specifically at Senior Capitano Francisco, a black man commissioned by Spain who sat accused of using the English "barbarously" at St. Augustine, Vezian forsook an appeal to English nationalism or Protestantism, going right to the most damning argument. "What a miserable State must a Man be in," he thundered, "who is Under the Jurisdiction of that vile and Cruel Colour." [56]

Other whites shared Vezian's predisposition, if not his tangled logic. When a storm crippled the sloop *Peggy* between Fayal and New York in 1769, the ship's company spent almost six weeks adrift. They even ate the pump leathers before casting lots "to determine which of them should be sacrificed for the sustenance of the rest." After white sailors rigged the lots, they selected a slave named Wiltshire, the sole African aboard. The survivors ate him. [57]

Situations far more mundane than shipwreck incited white sailors against blacks. During the American Revolution, when Lord Dunmore extended amnesty to American slaves who fled their masters for the British lines, Chesapeake bondsmen flocked not only to British warships but to several merchant vessels. According to two deserters from H.M.S. *Isis* in 1777, however, white sailors "boasted they would make their Fortunes by selling them in the West Indies," and the runaways "were kicked and cuffed on every Occasion." Criminal action books kept by a Boston justice of the peace from 1809 to 1816 reveal numerous incidents in which white seamen like William Poor and Robert Grant assaulted and beat black sailors like James Coen. [58]

Brutal white sailors abused John Jea on his first voyage, about 1806. "They used to flog, beat, and kick me about, the same as if I had been a dog; they also rubbed grease and dirt over my face and eyes; oftentimes they swore they would beat me till they made me jump overboard, but I never did; and sometimes they would call me a Jonah." Jea's inexperience, his vibrant Christianity, and his African heritage prompted white shipmates to torment him, "until it pleased the Lord to send the thunder and lightening." After he watched an abusive white sailor "burnt like a cinder" by lightening, Jea confessed, "My soul gave glory to God." As a committed pacifist, and one who, despite his New York upbringing, swore that he "was not an American, but . . . a poor black African, *a preacher of the gospel*," Jea remained separate from maritime culture and most white sailors, even though he made many voyages "for the glory of God, and the good of souls."[59]

Jea channeled his rage at the haughty domination of whites with a silver tongue. An American consul in France rebuffed him, saying, "We will cool your Negro temper, and will not suffer any more insolence in our office." Jea talked himself out of that jam. But few black seamen mustered his articulate poise. Most endured the degradation of race by bottling up turbulent self-doubt. Boston King remembered that "in the former part of my life I had suffered greatly from the cruelty and injustice of the Whites, which induced me to look upon them, in general, as our enemies: And even after the Lord had manifested his forgiving mercy to me, I still felt at times an uneasy distrust and shyness towards them." Some enslaved sailors stuttered, possible evidence of the psychological cost of quasi-assimilation into a white-dominated world.[60]

Reflecting the often contradictory nature of race at sea, black mariners' reactions to whites ran the gamut from fawning accomodationism to racist violence. Shipping out for six years after he evaded his abusive master, the ex-slave Peter Wheeler tried to convince himself that the white people he encountered in New York and New England around 1810 wanted to help him. By contrast, a slave boatswain who confessed to setting a house in Boston on fire in 1741 would have scorned such assimilationist naiveté: according to a contemporary, the boatswain "looked upon every white man as his declared enemy." Ultimately his fury consumed him. Most men who would neither cave, as did Wheeler, nor explode, like the boatswain, explored the limits of maritime culture within which blacks could assert themselves.[61]

Humanitarianism was not a cultural norm in the late eighteenth century: physical suffering, harsh punishments, and human exploitation were accepted in what was generally a brutal, if sentimental, age. Race reinforced those values. Blacks learned early that the white world was arrayed against them. Yet white sailors occasionally put themselves at risk to subvert slavery by helping slaves flee. When "a lusty Negro Man, named Prince, about 25 Years old," deserted from a vessel on the eastern shore of Maryland in 1746, one of the white sailors provided "a Certificate for his Freedom." A fray erupted at Old Harbour, Jamaica, when sailors protected a runaway from Maroon slave-catchers. White sailors' notorious dislike of authority and their openness to blacks, a reputation they maintained despite some irrefutable evidence to the contrary, induced blacks in need to sound them out.[62]

Maritime culture also had room for black leadership. Skilled black pilots regularly asserted formal authority aboard ship, and other black sailors assumed informal leadership roles. Insurrection simmered aboard the *Zant* in 1721, where several seamen "muttered" at their captain and "often wished that the said Ship was in the hands of the Pyrates." A "free Negro married at Deptford," a common foremast Jack, instigated the "wrangell." He "bred a Mutiney that we had too many Officers, and that the work was too hard, and what not," and his shipmates rallied behind him. The *Zant*'s captain tried to solve the problem by incarcerating the black man aboard a Royal Navy warship and shipping "a quiate fellow" in his place, but the seed had been sown and his shipmates challenged the captain again.[63]

When twenty or thirty men, mostly sailors, assembled in Boston's Dock Square on a winter night in 1769, looking for trouble with the British garrison and armed with hastily improvised cudgels, an Afro-Indian sailor named Crispus Attucks led the crowd. Attucks (at 6'2") towered above the rest. White onlookers claimed that his eerie "war-whoop" egged on the mob, and that he poked the red-coated sentry with his stick, calling him a "lobster" and swearing that he would have one of his claws. Attucks fell first that night. As on the *Zant* many years before, a crowd of mostly white sailors followed a seafaring man of color into danger; and this time, into history.[64]

Black sailors led whites in skilled operations, too. When in November 1794 the sloop *Sally* went aground near the entrance of Delaware Bay, all the captain's efforts to free her proved ineffectual. After five weeks the owner, Thomas Blount, suspected him of "mismanagement or neglect of Duty." Winter gales were in the offing and the Blounts became resigned to losing their vessel, when a black salvage master took charge. He floated *Sally* free, with minor damages, in short order. "The Negroe is a clever fellow," wrote an elated Thomas Blount, who gave him a bonus "for his industry and perseverance." More significant is that northern white men rarely deigned to work alongside, much less under, a black man. Sailors were the exception. All of the crew, save one, stuck by the stranded *Sally* and worked under the black salvage master's direction.[65]

A personalized view of the ambiguity of race at sea, and of how it often worked to blacks' advantage, can be garnered from the memoirs of Equiano. He had more contact with seafarers than with any other group of whites from the time of his childhood enslavement until well into middle-age. An accomplished seaman himself, he wrote from a sailor's perspective. Equiano wrote passionately against slavery and the moral ills it wrought on white people; he spelled out in detail the banality of accepted cruelties in the West Indies; and he revealed white man after white man—including some sailors—who had double-crossed him. Yet for the most part, white seamen receive sympathetic treatment in Equiano's penetrating critique of social relations in the eighteenth-century Atlantic world.

Equiano characterized the white sailors he met aboard the slaver bringing him from Africa as cruel and greedy. But after a short stint on a Virginia plantation, he found himself back at sea on a merchant vessel where "everybody on board used me very kindly, quite contrary to what I had seen of any white people before." Five years later, on the *Aetna*, "the captain's clerk taught me to write, and gave me a smattering of arithmetic." Aboard the *Aetna* Equiano messed with a white man named Daniel Quinn, who "soon became very much attached to me, and took great pains to instruct me in many things. He taught me to shave and dress hair a little, and also to read in the Bible, explaining many passages to me."[66]

Michael Henry Pascal, the Royal Navy captain who owned Equiano, perceived the black man as a commodity rather than as a British seaman. Having promised Equiano's freedom, and having already appropriated six years' worth of his prize money and wages, Pascal double-crossed him in December 1762, selling him to Captain James Doran of the *Charming Sally,* bound down the Thames for the West Indies. "If your prize-money had been £10,000," said Pascal on parting, "I had a right to it all, and would have taken it." As Equiano remembered, "I had about nine guineas, which, during my long seafaring life, I had scraped together from trifling perquisites and little ventures; and I hid it that instant, lest my master should take that from me likewise."[67]

The naval tars rowing the boat between *Aetna* and *Charming Sally* made it clear where their sentiments lay in this conflict between the African sailor and the British officer. "The boat's crew, who pulled against their will, became quite faint at different times, and would have gone ashore, but [Doran] would not let them. Some of them strove to cheer me, and told me he could not sell me, and that they would stand by me." Equiano himself challenged Captain Doran: "I have been baptized," he said, "and by the laws of the land, no man has a right to sell me." Ten years were to elapse, however, before Lord Mansfield would decree, when hearing the case of James Somersett, that "slavery . . . is so odious, that nothing can be suffered to support it, but positive law." In a decision discussed by captains, planters, and blacks throughout the English Atlantic world, Mansfield ruled that Somersett, a Virginian slave who had accompanied his master to England and lived there with him for two years, could not be detained in irons and sold to the West Indies because Parliament had never passed laws legitimizing slavery, as had American colonial assemblies. Somersett's case lay far in the future on the dreary day that Equiano argued his own aboard *Charming Sally;* and he had no lawyer. "Indeed, some of my old shipmates told me not to despair," remembered the disconsolate slave, "for they would get me back again; and that as soon as they could get their pay, they would immediately come to Portsmouth to me." Their hearty encouragement provided his only consolation. Some of them did return, "and sent me off some oranges, and other tokens of their regard," but the white sailors' good will could not overcome Pascal's power and greed.[68]

Equiano despised the Caribbean. Assessing white West Indians as more unscrupulous than any men he had encountered, save aboard the slaver, he found, nevertheless, that white shipmates in the Caribbean were still likely to be a black sailor's advocate. Humiliated by a Jamaican coasting captain, Equiano was able, "by means of a north-pole shipmate whom I met with in the sloop," to escape his clutches. Earlier, while working as steward on the ship *Grenada Planter,* Equiano was victimized by another white West Indian, who bought some goods from him and made "many fair promises, as usual, but without any intention of paying me." A black shipmate had likewise been duped, but the two of them got no redress from the man himself or from the justice of the peace. As black men they could not threaten their debtor without grave consequences, but as seamen they could turn to their white shipmates for help. Three white sailors to whom the man also owed money joined Equiano and his friend. They stripped the fellow, threatening to cut off his ears and to use him roughly—small satisfaction considering they never got paid, but rare satisfaction for black men in the heartland of slavery. Equiano's narrative makes it clear that from the perspective of at least one black sailor, white seamen were less likely than other whites to abuse blacks.[69]

Symbolic events also suggest considerable racial forbearance among sailors. No eighteenth-century ceremony aroused more attention than "crossing the line," the initiation of greenhands to southern latitudes. Sailors customarily demanded a treat from passengers, perhaps half a crown or a dollar with which to buy drinks when they crossed the equator, and they dunked those who refused. According to folklore, Davy Jones and his wife (or Father Neptune and his wife Amphitrite) "keep a kind of turn-pike gate here, which is impossible to pass without paying something to secure their friendship." Aboard ships without passengers, veteran tars initiated greenhands with rough play, and discipline relaxed for a frolic. As late as 1790, a passenger noted that the custom was so rooted that, if not granted, "it would occasion a dangerous cabal amongst the crew."[70]

Slaves aboard an East Indiaman figured prominently in the ceremony around 1790. A white sailor, "curiously rigged with a trident and stock fish at the top of it, with thick oakham to burlesque flowing locks," mounted one of the ship's gratings, with Madame Amphitrite at his side. "They were drawn upon the quarterdeck by two Africans, and attended by a numerous retinue of inferior Gods; and what was unexpectedly well timed, Amphitrite insisted on freedom being given to the Africans, swearing that the Gods would never countenance the inhuman slave trade." Temporarily in the spotlight when officers and passengers deferred to mariners, a white sailor scolded his betters in a galling critique of slavery.[71]

ENOUGH CONTEMPORARY ACCOUNTS of black mariners survive to reveal the contradictory workings of race at sea during the late eighteenth and early nineteenth centuries. These mini-dramas reveal that context, circumstance, and contingency condition human interaction. Boisterous and contentious, free-wheeling and egalitarian, eighteenth-century Atlantic maritime culture offered black men the opportunity to be accepted as individuals by white sailors, or to be joined in common cause "claiming a Right" against the men and institutions that perpetuated their dependency. Meanwhile, shipboard society remained ordered around obedience and toward suppression of individual sentiments, including racist ones, that might disrupt the ship's smooth functioning. This rigid hierarchy exerted a considerable leveling effect between shipmates. Black sailors benefited.[72]

Yet maritime culture never completely overcame the fissures of race. Black sailors bore their accumulated humiliations with the holy anger of John Jea, the political protest of Olaudah Equiano, and the conciliatory self-doubt of Boston King. Always they kept a weather-eye peeled for whites' duplicity—maritime culture notwithstanding. They knew that many white sailors believed that men of color were inferior. When Gideon Olmstead and other white Americans planned to seize the British sloop *Active*, on which they were captives in 1778, they told two black men aboard to remain quiet and stay out of the way.[73]

Allegiance to neither class nor race fully explains how black sailors and their white shipmates linked experience and meaning in their Atlantic world. Although most white sailors did not think of black men as their equals, neither did they accept unquestioningly a hierarchical view of their society or conceive of it in binary terms, as white against black, poor against rich, dependent against independent. Their shipboard culture included room for the psychological strategy in which Europeans and Euro-Americans saw themselves in positive terms because they were *not* black. Yet simultaneously, the exploitative system that stigmatized white seamen as dependents influenced and conditioned them to perceive the world from the vantage point of slaves—a term they often used to describe themselves.

Although black sailors justifiably distrusted most whites and seethed at the white-dominated social order, they also learned that their white shipmates would frequently disregard conventional racial etiquette. As a Jamaican wharfinger observed during the 1820s, "In the presence of the sailor, the Negro feels as a man." Equiano knew that black sailors sometimes risked their captains' wrath and their own lives to assist desperate white shipmates, putting their occupational identity (or their identity as men) ahead of their racial identity.[74]

Yet however much the very structure of their work drove black and white sailors together, the hierarchy of race in early America drove wedges between them. Despite black sailors' recognition that the way of the ship often served them well, despite black and white sailors' close physical proximity, and despite the similarities of their working conditions and their place in the Atlantic political economy, significant gaps remained between them.[75]

4. THE BOUNDARIES
OF RACE IN
MARITIME CULTURE

> When they approach me they see only my
> surroundings, themselves, or figments of their
> imagination—indeed, everything and anything
> except me.
>
> RALPH ELLISON,
> Invisible Man (1947)

LATE IN 1814, chilled by raw Atlantic westerlies blowing across the desolate Devonshire moor, nearly one thousand African American seamen and five thousand white shipmates slung their hammocks in the British Admiralty's Dartmoor Prison. As prisoners of war, they craved peace and liberty.[1]

Racial dynamics worked differently among seamen in Dartmoor Prison than at sea. If the forecastle of deep-water ships was sometimes a shared middle ground where emphasis on role and opposition to authority mitigated racial distinctions, the climate at Dartmoor encouraged blackness and whiteness to flourish.

Head and shoulders above the other prisoners, even without his bearskin grenadier's cap, towered a "stout black" privateersman named Richard Crafus—known in Dartmoor as King Dick. In a world where most sailors were under 5'9" (and the average height was 5'6"), Richard Crafus stood an imposing 6'3", with "a frame well proportioned" and "strength far greater than both height and proportions together."

Invincible as Stagolee and imperious as Haiti's Emperor Henri Christophe, King Dick was the best-known man in the prison, where he played to white sailors' stereotypes for his own purposes. Crafus, who also called himself Richard Seaver, quickly dominated the blacks' barracks after arriving in October 1814. Under his rule, African Americans organized, disciplined, and entertained themselves, but did nothing to discourage white inmates from visiting the black enclave as customers.[2] "In No 4 the Black's Prison," wrote a white sailor, "I have spent considerable of my time, for in the 3rd story or Cock loft they have reading whiting Fenceing, Boxing Danceing & many other schools which is very diverting to a young Person, indeed their is more amusement in this Prisson than in all the rest of them."[3]

Despite extensive interracial interactions and a prison-camp moment as pregnant with possibilities as it was burdened with despair, black and white sailors at Dartmoor organized themselves almost reflexively by race. Separation of the black men in their own yard and barracks nurtured distinctly black styles, though racial boundaries did not conform exactly to boundaries of stone and mortar. Men often passed freely from one yard to another. Yet most whites did not gravitate to black "amusement" or recognize black accomplishments without considerable denigration. Confronted by a vibrant black culture that contradicted what they had been taught about racial inferiority, most white sailors denied blacks' distinctive accomplishments. Blacks, meanwhile, capitalized on white sailors' uneasy fear of black political organization and their ambivalent attraction to black music, evangelism, and pugilistic skill. They collectively leveraged prison Number Four to prominence.[4]

AFRICAN AMERICANS were at the center of the War of 1812 long before incarceration. When His Majesty's ship *Leopard* forced the U.S. ship *Chesapeake* to surrender off the Virginia Capes in 1807, and sullied American national honor by impressing American men (an action eventually regarded as the catalyst for war), two of the four impressed sailors were men of color.[5] White-dominated national memory veiled that fact, just as white prisoners of war at Dartmoor denied black sailors' relative autonomy and assertiveness. For northern free blacks, however, sea service and imprisonment in the War of 1812 became a signal event that afforded an entire generation of young men the chance to fuse reputations and masculinity with patriotism and to link up with individuals from geographically diverse communities.

The prisoners' initial desire, however, was simply to survive. Dartmoor Prison was uphill from Plymouth, seventeen miles of arduous marching along a rutted, muddy track. None of the Americans just off ships had walked for a while, many were shoeless, and between the chilling rains and mist and "the Soldiers pricking us up with there Bayonets," the trek itself disheartened men already disconsolate.[6] The heath struck a melancholy chord in sailors brought so low. Many of their shipmates, including two black seamen from the privateer schooner *Rolla* of Newport, had died in captivity already. One "was buried with becoming solemnity" at sea aboard a transport to Dartmoor. His shipmates might well have remembered "the bell [that] was toll'd Dureing the cerimony" for him as they first saw Dartmoor's dark stone walls rising in the mist—an apparent charnel house on a forsaken moor.[7]

Three concentric walls limited the prisoners' freedom, and the heath stretched beyond as a natural moat. Failed subterranean tunneling operations and a few successful escape schemes notwithstanding, those obstacles forced the captives' attention inward.[8] Stacked in hammocks, more than one thousand men could be crammed into a single barracks not much larger than a ship of the line. Yet each of the seven barracks' yards connected with the others, and by the winter of 1814–1815 the prisoners had considerable freedom during the day to come and go as they pleased. Without cells, the smallest group assembled at any time were the inhabitants of one of the seven prisons, ranging from several hundred to more than one thousand men. At the rallying cry "Keeno," they intermittently mobbed guards or badgered the authorities.[9]

African Americans' distinctive prison society took time to emerge. After the first Americans arrived in April 1813, months passed before others followed. Initially, Americans were housed indiscriminately with veteran French prisoners for whom the facility had been built, but eventually all Americans were transferred to Number Four. Separated from the others by its own yard, that prison remained distinguished as the barracks for undesirables—at different times defined as renegade Frenchmen, Americans, or African Americans. By the end of September, the black population numbered sixty-two men. By the end of January 1814 and through the following spring, only seventy-six African Americans and between seven and eight hundred white Yankees shared quarters in Number Four. Living at large among white sailors, the blacks endured taunts and punishments exacerbated by race.[10]

Unlike most of their officers, who had been genteelly paroled to the town of Ashburton, and who had a daily allowance of one shilling from the American agent in London who was responsible for prisoners' welfare, the black and white sailors suffered intensely throughout their early months of confinement. During the summer of 1813, prison authorities restricted them to yard Number Four, allowing no market privileges. Food, clothing, tobacco, and soap were in short supply. Whereas paroled officers were granted liberty to stroll in Ashburton and spend their shilling, foremast men were left to die in the prisons from measles and small pox. Officers at Dartmoor paid the price. "If a man who had been an officer manifested a disposition to keep himself aloof," recollected George Little, "he was almost sure to be mobbed, and if he had kept a taut hand and good discipline on board of his vessel, on entering these prisons he was generally tied to the whipping-post and flogged." Even calls of nature were answered with risk. No lights were allowed at night, and the men groped for pots at the end of the barracks. A seaman from Rhode Island remembered being "forcibly struck when first entering these prisons," in the fall of 1813, "with the miserable, squalid, appearance of the prisoners."[11]

Racial segregation initially existed only within messes, the groups of six men who were issued food together. This changed once Americans mustered sufficient numbers to assert themselves against the French, and once the black population swelled enough that white sailors perceived it as threatening. Ten months after the first Americans arrived, some whites petitioned Captain Cotgrave "to have the black prisoners separated." They claimed that "it was impossible to prevent these fellows from stealing, although they were seized up and flogged almost every day." Blacks probably were stealing. White sailors picked pockets and swindled their shipmates, with "brothers and the most intimate friends stealing from each other." No evidence corroborates that the seventy-five blacks were more prone to theft than the whites, but part of the ideological backdrop for racial encounters in Dartmoor was whites' enduring image of blacks as thieves. In granting their petition, Cotgrave "greatly relieved" the white prisoners and suited the blacks as well. Blacks were moved to the cock-loft of Number Four, the lightest, airiest, and warmest—if smallest—quarters in the building.[12]

Conditions improved in the spring of 1814. Jailers opened Number Four's gates during the day so inmates could tour the prisons, visit the French, and have access to the market that operated six days a week in the guardhouse square. Sailors bought food, drink, and clothing from Devonshire farmers and peddlers, both for immediate consumption and for trafficking about the prison. Access to the external market promoted a vigorous internal one, and daily set men to work "makeing bone Ships, some making fiddles some making straw boxes, some tayloring, some Carpentering some making tin ware, some Shoemaking & some at every other different employment." Washermen and barbers provided services. Vendors hawked their wares "as tobacconists; others as potato merchants, [or] butter merchants." There were many stands "for the sale of ardent spirits" and beer, including stalls run by black prisoners. One mess of whites marketed stew "at a penny a pint under the classical name of Friego." Another white merchant sold plumgudgeons—boiled potatoes mashed and flavored with codfish. "Who'll buy nice large hot plumgudgeons for a penny-a-piece;—just now smoking from the frying pan, warranted to cure all diseases . . . crisping, nice and smoking hot—plumgudgeons for a penny." Elevating the prisoners' standard of living without expense to the authorities, the market made life bearable. Yet sailors despised the "innumerable shoals of Farmers, market Women & Jews," who, "knowing they had no competitors in the Market & that the Prisoners could not be supply'd elsewhere . . . have fatned on the hard earnings of the American Prisoners."[13]

Both blacks and whites marketed victuals, and in a white privateersman's envy and contempt for a black fritter-vendor we glimpse race at work in the prison yard. The black sailor, "with his platter of fritters piled chin high," had "gained the reputation of making the best in the prisons." Josiah Cobb saluted the man's "delicately flavored fritters" and commented on his knack for "making them appear double the size of others." Cobb also admitted that "his trumpet-toned voice has no small share in drawing buyers." Not the sales pitch itself—similar, in fact, to that of the white plumgudgeon seller—but its distinctive delivery caught the attention of hungry men with a penny. For blacks, the melodious hawking was a brother's bond, a spark to an ancestral aesthetic. For whites, it was an intriguing if not quite understandable expression of the other, an expression they deprecated while attempting to capture. "Fr-r-r-r-itters," Cobb imitated, "lighter dan da 'punge, bigger dan a nobodies—de pan so clean what fry um, a man can shabe heself in, or see he purty face, dout tearing it to tatters;—tur-r-r-r-it! tur-r-r-r-it! frit! ter-r-r-frit! ter-r-r-frit!"[14]

In the late summer of 1814, with Napoleon Bonaparte's defeat, the French began to depart and were replaced with Americans. By the first of September the African American contingent had swelled to 345 prisoners; by the end of that month, to nearly 500. Jubilee came on September 10, with the remaining white prisoners' exodus from Number Four. At the end of the month, white Americans occupied two prisons in the north wing and two prisons in the south wing; African Americans occupied the one in the center. Officials dictated that prisoners from the north, south, and center yards "were not permitted to have intercourse with one another . . . except on Sundays." Black sailors thus had the critical mass to establish their own institutions, and substantial autonomy, when on October 9, 1814, Richard Crafus strode through the massive oak portal.[15]

FROM THE BEGINNING of their imprisonment, whether aboard prison hulks or at depots like Dartmoor, white American sailors during the War of 1812 elected executive and judicial officers to enforce their own rules. Black men may or may not have had a vote in the election of these committees, but they definitely had recourse to them. In February 1814 a complaint "was brought before the Committee" aboard a prison ship in Bermuda. "A mess of Blacks informed [the committee] of some of the Cocoa pounders taking out some of the Cocoa which was [robbing] all hands." A trial ensued and the culprits,

found guilty, were punished. White sailors were proud of their committees' democratic tradition. At Dartmoor whites created committees
of twelve, elected with a president and chosen for terms that might
be as short as a week or as long as a month. Committees adjudicated
minor grievances, tried and punished men who broke communal
rules, and dispensed patronage with the prison's paying jobs as barbers, orderlies, sweepers, stablemen, and lamplighters.[16]

Once African American sailors in prison Number Four had sufficiently large numbers to distinguish themselves from the whites, however, they established their own mode of group discipline and government. Since the middle of the eighteenth century, blacks in certain
New England towns (including Newport, Rhode Island; Salem, Massachusetts; Portsmouth, New Hampshire; and Hartford, Connecticut)
had gathered on the legal election day to select their own dignitaries,
called kings or governors. For the black communities that celebrated
it, Negro Election Day became the highlight of the year. The Pinkster
holiday in some New York and New Jersey towns served a similar
function. These occasions provided slaves with an opportunity to feast,
dance, and socialize, and to celebrate openly a distinct black cultural
tradition. Although that often meant satirizing whites' ways, the focus
of these festivals was black conviviality and leadership. Many popular
kings enjoyed a long tenure. In Albany, New York, an "old Guinea
Negro" named King Charles, "whose authority is absolute," ruled
Pinkster from the American Revolution until about 1808. And some
kings and governors had considerably more than ceremonial functions. In Newport, Hartford, and Portsmouth, informal systems of
black government existed alongside white county courts. On complaints by either whites or blacks against black offenders, the African
American magistrate hearing the case would sentence the defendant,
and a black officer would punish him.[17]

African American sailors at Dartmoor adapted this system, vesting
command in one man—King Dick. Whether in the noontime market
or at the gambling tables; whether attended by his "two comely white
lads" or at the head of a mob of black and white sailors; whether
refereeing blacks' disputes or teaching boxing, Richard Crafus clearly
demonstrated his authority and represented African American sailors
to the prison at large.[18]

Despite their common work as sailors, much of what mattered to black seamen remained masked from whites. Steeped in the republican tradition of the American Revolution, white sailors failed to recognize their black shipmates' reliance on specifically African American political forms to govern Number Four. New World blacks, however, despite the shackles of slavery, already had well-established traditions honoring their own freely chosen rulers. In ports and colonies around the Atlantic including Antigua, Barbados, Haiti, Jamaica, Mexico, Venezuela, New Orleans, and Argentina, all familiar to African American sailors, annual festivals inducted or honored black kings and queens. Blacks in at least twenty-one New England cities and towns are known to have celebrated Negro Election Day. Twenty-eight percent of the African American prisoners at Dartmoor had been born in New England, and many of the men born in the South (33 percent) and the mid-Atlantic states (33 percent) sailed from New England ports. Many had participated in the festivals that defined much of northern blacks' public life. Most, it is reasonable to assume, had knowledge of Negro Election Day and Pinkster.[19]

The extent to which white sailors at Dartmoor misunderstood black self-rule is illuminated by an encounter that occurred during the American Revolution. A Connecticut slave told a Yankee soldier that he favored Great Britain out of respect for the monarchy. The irate soldier condescendingly refused to talk further, as it seemed to him that the black man's opinions had been formed by his Tory "betters." The white soldier ignored the long-standing tradition in numerous Connecticut towns of blacks' paying homage to local royalty, which they defined not only by election, but by beliefs in certain individuals' royal African genealogy. Imprisoned white seamen in Dartmoor were just as contemptuous of King Dick's centralization of power: "an exception to the democratical form of government" prevalent there. "Most tightly does he draw the cords of despotism around his good subjects," sneered Josiah Cobb. "His word is supreme, no higher authority can be appealed to than his." Cobb missed the nature of interactions between black "subjects" and their "king."[20]

Black kings and governors in New England generally were elected, but they were also appointed, and at times high-rollers simply bought the office. John Anderson, an enslaved sailor belonging to a British officer on parole in Hartford during the American Revolution, told local blacks that if they elected him, he would treat them with money earned aboard a vessel "where he had certain perquisites of his own." Locals told the outgoing Governor Cuff that as an outsider, and a Tory, Anderson could not win. So Cuff simply appointed him as the next governor of Hartford. Noteworthy, as the historian William D. Piersen argues, is that "recognition of the office, its formalities, and the festivities honoring the leadership of the black community" were more important than scrupulously observed democratic processes.[21]

White democrats conditioned by stereotypes of blacks as childlike and barbaric assumed that Crafus ruled by force, just as white New Englanders had long assumed Negro Election Day was nothing more than a parody of white political forms. Blacks captive in Dartmoor, however, knew Crafus would maintain order in a disorderly world; moreover, they effectively manipulated white fear of potent black masculinity by elevating him to the absolute authority of king. As undisputed leader of one of the five American barracks, Crafus negotiated with prison authorities and white sailors from a position of strength.

King Dick threatened white sailors in a way that black shipboard or mob leaders did not. The commonly accepted formal and informal leadership roles held by black mariners as pilots, salvage masters, or cocks-of-the-forecastle were honored precisely because those skilled blacks led inter-racial groups of seamen. They embodied sailorly skill or stoicism, not blackness. King Dick's independent leadership of a self-regulating black collective, one thousand men strong, unnerved even those white sailors accustomed to working under the direction of a black shipmate.

Black New Englanders traditionally selected men of great physical prowess as kings and governors. African-born Quash Freeman, the ruler in Derby, Connecticut, around 1810, rivaled Crafus for strength. So did Salem's King Mumford and Derby's Governor Eben Tobias (whose son became the United States minister to Haiti during Reconstruction).[22] Those crowned on Negro Election Day customarily dressed splendidly, spoke eloquently, and carried themselves with consummate dignity. They would have nodded approvingly at King Dick's bearskin grenadier's cap, a costly sartorial flourish in the drab prison economy. Crafus maintained his royal air long after repatriation. According to a chronicler of Boston's underclass, Crafus, who still taught boxing, "was a well-known character . . . about 1826–1835 [who] lived in one of the crowded tenements on Botolph Street and was the focus of all the colored population of that district." Whites, at least, still knew him as "King Dick." Dressed in a red vest and white shirt, crowned with "an old style police cap" and "swinging an Emmence cane," long a symbol associated with black leadership, he assembled black Bostonians each Election Day as "Master of Ceremonies." Crafus annually led the procession around Boston Common, and closed with a "patriotic speech." Twenty years after organizing prison Number Four, King Dick retained authority among Bostonians of color, who acknowledged him more as a leader than as a tyrant.[23]

Crafus maintained authority in Number Four by making daily rounds, checking each berth and mess for infractions. "If any of his men are dirty, drunken, or grossly negligent," noticed one white prisoner, "he threatens them with a beating; and if they are saucy they are sure to receive one."[24] But white myth-makers obsessed with Crafus's physique, command, and style shaped him into a larger-than-life figure. He played to their stereotype of the "barbarian king." No record of his election remains other than one white prisoner's passing comment that "from being president of the committee, [he] had contrived to depose his brethren in office and to usurp the sovereign sway." Crafus might have crudely bullied his way to dictatorship or been a persuasive demagogue: evidence suggests both to a degree. Two whites claimed that several "coup" attempts occurred, but that Crafus "always conquered the rebels." Black sailors in prison Number Four seem not to have chosen the committee system then prevalent in other barracks, deferring instead to a modified form of one-man rule for themselves, and vigorously promoting the image of an invincible king to whites, who acted offended by black royalty, even as their stereotypes allowed them to see nothing else.[25]

Yet others in Number Four clearly had a say in its governance, no matter how united their allegiance to King Dick appeared to outsiders. An impassioned Virginian Methodist named Simon, who gathered a congregation among the prisoners, exerted considerable influence. As W. E. B. Du Bois explained years later, "The preacher is the most unique personality developed by the Negro on American soil. A leader, a politician, an orator, a 'boss,' an intriguer, an idealist—all these he is, and ever too, the center of a group of men, now twenty, now a thousand in number." Simon's earnestness and adroit manipulation of others propelled him to preeminence. A man named John swayed his fellow prisoners, too. He had reputedly once been a servant in the household of Edward, Duke of Kent, before shipping on the American vessel from which he was pressed. Literate, worldly, and a "pretty clever fellow," John was "sometimes a judge in criminal cases" in Number Four, where decision-making remained far more complex than white sailors' caricature of African American autocracy. Blacks' mask of unity, and whites' stereotypical relegation of black authority to a superman figure, effectively shadowed the nuances of black self-regulation. Tellingly, however, when "two Black Men [were] Flog'd for Stealing" in Number Four, the culprits were publicly punished at a pre-arranged time—not thrashed by an impetuous and autocratic king.[26]

White commentators found it impossible to imagine that African Americans, left to themselves, could create a viable social organization founded on some principle other than raw power or toadying to whites. One diarist smugly suggested that Crafus remained in power partially through "the countenance he derived from the white prisoners." Another wrote that "Big Dick is a great favourite with the authorities of the Depot, and is allowed greater indulgence than any other within the walls." The historian Joseph P. Reidy argues insightfully that in New England elections, African Americans placed a "premium on internal group discipline as a survival mechanism." This, more than "their desire to do the Man's punishing for him," inspired self-regulation.[27]

King Dick's corporal punishments had precedents in New England towns. Black officials in Newport employed the same floggings and banishment (called "warning-out") as white courts, but according to one Newporter, they also included a more unique punishment by "bastinado with a large cobbing board." This meant beating the buttocks of the offender with a special wooden paddle, in which holes had been drilled so that round welts were raised on the skin. African American sailors in Dartmoor employed this form of correction as

Africans forcibly transported to the Americas as slaves had strong associations with the sea and vessels long before the horror of the Middle Passage. West Africans from Senegal to Angola not only traded, fished, and fought from dugout canoes, but believed their lives were integrally connected with the spirits of departed ancestors, who resided below the waters of rivers and the sea. Boats were understood as a means to that realm. Many Africans thus regarded ships and boats simultaneously as workplaces and as sites of spiritual power.

Canoemen were common in Africa. The upper image of Gold Coast canoes dates from about 1700; the lower left shows canoemen ferrying slaves to a Portuguese brig off the Bonny River in 1837. Survivors of the Middle Passage disembarked in colonial America, where canoes also were ubiquitous. Dirck Valkenburg painted those below in 1707 on a Dutch West Indian plantation in Surinam. Hewn from vast cyprus or silk cottonwood trees by skilled slaves, canoes were handled by black boatmen whose African skills and traditions were refashioned in the service of their white masters. And whether in the Chesapeake, Carolinas, or Caribbean, boat work gave maritime slaves constant access to ships.

Speights Town boat - Barbados

Plantations were part of a maritime system. Enslaved boatmen hauled sugar, rice, and tobacco to ships bound for distant markets, as shown in the coastal scene from Antigua in 1823 (upper left). Slaves frequently carried cargoes in pettiaugers, modified dugouts modeled on African and Indian canoes. P. G. F. von Reck sketched one in Georgia in 1739 (lower left). In every plantation society small coasters, like the Speightstown boat painted at Barbados in 1800 (above), were sailed by slaves. Boat slaves had considerable freedom of movement, and skilled boat sailors were frequently in demand aboard shorthanded ships.

By the middle of the eighteenth century, slaves were routinely sent to sea, especially in service roles that whites assumed most "appropriate" for blacks—cabin boys, cooks, musicians, and stewards. White captains gained status when served by blacks. But enslaved mariners, like the cabin boy drawn in 1785 (upper left) or the drummer in the aft cabin of a naval ship (above), painted in 1745 by William Hogarth, gained exposure to seaport cities and to the far-flung Atlantic community of color.

Sailors of African descent like Joseph Johnson created a black maritime tradition of their own. Too old to sail by 1815, he entertained for alms in London. Johnson's signature ship fused headdress traditions from West Africa and the Caribbean with his identity as a seaman.

Eighteenth-century seafaring routinely thrust black men among white
shipmates, brought them to foreign ports, and exposed them to danger—
as John Singleton Copley's *Watson and the Shark* suggests. Painted in 1778,
it was based on a real crew and an actual rescue in Havana.

Whether enslaved or free, many blacks acquired the skills necessary for rating as able-bodied seamen. This anonymous sailor, painted during the late eighteenth century, expresses proud confidence. Men who knew how to handle and repair all the rigging on a ship like the *Abula,* painted in 1806 with black men prominently on deck, found that skill sometimes mitigated the burdens of color.

JOHN JEA,
African Preacher of the
Gospel.

Among the most cosmopolitan of all slaves, seafarers like Olaudah Equiano (above) and John Jea (below) became leaders of various black communities and ardent abolitionists. Sailors, including Equiano and Jea, were among the earliest black autobiographers to write in English.

Roaming seafaring men connected blacks in communities as widespread as Providence, Rhode Island (above), and Charleston, South Carolina. The bustling Providence waterfront was engraved c. 1800; the chart of Charleston by Joseph F. W. DesBarres in 1777.

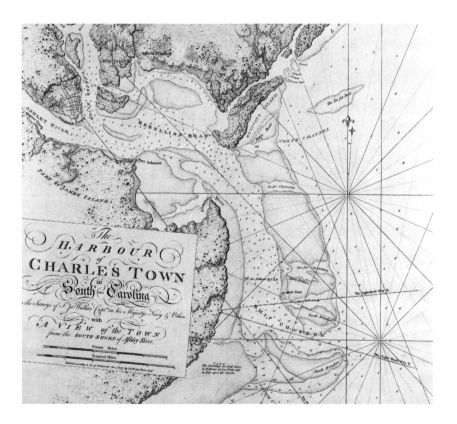

Traveling sailors disseminated news, rumor, and style among far-flung black people, contributing to the creation of a shared African identity and multiple black identities. The cudgelling match (above) was painted in the West Indies; the head-butting contest was drawn in Venezuela. Sailors from the eastern seaboard of North America frequented both places, mingled with local people, and competed in African-inspired martial arts contests.

During the American Revolution, enslaved sailors from northern states, like the Rhode Island privateersman shown above, often gained legal freedom through service at sea. The most influential black American after the Revolution was probably Captain Paul Cuffe of Massachusetts (1759–1817), respected for his profitable mercantile concerns, and for his advocacy of blacks in Africa and America. He led a back-to-Africa movement among free blacks.

After the American Revolution, seafaring became one of the few occupations commonly available to free black men. Although many maintained only a passing allegiance to respectable black society and families ashore, others used their paltry wages to support associations and churches, like the African Episcopal Church of St. Thomas in Philadelphia. Working aboard schooners like *The Young Brutus* (painted by Frederic Roux c. 1830 with black men on the foredeck), sailors often were separated from their families for months.

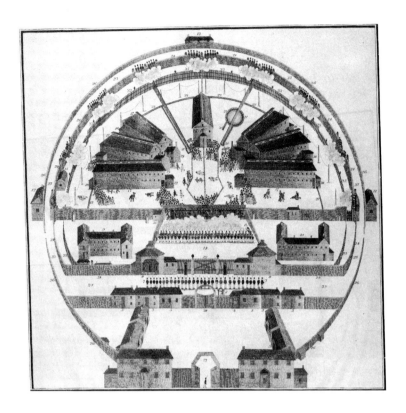

During the War of 1812, African Americans filled almost 20 percent of American sailors' berths. Black prisoners of war were incarcerated in the center barracks at Britain's Dartmoor Prison, where they organized themselves under the charismatic leadership of a privateersman named Richard Crafus—better known as "King Dick." Prominent in Boston after the war, Crafus is shown here in an engraving with his trademark hat and staff.

While approximately 90 percent of black Americans were confined to plantations during the antebellum era, most of them cultivating cotton, free black sailors roamed the world on whalers and merchant ships. Seafaring was dangerous and poorly paid, but sailors became the eyes and ears of black communities ashore. A Japanese artist painted these American whalemen in Japan in 1845.

Dirty, dangerous, and notoriously exploitative, whaling ships had a voracious appetite for labor. With limited options for employment, free blacks manned them in disproportionately large numbers. Slaves on the lam regarded whalers as a refuge, preferring to risk the vengeance of furious whales to that of slavemasters.

Blacks were often qualified for every station aboard ship, but few were allowed to command. As the master of the whaler *Industry* in 1822, Captain Absalom Boston was quite the exception. He sat for his portrait in gold hoop earrings and a white shirt and tie, revealing a man comfortable with several identities and conscious of his status.

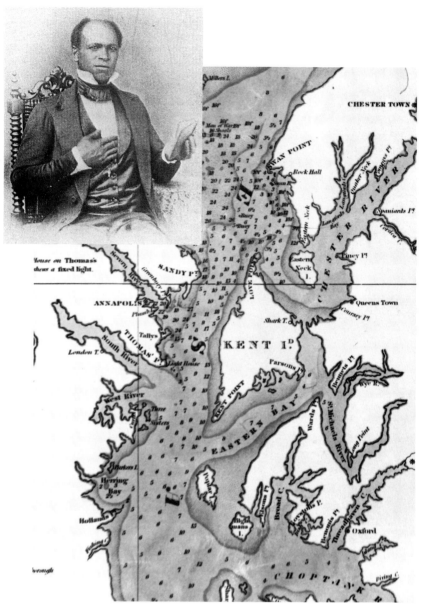

Ironically, slaves were more likely than free blacks to attain command. American social etiquette permitted skilled slaves to serve white masters, but forbade similarly skilled *free* blacks to ply their skill for themselves. During the antebellum years, enslaved captains like George Henry commanded cargo schooners throughout Chesapeake Bay—where he knew every river, shoal, and headland like the back of his hand. His self-assurance ultimately facilitated escape from slavery, but as a free man he had to step down from his high position as captain and sail instead as cook.

Enslaved pilots and watermen like Robert Smalls, who navigated the labyrinth of Carolina waterways, were well placed to strike a blow for freedom. During the Civil War, Captain Smalls and his crew of slaves commandeered the Confederate gunboat *Planter* (below), putting her at the disposal of the Union Navy.

Tens of thousands of African Americans served the cause of freedom during the Civil War, including the man in the foreground (top left) fighting aboard the *Hartford* at Mobile Bay. Fifteen African Americans were among the Union Navy crew photographed lounging on deck (above), taking a respite from war. Many black naval recruits were enslaved landsmen liberated as wartime "contraband," but many others had substantial sea experience. An all-black crew with white officers acquired such experience sailing the *Contest* (lower left) to Asia in 1863. Extreme clipper ships like the *Contest* were unforgiving racehorses, demanding seamen with nerve and skill.

But opportunities at sea for men of color ebbed after the Civil War. New forms of racist discrimination were intensified by a shrinking merchant marine and the loss of seafaring jobs. Following Emancipation, African Americans less frequently found positions aboard the ships that had so long been central to their economic survival and to the shaping of black America.

well. Accustomed to seeing the skin flayed off their shipmates' backs with the "cat-of-nine-tail," hardened sailors rarely displayed squeamishness over corporal punishment. Yet Benjamin Waterhouse, amanuensis for a white privateersman at Dartmoor, wrote that cobbing evoked "barbarity" and "ought never to be allowed where the whites have the controul of them." Black sailors' autonomy offended whites more than the cobbing. In their punishment by bastinado, as in their self-government, black sailors exhibited their own ways in Dartmoor, a place where "the whites [did not] have the controul of them."[28]

BACK IN AMERICA, economic exploitation maintained racial hierarchies. But in the prison yard at Dartmoor, white exploitation of black labor was absent; so, too, were white assertions of power such as slave codes, and dramatic inequities in material life. Walls created racial boundaries of a sort, as did a few British actions targeting blacks, but for the most part race was expressed through historical memory and cultural conventions—notably in the separate meanings sailors assigned to categories as varied as leadership, religious worship, and martial arts. Racial differences were evident in the ways black and white sailors got to prison, in their patriotic displays and manly sports, in their theater and dance.

The routes to imprisonment of the initial group of 24 African American men who arrived at Dartmoor on April 2, 1813, along with 226 white sailors, typify those of the 1,174 African Americans ultimately held at Dartmoor. More than 84 percent of the 6,560 American prisoners, black and white, were captured at sea. More than 1,200 American prisoners, however, were never captured in battle. George Higgens and John Odeen were black men "detained" in Gibraltar by British authorities intent on reducing the number of skilled mariners available to the United States. Press gangs seized George Dingall and Alex Petterson for the king's service. When given the choice, as detainees sometimes were, these blacks selected incarceration rather than enlistment in the Royal Navy. Cato Foster, a thirty-three-year-old black man from Marblehead, Massachusetts, was already in the Royal Navy when war broke out. He and at least 6 white shipmates delivered themselves up as prisoners of war rather than fight their own countrymen.[29]

At first glance, race seems immaterial in the ways Americans got to Dartmoor. Black and white seamen were captured by the British, and some of them refused to serve in the British navy when asked. Refusing to serve became more viable toward the end of the Napoleonic Wars, as the Admiralty reduced its personnel, offering Americans aboard royal ships incarceration in lieu of continued service. This policy was never uniform: American prisoners transported aboard H.M.S. *Talbot* in October 1813 "found there were four Americans on board that were impressed, that had frequently given themselves up as Americans, but were always flogged and made to do duty, viz. William Higgens of New London, William McCarty of Penobscot River, Thomas Hudson, a black man of Boston, and Peter Martin, a mulatto of Virginia." Ultimately, however, 1,011 of the American prisoners at Dartmoor came directly from the Royal Navy. And the lion's share were black.[30]

African Americans constituted 18 percent of the 6,560 American men admitted to Dartmoor, and about 18 percent of the contemporary American maritime labor force, then estimated at 100,000 strong. Any large sample of American mariners predictably would contain about 18 percent African Americans. But 33 percent of the 1,011 Americans exiting the Royal Navy were men of color—almost twice the expected ratio. Another, smaller sample of 221 prisoners impressed during the war who chose to go to prison rather than serve in the Royal Navy contained 30 percent African Americans. Race did affect how Americans got to Dartmoor.[31]

British pressure, black pragmatism, and a distinctive form of African American patriotism informed blacks' collective decision to withdraw from the Royal Navy. By the beginning of 1814, naval administrators were trying to reduce the number of blacks in the service. If not "the last hired," black sailors were "the first fired." A number of African Americans giving themselves up from the navy arrived at Dartmoor with fresh bruises and even fractures, feeding speculation that British seamen beat them when shipboard discipline turned a blind eye to race-baiting. In any event, though no systematic policy seems to have driven black Americans from the navy in 1814—black men, after all, were still being impressed—pressure from the British partly explains why more American blacks than whites volunteered for prison.[32]

Yet a larger number of black sailors made conscious decisions to leave the British navy. Black prisoners told clerks at Dartmoor that they had "delivered themselves up" as Americans, not that they had been drummed out of the service. African American men withdrawing *en masse* from the Royal Navy in 1813–1814 shared an appreciation of the historical moment for the race. They were fighting a desperate rear-guard action to disavow blacks' defilement in the national imagination and to defy the popular fusion of republicanism and whiteness that increasingly defined American citizenship by excluding people of color. Their actions were analogous to those of free men of color in Philadelphia and New York who offered to build fortifications during the late summer of 1814, as British naval squadrons lurked threateningly nearby. Despite exemption from military service, black New Yorkers dug in on Brooklyn Heights; and more than one thousand black Philadelphians helped fortify the west bank of the Schuylkill River. These former slaves or sons of slaves chose neither resentment nor apathy at a time of national crisis, but a pragmatic and calculating public show of citizenship.[33]

More black than white American sailors opted for prison rather than service against the United States because they had more to gain by getting out of the Royal Navy and more to lose by staying in. During this era of screaming-eagle patriotism, no black man who routinely associated with white Americans wished to be branded a traitor. Moreover, although Great Britain forbade slavery on its soil and publicly suppressed the slave trade, such abstractions were insufficient to overcome the more immediate and personal attractions of family, place, and habit that bound African American seafarers to the United States.

Much to the distress of British jailers, American prisoners managed to smuggle American flags into the prison almost from the beginning of their captivity. On July 4, 1813, when all of the six hundred Americans (of whom about seventy-five were black) lived in Number Four, they "divided into two columns and displayed [their] flags at each end of the prison." Whether the black men actively participated or not is unclear. The display led to a confrontation with the guards who tried to remove the flags; ultimately shots were fired and two prisoners wounded, ending the demonstration of patriotic solidarity.[34]

Once Number Four became all black, however, African American sailors participated selectively in patriotic rallies. Numerous occasions found "the American flag displayed on each of the Prisons." On December 31, 1814, sailors hoisted "saucy flags" emblazoned with "Free Trade and Sailors Rights" in large capital letters. "It humbles the British pride to see this Motto," wrote a privateersman. "This forenoon," he continued, "some English officers came up to see the prisoners & the [black] band of No 4 played up Yankee doodle dandy. O It galls them." Several months later, upon news of peace, "the musitions of all the prisons, formed a band and marched round the guards playing hail Columbia, and Yanky doodle, followed by a large procession." Meanwhile, "the star and stripe is flying on every prison." Black and white sailors shared public space, public processions, and public professions of patriotism to vex the British and express prisoner solidarity. At the same time, black men communicated to white Americans their hard-won rights to symbols of American freedom.[35]

Nationalist demonstrations by clannish sailors confronting an enemy abroad expressed honor, pride, and solidarity. They were similar to sailors' collective (and interracial) resistance to officers aboard ship. Black sailors hoisted the American flag or played "Yankee Doodle" in Dartmoor for reasons that transcended race. Consider John Johnson, a black sailor aboard the American privateer *Governor Thompkins*. After "a twenty-four pound shot struck him in the hip, and took away all the lower part of his body," according to his captain, "the poor, brave fellow lay on the deck, and several times exclaimed to his shipmates, "Fire away, my boys!—No haul a color down!" Johnson's dying words remind us that soldiers on the front line often fight more for their platoon (an immediate loyalty) than for the nation (a distant abstraction). Yet some whites contested what they regarded as blacks' presumptuous patriotism. When news of peace arrived in the prison on the last day of 1814, "the Prisoners of No 1 5 7 & 3 assembled in the Yard of No 3 and fired A Grand Salute of 17 guns—Composed of Rope Yarns and paper with powder inside." Black men were conspicuously absent.[36]

Black sailors' version of patriotism in 1814 asserted attachment to the United States and their right to belong. Whereas many of them regarded the American slaveholding republic in outright contempt, others were more ambivalent. For example, after being impressed into the Royal Navy, many African American men refused to enter their signatures in British man-of-wars' muster rolls. Doing so was to enlist officially in the Royal Navy, and to become eligible for a bounty, wages, and prize money. Refusing to sign the rolls consigned a man to the same work, food, and service as those who joined—but without the pay. Thus financial incentives and bullying were considerable. But many blacks refused. John Backus swore in 1811 that he "never Entered or took bounty," categorically refusing to profit by his unwilling service to a national enemy. "I . . . was treated very Ill because I would not Enter," lamented William Godfrey in 1799. "Neither have I," he wrote, "knowing myself to be an american as well as for what reason, I do not wish to serve them." Jacob Israel Potter refused to capitulate in 1811 after more than nine years of unwilling service "because I was an American and likewise I was a Citizen & beside I had a wife and family." [37]

To assume that men like Backus, Godfrey, and Potter were situating themselves as Americans simply to gain official American assistance, or to stick with white shipmates, is to ignore their conscious decision-making. A black sailor named William West under no such pressure explained his own patriotic identity in 1825. He "did not return in the schooner" *Albany Packet,* he said, "because she took Spanish colors at Havanna, and he did not choose to sail under Spanish Colors." Through the rage, pain, and endurance of their impressment, sailors like Backus, Godfrey, and Potter expressed an identity as black Americans at the turn of the nineteenth century, and a radical African American patriotism demanding black inclusion in the United States. [38]

Black and white seamen also shared respect for manly pluck in ways that were at once racially distinctive and overlapping. Physical bravery stood them in good stead in their rough-and-tumble waterfront world and in their frequent confrontations with officers. "Our seafaring people are brave," noted Benjamin Franklin on one of his many trans-Atlantic voyages, "being cowards in only one sense, that of *fearing* to be *thought afraid.*" Boxing, especially, validated manly qualities—personal valor, uncommon courage, and physical prowess. Seamen were the first Americans to embrace boxing as a sport, learning it from English tars for whom boxing, like cock-fighting, bull-baiting, and cudgel play, was a favorite past-time. At Dartmoor boxing was popular. Richard Crafus earned a reputation there as a masterful bare-knuckle boxer in a ring that knew no color line. Black and white students at his boxing academy pummelled each other, wrote one sailor, "for the amusement of the junior fry, who are yet to be the Cribs and Mollineaux of boxing celebrity, the most renowned heros in all christendom."[39]

If Crafus's notoriety remained limited to Dartmoor, the most awe-inspiring African American in England during the War of 1812 was Tom Molineaux, "the tremendous man of colour" who had recently contended for the national bare-knuckle championship. Born on the Chesapeake in 1784, Molineaux migrated northward by age twenty, where he found work as a porter and dock worker in New York. He probably began to box there with other longshoremen and British seamen, and apparently honed his pugilistic skills to a degree relatively unknown in America. In 1809 Molineaux signed aboard a trans-Atlantic ship as a foremast hand, working his way to England in search of a career as a boxer.[40]

Molineaux linked up with Bill Richmond, the free black American fighter who pioneered counterpunching and other defensive strategies in England, and who had created a sufficiently successful career as a prize-fighter to buy the Horse and Dolphin tavern in London. Close to fifty years old when Molineaux arrived, Richmond was still an active fighter, and he took the younger African American under his wing, becoming his "manager, trainer, patron, and second." Under Richmond's tutelage, Molineaux quickly dispatched his first two opponents and was soon paired with Tom Crib, the reigning bare-knuckle champion. They fought thirty-nine brutally punishing rounds in December 1810 before the African American challenger collapsed. According to a contemporary chronicler, "Molineaux proved himself as courageous a man as ever an adversary contended with . . . The Black astonished everyone, not only by his extraordinary power of hitting, and his gigantic strength, but also by his acquaintance with the science, which was far greater than any had given him credit for." Rumors flew that only duplicity by Crib's seconds and a boisterously pro-British crowd kept the title from the black American.[41]

Black and white sailors at Dartmoor found common ground in the boxing ring and as fencing and wrestling opponents. But it is by no means clear that all the underlying rules and meanings black sailors attributed to manly sports were identical with those of whites, even in this most common of arenas. Black sailors, for instance, competed in rough play and fought violently by butting heads. White sailors generally did not. Only in the "Rough-and-Tumble" scrapping of the southern backcountry, where "honor dictated that all techniques be permitted," did white men butt like black combatants.[42]

Head-butting contests in sport and anger were common throughout late-eighteenth- and early-nineteenth-century Afro-America. Battling a black overseer, the slave William Grimes "let him have it in old Virginia style, (which generally consists of gouging, biting, and butting.) I drove my head against him," remembered Grimes, "until he could scarcely stand or go." On board the *Alert*, the black steward "enraged the mate, who called him a 'black soger'; and at it they went, clenching, striking, and rolling over and over," recollected a white sailor. "The darkey tried to butt him, but the mate got him down." Men accustomed to butting perfected it for ends other than fighting. A black boatsteerer named Jack Sisson served in a special patriot expeditionary force during the American Revolution that, in 1777, captured British Major General Richard Prescott at his Rhode Island headquarters. Sisson broke down the general's door with his head, a feat subsequently immortalized by balladeers. Sixty years later one of the black servants of the Lafayette Guards, a New York regiment touring Boston, impressed onlookers with his remarkable butting.[43]

The African origins of head-butting are clear. Samba Jean, "a Mu Kongo expert in the martial arts of Africa," explained in 1990 that several head-butting styles of combat are currently practiced in Kongo. Afro-Brazilians, Venezuelans, and West Indians still rely on kicks and head-butts, as did nineteenth-century blacks on the Sea Islands off South Carolina and Georgia with their "knocking and kicking" combat. The butting characteristic of black sailors at the turn of the nineteenth century survived the Middle Passage to take root in Afro-America from New England to Brazil. Seamen propagated the art as they traveled from one region to another, forging diasporic links through martial skill.[44]

Butting was confined almost entirely to people of the African diaspora. Racially distinctive, it transcended other cultural and linguistic
divisions among blacks. Tarrying ashore at Guadeloupe in 1787, a
group of black and white English-speaking sailors watched a Sunday
gathering of slaves entertaining themselves. The males, according to
one white sailor, regarded butting as a "favorite amusement . . . for
which purpose their wooly hair is suffered to grow on the top of their
heads, whilst that from behind is cut away, and frizzled in amongst
that left on top, which forms a kind of cushion, or firm tuft of hair."
To "African music," the "opposing combatants dance with careless
gaiety, frequently exchanging smiles, and significantly nodding their
heads at each other," until they separate and advance toward each
other, "when as if by mutual impulse, both dart forward, head against
head, like two rams!" Intent on securing a reputation for himself, a
free seaman of color from Philadelphia named Tom Grace challenged
the local champion, a *patois*-speaking Guadeloupean slave, swearing
he would "capsize one of these fellows in a crack." He did, while his
white shipmates watched from the sidelines.[45]

As with sport and rough play, racial differences characterized sailors' theater. French prisoners had produced regular plays at Dartmoor "with very elegant scenery" and "appropriate comic and tragic
dresses." African Americans purchased sets, props, make-up, and cos-
tumes from the departing French, modifying them for their own
productions. Meanwhile, an all-white dramatic company in Number
Five composed of prisoners and Irish guards competed with the blacks'
troupe. Weekly or twice-weekly performances in Number Four cost
viewers six pence (four pence for seats in the rear) and included *The
Heir at Law,* a popular Scottish tragedy called *Douglas,* pantomimes
such as *Harlequin Revived,* and the central attraction—Shakespeare.[46]

Shakespeare was no stranger to African American sailors. During
the decades immediately after the American Revolution, Shakespearean productions outnumbered those of any other playwright in the
United States. The Bard of Avon became even more popular after the
turn of the nineteenth century, accounting for between one quarter
and one-fifth of all plays produced on the eastern seaboard. During
the 1810–1811 season in Philadelphia, just before war called sailors and
would-be privateersmen from the theater to enlistment rendezvous,
twenty-two of the eighty-eight plays performed were by Shakespeare.

Relegated to theaters' galleries, urban blacks invariably composed part of the audience. Theater-goers in Richmond, Virginia, expressed concern about the "overflowing of a riotous spirit among the coloured persons who nightly crowd there." In New Orleans, Mobile, and Richmond, playhouse managers catered to divisions within black society by providing separate sections for mulattoes or quadroons. In keeping with African Americans' theatrical tastes, a black West Indian named James Hewlett opened the African Grove Theater on the corner of Bleeker and Grove Streets in New York City shortly after the War of 1812. Hewlett led his repertoire company in several Shakespearean productions, dominated by *Richard III*, until white hoodlums wrecked the theater. Black sailors at Dartmoor produced the Shakespearean plays they knew, liked, and could sell.[47]

The theater in Number Four flourished. At a performance of *The Heir at Law*, a white privateersman recollected that "a ticket was of very little service as mob laws prevailed among the Prisoners [and] they made a rush in." He wrote, "I got along side of a great he Negro about seven feet high when he sat down 'twas with difficulty I could see over his head." Though side by side, the white and black sailors saw the show differently. White audiences enjoyed its professionalism; black actors, one white diarist had heard, "can perform as well as in any play House." Yet many whites also enjoyed theater in Number Four because they *expected* blacks to entertain them in a distinctive way. A white sailor claimed to have "witnessed a tall strapping negro, over six feet high, painted white, murdering the part of Juliet to the Romeo of another tall dark-skin." He also remembered that "the blacks were pretty well in pantomime—it seemed to be more natural to them." It seems likely that black patrons enjoyed black theater on many levels, not the least of which was black actors' masked mimicry of whites—a long-standing mainstay of African American performance. They undoubtedly were gratified, too, at the sight of whites' paying to see black productions.[48]

Blacks had long taught African-inspired art forms to white shipmates smitten with the mystique of black rhythm, a practice formalized for profit at the dancing school in Number Four. For African Americans, improvisational music and dance were essential forms of self-expression throughout the eighteenth and early nineteenth centuries, as accounts of Negro Election Day, plantation corn-shucking, and other cultural events invariably reveal. Some white listeners were disdainful; others participated robustly. Whites at Dartmoor were "regaled," wrote Benjamin Waterhouse, "with the sound of clarionets, flutes, violins, flagelets, fifes, and tambourines, together with the whooping and singing of the negroes." Whites on the waterfront already had well-established patterns of attending black performances. By the 1790s at Catharine's Market in New York, black dancers entertained themselves and competed with one another for the approbation of white people, who awarded dancers with fish or eels. These particular dancing competitions crested in the 1790s and early 1800s, though black sailors were still dancing for eels in Catharine's Market in the 1820s.[49]

Spontaneous interracial dances erupted at Dartmoor too, some with considerable energy. After a production of *The Heir at Law* one evening in Number Four, a white sailor wrote that "we had a grand dance & kept it up till daylight when the prison doors being open each one went to his own prison." Blacks in the early nineteenth century were notorious for dancing through the night, and interracial dances on black sailors' territory followed black customs with African roots.[50]

At black-run dancing schools and sailors' dances, racial encounters reflected the complex dynamics of stereotyping. White sailors who assumed that all blacks were natural performers gravitated to black shows, where they consciously and unconsciously imbibed black artistic forms. This, in turn, created targets for black parody, reinforcing black stereotypes of whites' gracelessness. Meanwhile, whites convinced themselves that the whole process reinforced their initial belief, whose role had been to separate white from black, even as the two converged. Black and white sailors interacted on common ground at Dartmoor in dance, theater, and manly sports, but their fraternization was colored by racial stereotypes. Cultural inheritance weighed heavily on immediate experience in Dartmoor's racial encounters.[51]

AT DARTMOOR, black and white sailors discovered common ground in a church established by a core of black men. Black sailors historically had found it difficult to practice meaningful religion in a predominantly white, and largely skeptical, community of sailors.

Coastal mariners had been the exception. In 1789, for instance, it was said of a Chesapeake Bay boatman named Will that he "frequently resorts among people who call themselves methodists." But practicing their faith proved difficult offshore. Pressed into the Royal Navy during the American Revolution, a black man named John Marrant "continued in his Majesty's service six years and eleven months." Marrant later felt shame "that a lamentable stupor crept over all my spiritual vivacity, life and vigour; I got cold and dead." Although "my dear Father in his dear Son, roused me every now and then by dangers and deliverances," Marrant wrote, it was not until after his discharge ashore that he again found the Lord. Boston King experienced similar spiritual isolation. Born into South Carolinian slavery, King fled to the British navy about the time Marrant succumbed to the press. He served a short naval stint, worked on a pilot boat out of New York, and then fished several seasons on the Labrador coast after joining the loyalist exodus to Nova Scotia. "One day when I was alone," he remembered, "and recollecting the patient sufferings of the servants of God for Truth's sake, I was ashamed of myself on account of the displeasure I felt at my ship-mates, because they would not be persuaded by me to forsake their sins."[52]

White sailors like King's shipmates had little time for "patient sufferings . . . for Truth's sake." Devotions at sea varied widely, but more often than not, prayers and psalms would be followed by "swearing, cursing and lying," according to Ned Coxere, and then a "laugh, scoff, and jeer." Most white seamen coped with their captain's tyranny and nature's terrors more through individual stoicism or group solidarity than through devotion to Jesus Christ. Black seamen, by contrast, were more likely to be religious. As the steward of a ship bound from London to Cadiz, Olaudah Equiano "heard the name of God much blasphemed, and I feared greatly lest I should catch the horrible infection." He would prefer, he wrote, "to beg my bread on shore, rather than go to sea amongst a people who feared not God." Although most seafaring slaves of this generation, fathers of the men languishing in Dartmoor, were less literate and less evangelically Christian than Equiano, King, and Marrant, they were not less oriented toward sacred belief systems. Religion created a racial divide within eighteenth- and early-nineteenth-century maritime culture.[53]

The Dartmoor church bore witness to black sailors' spirituality and to its limits. Jesse Almy, an African American from Newport, Rhode Island, joined the First Baptist Church of Providence in August 1806, when he was twenty. Three years later he applied for a Seaman's Protection Certificate with the intention of shipping out, and about the same time requested a letter from his church "to any sister church for transient membership." Almy determined not to let voyaging interfere with his church attendance. When the evangelical Sailors' Bethel movement first took shape on the river Thames between 1814 and 1817, a "pious youth of color" named Frederick Sanderson—"awakened by God on board a ship in 1815"—worked actively to convert sailors, despite "persecutions from watermen and ungodly sailors" who "raged . . . most fearfully." The devotions of black sailors such as these frequently irritated their white shipmates. "We have a Negro fellow on board," wrote the logkeeper on the *Panther* in 1822, "who is or pretends to be religiously crazed so much so that he is the common disturber of the peace. Is continually shouting for joy, passing from death to glory. Will break off from his work & have over a parcel of Methodistical exhortation." An officer unimpressed with fervent religion flogged him "with a piece of treble sinnet" in hopes that "his rational faculties will be restored to him."[54]

Evangelical religion was a mainstay of black community life ashore. During the eighteenth century, American slaves had embraced millennial aspects of Christianity, adapting it to their own dreams of deliverance from oppression. Believers understood that they could be reborn into eternal salvation through direct communication with the Holy Spirit, a religious practice that meshed easily with certain African forms of worship. Evangelical religion also challenged orthodox religious authority (which sometimes meant secular authority, too) and encouraged the faithful to think independently. Whites accustomed to rational religion, as many Yankee officers at the turn of the century still were, and suspicious of blacks' ploys to avoid work, often remained skeptical of black sailors' Christianity. Yet other whites found it extraordinarily attractive.

At Dartmoor, black religious leadership and style prevailed. Simon, "a methodist by Trade" and "an uncommonly large and muscular man," preached regularly from behind an improvised pulpit covered in green cloth, which doubled as a gambling table. Men of color constituted the majority of his congregation, even though most blacks did not participate. White sailors also regularly attended as communicants and spectators. Dartmoor's faithful found their only satisfying spiritual community and charismatic preacher in the cockloft of Number Four. No white minister rose from the ranks to gather an alternative church, and the preachers provided by the prison administration failed to galvanize large congregations.[55]

Simon's congregation represented much more, however, than the institutionalization of a heartfelt black desire for spiritual fellowship. Religious life in Dartmoor took its particular shape from black leadership in spiritual matters, whites' attraction to black preaching, and blacks' entrepreneurial impulses. Attempts at organized services in the white prisons fizzled because of the sailors' lackluster piety and the clergymen's ineptitude. When a visiting English minister shortsightedly offered "Prayers for his Magesty," outraged white sailors dumped him into the privy "to preach to the walls of the loathsome place." Moreover, white committees could not prevent gangs of scoffers, such as the Rough Alleys, from disrupting worship. Another English "Preacher from out side," the Reverend Mr. Jones of Plymouth, found safety and an audience only in Number Four, where he regularly preached on Thursdays.[56]

White seamen in general, however, seem to have feared no loss of racial privilege in deferring to blacks' spiritual leadership. Maritime culture associated devotion at sea with blackness. Shocked by an immoral naval chaplain, Commodore Thomas MacDonough replaced him with a pious black steward who offered prayers before the Battle of Lake Champlain, in 1814. White sailors afraid for their lives in the spume-tossed fury of a North Atlantic storm might turn to their black shipmates for spiritual help. Joseph Bates, a survivor of Dartmoor, thought his ship would founder during a gale in 1818. According to Bates, his captain implored the cook—"the only colored man on board" and a member of the Close Communion Baptist Church in New Bedford—to pray. "The cook knelt down where he could secure himself, the rest of us holding on upon our feet, and prayed most feverently for God to protect and save us from the dreadful, raging storm." Preaching or praying aboard ship did not garner profit or power. But at Dartmoor, Simon and Dick expanded black leadership and autonomy by using church services to attract whites and their money. As with the theater, blacks did not exclude whites from their church, a venture managed by the most influential men in the black barracks.[57]

Devout white sailors greatly appreciated Simon's church. Few embraced black religion as fully as Joseph Pittman and James Snow: after Simon baptized them in the courtyard pool, they were "taken into the Black Society" and "moved there Bags and hammocks into the Black prison." But a nucleus of white sailors regularly acknowledged Simon's spiritual leadership. During the most solemn time of their incarceration, after the massacre on April 6, 1815, in which seven Americans were killed and sixty wounded by British guards, white sailors like Nathaniel Pierce seeking solace and inspiration dressed "in clean Clothes & went to Church to hear Black Simon preach upon the Death of our fellow prisoners at the late Massacre."[58]

One appreciative white sailor recollected that Simon's services had "an imposing cast; and [were] often listened to with seriousness," not only by his black parishioners, from whom "sullen moans and hollow groans issue[d]" as he preached, but also from white men. Other white prisoners came for the spectacle or the music. "The musical performances at these meetings were in a wild, but not unpleasant style," wrote one sailor's amanuensis, "carried on entirely by the blacks." As a microcosm of Number Four, with its dancing and music schools, Simon's church provided a focal point for the celebration of black performance. Black sailors as a whole were sufficiently attentive to their preacher; on Good Friday, 1815, "all Gambleing was drop'd in the Black's Prison and a meeting held." Yet ultimately the hope offered by cards and dice outweighed that of salvation: in June 1815, when almost all the prisoners had been repatriated, Simon "left off preaching owing to some of his Church going to gambling tables & so he says he is done with the Glory."[59]

Simon's disgust signaled many black seamen's easy acceptance of both gambling and God's grace. This is not to say that some pious blacks did not eschew gaming, nor that many inveterate gamblers were not also religious scoffers. But black American culture remained at ease with what many whites considered inconsistencies. Thus black men at Dartmoor offered both bets and prayers without a nagging sense of conflict or shame.

In the wake of "a great stroke of Gambling . . . carried on in No 4," Thomas Catler of Newburyport won sixteen pounds and nineteen shillings. Catler displayed the liberality expected of a shipmate with ready money, but he did not distribute all of his largess in the black barracks. The next morning he bestowed on a mess of white townsmen "a present of a two penny loaf & a pint of Coffee, which," according to the white Newburyporter Nathaniel Pierce, "was very good in him & a great present for Dartmoor." We do not know what Catler himself intended by his munificent present. Deference may have inspired his generosity, but, given Dartmoor's leveling, it is more likely that a sense of self-empowerment led him to out-do the white men who had been out-doing him all their lives. Like so many of the racial encounters at Dartmoor, Catler's gesture came from a black man living a new-found equality.[60]

The nature of prison life meant that interracial fraternization occurred more nearly between equals in Dartmoor than in seaports at home. Black sailors pushed the limits of racial restrictions while still accommodating themselves to the white majority's social and numerical power. Number Five's theater company, for example, had no black actors, but Number Four's troupe included whites. Meanwhile, Number Four always housed a small contingent of white men who found the black prison more to their liking because it provided a haven from the marauding gang known as the Rough Alleys, and because Simon offered religious fellowship unavailable elsewhere. But no black men lived in the white barracks. What is more, the black community occasionally endured gross insults: three Frenchmen "Detected in the Act of buggery" received as severe a flogging as they could bear; and were then "turned in to No 4 among the Negroes."[61]

But white sailors always overstated the acquiescence of blacks. Interracial fraternization notwithstanding, black sailors built a nation-within-a-nation in Dartmoor Prison, trading and negotiating with the white Americans who surrounded them, but largely controlling their own territory and asserting their right to public space in the market square and in mixed-race parades. The apparent lack of interracial fights in the turbulent prison world attests to their collective strength, for bloody fights within racial lines and against the authorities broke out routinely and were noted by diarists along with suicides, natural deaths, and murders. One white sailor lost a foot during a fight;

another suffered the fury of a mob that "crushed him most to pieces." When a black man knocked down another in Number Four and "stamp'd upon his Breast," the loser "was taken up apparently dead." As groups, however, black and white prisoners were aware of each other's strength. Both were sufficiently self-policing to defuse confrontation—a far cry from whites' stereotypical presentation of black sailors as meek and acquiescent.[62]

Black seamen jealously guarded their hard-won autonomy, distinguishing themselves as equal players in inter-barracks rivalries. Sometimes they faced off against all the white barracks; at other times they joined certain white barracks against the rest. In February 1815, a one-week altercation ensued between the Americans and the prison authorities after a white sailor escaped from solitary confinement and was hidden in Number Seven. Initially all the barracks, including Number Four, agreed unanimously not to surrender the escapee. When the authorities stopped all "indulgences," such as marketing and visiting, "the Prisoners in retaliation put on an Embargo & would not allow the lamp trimmers nor any of the workmen [to work], nor allow anyone to trade with the Soldiers." Five days into the stand-off, for reasons known only to them, the blacks decided to break ranks: "the lamp Trimmers [an occupation monopolized by blacks] are permitted by the Blacks to go to their former duty." Sailors in Number Four might break ranks, but they did not defer to the white prisons.[63]

Black influence extended well beyond the limits of Number Four. When in January 1815 officials denied market privileges to all prisoners "on account of some boards being taken out of No. 6 Prison," the culprits' messmates tried to shield them from punishment at the hands of Captain Shortland. But prisoners in the other barracks chose not to suffer without the market, "being destitute of Coffee and other Necessaries." White prisoners in Numbers One, Three, and Five, joined by the blacks in Number Four, sent a letter to Number Seven "to inform us that if we did not deliver up those three Men to Capt Shortland that they would come and take them by force." That afternoon, "sixteen hundred Men assembled" and "came in a mob headed by Big Dick, A 7 foot Negro, and by force of Arms took out the offenders, and carried them before Shortland."[64]

Although much of the behavior of blacks and whites served to reinforce racial differences, mundane daily encounters reveal an easy familiarity between men of each race. "In the Afternoon I made a Tour through No one three & four prisons in Company with Joseph Gwinn of Salem and several more of my Acquaintences," wrote the white diarist Joseph Valpey, who lived in "Prison 7, Mess No. 129." He listed at least ten white acquaintances who visited Number Four with him over the course of months, and explained their excursions across the color line. "I went into Number four Prison for to see the Fashons and pass the time"; "to hear the News of the day"; to "see two Black Men flog'd for Stealing"; "to pass a dull and tegeous hour"; "to hear the Black Preacher"; and "to hear the Word of God Preached by a White Minister." Valpey did not denigrate blacks as he did thieves, gamblers, British officials, and the unfeeling American agent. And neither Valpey nor the white men of his Salem circle made any move to ostracize the two whites baptized by Simon: expressing "surprise," he continued to socialize with them.[65]

Black and white sailors banded together in other ways. Tensions pitted Americans (white and black) against the British; evangelicals (white and black) against the blasphemous; boxers and gamblers (white and black) against outsiders. Constantly shifting alliances and struggles between groups of white sailors, black sailors, and white British officials blurred what were assumed to be racial boundaries. But though black and white sailors gambled, prayed, talked, and formed mobs together, racial expectations in Dartmoor exercised more influence than did shared experiences.

One white privateersman could not imagine that imprisoned white sailors would seek spiritual inspiration from a black preacher: he grudgingly reported that white men listened to Simon's sermons "without any expressions of ridicule." Another white privateersman found independent black leadership so unsettling that he denied Simon's humanity, describing him as "with exception the ugliest looking Negro that I ever saw." Confronted by life behind the walls in Number Four—by valid African American institutions and black men's authority and expertise—many white sailors continued to catalog blacks as brutes, or to couch black leadership in incredulous terms.[66]

LONG BEFORE the last ragged sailor marched out of Dartmoor in July 1815, the prison spawned stories about British tyranny, American fortitude, and race. Blacks achieved a rare degree of autonomy at Dartmoor, where "the whites [did not] have the controul of them." African American sailors asserted themselves in mob actions, political processions, inter-barracks wrangling, and marketplace transactions. They survived by regulating themselves effectively in their own quarters and by capitalizing on whites' ambivalence toward blacks. Survivors long told tales of those grim and heady days when race was defined not by material differences, such as slavery or poverty, but by cultural differences. Black men more than held their own. Yet most white storytellers, as their reminiscences reveal, could see what they were experiencing only through the distorting glass of race.

It is easy to forget that few other multiracial groups of Americans in 1815 shared as much as black and white sailors at Dartmoor. The structure of their work and the psychology of voyaging drove these men together. Yet despite their cultural borrowing, their moments of easy familiarity, and their shared imprisonment, wary interactions affirmed race as the primary relationship among seafaring prisoners of war. At sea black and white hands together still clasped topsail braces and windlass handspikes. But ashore, even in unusual circumstances such as those at Dartmoor, where rules were challenged and possibilities expanded, sailors still segregated themselves by race.

5. POSSIBILITIES
FOR
FREEDOM

My country, the land of my birth,
   Farewell to thy fetters, and thee!
The by-word of tyrants, the scorn of the earth,
   A mockery to all thou shalt be!
Hurra for the sea and its waves!
   Ye billows and surges, all hail!
My brothers henceforth—for ye scorn to be Slaves,
   As ye toss up your crests to the gale;
Farewell to the land of the bloodhound and chain,
My path is away o'er the fetterless main.

BLACK SAILORS' SONG,
FROM MARTIN DELANY,
Blake, or the Huts of America (c. 1861)

ARRIVING OFF BLACK RIVER BAY, JAMAICA, in the six-hundred-ton ship *Sir Godfrey Webster,* M. G. Lewis noted in 1815 that "a black pilot came on board yesterday in a canoe hollowed out of the cotton-tree." Enslaved pilots were common in maritime slave societies throughout the Americas, where whites expected bondsmen to provide a multitude of skilled services. Yet as the slave climbed to the maindeck, he ascended into an uncommon position of authority and honor. "A Vessel, whilst the *Pilot* is on Board, is an Emblem of Feeble *Monarchy*," the veteran sea-voyager Ned Ward once wrote, "where the

King has a States-man in his Dominions Greater than himself." En-slaved pilots delighted in their temporary authority. A West Indian slave who truculently announced to an inbound white crew, "I let you know I king pilot," challenged slavery's power relations and spoke of an identity created from the material and symbolic dimensions of his work.[1]

Slaves regularly took charge of coastal vessels in the West Indies, the lower South, and the Chesapeake, managing their crews, their naviga-tion, and their lading. Seamanship became an emblem of black ac-complishment and (at propitious moments) an arrow in the quiver of black resistance. More than one skilled slave willingly piloted enemy ships into his master's territory in wartime, or stole both himself and his master's vessel.

Enslaved captains reconciled the self-assertion, coolness, and deci-siveness of the sea captain with the abject servility and docility that slavery demanded of male bondsmen. But the internalization of these two sets of conventions generated great tensions. Elite maritime slaves able to pursue freedom did so with an urgency born of the individu-alism fostered by command.[2]

As Ned Ward well knew, it was the pilot who handled the ship when she was "on soundings," and thus in greatest danger. It was the pilot who decided when to tack or wear ship, when to shorten sail, and where to let go the anchor. It was the pilot who gave the commands. Many harbors in slave territory were notoriously tricky, such as the coral-studded entrances to Christiansted, St. Croix, and Hamilton, Bermuda. Shifting bars, or swashes, and breaking seas challenged mariners at Ocracoke, North Carolina. Fierce tidal currents swept the Savannah River with each ebb and flood. Yet in all these ports, the cargos on which prosperity rested, and the warships detailed to protect that commerce, were entrusted to slaves. A North Carolina law of 1783, typical "for facilitating the navigation, and regulating the pilotage of the several ports of this state," stipulated "that negroes after undergo-ing an examination . . . shall be entitled to a certificate to act as pilots, upon their masters' giving bond." Lieutenant Evans of the Royal Navy wrote of the skill with which Jemmy Darrell—a slave recently manu-mitted for his skill as a pilot—brought a frigate through Bermuda's North Channel. "With great coolness and presence of mind," Evans wrote, Darrell "had the vessel's sail shortened, backed her through the more intricate part of the channel . . . and then proceeded by the usual course."[3]

Slave pilots practiced their trade right to the end of slavery. Robert Smalls is the best known of the "contrabands" who volunteered their services to the Union Navy in the war for freedom. Smalls boldly appropriated not only himself and his enslaved crew (along with their families), but the Confederate steamer *Planter*, which he brazenly steamed past the Confederate battery at Fort Sumter by impersonating the captain. Turning over C.S.S. *Planter* to the Union navy instantaneously put Smalls in the pantheon of black war heros. Numerous slave pilots made Union operations throughout the low country possible. "Charles Tatnall, our contraband Pilot, whose services have been valuable, I have rated seaman," wrote Lieutenant Penrod Watmough in 1862 aboard the U.S.S. *Potomka*. "His knowledge of the entire inland water course is perfect." Commander T. H. Stevens wrote from the ironclad *Patapsco* "that for intelligence, quickness, coolness in danger, and capacity as a Charleston bar and harbor Pilot," the contraband Gabriel Pinckney was "worthy of promotion." Smalls, Tatnall, and Pinckney were among the last enslaved captains and pilots to serve white owners, but they represented a tradition that stretched back two centuries.[4]

Pilots and captains were the elite of maritime slaves, but even boatmen resisted the routinization of slavery by cultivating independent habits and behavior, often by hiring themselves out. Caribbean slave boatmen, like those in other regions, worked under less regimentation than enslaved domestics or field hands. Barbados planters such as Joseph Senhouse "paid the Negroes in [the] Pettiauger for Rowing" between plantations, an intermittent job that allowed stretches without hard labor or supervision. All the wherries plying between Passage Fort and Port-Royal, Jamaica, with passengers in 1773 were "navigated entirely by Negroes," who measured possibilities for freedom in hours or days without white interference. For the lucky or talented few— such as an Antiguan "stout negro man, a good sailor and fisherman, capable of taking charge of a vessel, and a good pilot for this and all the neighboring islands"—a somewhat independent existence could be created within the bounds of slavery.[5]

"One of the most intelligent of the negroes with whom I have yet conversed," observed M. G. Lewis on a visit to Jamaica in 1816, "was the coxswain of my Port Royal canoe." The slave waterman hired himself out to people like Lewis, paying his master ten shillings a week and pocketing any profit that remained. He circulated between enslaved Jamaicans and whites, between porters, wharfingers, hucksters, and sailors. Keeping abreast of news and politics through his waterfront job, he struck Lewis as something of a philosopher—an independent thinker as well as a semi-independent worker. The coxswain had his own sense of historical change in Jamaica, influenced no doubt by the Haitians' successful revolution a scant hundred miles to the northeast. He told the English proprietor that "blacks must not be treated now, massa, as they used to be; they can think and hear, and see, as well as white people: blacks are wiser, massa, than they were, and will soon be still wiser."[6]

Drogher crews and boatmen throughout the Caribbean managed their own time to a degree, with work dependent on the vagaries of wind as much as on their masters' demands. All the Caribbean islands lie in a zone of easterly trade winds, which, during the winter months, blow especially hard through the day. The breeze often comes up with the sun and moderates at dusk. Mountainous island coasts get the "land breeze" blowing offshore in the evening as cooler air descends down mountain slopes. "By aid of this land-wind, small vessels can readily sail along the coast to windward ports," remembered the Jamaican wharfinger James Kelly, "which they could hardly do against the daily sea-breeze." Caribbean boat slaves thus made mileage to the eastward at night. Wind patterns also affected the working lives of "wharf Negroes." Kelly allowed his slave stevedores to "go where they were inclined" when the midday breeze prevented the loading or unloading of vessels because he "could, with confidence, count on their attendance" once the wind moderated.[7]

Whereas West Indian field hands turned out to the driver's conch-shell horn each dawn for another day of regimented labor, maritime slaves worked irregular hours night and day. Their regimen allowed a certain mobility without supervision, but it also precluded the dawn-to-dusk free time accorded other slaves. Nevertheless, slaves routinely put vessels to their own ends; for example, the crew on Jamaica's Holland estate in 1826 "have, or had lately, a coasting-vessel, which they employed in carrying plantains, yams, edoes, and corn from the estate's wharf to Kingston, a distance coastwise of sixty to seventy miles."[8]

Coastal maritime work created a distinctive identity among boat slaves. An enslaved schooner captain with years of experience on Chesapeake Bay, the Virginian George Henry recollected that he arrived home from his first voyage "with knowledge to impart to my friends, and with double zeal to increase my knowledge of the world." Returning to the quarters from each successive trip, Henry boasted of "many strange tales to tell, because I had been in another strange place." Frederick Douglass recalled that slaves normally confined to the circumscribed world of Talbot County, Maryland, plantations during the 1830s respected slave-sailors for their worldliness. "My cousin Tom . . . was sometimes a cabin boy on board the sloop *Sally Lloyd* (which Capt. Thomas Auld commanded), and when he came home from Baltimore he was always a sort of hero amongst us, at least till his trip to Baltimore was forgotten."[9]

Whites understood at least dimly the implications of well-traveled slaves' talking to other blacks. "From the nature and position of these islands," reported a committee of the Bahamian House of Assembly in 1826, "a number of the male slaves are employed in navigation . . . which is, almost of necessity, calculated to disseminate among the Slave population generally a taste for many of the comforts of civilized life." Black sailors knew that civilized life meant more than commodities and comfort, stemming fundamentally from the right to liberty, the proceeds of one's labor, and the guarantee of personal security under the law.[10]

Enslaved mariners who worked coastwise won tangible concessions from whites, including considerable amounts of time without white supervision; substantial freedom of movement; and an independent income from perquisites and petty trading. A slave pilot named Bluff assisted a group of Tories fleeing Charleston in 1778. According to Louisa S. Wells, they promised him "a hundred dollars Congress, if he would carry us safely over the Bar," in addition to his master's fee. An enslaved Savannah River pilot named Dallass, who "Always followed that business," according to his wife, hired himself out for years prior to the Civil War and accumulated some property.[11]

Intangibles mattered too. Handling vessels in tight quarters or thinking one's way out of a ticklish situation fostered a sense of self. Robert Smalls was long remembered with pride in Charleston as having evidenced self-assurance at an early age. As a hired slave employed by John Simmons, a local rigger and sailmaker, Smalls labored on the wharves as a stevedore, and then as an apprentice rigger and sailmaker, until Simmons noted his talent and put him to work on coasting schooners. Smalls later handled those vessels with aplomb. At the bar on an ebb tide he disdained dropping anchor and waiting for the flood, preferring instead to back the schooner in on the swells. Skilled slaves like Smalls developed a sense of self-worth from handling people as well as vessels, something that may have been heightened among Caribbean slaves who commanded free black sailors. "I have frequently known such slave captains," wrote Alexander Barclay of men who sailed Jamaican coasting vessels in the 1820s, "commanding free people."[12]

Most slaves were restricted to menial laboring jobs with no opportunities to develop skills, promote self-discipline, inculcate responsibility, or take pleasure from a job well done. Schooner captains, by contrast, invested themselves in their work. Captain George Henry remembered that when the foremast sprung on the schooner *Llewylen* he had to act quickly lest "we would have gone on [a] lee shore, and the vessel and all hands would have been lost." He recounted with pride his master's ordering a new vessel, the *Susan Ellen*, of which he was to take command. "We . . . rigged her out as fine as a schooner could be rigged. I took a delight in having everything put in first-rate order. I had mainsail, foresail, square-sail, jib, flying-jib, and main topsail."[13]

Slaves like Bluff, Dallass, Smalls, and Henry were fortunate enough to find important psychological perquisites in the workplace, including honorific titles. Slaveholders wanted bondage to infantilize blacks. Their restrictions forbade most slaves to have a surname, or a surname different from that of their owner, much less a title. Whites hoped slavery would both degrade blacks and serve as a great equalizer among them. African Americans consistently defied their masters, maintaining important last names of their own choosing. Significantly, slaves called their last names "entitles," or "titles." E. W. Hooper, a Union army general's aide-de-camp, observed, "Their masters never allowed them to use titles and would whip them if they used a second name." Yet Hooper remembered, "Each had a title as near as I can learn." Powerful white people in the slaves' world also possessed titles—the omnipresent "master," as well as "judge," "colonel," or "captain." In the Pre-Emancipation Caribbean and the Old South, where honor and reputation often carried more weight than individual merit, white people cherished such titles.[14]

"Captain" also meant a lot in the slave quarters. Within the truncated social hierarchy that bondage imposed on slaves, social distinctions and terms of respect were highly regarded. Olaudah Equiano was en route from Georgia to Montserrat when his captain died. Recently manumitted, Equiano had studied navigation clandestinely while a slave and had made that particular passage several times. Thus armed, he navigated the sloop from mid-ocean to a safe anchorage off Montserrat.

> Many were surprised when they heard of my conducting the sloop into port; and I now obtained a new appellation, and was called "Captain." This elated me not a little, and it was quite flattering to my vanity to be thus styled by as high a title as any sable freeman in this place possessed . . . The sable Captain lost no fame; for the success I had met with increased the affection of my friends in no small measure.[15]

Like Equiano, an enslaved Virginian drew on his occupational identity to resist the dependency that his master and other whites projected on him. African-born, but raised from boyhood as a river pilot, he *acted* as a free man during the era of the American Revolution, according to a white man who knew him, because of his skill and the estimation in which he was held. Most telling is that though local whites called him "Uncle Mark," the African pilot repeatedly introduced himself as "Capt. Starlins."[16]

The opportunities for freedom at sea provided pilots with more than semantics to bedevil their masters. A slave who piloted the schooner *Betsy* from Washington, North Carolina, to sea in 1802 seized his freedom. Once the *Betsy* was across the shoal bar at the mouth of the inlet, the wind "freshened up & blew so heavy that it was impossible" to return the man to the pilot boat; so Captain Gilpin of the

Betsy carried him to Alexandria, Virginia. But Gilpin claimed not to know the pilot was a slave, and he paid him "Seamans wages from the day we left the bar untill the vessel was discharged" in Alexandria. On their arrival, the slave pilot initially told Captain Gilpin that "he wished to Return," and Gilpin "engaged him a passage on board of a vessel bound" back to North Carolina. When the vessel was ready to sail "he declined going," according to Captain Gilpin, who was then writing to the runaway pilot's irate owner, "as he said he had Ship'd on Board a Vessel bound to the Northward." The black pilot subsequently sailed to Boston and back as a hand before the mast with Captain Peter Butler. When the slave arrived in Alexandria a second time, Gilpin's father "saw him on the Wharf & asked him if he did not mean to go back to Carolina to which he answered that he intended to make another trip to the Northward before he returned."[17]

This pilot's story suggests not only blacks' communications between North Carolina, Alexandria, and Boston, but the limited nature of the space between slavery and freedom. It is unknown whether the lure of family and place ever brought the man back. However, few black Americans at the turn of the century had much leeway to create autonomous lives as freemen or freeholders. They might strive to achieve some independence and autonomy, and hope to facilitate a better life for their children, but running away from one's legal master did not free a recent bondsman of the inquisitive challenges of other white men, nor free him from a white-dominated society that presumed he was inferior. Thus the realistic option for many slaves, even seafaring ones with a worldliness and knowledge denied to most bondsmen, was to run off for a while, to experiment with freedom, to toy with the psychological changes necessary for independent living—but not necessarily to burn all one's bridges at once. Maritime slaves moved in and out of that gray area between slavery and quasi-freedom through flight, voluntary return, and recapture.

Enslaved pilots like the North Carolinian runaway proudly asserted themselves, berating the white sailors temporarily under their command. Slaveholders with real power condoned what normally would have been perceived as black effrontery because they believed that such displays benefited the white men whom the pilots served. An enslaved pilot in Martinique whose colorful clothes prompted laughter from a white sailor arriving there in 1805 immediately put the man in his place. "Who you laugh at, you bloody bitch?" swore the slave, who then ordered the chastened sailor to "Go in the chain and heab de lead," that is, to stand on the platform outboard of the forerigging and measure the depth of the water with a leadline. He also berated the white helmsman. His defense against the demeaning nature of slavery was to make sailor Jack jump. White sailors who respected ship captains with some of the same skills smirked at what they saw as hollow posturing by a black man. They could not separate the significance of a skilled slave's handling a ship or asserting his authority from their assumptions about black inferiority. But for the pilot and his black acquaintances, real accomplishment deserved real respect.[18]

Like their white counterparts, enslaved black captains often recounted instances of their voyaging in the first-person singular, indicating close personal identification with command. To hear Moses Grandy tell of sailing canal boats and lumber schooners in North Carolina and Virginia, one would think he had sailed the vessels and handled the cargo on his own.

> Mr. Shaw . . . said . . . he had nobody he could trust with his goods; he offered me five dollars to take the vessel down . . . The wind was fair, and the hands on board so I agreed . . . I ran the vessel down to the mouth of the creek and anchored; when the moon rose I went up the river. I reached the wharf, and commenced taking out the goods that night.[19]

By making no mention of the "hands" who worked the ship, slave captains such as Grandy invested themselves with the responsibility and success of their voyages. Occupational identity fostered a pronounced sense of self-importance.

Enslaved captains and pilots had little real power over whites, as the pilot who swore at William Nevens in Martinique well knew. They could lord over their black crews, however, reflecting the obsession with honor and ranking prevalent in plantation society, where a prominent pecking order encouraged contempt for lower-ranking individuals. "Everybody in the South," remembered Frederick Douglass, "seemed to want the privilege of whipping somebody else." Slave captains drove their crews and raced other captains. George Henry remembered that when he began as captain, the "noted skippers" (also slaves) "were all down on me; and said the vessel was lost." As he tells it, however, he began "Making shorter and quicker voyages than any other skipper that ever went out of that river . . . The more they talked the harder I drove them." Being in command caused some slave captains to become obsessed with personal achievement. Searching for freedom, they distanced themselves from other slaves.[20]

Whereas coasting captains worked primarily with other blacks, slave pilots worked in a veritable contest with the white captains and mates who continually judged them. Unlike coasting captains, who had days without white supervision, slave pilots always had the white captain at their elbow. And while most seamen did their work out of the public eye, harbor and channel pilots often worked within sight of crowds of shipowners, slave women, and other seamen ashore. Pilots' professional merits—and their mistakes—were common knowledge. Collectively, however, slave captains and pilots had one of the easiest lots in slavery. The labor required of them was by no means grueling, and they had much more autonomy than most other bondsmen. They should have been among the most contented of slaves. That they were not is a warning to look beyond material considerations in evaluating both the impact of slavery and the meanings that slaves gave to their experiences.[21]

Bondsmen with a degree of autonomy, including the maritime elite, some craftsmen, and those urban slaves who hired themselves out, were substantially more socialized to commercial practices than were the bulk of field hands, day laborers, and domestics. Slave captains such as Moses Grandy and George Henry frequently participated in market transactions. "I gave [my master] one half of all I received for freight," recollected Grandy of his North Carolina lumber freighting, "out of the other half I had to victual and man the boats, and all over that expense was my own profit." Captain Henry carried grain from around the Chesapeake to commission merchants in Alexandria and Baltimore. "When the grain was sold" by the merchant and "his fees taken out," Henry wrote, "the balance of the money was handed over to me. I always paid my bills, got my stores, paid the hands, and paid the balance of the money to the owners on my return home."[22]

The psychology of enslaved captains was influenced by the underlying assumptions of commercial norms. The market that became the hallmark of American society in the late eighteenth and early nineteenth centuries was based on private property, personal trust, and contracts between autonomous individuals. The liberal capitalist values that allowed this market to flourish, and that, with its flourishing, penetrated ever deeper into the recesses of American society, included "the absolute property of each individual in his or her own person, and the transformation of labor-power into a commodity." On a grand scale this meant that as the market economy grew, and as market discipline and the market mentality spread, slavery appeared ever more anomalous in the face of free labor and individualism. No people were more strategically situated to experience this disjunction than slaves daily involved in commerce. Making transactions and decisions with real consequences in the marketplace, they lacked control over their own persons.[23]

Captain Moses Grandy, for instance, remembered Mr. Myers, a white merchant in North Carolina, speaking of him to another white man: "Here is a captain doing business for you." Grandy relates that Myers "said I was one of their old war captains, and had never lost a single thing of the property intrusted to me." Myers valued the slave's trustworthiness, yet Grandy had to purchase his own freedom *three times* because in each of the first two transactions he was defrauded by his white owner.[24]

"I knew that the vessel and cargo was entrusted into my hands," wrote George Henry on the eve of his flight to northern freedom. "I could wait until the cargo was sold and come away with $1800, as well as to come away without anything, but I was too much of a man." Although fear of reprisal for felony theft probably deterred Captain Henry, there is no doubt that some elite slaves defined themselves in part through commercial society's ethos of trust, exemplifying it as a form of black pride. They separated the hypocrisy of white slaveholders' unmitigated theft of their persons from the value they placed on personal honor defined by commercial society.[25]

"What can a man do who has his hands bound and his feet fettered?" wrote the Baltimore slave Anthony Chase in 1827. "He will certainly try to get them loosened by fair and honorable means and if not so he will ceartainly get them loosened in any way that he may think the most adviseable." Honor mattered to Chase, even though his mistress "would not consent to anything that would melorate my condition . . . So I shall go to sea in the first vesel that may ofer an oppertunity and as soon as I can acumulate a sum of money suficent I will Remit it to my mistress to prove to her and to [the] world that I dont mean to be dishonest but wish to pay her every cent that I think my servaces is worth . . . I dont take this step mearly because I wish to be free but because I want to do justice to myself and to others and also to procure a liveing for a family."[26]

Anthony Chase and Captain George Henry sought what for them would be an honorable freedom because they had internalized the values of commercial society that most slaves rejected outright. "Slaves have their *code of honor,* and their *tricks of trade,*" the Reverend John Dixon Long wrote in 1857. "They say: 'We do the work; we raise the corn and wheat; and part of it is justly ours.'" Slaves' folk tales pitted witty figures against strong ones and instructed listeners to beware of deception. Antagonists in the tales constantly manipulated their aggressors, often succeeding by guile. One moral, not lost on a black storyteller, was "You nebber kin trus Buh Rabbit." These were the maxims through which agricultural slaves made sense of their world. Although such slave-quarter wisdom provided a framework for the actions and experiences of elite maritime slaves, context always conditioned the construction of meaning. Enslaved captains were among the few bondsmen with real responsibility—not only for their masters' vessels, but for an enslaved crew, their own reputations, and the ideal of black competence. They learned to value the trust that had been placed in them. Acting as individuals, they were often fully convinced that they were acting for the good of the race.[27]

The market influenced enslaved captains' behavior to an unparalleled degree. The most profound difference between agricultural and maritime slaves lay in their respective positions vis-à-vis the market. Field hands and drivers worked within plantations: enslaved coasting captains maneuvered in an orbit physically removed from the plantation and integral to the larger market economy. Frederick Douglass acknowledged their different experiences when he spoke of the "isolation" of his boyhood plantation. "Not even commerce, selfish and indifferent to moral considerations as it usually is," said Douglass, "was permitted within its secluded precincts . . . Every leaf and grain of the products of this plantation and those of the neighboring farms belonging to Col. Lloyd were transported to Baltimore in his own vessels." For Douglass, plantations were "secluded and out-of-the-way places . . . seldom visited by a single ray of healthy public sentiment."[28]

Slave captains such as George Henry and Moses Grandy, however, and slave sailors like those on Colonel Lloyd's vessels, were frequently exposed to the rays of "healthy public sentiment." Confined to sailing within slave territory, they nonetheless moved constantly in and out of commercial centers. Although captains conducted business on behalf of their masters, captains and sailors alike bought and sold their own personal "ventures." They necessarily spoke the language of the market. As with all people, their language not only expressed their thoughts but shaped and conditioned them. Aspiring to economic advancement and individual freedom, they began to act and define themselves through the standards of the commercial world.

The catch, of course, is that they were still slaves, "under fear in every word they speak," according to Captain Moses Grandy, who knew what it meant to be whipped. Conversant with the commercial world, in which life was open-ended and subject to improvement, and in which a talented individual could affect his own destiny, enslaved captains could not abide their slavery. Compared with plantation drivers, they had more access to freedom. Equiano and Grandy earned enough at their maritime trades to buy their freedom. Robert Smalls steamed the *Planter* out of bondage. George Henry escaped to the North after being insulted one time too many by his master, for whom he said he "was making money . . . just the same as if you were shaking it off a tree." Each subsequently employed the talents for leadership he had honed in slavery to work on behalf of black people.[29]

The experience of enslaved coastal captains and pilots speaks to the stratified structure of slave society, and to the fact that a small percentage of elite slaves developed tangible skills, a fundamental sense of self, and leadership abilities within bondage—all while negotiating around and accommodating the substantial power of their masters. Confined to slave territory in all-black crews, enslaved captains created a degree of physical and psychological freedom aboard their vessels unthinkable on land. Their jobs emphasized their individuality. Yet captains and pilots, more than almost any other slaves, sailed harrowing seas between the world of bondage and the world of commercial society. Responsibility for vessels and exposure to marketplace values, juxtaposed with the degradation of slavery, created rising expectations and competing allegiances that racked these men. Although possibilities for real freedom were limited and circumstantial, elite maritime slaves occasionally drew on their skills to escape for good. But whether they remained in the plantation system or began a new life outside it, black captains and pilots who had learned to command vessels in slavery developed an extraordinary sense of self-worth.

Possibilities for black freedom on a much larger scale erupted during the late summer and fall of 1791, when French West Indian slaves began torching plantations on the north coast of St. Domingue. They kindled a New World slave rebellion of unprecedented magnitude. When news that whites were fleeing the ravaged colony arrived in Caribbean and mainland ports, it dealt a crippling blow to the belief in the inevitability of white supremacy on which slave societies rested. Black sailors (and slaves evacuated along with their white masters) carried their versions of events to blacks all around the Atlantic rim. Revolutionary St. Domingue embodied a potent symbol of the possibility of black freedom for slaveowners, statesmen, and free blacks everywhere. Yet the foreigners most able to convert the uprising's possibilities to their own advantage were seamen of color who experienced firsthand the revolution in St. Domingue and the black republic in Haiti.[30]

More than ten years after the insurrection began, battles still raged throughout the countryside around Cape François, the northern port in St. Domingue that would later be called Cape Haitian. Nevertheless, in April 1802 some eighty American merchant vessels rode at anchor in search of trade and a market. The town lay in ashes, burned by the rebel general Henri Christophe in February; and most American seamen were loath to venture ashore. Capitalizing on a world turned upside down by successful slave rebellion, however, "a Certain Coloured Man Named *Joseph*" deserted from the American brig *Lydia*. Captain John Leonard, hurrying ashore to retrieve the sailor for "his rightful owner," heard from "the officers of Police that the said Joseph claimed the protection of a french citizen to which he was entitled, that he was now at full liberty and no longer a Slave." After Joseph returned with black soldiers to retrieve his clothes and bedding, Captain Leonard never saw him again.[31]

Episodes like Joseph's escape were significant, not only in terms of individual freedom, but for the developing consciousness of the black Atlantic community. Once in revolutionary St. Domingue or in republican Haiti, black seamen from all over the hemisphere were able to rely on the assistance of revolutionary governments in challenging the authority of white shipmasters and American commercial officials. This was an unprecedented situation for sailors, especially black sailors, who rarely had governments working on their behalf. Black mariners spread individual stories of freedom throughout the Atlantic, firing the imaginations of slaves with untold possibilities. After becoming honorary "citizens" of Haiti, they returned to the sea, acting as roving ambassadors of the black sovereignty they had discovered in Haitian ports.

Well-founded estimates suggest that thousands of black seamen voyaged to St. Domingue and Haiti between 1790 and 1830. Americans carried on a brisk trade there both before and during the uprising. In February 1790, the year before the Haitian Revolution began, one Rhode Islander at Cape François saw "about fifty Sail of american Vessels now lying here and others arriving daily." In 1797, as civil war raged, 600 American ships manned by approximately 5,000 American sailors traded with the colony. Given that about 15 percent of the seamen aboard American merchantmen were African Americans, 750 black Americans voyaged to St. Domingue that year alone. Among a group of 103 blacks outbound from Philadelphia in 1803, 12 departed for St. Domingue—more than 10 percent. As late as 1826, more than half the ship tonnage trading in Port-au-Prince was American. Although the number of ships conducting trade in Haiti in 1826 was greatly reduced from what it had been during the commercial heyday before the war, black sailors continued to have access to the island.[32]

Certain mariners of color went to great lengths to make a pilgrimage to Haiti during the rebellion. Jamaica's *Royal Gazette* announced that in May 1792 a free man of color, "said to be employed in a small vessel that trades from Port-Royal to Hispaniola," assaulted a naval officer who refused to issue him a clearance—most likely for the French section of Hispaniola, then in revolt. The following year the captain of a schooner bound for Curaçao was murdered by a mulatto seaman, who "took command of the vessel, and ran her into the French part of St. Domingo."[33]

African American sailors expressed pride in what they found on the island. When the brig *Traveller* arrived in Port-au-Prince about eight years after the declaration of Haitian independence, one of the sailors in her all-black crew watched President Jean Pierre Boyer's bodyguards with fascination. "They appeared to understand military tactics to perfection," he wrote. "They were elegantly dressed in red frocks and trousers, faced with blue and green . . . Boyer was most superbly dressed and equipped, and on horseback made an elegant appearance." Here was an incarnation of black achievement and power. Other, more desperate black mariners also sought freedom there. After the all-black crew on the American brig *Holkar* murdered their captain, mate, and passenger near Curaçao in 1818, they bore away for St. Domingue. Scuttling the brig in deep water, the men went ashore in the boat at Bennet with a box of gold, and walked to Jacquemel.[34]

A magnet for blacks, the inspirational rebellion that launched black independence in St. Domingue had an unintended effect on seamen of color in other slave societies. Perceiving black mariners as *agents provocateurs*, the Jamaican Assembly in 1792 directed officials to "take account" of people of color aboard inbound vessels, and to guarantee that sailors of African descent would depart on the vessels on which they had arrived. As "the dangerous designs and machinations of certain french West India negroes" dominated slaveholders' conversations in South Carolina, whites there applied pressure to black sailors. Those assembled at an extra-legal citizens' meeting at Charleston in June 1794, fearful of the contagion of rebellion, called on the governor and General Assembly to address the problem of black immigrants from St. Domingue, and demanded lists from every in-bound ship "stating what number of negroes or other people of colour sailors or others are on board." In 1797 the governor of South Carolina himself recognized the danger, ordering incoming captains to report the numbers of blacks aboard their ships. White petitioners that year also suggested that captains with free seamen of color should be "obliged to give bond to the State, to secure their re-exportation." But despite outcries from alarmed slaveholders, none of these measures concerning transient black sailors became law in South Carolina during the 1790s; and the policing of black sailors in Jamaica was abandoned within a year because of its cost and the disruption to trade.[35]

Black seamen concerned with freedom knew that the Haitian government actively encouraged black immigration, hoping to enlarge its army and swell the war-ravished male population. As early as 1804, the governor-general of Haiti had offered American ship captains financial incentives to carry African Americans there. Before the new nation was unified after the war, and while Emperor Henri Christophe reigned in the north, his secretary-general, Joseph Balthazar Inginac, encouraged New York blacks to emigrate. So did other prominent Haitians. "Make known, sir, to the unfortunate descendants of Africans, in the United States," wrote one of President Boyer's aides to a Massachusetts correspondent in 1824, "that when they may be at liberty to come hither, they will find in us brothers ever ready to receive them." Haitian President Alexander Petion, displaying diplomatic indifference, offered a refuge to African American seamen at the risk of angering the United States. "Petion is extremely obstinate," the U.S. commercial agent William Taylor wrote to James Monroe in 1814, "and claims every negro or mulatto (no matter of what nation), who enters this port and will go every length to seduce them from their bounden duty."[36]

Haitian officials did not have to "seduce" black sailors. Desertion was a crucial weapon in the limited arsenal of every seafaring man. Following Haitian independence, however, black sailors from around the Atlantic learned that they could desert in Haitian ports with impunity. Taylor lamented to Monroe again in 1814 "that among . . . seamen on board of our vessels . . . are sometimes found *natives of this island.*" "Such men on their arrival here," continued the agent, "immediately desert their vessels and such is the situation of this country, that there is neither authority, nor inclination, to compel them to return." A black sailor signed articles for a cruise on the American privateer *Fox* "at New Orleans where he had resided many years." In Port-au-Prince, the sailor took on a new identity: he "called himself a Haytian, but," wrote Taylor, "as far as I have been enabled to ascertain the fact, [he] is a native of Martinique, and was never until now in Haiti." For Taylor this swearing and counterswearing was pure duplicity, a breach of the code of honor that supposedly regulated men's actions. For the unnamed French West Indian man of color—a resident of Martinique, New Orleans, and Haiti—a declaration of Haitian citizenship at once freed him from his captain's power and affirmed blacks' rising protest in the Atlantic of 1814.[37]

Enslaved seamen found freedom in Haiti because they were regarded as brothers to be liberated and as actors in the contest between the dominant hemispheric slavocracy and a nascent black republic. The first article of the Haitian constitution expressly forbade slavery, and many Haitians took seriously the implied emancipation of enslaved sailors. Captain Nathaniel Raymond sailed the American schooner *Baracoa* from Baltimore to Cape Haitian in December 1820 with a hired slave seaman named George Rayner. As the crew discharged the cargo, Rayner absconded. Captain Raymond employed "every possible exertion" to get him back, including "a reward of twenty dollars [that] was offered for his apprehension." At liberty for several days, the ex-slave was ultimately apprehended and "lodged in the Guardhouse," but only as a sop to the captain, for he was soon "suffered to escape." The captain located him again and brought him aboard the ship, but the next day "the Government Boat with an armed force came on board" and carried Rayner off. Captain Raymond continued to protest, and he received many empty promises from the commanding general of the port that Rayner would be returned to him, but when the *Baracoa* departed for New Orleans, George Rayner remained in Haiti.[38]

Most historians have seen runaway slaves as an exasperating inconvenience to their masters, and as a constant reminder of the hollowness of their masters' professions of paternalism. Rarely have they been viewed as a real threat to the slave system. Few runaways were as bold as the four blacks who desperately mutinied against their captain near St. Kitts in 1790, seizing the sloop *Nancy*. Such open resistance was a high-stakes venture from which there were few alternatives other than death at the hands of a court or self-imposed exile. *Nancy's* crew dropped from sight, lost at sea or absorbed into the maritime underclass. In the longer term, the extensive influence of runaways, especially seafaring runaways, must be traced outward to the West Indies, to Europe, and to the northern United States, as well as inward to local black societies. Ultimately, the presence of runaways in capitols such as London, Boston, and Philadelphia fueled the embryonic antislavery movement. Moreover, few runaways conveyed more compellingly the possibilities for freedom than sailors who jumped ship in Haiti but subsequently returned to America with tales to tell of blacks' revolt and assumption of rights.[39]

Seamen liked the fact that Haitian courts were especially receptive to free blacks' accusations of "man-stealing," and as foreign nationals they used those courts to embarrass and prosecute their captains. Robert Baker, the cook on the American schooner *Hancock*, filed a suit in 1822 against Captain Ezra Ryan in a Haitian court, charging that Ryan had threatened to sell him as a slave in North Carolina. The commercial agent Andrew Armstrong interceded on behalf of Captain Ryan with the grand judge of Haiti. "The difficulties he would have met trying to execute such a plan," wrote Armstrong, "shows its almost impossibility & he knew that the laws punish such crimes with death." But the seaman Baker and Judge Fresnel knew otherwise. Hundreds of free seamen lost their liberty to man-stealers in precisely that fashion. Vulnerable at sea to a captain without scruples, Baker could seek restitution in Haiti.[40]

By the end of 1821, American officials remained ruffled by the Haitian government's favorable treatment of free black seamen. The American agent in Port-au-Prince conceded to President Boyer "that if a *slave* is brought to this country in a foreign vessel, he may take the benefit of the laws of Haiti, and leave the vessel with impunity, but the case is very different with a free man." The agent tried to argue hypocritically that "it is no matter whether a citizen of the U.S. is white or black—if he is a free man our laws make no distinction respecting colour." Boyer knew precisely how race factored into decisions of the United States government, and of American state governments, and he determined to maintain Haiti as an oasis for people of color. African American seamen arriving in Haiti, "either with or without cause of complaint" against their shipmaster, according to Agent Armstrong, "have only to say they have been maltreated, wish to become, or are citizens of Haiti, and they immediately obtain their desire."[41]

William Dalton sought in Haiti the protection of citizenship that his native country denied him. In April 1822 Dalton, who was the cook of the schooner *Francis* of Boston, "wente ashore Att St. Demingo and with a parsel of blackmen Wente to Governor Bashalere" demanding his discharge. The governor commanded Captain Stephen Burgess to appear, dismissed his protestations that "it was againste the Law of the United State to Discharge any of our Seman in a forreng porte," and instructed the captain "that the cook Was a negro and had appleyed to him and that he Must order his discharge." The cornered white man tried one more tack—to no avail. He claimed that Dalton "did not belong to that Island but that he was a native sittersan [citizen] of the United States." As the minor drama closed, the Haitian captain of the port arrived on board the *Francis* "with 3 armed negroes" to retrieve Dalton's belongings—"a chest of cloathing one Bed and sundray articles."[42]

Sailors such as Dalton recognized the mountainous island nation as an outpost of black liberty in a sea of slavery, and as a place where race conferred more privileges than did nationality. Aaron B. Nouez, the commercial agent of the United States at Aux Cayes, complained bitterly to the president of Haiti in 1821 that he had frequently applied to the Haitian authorities to help apprehend "seamen, men of colour and citizens of the U.S. who have deserted from their vessels in this port." But, he continued, "instead of affording that aid, due to me as the Agent of my Government," the Haitian officials "invariably protected such deserters, and in no instance have I succeeded in obtaining them."[43]

The American agent vainly invoked nationalism, neatly ignoring the fact that, in the hemispheric politics of the early nineteenth century, race often transcended nationality. Slavery and black oppression were international and transcultural systems against which the republic of Haiti was valiantly struggling. Haitian nationalism erupted as a response to the history of slavery, and Haitian politicians resolutely defined Haitian citizenship in terms of African descent, especially for the benefit of foreigners. After the cook of an American schooner from Philadelphia was "chastised" by his captain on a voyage to Aux Cayes in 1821, he deserted and "made his complaint before the justice of the peace, Mr. Solomon Fils, who immediately sited [cited] the captain to appear before him." The American commercial agent at Aux Cayes attempted to intercede, explaining that because the matter had occurred "between the master & Seaman of an American" ship, it should properly be resolved by the American agent. Fils interpreted the case as racial politics instead of Admiralty law. He commanded the captain to pay a fine and court costs, liberated the cook from his contract, and—in a blow to American national pride—forced the captain to hand over the black seaman's official American protection certificate. In effect, Fils awarded the African American sailor dual citizenship by offering him asylum in Haiti and simultaneously letting him keep his American "passport."[44]

This was exactly what most African American sailors wanted: the chance to manipulate the political situation in Haiti against their captains and employers, while retaining the option to return to their own country when they chose. It is probably fair to say that most black seamen—even if they jumped ship in Haiti—did not want to become permanent expatriates. The commercial agent Armstrong complained of black seamen in Port-au-Prince who petitioned him for passage back to the States. These sailors, like the several thousand African American emigrants who voluntarily went to Haiti in the mid-1820s but then returned to the United States, found themselves in a foreign society that for all its racial pride still spoke Haitian Creole, practiced a creolized Catholicism, and countenanced an exploitative plantation economy.[45]

Unsympathetic to blacks' freedom struggle, American agents had a more rigid understanding of nationalism and citizenship than did Haitian officials. They fumed that when African American seamen accepted the privileges and protection of Haitian citizenship, the sailors' American protection certificates should be surrendered. They did not want black men who circumvented their authority with instantaneous Haitian citizenship later to claim American entitlements, including hospital money, repatriation, or employment.

Solomon Fils and other Haitian officials understood Haitian citizenship in more mutable terms. Fils recognized that a transient black man's "citizenship" in Haiti did not preclude that same sailor's continued citizenship in the United States, because the former—as extended to seamen of color—was as much an affirmation of pan-Atlantic black freedom as an extension of specific national privileges or responsibilities. Haitians, African Americans, and West Indians of color intermingling in Haiti helped create a diasporic black sensibility, which seafarers transported abroad. The "Brig Saco, sold here," wrote the American commercial agent at Cape Haitian, "is now Haytien. Her crew (all black) reshipped here as Haytiens, and returned to New York in the same vessel." Refashioning themselves as "Haytiens," those English-speaking black Americans returned to the United States under the red-and-black Haitian flag, with tales of resplendent black troops, obliging officials, and a nation where all black people were citizens.[46]

Needless to say, Haiti was not a paradise for every sailor of color. Caste, class, criminality, and the greediness of other blacks affected mariners' experience in the black republic. In 1802 the American consul at Cape François referred to an American mulatto from the schooner *Neptune* who "was taken up . . . and is now in prison" along with several white Americans arrested for theft and vagrancy. In 1824, a Haitian court sentenced two British "coloured men" to hard labor for piracy.[47] Haitian nationals, moreover, were not beyond returning foreign black seamen to their white shipmasters for a price. A black sailor named Nugent deserted from the U.S. naval ship *St. Louis* in 1837 and sought refuge in Port-au-Prince with a local man named Jerome Taylor. After *St. Louis*'s officers posted "the usual reward" for Nugent's apprehension, Taylor betrayed him. At that point, rather than enlisting the local constabulary to arrest Nugent and return him to the ship, several American naval officers chose to apprehend him themselves, accompanied by two Americans familiar with the area. Four miles out of town, in the neighborhood of Sarthe, according to the *Feuille de Commerce* newspaper, "they seized, by force of arms, a man who had taken asylum against the manacles of slavery."[48]

It mattered little to the editors whether Nugent was technically slave or free: if he was a free man, "the white Americans, who as everyone knew had an abominable system of slavery," were obliged to request Haitian authorities to arrest him. "But if Nugent is, as we are assured, a slave of Captain Payne, or of another officer on board the American ship, Captain Payne certainly ignored the general laws of our free country." Such laws were no match for arrogant American officers backed by artillery and marines on a ship-of-war. The spirit of the laws had not even prevailed with the Haitian betrayer, inspired more by self-interest than racial allegiance. Black sailors' possibilities for freedom were always circumscribed—even in Haiti.

Although Haiti may have seemed to many a tropical Promised Land, it was but one-third of one island in the Caribbean. Given that its impact on the racial tug-of-war in the Atlantic was disproportionate to its size, and given that it burned like a beacon for many African Americans, the black republic's extension of freedom had very real limits. Nevertheless, foreign black seamen took justifiable pride in Haiti, delighting in their new-found ability to play off the Haitian state against shipmasters and consular officials. Haitian sovereignty united their pragmatic concerns about securing wages and receiving independence from their captains with the ideology of racial liberty. As they voyaged onward, their tales of tactics and triumphs reinforced the consciousness of freedom among blacks around the Atlantic world.

THE AMERICAN REVOLUTION had provided northern blacks with the first large-scale possibility for freedom. Before the war, nearly every person of color throughout the British North American colonies was a slave; by war's end, almost 60,000 black Americans had their freedom. During the Revolution itself, numerous black men served aboard privateers, or on ships in the Continental navy. The Connecticut and Massachusetts state navies were known for enlisting all the black sailors they could recruit; slaves also served in other navies, including those of Virginia, South Carolina, and Georgia. Seafaring slaves in the lower South were rarely liberated, but in the North, revolutionary naval service or privateering sometimes became a means to individual freedom. An enslaved mariner named Prince from Lyme, Connecticut, turned over his privateering proceeds to his master, Captain Joseph Mather, and was freed in 1779.[49]

The Revolution had profound implications for black mariners and black society as a whole, however, as a crew of enslaved privateersmen from Bermuda discovered. In May 1782, the sixteen-gun Bermudian privateer *Regulator*, manned by seventy slaves and five white men, was

captured by the American frigate *Deane*. The American commander
sent the *Regulator* and her crew to Boston as prizes, counting on the
Admiralty Court there to auction all that was saleable. Lawmakers in
Massachusetts had recently decided, however, that slaves captured on
the high seas were not to be sold as prizes—a departure from the
norms of eighteenth-century warfare at sea. Stating clearly that they
would not be sold, the court offered the seventy privateersmen the
choice of freedom in Massachusetts or return to their homes in
Bermuda. For many seafaring blacks the most significant development
following the American Revolution was the abolition of slavery in
northern states. Northern men of color henceforth would enter the
maritime labor market as free men; and mariners from slave societies
would have the possibility of seeking a haven in societies without
slavery.[50]

Deep-sea maritime slavery became a casualty of slaves' chronic
flight and the easy access to free territory after the revolutions in the
United States and St. Domingue. The coastal versions of maritime
slavery found in plantation societies did not collapse outright, but they
evolved toward free labor. A Jamaican planter claimed in 1826 that
"twenty years ago the coasting vessels of Jamaica were almost exclusively manned with slaves. From the increase of the free population the coasting vessels are now more commonly manned with free
men." Given the problems of controlling enslaved maritime workers,
planters and merchants came to realize that a free market in labor
would be more efficient and tractable than the continued use of
seafaring slaves.[51]

Nowhere was the decline of maritime slavery more evident than in
Chesapeake Bay, where hiring slaves for international voyages became
ever more problematic during the early nineteenth century. When in
1802 Captain Conner hired James Perry for a voyage from Baltimore
to Hamburg and back, he did not expect the Maryland Court of
Appeals to hold him responsible for Perry's escape. They did. This
decision warned Conner and other captains that the apparent economy of hiring slave sailors could be more than offset by expense and
aggravation if the slave fled. In 1813 Jane H. Slacum agreed that her
slave David would serve as a mariner on a voyage from Alexandria,
Virginia, to Lisbon and back. When she agreed to enter him on the

shipping articles, the court ruled that she effectively "bound herself that her slave should conduct himself as a seaman, agreeable to the articles." So when David fled in New York, having returned from Portugal, she lost both his wages and the value of David himself. When three slaves hired to the master of the brig *Sophila* for a voyage from Alexandria, Virginia, to Amsterdam in 1809 deserted in Liverpool, they were "totally lost" to their owner. He attempted to hold *Sophila*'s captain responsible, but by the time the case had worked its way from the District of Columbia's Circuit Court to the United States Supreme Court, Chief Justice John Marshall held that all the risk was the slaveholder's. "These slaves were received on board the vessel as mariners on the usual wages, and without any special contract," wrote Marshall. Their owner "knew his property might be exposed" to "the danger of their escaping." Whereas courts in slave states such as Maryland continued to protect slaveholders' human property, the notoriously procommercial federal courts of the early republic were more likely to support commerce than individuals' property in slaves, thereby accelerating the erosion of deep-sea maritime slavery.[52]

During the Napoleonic Wars, mariners' wages skyrocketed and seamen were in short supply, especially in the profitable era of "neutral trade," from 1793 to 1807. But in 1806 slaves constituted only about 1 percent of seafarers shipped in Baltimore for international voyages. Although black sailors as a whole filled 14.5 percent of the foreign-going berths in Baltimore that year, maritime slavery was on the wane.[53] This decline in the Chesapeake region was evident in runaway slave advertisements in Virginian newspapers. From 1736 to 1801, mariners constituted 24 percent of the skilled slave runaways. But between 1815 and 1832, only 13 percent of skilled slave runaways were maritime workers. The maritime sector became one of the first labor forces in slave society to make the transition from enslaved to nominally free wage labor.[54]

Evidence from the Caribbean and the Carolinas suggests similar patterns. Maritime slavery may have been more prominent in the urban areas of the Carolina low-country than in Caribbean towns. The historian Philip Morgan found that 20 percent of the male slaves belonging to Charleston residents between 1730 and 1799 were "watermen," "boatmen," "fishermen," or "pilots." In a similar analysis of

British Caribbean towns around 1820, Barry Higman found only 5 to 8 percent of all urban slaves involved in maritime work. The discrepancy may hinge on regional differences; more likely, though, it is an index of how free blacks were replacing slaves in Caribbean maritime work after 1800.[55]

The exact proportion of enslaved seamen departing South Carolina and Georgia on international voyages during the eighteenth century is not recoverable, but slave sailors were undoubtedly more numerous then than during the nineteenth century. Nineteenth-century crew lists from Savannah reveal that only 1 to 2 percent of foreign-bound sailors' berths were filled by slaves between 1803 and 1819 (the earliest period for which data are available), an era in which black sailors as a whole filled 12 to 15 percent of such berths. Although by the 1820s deep-sea maritime slavery was virtually moribund in Georgia, some low-country entrepreneurs continued to organize seafaring labor in what had become an anachronistic manner. Merchants in the Charleston Marine Society lobbied from 1825 to 1830 against state laws restricting the movement of slave sailors, arguing that "the crews with which our vessels are manned are principally, if not altogether, slaves." They spoke of the "great pains and trouble" with which they prepared those slaves "for the duties of mariners," and insisted that slave sailors were still vital to South Carolina "because there are no white seamen belonging to the state, and in the summer season particularly, none are to be procured." They also opposed state laws forbidding the return to South Carolina of slaves who had been abroad.[56]

The laments of merchants in South Carolina prefigured similar complaints from shipowners in Grenada, who claimed in 1832 that hired slave mariners constituted "a chief part" of the crews of vessels trading between the islands and North America. Merchants in Grenada opposed the new Royal Customs Service's refusal to clear vessels manned by slaves unaccompanied by owners. Although designed to suppress the intercolonial slave trade, the regulation crippled maritime slavery. British West Indian merchants and ship captains could no longer hire slaves as sailors. By 1834, when commissioners accurately listed the occupations of British Caribbean slaves, only 7,238 bondsmen worked in "wharves, shipping, etc."—2.2 percent of the male slaves throughout all the British Caribbean colonies.[57]

Within the maritime slavery that persisted in the coastal regions of plantation societies, however, enslaved sailors and captains like Moses Grandy propelled themselves toward freedom. And by the first quarter of the nineteenth century, international seafaring throughout the Atlantic had become the province of free men of color. As independent wage-earners, they defied white predictions that free blacks would be incapable of making their way in the world.

DURING THE AGE OF REVOLUTIONS, in which American, French, and Haitian upheavals successfully challenged the old order, restive black sailors discovered that free territory was expanding around the Atlantic. They found a special welcome in Haiti. Nevertheless, limitations on all black sailors' freedom remained severe. Successful runaways could rarely do better than exchange the lifetime domination of one owner for the crap-shoot of a series of captains. And free sailors' wages never allowed real independence. Ironically, enslaved masters of vessels found a degree of physical and psychological freedom *within* maritime slavery. Their exceptional talents and workplace opportunities subtly combined with the influence of market values to transform them. Forging individual freedom, elite maritime slaves became forces for change because they grasped revolutionary ways of imagining the world and their place in it. Although most remained enslaved, the combination of skill and determination led many of them to escape.

Black sailors in revolutionary Haiti, drawing strength from an explicit black community, and elite slave mariners in plantation societies, acting primarily as individuals, affirmed various possibilities for black freedom in an age of slavery.

6. PRECARIOUS PILLAR
OF THE
BLACK COMMUNITY

*Ships at a distance have every man's wish
on board.*

ZORA NEALE HURSTON,
Their Eyes Were Watching God (1937)

DURING THE EARLY NINETEENTH CENTURY, free black men throughout the North gravitated toward ships in search of a livelihood. Although shipping had stagnated as the first free black communities took shape during the decade after the American Revolution, the outbreak of the Napoleonic Wars in 1793 catapulted American merchants into a lucrative niche as "neutral" carriers. Seafaring jobs multiplied exponentially until 1807, and continued to grow at a slower pace thereafter. American tonnage quadrupled between 1815 and 1860, and shipping remained one of the few expanding industries open to men of color.[1]

Free blacks found it exceedingly difficult to acquire productive land, and they invariably faced discrimination in most trades. With few options for employment, free sailors of color from Boston argued in 1788 that seafaring was one calling in which "thay might get a hanceum livehud for themselves and theres."[2] Black New Englanders thus turned to the sea to hold families together, acquire property, and attain respectability. The Cuffes and Wainers in Bristol County, Massachusetts, the Browns in Providence, Rhode Island, the Bostons in Nantucket, and the Smiths in southeastern Connecticut all made the difficult transition from slavery to freedom on the strength of maritime work. Each family relied on seafaring wages, whaling shares, and entrepreneurial coastal trading for economic survival, sometimes for as many as four generations. Their menfolk were fixtures in their communities whose arrivals and departures were noted by friends and family.[3]

Yet free blacks in New England and elsewhere recognized the ironies associated with seafaring. Although relatively important for the financial support of families and newly founded black organizations, shipping drew away many of the best and brightest young men just as free black communities were trying to establish themselves. Furthermore, the values inculcated by maritime work rarely promoted the responsibility and respectability so important to free black society in its formative stages. From elders' standpoint, all too many sailors were rolling stones who owned nothing but what they could carry, and whose ties ashore were fleeting at best. Seafaring remained a pillar of early-nineteenth-century northern free black society, but its perilous nature and meager wages made it a precarious one. By mid-century, changes in maritime hiring and worsening conditions for all sailors further alienated black seamen from black society ashore.

BLACK MEN often had few alternatives to maritime employment as a means to establish households and raise families. William J. Brown noted that his father was married in Cranston, Rhode Island, in 1805, "and commenced keeping house in that town, but being engaged in a seafaring life he removed to Providence and rented a house of Dr. Pardon Bowen." Noah Brown continued to ship out on deep-water voyages for another decade. The "Return of Coloured Persons Being Housekeepers," compiled in Providence in 1822, listed a number of black sailors, including Fortune Dyer, whose wife and child profited from a boarder's company in his absence. By the time the Providence City Directory was published in 1832, one quarter of African American household heads were mariners. These Rhode Island sailors were by no means anomalies: city directories from Portland, Maine, to Baltimore consistently listed seafaring among the three or four most common occupations pursued by free black men.[4]

When members of the Providence African Union Society (the city's first black benevolent group) drafted bylaws at the turn of the century, they acknowledged the importance of maritime work to eminent black citizens by agreeing to a common sacrifice: members swore not to serve on slavers, although such ships were prominent in the Newport and Bristol fleets. Other African American mutual aid and fraternal organizations recognized the prominence of seafaring in their members' lives, as well as its ever-present dangers. The African Marine Fund incorporated itself in New York City in 1810 "For The Relief Of The Distressed Orphans, And Poor Members Of This Fund." The sole occupation specifically mentioned in the constitution of the Brotherly Union Society, founded in Philadelphia in April 1823, was seafaring. The society maintained moral standards not usually associated with seamen, reinforcing the fact that many black men seeking respectability were then shipping out. The Brotherly Union Society expelled members for "fraudulent, base or immoral conduct" or "for gambling, tippling in shops, or spending time in brothels."[5]

Aspiring to middle-class status, the "best" black families in the North sent their sons to sea. Born a slave in 1790, James Mars bought his freedom, married, and became prominent in antebellum black Connecticut. Later, three of his four sons shipped out. Paul Cuffe, an internationally known Massachusetts merchant and shipmaster, and James Forten, a Philadelphia sailmaker who patented a device for handling sails, exemplify the financial success and respectability of northern black Americans. Each of them had sea experience, as did other men in their families.[6] But though many an enterprising black man shipped out in the early and mid-nineteenth century, seafaring never attained the status of barbering or other dignified professions in the black community ashore. It was always stigmatized by the taint of immorality. Henry Highland Garnett, a respected black preacher and abolitionist who had been to sea as a boy, wrote from Jamaica in 1852 that "West Indian towns are generally notorious for immorality, and the reason is they are usually seaports."[7]

Despite temptations in ports-of-call, some resolute seamen were able to delay gratification. For the few who did not draw on their wages, one of the attractions of seafaring was its lump-sum payday. "My entire savings up to the period of my return from this voyage," remembered Moses Grandy of his trip to the East Indies aboard the ship *James Murray,* "amounted to $300. I sent it to Virginia and bought my wife." Ambitious men looked to seafaring for capital accumulation. "I was born free," recollected Dempsey Reid, a Virginian farmer from Nansemond County who sailed during the 1830s and whose life story would have pleased Horatio Alger. "I worked hard for the property. I went to sea and afterwards bought a team and went to teaming and saved enough to buy my land etc." These men more than fulfilled society's expectation that they provide for their families.[8]

All sailors' pay was poor, but at least aboard ship blacks often earned pay equal to that of whites in the same position. Voyages originating in the South were the exception. There, as in much shoreside employment in the North, blacks made do with significantly less. In 1813 free black seamen in Charleston earned only $17 per month, whereas their white shipmates earned $30. Similar inequities prevailed *ashore* in the North. In Rhode Island in 1810, white laborers "receiving ballast" pocketed half again as much as blacks. But aboard the Rhode Island brig *John* in 1806, seamen of color earned $4 per month more than the white cook and ordinary seamen. A black was the best paid sailor aboard the Rhode Island brig *Mary* in 1819. These patterns prevailed through the 1850s. Blacks mariners in Baltimore and Charleston were paid less than whites, whereas black deckhands shipping from Liverpool and New York were paid equally.[9]

Black whalemen in the same station as whites were also paid equally. Lays (that is, shares) on the whaleship *Bowditch* in 1843 were assigned by berth, regardless of race: 1/185 for greenhands and 1/150 for seamen. An analysis of thirty-five whaleships sailing from southern New England between 1837 and 1853 reveals this to have been customary. Equal remuneration aboard ship reinforced blacks' claims of equality.[10]

Free black communities had begun to form during the 1790s, when demands for seamen on risky but profitable "neutral" voyages boosted seafaring wages threefold. Never thereafter would sailors' pay range so far ahead of the price of essentials such as food, fuel, and lodging; and never again would the promise of seafaring for poor laborers seem so great. Maritime wages fell with the resumption of peace in 1815, and slumped considerably after the Panic of 1819. Nevertheless, work at sea still appealed to some blacks. Wages, though never high, often equaled those paid to shore-bound laborers through the 1850s. In addition, shipboard work included victuals and accommodations—an important consideration for poor laborers. Even the irregularity of sailors' work was not an impediment to black men: a job that promised to last several months remained an almost unheard-of luxury in the black community.[11]

Along with room and board, the use of cargo space for sailors' own entrepreneurial ventures remained a customary part of the wage, although it was never guaranteed. Sailors transported goods they had purchased—such as shoes, shirts, or sugar—to sell for profit in the next port. Masters hoped this would give mariners an interest in their voyage; sailors themselves saw it as a risky way to augment their pay. Four free black sailors aboard the *Young Johannes* of Curaçao were "concerned in Twelve Seroons of Cocoa" in 1747. Some free black seamen maintained this privilege into the antebellum period, trying to parlay it into increased family earnings. Enos Cuthbert, the steward of the schooner *Splendid* sailing from Porto Bello to New York in 1830, "had a venture on board consisting of Indigo, 4 bales." Sailors occasionally found access to other perquisites that established their reputations at home. A white woman from Marblehead, Massachusetts, lamented in 1779 that they "go a privateering, & bring home their black Ladies such things, as enable them to look down, with Contempt, upon many of the Whites."[12]

Northern free blacks in the early nineteenth century looked to exemplary mariners as role models and community leaders. Men of color rarely achieved the pinnacle of command, but when they did, class distinctions among blacks were subordinated to racial pride. Born in 1785, Absalom Boston became a mariner and laborer who at one time obtained from the Nantucket county commissioners a license to run a "public inn." He gained notoriety in 1822, however, as the master of an all-black crew aboard the whaling schooner *Industry*— something "quite strange," according to one of his sailors. Upon his death at age seventy, Captain Absalom Boston owned three houses, a store, a garden lot, and a mowing lot on Nantucket. Few black seamen approached such wealth. His brother Reuben, also a mariner, faced the constant poverty typical of most black New Englanders.

The self-described "coloured tars" who sailed under Captain Boston extolled his leadership rather than vilifying him, as white sailors often did their commanders. "Here's health to Captain Boston, His officers and crew," ran a ballad composed in honor of a professedly racial enterprise, "And if he gets another craft, To sea with him I'll go." Captain Boston's seamen shared the Promethean burdens of an all-black venture during an era of rising Negrophobia. A routine gale provoked fear of "losing caboose and boats," for "then our voyage is done"—something none of those sailors wanted under any but the most auspicious circumstances.[13]

Maintaining a home on a sailor's wages, and with a sailor's schedule, was almost as difficult as attaining command. After the War of 1812, remembered Abraham Williams, "I then thought of having a home of my own." Stolen from Africa about 1800, Williams had made voyages enslaved to a Bahamian and then sailed as a free man from Massachusetts. After marrying, he circumnavigated the globe three times in the China trade—each voyage lasting more than a year—to support a household. For blacks in the first generations of freedom, moving out from under the roof of a white master and creating a home often entailed long absences. Even short-haul coasting voyages took a week or two; sailors bound on coasting trips to the South, or on European or West Indian voyages, commonly were gone for three or four months. Whalers could be away for years. During an eighteen-year period, the whaleman Ebenezer Hunt of New Bedford spent only twenty-three months ashore, though he remained listed in the New Bedford City Directory as the head of a household because his wife resided there. In spite of such absences, black men balanced home life and maritime work. Charles Williams testified in 1830 that his "permanent residence is in New York where he has a family, has been a seafaring man off and on for twenty-two years."[14]

A small group of black seafarers in New England earned enough to purchase houses, or at least to rent steadily and forestall disruptive moves. Their tenure was always precarious. John and Sarah Brown lived on Belknap Street in Boston, "in an alley leading from the court in which the African Church was." According to his wife, Brown owned the house for a number of years, having "bought it of a man named Hartshorne, a gentleman," until it was taken by Mr. Parker in the early 1830s, "it being mortgaged to him by Brown." Mrs. Brown

remembered that "she went out washing & he went to sea." Black
sailors in Portland, Maine, had a degree of residential and occupational stability atypical in larger cities such as Baltimore or New York.
Of thirty-three black seamen listed in the city directory in 1830, nine
lived there sixteen years later, most still shipping out, and many at the
same addresses. Five of thirty-one black seafaring householders in
New Bedford owned real estate in 1838. In every port, most African
American seamen changed domiciles frequently or bounced between
boardinghouses and forecastles, while a core group strove for respectability with purchased or rented accommodations.[15]

The most stable seamen of color in New England lived among the
Indian populations at Chappequiddick, Gay Head, and Christiantown
on Martha's Vineyard and at Mashpee on Cape Cod. Referred to as
"amalgamated," these people were considered "a mixture of the red,
white, and black races." Virtually all the men, according to the Indian
commissioner of Massachusetts, "engage in seafaring as an occupation." Subject to white "guardianship" since 1693, they had no political
rights, and by 1861 they numbered only 1,600. But coastal Indians were
prominent beyond their numbers, generating leaders such as Paul
Cuffe and Samson Occam. And unlike most seamen of color, they
owned land.[16]

The men still sailed because their white neighbors' depredations
made it impossible for them to eke a living from the land. About 1805,
"the Indian natives and colour'd People inhabiting the Indian lands"
on Chappequiddick complained that they "consider [themselves] injured and oppress'd by many of the White Inhabitants of Said Island."
In 1828 the people of Christiantown complained about the unequal
"division of our lands by the commissioners." Dependent "on other
People for the privilege of watering our stock," they lamented "that
they follow the sea and [were] absent when the division was made."
According to nineteenth-century political economists, land allowed
independence and might forestall families from indenturing their
children to service. More than a few black and white Americans
shipped out with the hope of investing their wages in a farm. But the
largest group of northern landowners of color found that their dreams
of financial independence were a mockery because of political pow-
erlessness. James Williamson, "a Negro man," owned seventeen acres

of "upland" in Christiantown. Needing cash, he shipped aboard a whaler in 1828. By 1840, whalemen's lays provided 69 percent of the reported income at Chappequiddick and Christiantown. Landowning "Indians and People of Color" there had been thoroughly proletarianized.[17]

Although some blacks who aspired to respectability or independence looked seaward, black deep-sea sailors with residential stability were the exception. This was especially true in large cities by mid-century. Only 9 percent of the black mariners sailing on foreign voyages from Philadelphia in 1850 who claimed to reside there appeared in the 1850 census. Employment was crucial for these men: all had wives or children in their households. Only 4 percent of a group of 223 black sailors shipping on foreign voyages from Baltimore in 1857 appeared in the city directory. Clearly, by 1850 blacks in the deep-sea merchant marine were either uninterested in families or unable to support them with sailors' wages and sailors' schedules. Seamen seeking respectability and family homes worked in the coastal trade. For instance, 116 free black householders in Baltimore who described themselves as mariners in the 1857 directory did not appear on crew lists of sailors making international voyages. Although evidence regarding coastal shipping is sketchy, it appears that by the 1830s a fault line separated respectable black sailors with families from unattached boardinghouse dwellers. Family men oriented themselves toward coasting; reputation-seeking rakes and angry dissenters, toward deep-sea voyages.[18]

Black seafaring men who took seriously their role as providers lived with the constant tension of separation from their families. A Philadelphian named John Gardner wrote to his wife's employer in 1814 from on board ship, "I hope all my wife's friends are well my love to her, I hope to see her again." Sheppard Bourne wrote to his mother, "I am very antious to get hom to my wif and famly if not to you."[19]

Families already stressed by poverty were made vulnerable by sailors' long voyages. A Rhode Islander named John Gardner, who acknowledged in 1831 that he "follows the sea mostly," married Mary Ann Elizabeth Stewart in a Presbyterian service at her father's house in Providence. She contributed to the household they established on Olney Lane by doing laundry for the steamboats and taking in sewing and washing from other black people in the Hardscrabble neighborhood. Always pressed financially, however, Gardner spent time in jail for debt and reluctantly shipped out again in 1835. During that absence, three drunken white men gang-raped his wife.[20]

Black women bore burdens enough in the best of times. "Honey, de white man is de ruler of everything as fur as Ah been able tuh find out," lamented Janie Sparks's grandmother in a Zora Neale Hurston novel. "Maybe its some place way off in the ocean where de black man is in power, but we don't know nothin' but what we see. So de white man throw down the load, and tell de nigger man to pick it up. He pick it up because he have to, but he don't tote it. He hand it to his womenfolks. De nigger woman is de mule of the world so fur as Ah can see."[21]

Seafarers' womenfolk knew all too well about being "de mule of the world." Like Mrs. Charles Benson, of Salem, they took in "Washing and Ironing for Mrs Haraden at one dollar per dossen," or "commenced work for Mrs. Mary Chandler . . . at two dollars per week." Mrs. Benson's washing and domestic service typified most urban black women's employment options. With her husband earning twenty dollars per month as the steward aboard the *Glide*, then on a nine- or ten-month voyage to East Africa, her contribution to the household budget was substantial. Less fortunate wives abandoned by their husbands turned to prostitution to support themselves and their children. The few who owned land put in crops, tended animals, and kept their houses in repair. A. L. Wainer wrote to her brother aboard a whale ship in 1850 from their home in Bristol County, Massachusetts, "We are yery bizy harvest ing at this time potatoes about 50 bushels." She had "swapt away the old horse" and was trying to collect debts while taking care of their elderly mother. She took it all in stride: "We are getting a long comefortable."[22]

Within struggling free black communities, where women routinely worked just as hard as men for wages, providership nevertheless remained an important dimension of masculinity. And defining themselves as men was important to black landsmen and seamen alike. The abolitionist William Wells Brown addressed a New England Convention of blacks in 1859 by saying, "We must take a manly stand, bid defiance to the Fugitive Slave Law, Dred Scott Decision, and everything that shall attempt to fashion fetters upon us." The boardinghouse keeper William P. Powell often used references to masculinity to affirm black mariners' skill and equality. Introducing Mr. Charles Flowers to William Lloyd Garrison by letter in 1853, Powell wrote: "Though one of the Sons of *Neptune* he is every inch a *man* and entitled to be respected as such wherever he may go." Black seamen like Powell linked assertions of equality with a clearly defined gender identity. They saw manliness as common ground among all men, even though education, wealth, and status were denied to blacks by a white-dominated society. Black men oppressed by almost insurmountable burdens fell back on claims of manhood rather than appeals to a common humanity, because the canons of nineteenth-century masculinity invested manhood with a special dignity. Referring to manliness, the historian David Montgomery noted that "few words enjoyed more popularity in the nineteenth century than this honorific, with all its connotations of dignity, respectability, defiant egalitarianism, and patriarchal male supremacy."[23]

Black mariners' professions of masculine equality and providership notwithstanding, whites expected them to sail as cooks or stewards. These were service-oriented positions (even "feminine" jobs in the minds of some whites) not defined by nautical skill and physical courage. This is not to say that cooks were rarely skilled sailors: many had prodigious experience at sea. A mulatto seaman spoke admiringly of "old Alec Rolling, our Negro cook, who was also a thorough sailor."[24] It is to say that whites pigeonholed blacks for berths that white society associated with service and retrograde masculinity: of 667 white mariners departing Philadelphia in 1803 and Baltimore in 1806, only 2 were cooks or stewards. The captain's son aboard the brig *Palestine* in 1832 chortled gleefully about "our Steward—alias Kitchen Maid," because he was "a black *man!*" Lamenting the shortage of white stewards for the Revenue Cutter Service, Captain W. W. Polk noted in 1831 that "the custom which prevails at the port of Philadelphia of having coloured persons for cooks & stewards, renders it very difficult to procure suitable white persons to fill those stations."[25]

Conforming to values forged in the black community, African American mariners did not necessarily resent sailing as a cook or a steward, and they often considered such jobs theirs by right of race. They played to whites' expectations for their own purposes. Arriving at New Bedford, the fugitive slave John Thompson was told that "great responsibility rested upon the cook, or steward, of a whaling vessel." But Thompson explicitly said that he "preferred" one of those berths. A mulatto steward named Charles Benson confided to his diary in 1862 that though he expected to find the crew "a pack of fault finding ignorant men," he also expected his berth as steward to shield him from them. And getting paid more than sailors was part of the attraction of the cook's or steward's job, at least by 1850.[26]

The relative rise in seacooks' pay was one of the few changes within the maritime industries that benefited blacks as the nineteenth century progressed. Until about 1820, cooks and stewards had the worst-paying jobs aboard ship; and many more blacks than whites filled those positions. By no means were most black mariners cooks, but almost all seacooks were black. Cooks' pay averaged about five dollars per month (33 percent) less than sailors' before 1820, but it improved with time, equaling sailors' from approximately 1820 to 1850. The introduction of iron stoves into the galley, and the growing emphasis on culinary skill at sea—an offshoot of the rising emphasis on domestication ashore—meant that cooks and stewards routinely earned more than seamen after 1850. During the 1850s and 1860s, the cook's pay often equaled that of the second mate, allowing many blacks the opportunity to earn more and provide for a family.[27]

One of the lateral career tracks open to black men in the nineteenth century was using catering or restaurant experience to get a job cooking at sea. William C. Nell apprenticed to Jehu Jones, an aristocratic free man of color who kept one of Charleston's most celebrated hotels, then shipped as steward of the *General Gadsen* in 1813. John Robbins, a waiter at the Mansion House, left New Bedford to go whaling and then worked in a New Orleans packet. African American men shipping in Baltimore for naval service during the Civil War had considerable hotel experience. Wesley Wilson shipped as steward for the commander of the U.S.S. *Flagg* after two years of waiting tables at "a respectable hotel."[28]

Thus right up to the Civil War, many black men paradoxically assumed the most "feminine" roles aboard white-dominated ships to maintain their masculine roles as respectable providers in the black community. Charles Benson, who occasionally worked ashore as a caterer, sailed out of Salem and Boston from the late 1850s until his death at sea in 1881. His diaries indicate how one "Kitchen Maid" took seriously his duties as husband and father. Writing to his wife in 1862, a homesick Benson complained, "What a miserable life a sea fareing life is. I will stop it if I live & that soon (that is if I get anything to do on shore). You & the children must have things to eat drink & were [wear] & I must get it some were [somewhere] if not on land, on the sea." Sixteen years later his tune had not changed much: "How can I ern my bread without it on the Mighty Deep?"[29]

Benson's identity as a seaman incorporated Victorian society's masculine virtues: stoicism, prestige, and providership. "Was there any comfort any time, any where at sea? I cannot really say I ever [found it]. It is the excitement, danger, and money that a sea life Brings, that keeps me at sea. Nothing else. 226 days from home." Benson did not envision himself as a domestic. He took pride in his work and in the self-image formed through it. As steward, he was the captain's servant. But he was also the ship's barber and doctor and the man responsible for all the provisions on voyages to East Africa. In his own estimation he was an honorable provider for his family and a man respected ashore. Other black stewards also took seriously their roles as providers. Jesse Scott, formerly a slave to General Robert E. Lee, and by 1868 the cook and steward aboard the brig *Charles Albert* of Baltimore, opened a bank account between voyages. He made it "subject to the order of my children Letty & James Scott."[30]

Patterns of prolonged absence and return created an emotional roller-coaster for families. Two hundred and twenty-seven days out on a passage to Mozambique, Charles Benson confided to his diary, "How I want to get home & yet I some times dread the thoughts of going home; for it seems to me at times as though I was not wanted there, is it so? Am I not in the way sometimes?" Of course he was in the way. His wife customarily worked, went to church, visited with women friends, and tended her children without him. At sea for more than twenty years, Charles Benson became an intruder in his own house and a stranger to his children. Countless other black children lost their fathers to the sea permanently. Susan Rex remembered that her father was "supposed to have been shipwrecked" and "dec'd at sea when she was small." Andrew Laurey of New Bedford spoke of his father, Perry, who "died at Sea near home in Ship Planter. Was brought home and buried here." Andrew was then living with his grandmother, and he remembered going with her to the funeral when he was about seven years old, in 1823. Preserving the memories of dead husbands and fathers, widows and children testified to mariners' attempts to be responsible providers. Their loneliness and hurt revealed the personal cost of a seafaring livelihood.[31]

Common white sailors rarely had families to be threatened ashore in their absence, as Nathaniel Ames indicated in his *Nautical Reminiscences.* "I do not know that I ever sailed in an American ship," he recalled, "with an individual before the mast that was a married man with the exception of one Negro cook of Boston." The fact that black mariners had families ashore made them more likely than footloose white deckhands to ship out of a homeport regularly and keep returning there. It also meant that maritime tragedies struck directly at the black community struggling for stability and respectability on shore. Betsy Watson of Providence lost several husbands to the sea around the turn of the century; by 1822 she had married a fourth time—to the seaman Henry Gray.[32]

Seafaring, then, meant something very different for black men and white men, especially in the early nineteenth century. White sailors—whether gentlemen's sons inspired to dare "an insight into the mysteries of a sailor's life," ambitious boys eager to gain a command, or "rebels who left the land in flight and fear"—were geographically mobile, unmarried, and unlikely to stick with the sea unless promoted. Black sailors were older than their white shipmates; more rooted in their homeports; more likely to be married; more likely to persist in going to sea; and more likely to define themselves with dignity as respectable men because seafaring enabled at least some of them to provide for their families.[33]

As the antebellum period progressed, and domestic economic development accelerated, the proportion of American commerce in coasters rose faster than that in deep-water ships. The "Philadelphia Commercial List" estimated that 15,957 seamen (black and white) worked aboard vessels engaged exclusively in the Philadelphia coal trade in 1837, and Customs House statistics reveal that 4,800 of the 8,011 vessels arriving at New York in 1847 were coasters. In 1800, by contrast, merchants had looked overseas for goods and markets, and fewer vessels sailed coastwise. Coastal voyages allowed seamen with families to stay closer to home, and coasting became the job of choice for black mariners with dependents.[34]

William J. Brown remembered that "father married and settled down" after years of seafaring in the early national period, "intending not to take any more long voyages, but labor along shore or go coasting." Noah Brown "ploughed his land and began to cultivate it; and for several years raised enough vegetables to supply his family." In the meantime, he "followed coasting, running from Providence to New York on a vessel commanded by Captain Comstock." A black Bostonian named William Black sailed as the cook and steward of the coasting schooner *Bonna Boat.* "A steady sober man," according to his captain, "he wished to go on shore to see his daughter." A white pamphleteer recognized that men like Noah Brown and William Black were motivated by concerns different from those that motivated deep-water sailors. "The men engaged in the fisheries, the coasting trade, and in steamers," wrote John Codman, "are generally of a better class. They are not the bondsmen of [landlords], but are bound to their homes by domestic ties." Like other moral reformers, Codman believed that "the sacred influence of home" worked a salubrious effect on seamen. He suspended attention to the financial difficulties faced by most coastal mariners. Two black sailors named Haskins and Ellis left New Bedford for Baltimore to go coasting in the winter of 1853, and their wives had to apply to the Overseers of the Poor for relief. Intermittent work and poor pay did not provide them with the barest necessities for the kind of home reformers envisioned.[35]

Coasting offered other promises to a fortunate few. The capital required to invest in a modest coasting vessel was significantly less than that needed for an ocean-going craft, and coasting occasionally provided important opportunities for entrepreneurship to nineteenth-century blacks. The intermarried Cuffe, Cory, Wainer, and Johnson families, the elite of Massachusetts's colored society, had sufficient capital to organize coastal trading voyages to southern states before the early 1820s. Their all-black or primarily black crews frequently attracted attention: the collector of customs at Norfolk once denied Captain Paul Cuffe a clearance because of his race. Despite official obstacles and personal abuse, the Cuffes and other black entrepreneurs from southeastern Massachusetts persisted in the coastwise shipping ventures on which economic survival and respectability rested. "My brother is not at home," wrote Captain Cuffe's daughter Ruth in January 1819. "He is gone to north Carolina . . . I don't expect him home not in 3 or 4 months. When we heard from him he and his pardners was Selling off their Cargo."[36]

Free blacks in the upper South also embarked on coastal freighting ventures. Standley Battou bought the 43-foot schooner *Resolution* in 1797 at Oxford, Maryland. *Resolution* had been built along the Choptank River thirteen years earlier and was near the end of her usefulness: Captain Battou paid only $130 for her. She was still sufficiently seaworthy, however, for Battou to enroll her for coasting. He probably freighted wood, grain, and produce in the northern part of the Chesapeake Bay. Ben Legg, a free man of color, owned and navigated a coasting schooner in Virginia in 1819. His vessel was generally "found at Richmond, Norfolk, Petersburg, or Smithfield when in port," noted the irate master of his enslaved nephew, but "Legg sometimes makes a trip in her to Baltimore, Philadelphia and New York." The angry master feared that his slave "will make for this schooner under the hope that his uncle will carry him off."[37]

Blacks' maritime entrepreneurship suffered a double blow during the 1820s. In 1821, the year before South Carolina began to incarcerate all free black sailors under the new Negro Seamen Acts, the collector of customs at Norfolk, Virginia, questioned whether a free black man could legally command an American merchant vessel. Protectionist legislation required commanders of American vessels to be "citizens." But whites intent on limiting free blacks' upward mobility wanted that law to exclude black men from commands. In 1821 the U.S. attorney general, William Wirt, ruled that "free persons of color in Virginia are not citizens of the United States, within the intent and meaning of the acts regulating foreign and coasting trade, so as to be qualified to command vessels." Captain Ben Legg was out of business.[38]

Wirt's ruling, compounded by South Carolina's Negro Seamen Acts, reduced the ability of black maritime entrepreneurs to operate larger vessels, especially in southern states. The precarious financial stability of old black maritime families like the Cuffes collapsed quickly: Captain Paul Cuffe's namesake son spent a life at sea as a common sailor, and his granddaughter Joanna was reduced to public assistance in New Bedford by 1864. Legal restrictions did not keep men of color from owning or operating vessels locally, where profits were much more modest. Jerry Jeffers sailed as master of a sloop on Delaware Bay in 1843, "trading from Slaughter creek. Jeffers sailed the vessel," according to a court record, "for a share of the freights." Captain Daniel Drayton, intimately familiar with commerce on Delaware Bay, wrote that a skipper such as Jeffers would victual the sloop, hire and pay the hands, and receive 50 percent of the net profits after deducting the expense of loading and unloading. Someone else owned the vessel, but Captain Jeffers operated a simple business as a managerial capitalist.[39]

Slave states increasingly restricted free black maritime entrepreneurship as the abolitionist crusade gained momentum. Contacts between slaves and northern seaports, like the voyages once run by Ben Legg, were squelched. In Maryland, a bill was introduced into the House of Delegates in 1833 to prevent owners of vessels from allowing their navigation solely by blacks. African Americans commanding a Bay vessel petitioned against it, and the Senate rejected the bill. But several years later the House precluded blacks from legal command. By 1835, wrote E. A. Andrews, free blacks in Maryland were not "excluded from any trade or employment which may be practiced by the whites, except from the vending of spirituous liquors, and from the command of vessels." Captain Standley Battou, who thirty-eight years before had been operating the *Resolution* out of the Choptank River, would have been high and dry. A free black petitioning the state in 1838 to sail his own boat was rejected, and in 1854 a schooner was condemned after having been sailed by a black man in violation of the law.[40]

Small-scale maritime entrepreneurship kept black families financially afloat in both northern and southern states, but rarely surpassed subsistence. Silas Moore identified himself as "a Waterman, Master of a vessel," and explained that he was "half-owner of the schooner 'Susan' which plied in the river Neuse and freighted wood for the benefit of the citizens of New Bern," North Carolina, before the Civil War. Obviously proud of his vessel, Moore described *Susan* as "a two-mast schooner, with jib and topmast, foresail and mainsail. She was about 40 feet . . . oak timbers and cypress plank, well-caulked and painted, cabin and all conveniences." His free-born father owned the other half as well as a schooner named *Water Witch*. But these free black maritime entrepreneurs from North Carolina confronted much more circumscribed opportunities in the 1850s and early 1860s than had earlier black mariners such as Ben Legg or Standley Battou. They were rigidly restricted from sailing beyond state borders.[41] No record exists of Dudley Wright's financial circumstances, either before or after the Civil War, but his savings account passbook at the Norfolk branch of the Freedmen's Bank indicates a strong occupational identity and self-esteem. Married, with six children, Wright described himself as "CAPTAIN OF SCHOONER Works for SELF."[42]

The attorney general's decision that blacks could not legally be coasting captains because they were not "citizens" seems to have been ignored in the North. In 1845 the New Bedford City Directory listed James Lang, colored, as a master mariner and the head of a household on Orchard Street. An occupational census of black men in Philadelphia noted two "Captains of Coasting Vessels" in 1859. Six years earlier, "Captain Potter, a colored man," bought the schooner *Jerome* in Portland, Maine. *Jerome* carried about 150 tons of cargo, and when Potter bought her she was hauling coal from Philadelphia to New England, grossing approximately $3.50 per ton in the winter. Secretary of the Treasury Salmon P. Chase noted in 1862 that "colored masters are numerous in our coasting trade." Financial constraints hindered aspiring black owner-operators more than the attorney general's decree.[43]

One of the few mid-century changes in the maritime industries that worked to blacks' advantage was the repeal of their legal exclusion from coasting commands. After the captain of a U.S. Revenue Cutter detained the schooner *Elizabeth and Margaret* at Perth Amboy, New Jersey, in 1862 because a black skipper commanded her, President Lincoln's attorney general, Edward Bates, reversed William Wirt's decision. If born in the United States and otherwise qualified, Bates wrote, a black man "is competent according to the Acts of Congress, to be master of a vessel engaged in the coasting trade." This vindicated William P. Powell, who had argued constantly that "the coloured sailor is every way qualified to man and command vessels of any class to any part of the world." He swore that "if sufficient pains were taken to collect all the facts" concerning black captains, "what a mass of evidence we could have at hand to refute the *foul* calumnies daily heaped upon us."[44]

The responsibility of command combined with business competition openly challenged black subordination. Numerous black coasting masters enjoyed not only a degree of economic independence, but the intangible benefits of personal and racial affirmation. By the time legal restrictions on blacks' command of coasters were removed, however, northern free blacks as a whole had less capital and fewer opportunities to invest in coastal vessels than they had during the 1810s and 1820s. Theirs was a hollow victory.

NOTWITHSTANDING the determination of many mariners of color to provide for their families, the perilous nature of seafaring in the age of sail undermined the efforts of even the most responsible men. When Money Vose died at sea about 1813, his family was torn apart. One boy became a ward of the town; another went to sea and was never heard from again. One daughter resorted to prostitution in Boston; another to domestic service. When Francis Silva died in Honolulu aboard a whaleship in 1863, his thirteen-year-old daughter went to domestic service, and her mother to the almshouse. Silva's eighteen-year-old son was already whaling and beginning the cycle anew. Try as black northerners might to hold families and communities together, maritime employment provided a very precarious livelihood.[45]

Maritime labor markets routinely excluded men of color during financial slumps. Throughout President Thomas Jefferson's embargo on shipping, which lasted from late 1807 to 1809, the number of available berths going to African Americans in Providence fell from 22 percent to 15.5 percent. The Panics of 1819 and 1837 each adversely affected blacks' employment. In New Orleans, African Americans filled nearly 20 percent of sailors' jobs in 1819. The next year, as the panic rippled through the economy, black men filled less than 15 percent of available berths. In fact, every recession constricted blacks' employment prospects. Albro Lyons, the superintendent of the Coloured Sailors' Home in New York during the Panic of 1857, wrote that "the great revulsion in the commercial affairs" limited "situations for cooks and stewards especially—which cause many to Remain a long time on his hands."[46]

Even in good years the color line determined what a black man might do aboard American ships. With the exception of a few remarkable masters such as Captains Paul Cuffe and Pardon Cook, African American mariners found few promotions outside whale ships and small coasters—especially after the 1830s. Occupational mobility on merchant ships was virtually all lateral, between cook and steward and seaman. Of 3,500 merchant ship crews outbound on foreign voyages from Providence, Philadelphia, and New York between 1803 and 1856, only 3 had an officer of color. George Henry, an ex-slave who escaped to Providence after years of commanding a coasting schooner in his native Virginia, curtly recalled, "I found prejudice so great in the North that I was forced to come down from my high position as captain, and take my whitewash brush and wheelbarrow and get my living in that way."[47]

Despite entrenched barriers to promotion in the merchant service, young blacks vainly aspired to officers' billets. Noah Brown took lessons in Providence from a Quaker schoolmaster "celebrated for teaching the Mariner's art." In the late 1820s, the New York African Free School added navigation to its curriculum. But schooling for a trade, especially a seafaring one, was by no means common among young black men in the early republic. The uncertainties with which they lived did not allow for much sustained planning, and most understood work as God's curse on Adam.[48]

Whaling was the service of choice for some seamen of color because they felt that its particular workplace conditions encouraged them to act with a manly bearing. J. Ross Browne, a white southerner on a New Bedford whaleship during the 1840s, remembered that "it was . . . particularly galling to my feelings to be compelled to live in the forecastle with a brutal negro, who, conscious that he was upon an equality with the sailors, presumed upon his equality to a degree that was insufferable." Browne's ship was not extraordinary. "There is not that nice distinction made in whaling as there is in the naval and merchant services," wrote a black boardinghouse master. "A coloured man is only known and looked upon as a man, and is promoted in rank according to his ability and skill to perform the same duties as the white man."[49]

Whaling ships offered the best chances for promotion and responsibility to blacks, but they were notorious for poor pay, and conditions aboard the floating factories that butchered and processed whales were abysmal. When the *Cavalier* departed in 1848, during the heyday of whaling, a black second mate headed one watch. Some 700 men of color then sailed as officers and harpooners on American whalers, substantiating blacks' claims of masculine equality and challenging white newcomers' assumptions about race. Questioned by an imposing black seaman moments after joining the *Cachelot* in New Bedford, Frank Bullen

> said "yes" very curtly, for I hardly liked his patronizing air; but he snapped me up short with "yes, *sir,* when yew speak to me, yew blank limejuicer. I'se de fourf mate ob dis yar ship, en my name's Mistah Jones, 'n yew jest freeze on to dat ar, ef yew want ter lib long 'n die happy. See, sonny." I *saw,* and answered promptly, "I beg your pardon, sir, I didn't know."[50]

The promise of promotion notwithstanding, most sailors preferred a dash to the West Indies or a six-week Atlantic crossing to the eternity of a whaling cruise—which routinely lasted for months or even years, until the ship's hold was filled with whale oil. And every whaler was by no means free of customary prejudices. One white seaman aboard Nantucket's *Rambler* in 1822 noted that "the white portion of the hands" lived in the steerage with the boatsteerers, "the forecastle being filled with darkies."[51]

Most blacks aboard whaling ships from 1790 to 1860 were transient, not permanent, workers. All the undesirable aspects of seafaring were magnified in whaling: it was dirtier, more dangerous, more estranging, and worse paying than merchant or coastal shipping. Of 3,189 black men on New Bedford whaling ships between 1803 and 1860, only 20 percent made multiple voyages out of New Bedford. Most men of color in the antebellum whaling fleet were newcomers, for whom one voyage was sufficient.[52]

The likelihood of black men becoming career seamen aboard merchant ships declined with time. As economic conditions worsened in the antebellum black community, and as racism increased in urban America, fewer blacks persisted at voyaging. Blacks became casual sailors at a higher rate than whites by the 1850s. In the first decade of the century, 21 percent of the African American men sailing out of Providence made at least three voyages in a seven-year period; during the 1830s, 24 percent did. But by the 1850s, only 7 percent made that many voyages. Drawn by the security of a few months' wages, black men flowed into the maritime labor market when it could absorb them, and then later drifted—or were bounced—back ashore to ditch-digging, boot-blacking, wood-chopping, and unemployment.[53]

Nevertheless, a core group of black mariners remained wedded to the sea. These men grew gray before the mast as white youngsters came and went. Many "old salts" on American sailing ships were black men with nowhere else to go, seamen like Prince Brown, who in his mid-forties made at least six voyages from Providence. "Of our entire crew," remembered Charles Nordhoff about a whaling voyage to the Indian Ocean, "none but one Portuguese and the black cook really cared to stay."[54]

Equal pay with northern white mariners in the same job, and the occasionally profitable venture notwithstanding, seafaring rarely alleviated the grinding poverty faced by most nineteenth-century blacks. Quarterly reports from the Coloured Sailors' Home in New York highlight black mariners' destitution. That particular boardinghouse catered to the most respectable clientele, and men staying there were as likely as any to be temperate and thrifty. Yet in 1843 the superintendent exhausted his resources aiding "seamen . . . without a cent to help themselves," and 13 percent of his boarders were "true objects of charity." Their plight threatened the financial stability of the home itself, which existed on a shoe-string because of its guarantee that shipwrecked or impoverished black sailors would always receive shelter, food, and clothing without charge.[55]

New England whalers' real pay deteriorated more substantially in the antebellum years than did that of merchant mariners in ports such as New York; and black men (on a per capita basis) were about twice as likely as whites to work in whaleships. Declining pay on whaleships thus hit blacks especially hard. The peculiar nature of whaling's share system, which was skewed to protect shipowners' profits, meant that at the end of a two- or three-year voyage whalemen might earn nothing or even owe the ship. Their plight foreshadowed that of sharecroppers after the Civil War. Skinflint whaling merchants amassed substantial profits by delaying workers' pay and defrauding them.[56]

In whaling ports such as New Bedford and New London, out-of-work black whalemen constituted a significant homeless population. "George Miller, Colored Seaman, destitute for the night," was "taken in to Lodge & discharged" by the New Bedford Night Watch in 1849. The Overseers of the Poor there assisted numerous "sick & destitute" black seamen like Henry A. Lewis, who by age fifty-one was "palsied and unable to do anything." A widower, Lewis told the Overseers that "he has always followed the sea, never owned any property, never paid any taxes." His grown daughter Amelia boarded with a local barber, but she had been "sick a long time" with "a Cancer." Whaling's economic ramifications for most were not substantially different from what blacks had come to expect in the economy at large: unappealing work, offered intermittently, and rewarded with grinding poverty.[57]

Death and danger accompanied every voyage, whether on whalers or merchant vessels. No industry other than mining took such a toll in lives as did seafaring, which drained communities of vigorous young men. Although mortality statistics are not available by race, an estimate made at Lloyds of London about 1852 fixed the annual decrease of seamen by death at 8 3/4 percent. Black sailors succumbed to venereal complaints despite doses of "jalop and calomel," to tropical maladies, to accidental drowning, and to whale attacks. "This afternoon while the sailors were pulling on the top gallant halyards the runner broke & down came block & all," observed a passenger aboard the clipper *Contest*, then manned by an all-black crew. "The block in its fall struck one of the niggers on the pate and knocked him senseless."[58]

Overshadowing the terror of faulty gear, frenzied whales, and hurricanes loomed the endemic violence of the maritime workplace. Physically coercive labor control, exacerbated by flaring tempers and confining spaces, threatened the "hanceum livehud" that black men pursued. "You damned Negro," swore Captain John Moore to his injured cook in 1835, "you have played with me long enough, and the sooner you get out of this vessel the better it will be for you." A sailor named McCourtland claimed in 1820 that Captain Daniels swore "he would have given them 5 Dozen a piece until the blood run out of the scuppers." Congress abolished flogging in 1850, but it continued nonetheless. A seaman on the *Lion* overheard a conversation between his captain and the captain of the *Enterprise* in 1853. "Capt. Nichols said he didn't care, he sailed under the old law, & he should trust himself and that he should flog as much as ever."[59]

In this brutal environment, class violence and racial violence reinforced each other. William P. Powell spoke of sailors' "hard usage at sea, wholly at the mercy of tyrant captains and brutal officers, (more especially the coloured sailor) subject as he is to the unholy prejudice, in consequence of the *usage, customs* and *laws* of his native country." Powell had in mind blacks such as Sam Coursey, killed in 1827 by Captain Abel Dungan—a man "of hasty and violent temper." Dungan hit Coursey on the head with a porter bottle and iron sauce pan, flogged him with several large ropes, drenched him with cold water, and finally scrubbed him with a hickory broom, leaving the man exposed to die on deck in bitter Cape Horn weather. When an American ship arrived at Havre, France, in January 1856, the slaughter that passed as discipline appalled a chaplain there. "Her papers showed a crew's list of twenty coloured men, only seventeen of whom lived to reach the port, and eight of those so terribly bruised and mangled, as to be sent at once to the hospital." The hospitalized sailors swore "that the three missing men that were thrown into the sea like so many dead dogs, were literally beaten to death."[60]

Working conditions at sea encouraged African American mariners to create manly reputations through toughness and bold exploits, which were far easier to achieve than the respectable ownership of property ashore. A free sailor named Moses singlehandedly recaptured the brig *Betsies* in 1800 from five French privateersmen, "then took command of the vessel, and put her head to the northward to bring her home." A black named George, "a bold, ambitious, adventurous fellow," responded with all hands aboard the *Dudley* at their captain's summons to fend off another vessel. Warned to avoid danger, George nonetheless took up a position outboard of the bulwarks as *Neptune* approached. His reputation for boldness came at a price: as the two vessels collided they crushed his leg. Actions like these prompted a white sailor to observe astutely that "an overstrained sense of manliness is the characteristic of seafaring men . . . and any expression of pity, or any show of attention, would look sisterly, and unbecoming a man who has to face the rough and tumble of such a life."[61]

Unwilling to be considered fearful, seamen often risked life and limb in merchants' service. They also acted on concerns about mistreatment aboard ship. Black sailors were among those who rebelled against unacceptable working conditions with protests and mutinies. Angry about his treatment en route from Genoa to Malaga in 1836, Lewis Willett assaulted his captain with an axe and inflicted on the chief mate "a severe and dangerous wound in the left temple with a large knife." Aboard the whaleship *Chelsea* in 1841, "George Bacon a Collard man refused to hoist out the Oil." According to the first mate's log, Bacon "appeared to like to make a Difficulty Among the Crew."[62]

Less dramatic forms of labor activism also effectively balked masters. When wronged by officers, seamen commenced "'Tom Cox's traverse'—three turns round the long-boat, and a pull at the scuttledbutt." That was sailor jargon for motion without production. A black American named Amos Richards "shipped at Liverpool as an able seaman," but according to the abusive third mate of the *Neptune*, "he was no seaman; ask him to haul the main topsail halyards he would go forward . . . Richards was what I should call a skulker." Except for lazy men with little pride, sailors decided when to apply themselves "like men" and when to act upon their understanding of exploitation. If much of their job was a venue for demonstrations of manly competence—work as that might to their employers' benefit—certain situations demanded masculine defiance of shipboard order.[63]

Fusing quests for reputation and respectability, black labor activists formed the American Seamen's Protective Union Association at the port of New York in 1863. The ASPUA was "a transitional type of organization standing somewhere between the oldstyle benevolent society and the Negro labor unions that burgeoned" after the Civil War. Apparently the first union or proto-union organized by sailors in the United States—black or white—the ASPUA attempted to guard its members' interests more militantly than had black organizations such as the Stewards' and Cooks' Marine Benevolent Society, formed at New York's Phoenix Saloon in 1837. It welcomed cooks, seamen, and stewards of color—but not officers. The black seamen who founded the ASPUA embodied many of the contradictions that defined seafaring to nineteenth-century black America. Mariners of color were citizens of the world, but residents of poor neighborhoods; they identified with their trade, but loathed its exploitation; they were committed to bourgeois self-improvement, but proud of their manly reputations.[64]

Able-bodied seamen versed in "the Mariner's art" were admittedly a minority among black seamen; but men like Daniel Watson, who made five foreign voyages from Providence between 1803 and 1810, cultivated professional identities as seamen. As sailors, they wove together worldliness, skill, and class. Watson, and men such as the African-born David O'Kee, an ex-slave who made at least eight voyages from Providence during the 1830s, were fully socialized to the world of the ship, and probably more at home there than ashore. A blind sixty-year-old black Philadelphian introduced himself to the census marshall in 1850 as a "Seaman," though his voyaging days were over. The pride black men felt in being identified as seamen is evident in the possessions left by Henry Robinson, a black laborer who died in Boston in 1849. Robinson owned the clothing, chairs, and stove that one would expect, but he also lived among a stock of curios that seem to have been collected at sea. Cases of "sea shells of several kinds," "two coral baskets," "one statue," "one toy ship," a series of pictures, and "two african swords and arrows" perpetuated images of a life considerably more exotic than the one that ended in a down-at-the-heels Boston tenement house.[65]

Voyaging's psychological impact persisted, and was considerably more profound than that associated with other unskilled and semi-skilled work. Seafaring rarely alleviated poverty, but throughout the nineteenth century it affirmed blacks' capacity for masculine bravado and transcendence of the ordinary.

ON SHORE, the boardinghouse was the most dominant institution in mariners' lives. Regulations to prevent plunder and fire in ports such as London forbade sailors to live aboard ships while docked. Elsewhere, custom and preference drove sailors ashore from smokeless hearths and lifeless ships. New York City alone had 153 sailors' boardinghouses during the mid-1840s—with at least 16 for "colored seamen."[66]

Sailors' boardinghouses had long existed, but boardinghouse keepers exerted more influence on seamen as the century progressed. Household arrangements for most workers in American cities were changing during the 1820s and 1830s, and seamen were affected with the rest. In an important cultural shift, "masters" of slaves and servants became "bosses" of wage-earners, and most workers other than domestics moved out from under their employer's roof. As immigrants and laborers working in new industries sought independent lodgings, rents rose; and seamen faced increasing competition for rooms ashore. A variety of living arrangements thus arose in the early nineteenth-century city, including new forms of boardinghouses that catered to sailors' needs and exploited their vulnerabilities.[67]

Boardinghouse keepers hired runners to corral arriving sailors who were flush with money and who had not drunk anything stronger than coffee for months. Runners enticed men to come to the boardinghouse for a frolic. They promised plenty of hot food, lots of booze, and willing girls—a vision for which Jack had been working—and they pressured hold-outs to conform to the group. Many sailors had no ready alternative, and reputations were at stake. In the enforced conviviality of the quayside, drinking together was presented as the final mark of true shipmates. "Full of money as a dog is full of fleas," observed William Brown, sailors trapped by their shipmates' expectations and a well-oiled system "generally fell a prey to the landlords and their accomplices." Destitute sailors frequently arrived at the Coloured Sailors' Home looking for help after they "fell into the hands of white and black land-sharks, and were stripped of all their clothes and money." Not until post–Civil War laws reformed payday practices and regulated boardinghouses were seamen spared from an exploitative system.[68]

Within black society there existed a hierarchy of boardinghouses. Every seaport had "low houses where colored sailors resort," "the worst groggeries and dens," or "hovels" in which the "premises both inside and out were in the most filthy condition." James Dyre kept such a squalid house in New Bedford in 1834. Ostracized by local blacks, he took in destitute Sandwich Island whalemen "to get his pay for their board by shipping them on board of the outward bound ships." Dyre became newsworthy when cholera began killing people in his house. Other dangers lurked in boardinghouses: the New York Committee of Vigilance hinted at man-stealing when it launched an investigation in 1838 on behalf of "colored seamen" shipped "from the port of New York by unprincipled landlords." But safe havens were available. William P. Powell kept a "Sailors' Temperance Boarding-house" in New Bedford during the late 1830s, and then opened a boardinghouse he called the "Golden Farm" at the corner of New York's John and Gold Streets in November 1839. His establishments were "intended for the better class of colored seamen." Powell later moved his boardinghouse to Cherry Street and then to Dover Street, renaming it with a cosmopolitan flourish as "The Globe Hotel." Of course, the "best" boardinghouses excluded sailors entirely. Mr. Thomas Reed, "considered the upper crust of the colored population" in Providence, "kept a fashionable shaving saloon . . . using the rooms upstairs as a genteel boarding house. He did not accommodate sailors," remembered one, "and thus regained the reputation of the house, which had previously been occupied and patronized by the lower classes." [69]

Clannish sailors depended on boardinghouse keepers who were ex-seamen themselves and, oddly enough, often trusted them. Jimmie Axum kept a house on Providence's Power Street during the 1820s. "He was a sailor, every inch of him," remembered William Brown, "and his wife Hannah was an Indian woman of the Narragansett tribe." Born in Virginia, Axum migrated to Providence and shipped out in 1799. In his forties he gave up active seafaring and began to rely more on fiddling and fleecing. "When a ship's crew of sailors came ashore to board they would all go to Uncle Jimmie's," wrote Brown. "There would be drinking and dancing throughout the day and evening, and every half hour someone would take a pitcher and go after liquor." Seamen staying there would "be stripped of nearly all their money by Uncle Jimmie and his wife, and the females which hung around there." Reformers liked to describe seamen as landlords' victims, and to some extent they were. But sailors contributed to their own victimization. Knowing what awaited them, they repaired to boardinghouses and frequently depended on landlords for access to entertainment and relaxation. And by no means did sailors unequivocally resent boardinghouse keepers like Uncle Jimmie. Many sailors had nowhere else to turn, and they surrendered their money willingly enough to stay in familiar surroundings with men of their own kind.[70]

Things were different at the Coloured Seamen's Home in New York. No individual championed the respectability and well-being of black sailors more vigorously than William P. Powell, who for more than twenty-five years managed that establishment. Boarders dined under a picture of Crispus Attucks, the seafaring martyr of the Boston Massacre, and Powell reiterated to them that they were "truly the nation's benefactors." Powell actively involved seamen in the fight against slavery, rescuing fugitive slaves from man-stealers and leading political discussions that received accolades from Frederick Douglass. Evidence indicates that he strongly encouraged seafaring men of color to assert themselves as men and citizens. Between 1836 and 1838, Powell opened his first seamen's temperance boardinghouse in New Bedford. Simultaneously, the number of black seamen listed in the New Bedford City Directories almost quadrupled. Twenty-five years later his Globe Hotel in New York was "heated throughout with hot air, abundantly supplied with hot and cold water baths for the use of the boarders . . . kept neat, airy, and well arranged for the promotion of health, and is designed to be a Home, with its religious, moral, and social influences for our colored seamen." Powell advocated self-restraint and self-improvement, and he prohibited profanity and gambling. Seamen also stayed at his house for substantially shorter periods than at most sailor haunts, "averaging *four* days board," according to the proprietor. Unwilling to entertain men indefinitely just so they would run up a bill, Powell encouraged them to either ship out or go home, and to pay their bills on time.[71]

A rough survey of the shoreside residences of black seamen sailing out of New York in 1846 showed that of twenty-two hundred black seamen, only one hundred, or less than 5 percent, lived with their families. Four hundred more boarded at Powell's staunchly temperate Globe Hotel. Another one hundred boarded "at that earthly pandemonium, the Five Points"—a notorious crime and vice district. The remaining sixteen-hundred found quarters at sixteen other black sailors' boardinghouses, "every one of which is anti-temperance" and managed by landlords "hostile to reform." About three-quarters of these sailors obviously voted for a good time—for barrooms, music, and the kind of "Boarding houses for colored seamen" where, according to one reformer, "the rear of the building is rented for bad women." [72]

By the 1840s, most black seafaring men in major seaports clearly did not embrace the domestic virtues and morality that William P. Powell cultivated in the Coloured Sailors' Home. Crew lists, city directories, and censuses from Baltimore and Philadelphia reveal just how unattached most black sailors were. Among 110 blacks sailing on international voyages from Philadelphia in 1850, each of whom claimed to reside in that city, more than 90 percent did not appear in the census. Among 223 blacks shipping on foreign voyages from Baltimore in 1857, only 9 appeared in the city directory. Few sailors of color then had dependents or regular addresses, a tendency that seems to have increased after 1800. [73]

Coming ashore in whatever port, unattached sailors headed for places like the "Subterrainian" in New Bedford, where black and white men and women were frequently arrested by the Night Watch for fighting and late-night revelry. The west end of Olney Street in Providence was the site of great sprees. "Here were a number of houses built and owned by white men," wrote William Brown, "and rented to anyone, white or colored, who wanted to hire one or more rooms, rent payable weekly." More respectable landlords, he pointed out, collected quarterly. "Some of these places had bar-rooms, where liquors were dealt out, and places where they sold cakes, pies, doughnuts, &c. These they called cooky stands. In some houses dancing and fiddling was the order of the day." Brown recognized that "this street had a correspondence with all the sailor boarding houses in town, and was sustained by their patronage." [74]

Every seaport had "houses kept by unprincipled men and women for the vilest purposes," and sailors expected to purchase sex when they came ashore. In 1826, when "the prohibition forbidding lewd women visiting the Ships was renewed" in Oahu, Hawaii, a mob of naval and whaling tars threatened to "demolish the houses" of missionaries and chiefs who had shut off "the accustomed means of licentious indulgence." A black madame named Mary Craig Lopez ran colored whalemen's favorite haunt in New London, Connecticut, during the 1840s, before being jailed for her work. But purchased sex was only one reason brothels were attractive.[75]

For some black sailors a favorite brothel was not merely a way station of pleasure, but a variant of boardinghouse life and the nearest they could muster to a permanent residence ashore. Court records from Providence in 1831 reveal that a man could store his prized possessions in a brothel and reside there. William Jordan testified at age thirty that he had been born in Baltimore, but that he lived in Ezekial Burr's house on Olney Lane, "in the upper story with a woman named Mahala Green and has lived there for nearly five years." He clarified his living arrangements, however, by explaining that he "follows the sea and lately returned from India in the ship N.J.," a voyage of about a year's duration, "and was at work in Providence calculating to go out in the ship Ann & Hope." The black man who kept the "Cook Sellar" underneath Ezekial Burr's house stated frankly that "the upper part of the house was occupied by black and white prostitutes, and others used to frequent there, and sailors used to resort there."[76]

Although we do not know how Jordan and Mahala Green understood their living arrangements, it is clear that Jordan regarded Burr's house on Olney Lane as his residence. He "had a gun or guns up in his apartments," a black friend said, which he never would have taken to sea, "and he used frequently to be out gunning." Moreover, his friend (another black sailor), referred to Green as Jordan's "wife." Whether Jordan was procuring for Green or whether Green was his "wife" only when he was in port we do not know. But the sheriff had cited her twice in two years for keeping "a house of ill-fame and disorder." William Jordan's accommodations were common for black sailors. Caught ashore between inhospitable ships and expensive lodgings, they lived and died in boardinghouses, whorehouses, and flophouses. John L. Morris, born in Norfolk, expired in New Bedford in 1864 "in house of ill-fame No. 3 First St."[77]

William J. Brown understood that black seamen streaming ashore at Providence in the 1820s defined themselves as men through reputations built on their worldliness, bravery, and skill at sea, complemented by their liberality ashore. He knew that working too hard and valuing money too much detracted from a man's reputation among his drinking companions. At the same time, Brown recognized that his father—well respected in Providence's black community—had supported a family on seafaring income. In Providence, as in many other ports, seafaring was fundamental to blacks' survival, especially in the early nineteenth century. As time passed and conditions worsened, seafaring remained central to masculine identity-formation, but it increasingly reinforced the poverty and fragmentation of black communities.

Boardinghouse masters exerted growing control over the maritime labor market as the first half of the nineteenth century progressed, gaining a virtual lock on supplying sailors to captains. According to an ex-tar, they conspired to stop a man from shipping "unless he would consent—even if a married man, to leave his home and become a denizen of" the boardinghouse. In New York in 1863, "a combination of colored sailor landlords" strove bitterly to prevent "the shipping of seamen from Mr. Powell's house" because of Powell's crusade against their hustling. During the early nineteenth century, black family men like Noah Brown lived at home between voyages. As decades passed, however, it became increasingly difficult to get a seafaring job *unless* a man stayed in a boardinghouse—even in his homeport. Boarding-house keepers had become middlemen who supplied labor to ship-masters and room, board, and jobs to sailors. By the 1830s black sailors with families were being caught in the squeeze: relegated to seafaring to support their families, they were prevented by boardinghouse masters from even living at home. The changing nature of maritime hiring made the seafaring pillar of the black community ever more precarious.[78]

SEAFARING WAS CENTRAL to the community life and masculine identities of northern free blacks between the American Revolution and the Civil War. A core of career black seamen, some with dependents, sailed year after year—increasingly in the expanding coastal trade. Striving to create opportunities, a few skippered small coasters or sought positions as deep-sea officers. Many sailed as cooks or stewards to support their families. Some were community leaders, stalwart members of black benevolent societies, and responsible providers. A few even managed to purchase homes, especially in New England seaports. Among common Jack Tars, black sailors were more likely than whites to be older and to have ties ashore.

But the paradoxes of maritime work undermined free black society, especially as the decades passed and it became increasingly difficult to get a seafaring job without living in a boardinghouse. Blacks strove to be "men" in a proletarianized occupation whose physical abuse, dan- ger, and exploitative wage structure virtually knocked the manhood out of them, preventing almost all from achieving the independence and dignified providership they sought. Most mariners of color thus remained casual seafarers, drawn from the reservoir of underemployed black laborers who waited in every city. They careened between fore- castle and galley, or boardinghouse and brothel, substituting the repu- tations of deep-water men for more enduring attachments. As chasms in northern antebellum society widened between capital and labor, and between white and free black workers, black mariners fought a losing battle to maintain seafaring as a pillar of free black society.

7. FREE SAILORS AND THE STRUGGLE WITH SLAVERY

If it had not been the Lord who was on our side, when men rose up against us: then they had swallowed us up . . . Blessed be the Lord who hath not given us as a prey to their teeth.

PSALM 124

DURING THE FIRST HALF of the nineteenth century, as cotton became the mainstay of the American economy, more and more ships sailed into the lower South. Political polarization between North and South simultaneously caught black sailors firmly in the vise of racial conflict. Regarded by white southerners as "colored emissaries from the North," free black seamen on board ships in the South confronted an intimidating local population. Southern racial ideology demanded that free blacks be submissive and dependent—essentially "slaves without masters." Northern black sailors claiming freedom and respectability challenged the underpinnings of southern society. Yet, without local patrons or any essential niche in the southern economy, independent black sailors became lightning rods for white southerners' fury.[1]

As early as 1822, lawmakers concerned with the contagion of liberty emanating from northern ships began to require black sailors' incarceration during southern port calls. Free black sailors deferred to whites' formal demands as needed for self-preservation, but many also empathized with slaves. They tippled with slaves in unobtrusive back alleys and brought tidings of the black world beyond the South. Bold black sailors stowed fugitives aboard ships. Whether guerrilla fighters in the war on slavery or merely black strangers in a hostile white world, free black mariners voyaging south sailed in harm's way. For this, they paid dearly.

FREE SAILORS appeared as angels of liberty to some slaves. Working as a stevedore aboard the brig *Casket* in Savannah in 1818, a slave named William Grimes "got acquainted with some of these Yankee sailors." The evening before *Casket* sailed, Grimes "went with a colored man (a sailor on board) up into town and procured some bread, water, dried beef, and such other necessaries" and then clambered into a prearranged space in the deckload of cotton bales. "After we had got into the ocean the sailors gave three hearty cheers, and gave me to understand that I was clear; we were out of sight of land, they said." He got ashore safely in New York.[2]

During the decade before Grimes's successful escape, cotton had become the centerpiece of American commerce. Cotton sapped the lives of millions of slaves toiling from the Georgia uplands to the Mississippi delta. For merchants in northern commercial cities, the sealanes to cotton ports such as Charleston, Savannah, Mobile, and New Orleans became paths to prosperity. For Charleston slaveholders, racial worries shadowed commercial profits. "Scarcely a vessel . . . arrives in our port from the North," they lamented in 1823, "which has not two or three, or more black persons employed." Whites prophesied that their slaves would "be seduced from the service of their masters in greater numbers" and that "Abolition Societies of the North" would "intrigue, through this class of persons, with our slave population."[3]

By 1822, southern cotton, tobacco, naval stores, and rice constituted 55 percent of New York's domestic exports. As ships and schooners collected southern commodities for New York merchants, many of the approximately 2,500 black seamen annually shipping from that port sailed south. Working side by side with enslaved stevedores like William Grimes, free black sailors from the North had a close encounter with slavery.[4]

Free black seamen traveled with relative impunity between northern ports, Haiti, and the lower South before 1822. An all-black crew with white officers aboard the brig *C. Perry,* for instance, sailed from Philadelphia to Savannah, then to St. Thomas in the Danish Virgin Islands, to Cape Haitian, and back to Savannah. Sailors on St. Thomas formed lasting impressions of merchants and artisans of color, roles traditionally closed to American free blacks. African American sailors swaggered along the French colonial boulevards of Cape Haitian, on which Henri Christophe's black legions had routed European armies, and chatted with slaves in Savannah. August Lemonier was such a freewheeling black sailor. He shipped aboard the brig *Hercules* for a voyage from New York to Mobile. When *Hercules* was stranded on Carysfort Reef and was taken to Key West by salvage-masters, Lemonier left her and, as he told it, "shipped on board Captain Johnson's schooner and went to Savannah." From there he joined "the Ship Garones, Capt. Story, and went three voyages with him to Havre," France. Seamen like Lemonier circulated freely ashore, with as much liberty as black men ever had in slave societies to discuss whatever they wished with whomever they wished.[5]

A certain permissiveness characterized American slavery in the settled regions of the East during the 1810s and early 1820s. As upstart planters made slavery particularly harsh on the southwestern cotton frontier, genteel planters with deep roots in the Carolina tidewater were experimenting with "the loosest paternalistic control they would ever deploy." Striving to reconcile the republican democracy they prized with the tyrannical slavery that sustained them, seaboard slave-holders envisioned themselves as benign paternalists, coining euphemisms such as "Peculiar Institution" to camouflage their savagery. According to their logic, slaves did not insist on liberty because they realized their inferiority and dependence. Riddled with inconsistencies, not the least of which was blacks' disdain for submissiveness, this ideology nevertheless nurtured a relatively tolerant style of slave control in Charleston by 1822. Paternalists wished to rule with what they called "affection and gratitude" rather than coercion.[6]

Into this breach stepped Denmark Vesey, a skilled free black carpenter and ex-sailor of great strength and energy. Vesey was a charismatic visionary who dreamed of bloody atonement for blacks' sorrows and slights. Capitalizing on whites' laxity, and threatening death to blacks who would not follow him, he planned one of the largest slave conspiracies in American history during the summer of 1822 in Charleston. Although Vesey had been freed through his own luck in a lottery, his wives and children yet bore the shackles of slavery, as did seven of every eight blacks in that city. Vesey sustained his vision of freedom by reading the Declaration of Independence, the Old Testament prophets Zechariah and Joshua, and debates on the Missouri Compromise. "Even whilst walking through the streets in company with another, he was not idle," recollected a contemporary, "for if his companion bowed to a white person he would rebuke him, and observe that all men were born equal." Denmark Vesey's eventual betrayal by an unreliable conspirator led more than thirty plotters to the gallows. His near success unleashed repressive new laws, including ones aimed specifically at black seamen.[7]

Confessions extracted from several of the leaders (though not Vesey himself, who remained silent until death) pointed to black seamen as links in the chain of rebellion. Vesey had been a mariner as a youth—a fact well known to his followers, who respected and exaggerated his cosmopolitanism. Monday Gell, a chief lieutenant, testified that Vesey "had travelled through almost every part of the world with his former master Captain Vesey, and spoke French fluently." According to Gell, Vesey wanted to "open a correspondence with Port-au-Prince in Santo Domingo, to ascertain whether the inhabitants there would assist us . . . He brought a letter to me, which was directed to President Boyer, and was enclosed in a cover, which was directed to the uncle of the cook of the vessel by which it was sent." A conspirator named Prince said that the brother of William, the mariner "who was to carry the letter to Santo Domingo, was a General, as I understand, in Santo Domingo." Vesey, Gell, and another leader named Peirault hand-delivered the letter to William aboard his schooner at Vanderhorst's Wharf. Should the insurrection have been even partially successful, according to several of the conspirators, Vesey intended "to sail for St. Domingue with his principal adherents."[8]

With the maritime dimensions of the conspiracy so evident, and a paranoid belief among white Charlestonians that no "evil of greater magnitude" could exist "than the constant intercourse which is maintained between the blacks of the North and the South," black sailors became prime targets of the state of South Carolina. As early as 1809, recollected a Charleston magistrate, "several hundred pamphlets of an insurrectionary character were brought to Charleston, in the ship *Minerva,* from New York, by her steward who was a black man." During the Vesey trial, local justices claimed that "inflammatory pamphlets on slavery brought into Charleston from some of our sister states, within the last four years (and one from Sierra Leone), and distributed among the colored population of the city," had contributed to the plotters' near success. This inspired Governor John Wilson to refer to transient free black sailors as "those afflicted with infectious disease." [9]

Black seafaring men may have cross-pollinated a free black congregation in Philadelphia and the African Church in Charleston in which Vesey preached freedom. They definitely talked with enslaved men and women in the streets and cook shops of that loosely regulated seaport. But no conclusive evidence pointed to transient seamen as instigators. Men such as sailors, without a stake in the community, would have lacked the authority to enlist locals for a venture whose outcome was almost certain death. Yet slaveholders later claimed that the "planned insurrection was advised, set on foot, and arranged by the agency of free Negro sailors on board Northern vessels." Such claims helped to justify the systematic and legal oppression of black seamen. [10]

South Carolina's legislature passed the original "Act for the Better Regulation and Government of Free Negroes and Persons of Color" in December 1822, within months of the Vesey plot. The new law stipulated "that if any vessel shall come into any port or harbor of this State . . . having on board any free negroes or persons of color as cooks, stewards, mariners, or in any other employment on board of said vessel, such free negroes or persons of color shall be . . . confined in jail until said vessel shall clear out and depart from this State." Should the captain not carry away his free black sailors, or should he not pay the expenses of their detention, they would be "taken as absolute slaves, and sold." Legislators later removed the provision for the sale of free men, substituting whipping. These laws institutionalized the debasement of African American seamen and spurred their politicization and protest in the war against slavery. A legislative committee in South Carolina conceded that black seamen were "prompted to efforts of this description by the supposed wrongs inflicted on them."[11]

Warily assessing the act, sailors initially were not convinced that it would be implemented. People of color had long maneuvered around unenforced statutes designed to repress them. Throughout the upper South, laws required free blacks to register with commissioners and carry free papers. Few did, preferring the risk of a penalty to visiting the sheriff. Free blacks in the lower South similarly circumvented rules stipulating that they have white "guardians." Aware that such laws could be enforced at any time, black people guardedly skirted them when they could. Substantial numbers of black mariners thus landed at and departed from Charleston without being incarcerated during the early months of 1823—hard on the heels of the promulgation of the new law. Shortly thereafter, however, enforcement bore down brutally on Amos Daley.[12]

Daley arrived at Charleston aboard Captain Rose's schooner *Fox* on April 22, 1823. The authorities promptly jailed him under the law requiring incarceration of free black sailors. Thirteen days later, having been warned "never to return here again," he was escorted to the wharf. According to Justice Andrew Bay, the magistrates warned Captain Rose "of the consequences which would ensue should he be brought into this State." Nevertheless, within six weeks Daley was back. Apprenticed to Captain Rose, Daley protested that "he . . . could not prevent it." Daley also may have been overly optimistic about how he would fare because the law had provided certain exemptions. No black men were safe, but Indians were. In his own eyes, Amos Daley was an Indian—the son of a Narragansett Indian woman "with straight black hair." Daley even carried a certificate from the town clerk of North Kingston, Rhode Island, explaining his parentage and status. The mate aboard *Fox* swore that he "had no doubt that the prisoner was a free Indian," even if "it was customary to call Indians colored men." But in Charleston, Daley's fate hung on the curl of his hair. A magistrate with an eye for African descent deposed that "the hair of the prisoner [was] rather against him." The sheriff bluntly sneered that "the prisoner's hair was wooly." Given the extenuating circumstances, the justices thought they let him off easy with only twelve lashes on his bare back.[13]

Nonetheless, luckier black seamen freely roamed Charleston's streets early that summer, before a new vigilante group called the South Carolina Association unleashed the full force of the statute, making the harbor master corral all sailors of color. From late July through September, 154 black mariners arrived at Charleston—118 from northern ports, 15 from the West Indies, and 21 from Europe. All went to jail. "In so short a time, and principally during a season when there is little or no trade," argued the South Carolina Association, "so many have arrived here, some idea may be formed of the number which must enter into our limits in the course of the year." Jail expenses became considerable for the shipowners who were held legally liable, and devastating for the wage-earning sailors to whom the owners passed on the cost. Captain David Low of the Boston brig *Arctic* paid $10.44 "for arresting," "for warning and affidavit," and for thirteen days maintenance in jail for "a free col'd Man named Jefferson Allston," when seamen like Allston earned only $10 to $14 per month. "Denied a sufficiency of food, and compelled to perform various menial and disgusting offices in the prison," hundreds of imprisoned sailors bore this new degradation with melancholy and rage.[14]

Vesey's inspirational but suicidal campaign for freedom had been limited to Charleston, as were the repercussions black sailors felt in its wake. Nevertheless, for men with few other options in the labor market, it was easy enough to find a ship bound elsewhere. Magistrates obsessed with color and the curl of a man's hair could not derail northern free blacks' reliance on seafaring. Pressures remained, but they were the kind of random assaults that blacks always faced. "Bradford Mowry, a coloured seaman . . . from the American schooner *Ann*" of Norfolk, encountered that pervasive racism at Antigua in 1824. "Although [Mowry] has committed no other crime but that of desertion," wrote the American consul, emphasizing his point by underlining the operative phrase, "duty" demanded that he "make an example," Mowry *"being a coloured person."* The consul and *Ann*'s captain had Mowry repatriated to Virginia and "lodged in Prison" for prosecution.[15]

In 1829, goaded by the insults and degradations endured simply for "being a coloured person," a black nationalist thinker named David Walker published the most bitter denunciation of American freedom yet written by a man of color. Walker wrote and published his inflammatory *Appeal to the Colored Citizens of the World* in Boston, but his intended audience was the enslaved masses in the South. "We, (coloured people of these United States of America) are the *most wretched, degraded* and *abject* set of beings that *ever lived* since the world began," Walker railed. "The whites want slaves, and want us for their slaves, but some of them will curse the day they ever saw us. As true as the sun ever shone in its meridian splendor, my colour will root some of them out of the very face of the earth." The apocalyptical *Appeal* turned up first among disbelieving whites in Savannah, and rapidly thereafter in Richmond. In Walker's native North Carolina, officials found it in Wilmington. "An open appeal to [bondsmen's] natural love of liberty," claimed a police magistrate in Wilmington, Walker's book was "totally subversive of all subordination in our slaves." A jailed slave was heard discussing it nearby in the small port of Newbern. Sailors, preachers, missionaries, and other radicals circulated it in South Carolina and Louisiana. Like Vesey, Walker sought to unite free and enslaved people of color in a revolutionary campaign for dignity and the return of the proceeds of their labor. Unlike Vesey, however, Walker left his mark throughout the seaboard South.[16]

From the used-clothing store that he operated on Brattle Street, near the Boston wharves, Walker buttonholed sailors and asked them to spread his message. It was no coincidence that the *Appeal* circulated first in seaports. As had been the case for centuries, those in the orbit of a port often were the first to hear news from near and far. A sophisticated propagandist, Walker had stressed to the General Colored Association of Massachusetts in 1828 the need "to unite the colored population, so far, through the United States of America, as may be practicable and expedient; forming societies, opening, extending, and keeping up correspondences, and not withholding any thing which may have the least tendency to meliorate *our* miserable condition." An active agent of several black newspapers, and one of the most powerful published black voices of his generation, Walker nevertheless realized that the clandestine and far-flung distribution of radical ideas among the black population could best occur by word of mouth.[17]

Walker, and the brave messengers who carried his book in their sea-chests, provoked the Georgia legislature into imposing a forty-day quarantine on all vessels with free black seamen aboard, and requiring the incarceration of any black sailor ashore or in contact with slaves. Despite Vesey's conspiracy in neighboring Charleston, Georgians had never singled out black mariners. Restricting free black access to the state in 1818, the legislature previously had exempted seamen. The appearance of Walker's *Appeal* in Savannah, where fleets of cotton ships tugged restlessly on their hawsers, changed that. According to the governor, sixty copies had been "carried to Savannah by the Steward of some vessel (a white man), and delivered by him to a negro preacher for distribution."[18]

Stringent legislation restricting black seamen's freedom and livelihood snowballed during the 1830s, in the wake of Walker's *Appeal* and its apparent circulation by seafaring men. North Carolina's legislature rapidly passed a law emulating Georgia's. The next year Florida's legislators prohibited all free blacks, including sailors, from entering the territory on pain of imprisonment. Authorities there subsequently sold into slavery a free black seaman from Nassau who returned despite a prior warning.[19]

Gulf coast states were not so quick to impose sanctions on seamen of color, which meant that sailors in the cotton trade continued to enjoy mobility there for several years. In 1836, when Georgia's law had reduced blacks to only 2 percent of sailors in Savannah, they still accounted for almost 10 percent of sailors in New Orleans. The French and Spanish cultural roots in Gulf coast societies had resulted in a three-tiered racial system there. "Gens du coleur" had established rights, and thus inhabited a southern milieu distinctly different from that experienced by free people of color elsewhere. As late as 1856, the Louisiana Supreme Court reiterated that "in the eye of Louisiana law, there is . . . all the difference between a free man of color and a slave, that there is between a white man and a slave," a notion that would have seemed preposterous on the Atlantic coast.[20]

Languid New Orleans also extended more earthy attractions. If savory creole cuisine made salt beef appear as bad as it really was, the remembrance of sweet caresses got many a sailor through lonely night watches. Black shanteymen sang, "When I was a young man in me prime, I chased them yaller gals two at a time," prompting their shipmates to recollect the intersection of Bourbon and Orleans Streets, where salt-crusted men starved for female company were rejuvenated in bawdy houses. Despite these pleasures, black sailors were under no illusion that Gulf coast societies' three-caste system automatically included them. Legal and social perquisites for free people of color hinged on local lineage, just as sailors' freedom of movement hinged on the sufferance of state legislators.[21]

During the late 1830s and early 1840s, the fear of alien free blacks prompted lawmakers in Alabama, Louisiana, and the Spanish Caribbean to imitate South Carolina's Negro Seamen Acts. Worried Cuban slaveholders such as Capitan-General don Francisco Dionisio Vives, concerned by minor slave revolts and rumors of more, claimed that "the existence of free blacks and mulattoes in the midst of the slavery of their companions is an example which will become very dangerous one day." In 1837 a royal order prohibited all free persons of color— including seamen—from landing in Cuba or Puerto Rico under any pretext. Americans at that time carried on a brisk trade with Cuba. More than two hundred vessels sailed between Cuba and New York alone in 1835. The *Colored American* newspaper alerted black seamen to the new danger, and William P. Powell bluntly told men at the Coloured Sailors' Home in New York what awaited even the most apolitical. "Every negro seized with *wooly* hair, no matter how *white* his complexion may be, is thrust into prison." Alabama shut its ports to blacks in 1839. Three years later Louisiana's legislature required New Orleans police to arrest incoming sailors of color (other than state residents) and imprison them until their vessel's departure.[22]

Within twenty short years following Vesey's and Walker's bold thrusts for freedom, and accompanying the phenomenal rise of organized abolition, an apparatus of systematic state coercion beset black sailors. In 1822 they had circulated relatively freely around the Atlantic, limited only by their employers, irascible consuls, and the threat of kidnappers. Supporting fledgling northern black communities, and smuggling slaves to freedom whenever possible, sailors linked black America—free and slave, North and South. By fulfilling this part of

David Walker's nationalist dream, seamen of color attracted the wrath of wary white legislators. Although free blacks everywhere in these pre–Civil War decades confronted reduced manumissions and declining opportunities, no other black occupation was threatened as extensively as seafaring.

Negro Seamen Acts made the financial circumstances of northern free blacks supported by mariners even more precarious. Virtually all the numerous seamen of color shipping from cotton ports had roots and responsibilities elsewhere. About 90 percent of the black seamen shipping from Savannah, for instance, were born outside the South. Thus the effect of the ban on black sailors in southern ports was to cut off the means of livelihood for seamen of color and their dependents in the North. One free sailor risking jail during the 1830s told a slave in Savannah "that his home was in New York; that he had a wife and several children there, but that he followed the sea for a livelihood and knew no other mode of life." Between 1803 and 1829, blacks constituted about 15 percent of the sailors in Savannah. The year after the state of Georgia quarantined and threatened to jail them, the figure dropped to 9 percent; and within a few years, to 4 percent, 3 percent, and 2 percent. Blacks in New York and Philadelphia reeled from racist decisions made at the statehouse in Milledgeville.[23]

Challenging sheriffs to jail them, African American sailors never withdrew completely from southern voyages, much less from seafaring. Avoiding ports one by one, under pressure, they returned when possible. After the Louisiana legislature passed a Negro Seamen Act in 1842, blacks' proportion of maritime labor in New Orleans fell from just under 10 percent to only 1 percent. Ten years later Louisiana lawmakers eased restrictions, substituting a passport system and shore privileges for imprisonment. African American sailors rebounded to fill more than 7 percent of sailors' berths by 1855, when some fifty to sixty thousand sailors and steamboat hands annually streamed through New Orleans.[24]

In addition to the legal constraints that threatened free black mariners in the South were illegal acts such as man-stealing, or the kidnapping of free sailors in order to enslave them. This practice existed before and after passage of the Negro Seamen Acts, and no northern free blacks were more vulnerable than sailors. Man-stealers scattered the sons of Jude Hall, a black Revolutionary War veteran from New Hampshire. "James was put on board a New Orleans vessel; Aaron was stolen from Providence, in 1807; William went to sea in the bark Hannibal, from Newburyport, and was sold in the West Indies." The Bostonian James G. Barbadoes recalled with anguish the travail of his brother imprisoned in New Orleans in 1816. For more than five months, Robert Barbadoes languished "handcuffed and chained," guilty only of being a strange black man in Louisiana. He was "deprived every way of communicating his situation to his parents. His [seaman's] protection was taken from him, and torn up. He was often flogged severely to be made submissive, and deny that he was free born." In desperation Barbadoes even pricked his own veins for ink, but jailers tore up the letter. The terrorization and kidnapping of men like these hobbled northern free blacks struggling to survive. Man-stealers not only snatched loved ones, but deprived embryonic black communities of earning power and of present and future numerical strength. The randomness of this piracy unsettled every free person of color, mocking their free status.[25]

During the 1840s, Mississippi River pilots practiced man-stealing on a grand scale. Large ships at New Orleans often finished loading several miles below the city, at Balize, and then arranged for crews to be sent down on towboats. Sailors, black and white, signed articles with shipping agents and collected their month's advance, sometimes not even knowing which ship they were bound for, and then embarked aboard towboats when needed. "Now," explained a black boarding-house keeper who had been informed by escaped seamen, "very often the coloured sailors get deceived. Instead of going on board of a ship at the Balize they are transferred and distributed among the pilot boats . . . The pilots will not pay them one cent of wages, and if they dare say they are free, they are whipped and punished with [great] cruelty."[26]

A Nova Scotian named Jacob Brown, probably a descendent of black American loyalists who emigrated there after the American Revolution, became a slave to New Orleans pilots in 1841. Brown sailed as the cook of the ship *Oceana* from Boston to New Orleans, and fled without wages when the captain and the mate planned to sell him. Broke and on the beach, he signed aboard the *Lafayette*, then lying at

Slaughter House Point and bound for Liverpool. Heading downstream on the towboat *Tiger,* he asked for the *Lafayette,* and was told she had gone farther down. "Upon the second inquiry [he] was told that he had shipped to the pilot boats at the Balize." As Brown told it, "there were sixty-eight free coloured men on board the several pilot boats at the Southwest and Southeast Pass, all made to work as slaves, some employed as pull-away boys, others repairing sails and rigging." Some died in the pilots' clutches, and others were sold into permanent slavery ashore. Yet others were cast off only to be taken up by the civil authorities and jailed, a fate that often meant the chain-gang. Nevertheless, some men like Brown were eventually freed. Pilots preferred not to pay for slaves' upkeep in slack times. But liberating captives as capriciously as they had been seized defined white men as the masters of the lower Mississippi. They trifled with black mariners simply to reinforce black subordination.[27]

Random enslavement of particularly vulnerable blacks, especially those associated with abolitionists, sent an unmistakable signal about the precarious status of free people of color. The Mississippi master from whom the enslaved sailor Isaac Wright fled in 1838 brazenly advertised him as "originally from New York," and conceded his northern free origins when he admitted that "Isaac . . . speaks quick, and very correctly for a negro." Removed from both the northern black elite and the white abolitionists who shielded free blacks in the North, nervous sailors approached southern ports apprehensively. Frustrating head winds forced Moses Grandy's vessel to "put back three times to Norfolk, anchoring each time just opposite the jail . . . I feared the mayor would find me on board, and sell me. I could see the jail, full of colored people, and even the whipping post, at which they were constantly enduring the lash."[28] Following British West Indian emancipation in 1838, island mariners became favorite targets of unprincipled man-stealers in the American South. In 1855 the British consul at Norfolk, G. P. R. James, wrote that this practice had lately increased "frightfully." According to James, the U.S. district attorney in eastern Virginia believed that in 1854 alone more than two hundred free British West Indian sailors had been sold illicitly.[29]

Ironically, the Negro Seamen Acts that were designed to prevent black seamen from communicating with slaves failed to do just that.

Incarcerated sailors were guaranteed contact with jailed slaves. Explaining why he had beaten a free sailor in 1835, the Charleston jailer said that he "found Jones harangueing three or four Negroes," and swore he overheard Jones say "that the negroes were fools for doing what he, Paine, ordered them." By 1843 concerned Charlestonians petitioned the legislature to incarcerate transient blacks "in a prison or building by themselves." Although South Carolina's legislators subsequently "required" the commissioners of public buildings in seaport districts to alter jails "to keep in safe custedy all free negroes and persons of color" separate from slaves "to prevent all communication between them," inertia and parsimony interfered. Authorities in the Charleston district never complied; and in 1854 lawmakers again futilely authorized separate jails for alien seamen.[30] A few years later liberalization of the law permitted free black seamen to stay aboard ships in Charleston, once again allowing unimpeded discussions with at least some slaves. "Ships having Collerd Crews from 14 to 16 Men," read a local complaint, "Commanded by Northern Men and Owned at the North hire your Slaves as Stevedores to Load and unload their Ships, and place your Slaves in direct communication with any emisary the North may think propper to send amongst us. Collerd persons are prohibited from Colecting together for any purpose, but on board Ships they can Collect from 40 to 60 at any time without any White Person among them, from 10 to 20 feet below decks."[31]

Shameless profiteering accompanied the intimidation of black sailors. Long before the convict-lease system that exploited black prisoners for profit became a hallmark of southern penology, southern authorities extorted labor from penurious free blacks. Their inability to pay fines, taxes, or jail fees often consigned people of color to lengthy servitude, as William Cook discovered after a voyage from Virginia to Pensacola in the early 1840s. Jailed for several months at the rate of 37 and 1/2 cents per day, and charged for doctors, printers, and the kidnapping itself, Cook ultimately "had bills of more than two hundred dollars against him." He had to work off the debt. Black sailors unable to prove their freedom in New Orleans "were compelled to work in chains on the roads in the burning sun for 25 cents per day, and pay in advance . . . for maintenance, doctor's and other bills." A Connecticut sailor named John Slate spent four and a half years on the chain-gang "employed ditching in the winter, and digging graves for the public cemetery." When sick and unable to work, he was charged one dollar a day to increase his jail fees. Slate finally arrived in New York, destitute and debilitated, "the iron shackle which he wore on his ancle . . . having chafed the flesh off to the bone." Recounting his twenty-one days in a New Orleans prison, one black mariner simply said, "They do treat coloured seamen very bad."[32]

Northern mariners of color and their families sought legal redress, but they were rarely successful against their oppressors. Writing to a friend in Boston from the New Orleans chain-gang in 1834, John Tidd claimed that his captain imprisoned him because "I was a little belaited with my supper and he gain to jaw me and I told him if he did not like et he might get somboday alse." The captain "carrid [off] my papers and clothing and by the information i can git he want to sall me." Tidd was an old hand in the courts: he had previously hired a Boston attorney to "sue for all wages due to me from the Captain and Owners of the Ship *Cameo*," and he now asked his friend to stop the captain "when he arrives . . . I want you to . . . gow to a lawyer and have them all stoped thair in tell I return that I can get recompense."[33] An African American widow living in Providence, shaken when her son was sold in New Orleans in 1834, contacted an attorney to prosecute his captain. Neither her suit nor Tidd's prevailed. A few individuals were redeemed during the 1830s when sympathetic white merchants traveling in the South intervened on their behalf, but this was by no means the norm, and it became ever more atypical as the abolitionist tempo increased. When the Commonwealth of Massachusetts sent agents to Charleston and New Orleans in 1844 on behalf of imprisoned black seamen, both were thwarted, and one almost lynched.[34]

Yet insisting that free people had rights, and distraught by the loss of loved ones, black citizens rallied collectively on behalf of sailors. Louisiana's act requiring the incarceration of free seamen sparked several African American meetings in Boston. The first, in 1842, petitioned both Congress and the Massachusetts legislature, and appointed a committee "to prepare and circulate petitions, and to correspond with our friends in the several States, to awaken an interest in behalf of their own seamen." In 1850, four hundred Bahamians signed what they called a memorial, or petition, and sent it to London to protest the poor treatment of black sailors in the United States, Cuba, and Puerto Rico. Black newspapers publicized changes in laws regarding seamen. Organized responses like these to the plight of colored seamen bolstered the abolitionist crusade, but African American communities remained essentially powerless to prevent the wholesale incarceration of sailors in the lower South.[35]

Overcrowded seaport jails burst at the seams during strict enforcement of the Negro Seamen Acts. A white man visiting black shipmates in the Charleston jail in November 1839 counted "fifty-two stewards and cooks in there." Several years later William H. Davis, imprisoned under the South Carolina act, counted seventy mariners confined at the same time. Whereas harassment had long been part of the life of every northern free black, broad-based roundups had not, nor had the galling ignominy of respectable men being paraded through the streets in handcuffs. Referring indignantly to New Orleans in 1846, a black boardinghouse keeper complained that "*nineteen* coloured men were taken out of vessels in one day." The simultaneous incarceration of large numbers of innocent men fostered camaraderie among them, allowed the rekindling of old friendships, and provided hours of tense boredom during which they swapped yarns and complained bitterly in low tones about their treatment. But even the hardiest quailed. For a captain "called by the Sheriff to put my negro in jail," inconvenience and expense resulted. For a sailor gripping his little bundle and sizing up the sheriff at the ship's rail, life-threatening uncertainty loomed. Each knew that not every seaman returned to his ship, and malicious sheriffs taunted free sailors with the insecurity of their freedom.[36]

Local circumstances dictated when and how mariners would be jailed. But the significant time lag between events in cotton ports and the dissemination of news through the waterfront grapevine in New York or Liverpool kept black sailors in the dark. In New Orleans during the early 1840s Joshua Baldwin, the Second Municipality recorder, rigidly enforced the incarceration of nonresident black sailors. After several years of large annual roundups, Baldwin came under fire for channeling the accrued fees into the Second Municipality treasury. State law stipulated that colored seamen were to be housed in the Orleans Parish Prison—not the municipality workhouse—and that fees were payable to the parish. Caught in a local political fracas, Baldwin relented long enough in 1845 to direct some sailors to the parish prison, but he ultimately circumvented his political opponents by instructing policemen in the Second Municipality to stop arresting black sailors altogether. Strict enforcement of the law alternated with periods of laxity on a port-by-port basis.[37]

Such minor inconsistencies in an oppressive law were not very reassuring to men concerned with their own freedom and with supporting their families. The roundups seemed relentless. From his proprietor's desk at the Coloured Seamen's Home in 1846, William P. Powell investigated the jailing of sailors in New Orleans and learned "that the average number is not less than thirty-five per month, for twelve months." Relying upon "men whose veracity I have good reason to believe," Powell deduced the numbers of black seamen he believed were incarcerated annually in several southern jails. His total, 1,168 men detained each year, broke down as follows: in New Orleans, 420 men; in Charleston, 240 men; in Savannah and Mobile, 204 men each; and in Cuba, 100 men. Alternative sources suggest that though Powell's calculations were exaggerated for Savannah, they were very accurate for Charleston.[38]

During the life of these acts, at least 10,000 free black seamen were man-handled and jailed before being freed to tell their tales. New Orleans police records confirm the arrests of 2,769 alien blacks from 1853 to 1862, of which approximately 88 percent (2,436) were seamen. The bulk of the arrests occurred during a two-year period from 1859 to 1862, when the acts were strictly enforced. In 1850, a Boston shipowner had testified that "certificates could be forwarded of more than one thousand imprisonments, within three years, at the port of New Orleans alone." This focus on New Orleans notwithstanding, contemporaries agreed that South Carolinians were the most vigorous enforcers. Scattered statistics suggest that at least 200 seamen per year were imprisoned in Charleston for 34 years—an estimated total of 6,400. Given that 4 other states and Cuba incarcerated black sailors as well, it appears that considerably more than 10,000 free seamen of color were jailed under these acts. And on pay day, at least 10,000 of them felt the sting of laws passed by slaveholders.[39]

Shipmasters passed on the costs of imprisonment to their black hands. "We had to pay our jail fees, the Recorder's and officer's bills," lamented a seaman after a stint in the New Orleans prison. The expenses were not inconsequential. In November 1843, Captain Dill of the brig *Penguin* paid $23.43 for "arrest, registry, dieting, etc. of Robert White, John Pluten, & Richard Fabler, colored seamen," in Charleston. In 1844 a ship's agent in New Orleans paid $8.25 "for taking the Cook out of jail." Cooks then earned only $16 to $20 per month, and seamen a few dollars less. Black mariners absorbing the cost of a southern port stay found weeks or even months of their wages deducted, giving new meaning to the shantey that ran, "O rouse an' bust 'er is the cry, A black man's wage is never high." Most seamen were hit twice for these voyages: wages invariably stopped for days when there was no shipboard work, during which a sailor often paid for the insult of menial labor and lousy meals in a filthy jail.[40]

Avoiding the cotton ports had its own costs. An ex-slave from the Chesapeake who shipped out for years refused to return to slave territory, poverty or not. "Every winter [Captain Baymore] used to trade South, and wanted me to go with him, but I refused him, because they would always take the stewards out and lock them up." Instead, "I was compelled to board during the winter in Philadelphia, and it took all my summer earnings to keep me through the winter." The compounded costs to northern black America were substantial in jobs lost, wages docked, and fees deducted. Local black economies simultaneously suffered in the cotton ports, as slaves and free blacks who had vended food, entertainment, or lodging to sailors of color lost their customers.[41]

Recompense for the southern authorities' plundering remained virtually out of the question, but northern captains were slightly more vulnerable. "These niggers have threatened to prosecute Capt Barber and me," complained the Yankee chief mate of an all-black crew loading cotton in 1854. "I shall have to stay and take the chances." In 1844 a black mariner sued the captain of the *Cynosure* in Massachusetts, seeking compensation for his imprisonment in New Orleans. He triumphed when the court ruled that he was "not liable for the prison expenses paid by the master." His was a partial victory. The judge refused financial damages because the sailor had signed articles agreeing to make a voyage to any port in the United States. His captain was thus exempt from liability for his "unconstitutional" imprisonment. Such verdicts never surprised black people, and the numbers who triumphed in court were tiny compared with the numbers who paid for their own incarceration.[42]

Confronting the awesome will of white southerners to debase and extort mariners of color, sailors devised various strategies for coping. Avoidance was a favorite. In 1836 Captain James Scott claimed that James Ware, a Rhode Island native and "a colored Seaman . . . was discharged with his own consent at Nassau not being willing to come to Savannah." But avoiding the South altogether was neither economically practical nor personally desirable for many black seamen.[43]

Discriminatory laws and extra-legal intimidation never entirely stemmed the flow of blacks into the South. Persistent sailors managed to circumvent Negro Seamen Acts on the very doorsteps of southern ports, although this required alliances with captains, who despite their irritation with meddlesome laws were rarely a black sailor's friend. Wesley Brown signed articles in November 1849 for a voyage from Saco, Maine, to any port in the Gulf of Mexico aboard the *Hungarian*. At New Orleans "she was moored out of the precincts of the city, to prevent [Brown] & other colored men of the crew being put in prison during the stay of the ship there." Brown and three other black seamen successfully requested that Captain Richard Hartley "procure [them] a berth on board another vessel going north, to relieve [them] of the danger of imprisonment."[44]

Louisiana's law of 1842 requiring captains to send African Americans to jail (and to pay for it) temporarily united sailors and captains against the state, as had similar laws in South Carolina and Georgia. At Charleston, remembered John Cory, his "Captain remonstrated, offered to be my surety for good behavior, offered to prove my birth, but all was unavailing." Not accustomed to having the captain on their side, sailors such as Brown and Cory manipulated the situation as best they could.[45]

But the class divide remained, and amendments to Louisiana's Negro Seamen's Act in 1852 (and to South Carolina's in 1856) opened black sailors to new forms of exploitation. The liberalized laws allowed black mariners to remain aboard their vessels. A sailor aboard ship, however, was the prisoner of his captain, and never more so than when the captain had the shoreside authorities' resources at his disposal. A federal judge recognized this in 1855. "A port in the slave states, where laws of this description prevail," he wrote, "is not a port of discharge for colored seamen . . . They are not free to go where they please, and to find other voyages . . . They cannot even leave the vessel without the hazard of being made slaves."⁴⁶ During the peak of southern enforcement, most captains did not want sailors of color. Jail fees and the invasion of ships by nosey sheriffs provided a new reason for racist exclusion at hiring time. Once laws were modified so that black seamen were forced to remain aboard ships, however, skin-flint Yankee skippers recognized a solution to the age-old problem of desertion. With regulations in southern ports making it dangerous for nonresident free blacks even to be seen on the streets, sailors of color became their employers' captives.

A captain hiring an all-black crew for a voyage to New Orleans or Charleston after the laws were liberalized during the 1850s knew that his sailors could not desert, and that he might coerce them into accepting low wages or force them to unload the ship. At New Orleans in 1857, "a crowd of unemployed workers congregated around a vessel on to which a group of northern negroes were rolling cotton bales," and they "seemed to envy the well fed and more fortunate blacks." A few years before, those blacks would have been in jail, and the "unemployed [white] workers" loading cotton. But black sailors bore their own crosses. An African American crew signed aboard the brig *Iddo Kimball* in Halifax, Nova Scotia, about 1854 for a voyage to Europe, and thence "to a port of discharge in the United States" at the rate of twenty-four dollars per month. In New Orleans they remained aboard, foregoing the pleasures of sailortown to avoid jail, and worked for the captain at local wages—fifteen dollars per month. Three weeks later he made the crew sign articles for the voyage north at the same low rate. Later arguing in the federal district court in Boston that they were entitled to their original wage, the *Iddo Kimball* crew prevailed because shipmasters legally could not use the laws of slave states to force lower wages on black sailors. But many captains continued to do so with impunity. State laws and the dominance of custom often took away with one hand what federal laws provided with the other. As illegal aliens in Louisiana, for example, out-of-state blacks could not file suits against white employers, opening them to serious exploitation.[47]

Blacks knew, of course, that white control was never absolute, and they subtly challenged white domination by choosing to make southern voyages. James P. Thomas first saw New Orleans as a runaway slave in 1839, and he returned in 1851 as a freeman hoping to settle there. Ultimately the steward on a Mississippi River steamer, Thomas traveled to nearly all the United States east of the Mississippi, the Caribbean, Central America, and Europe. The splendor of "Grand opera nights," the relative freedom of "large numbers of servants [who] managed to buy themselves, their families, and [who] had money and property besides," as he put it, and the sheer exuberance of New Orleans life made the Crescent City his kind of place. A slave himself until well into his twenties, and an eyewitness to the slave markets in New Orleans, Thomas still found an incomparable attractiveness in that cosmopolitan seaport on the Mississippi's great bend. He frequented New Orleans even during the era of the Negro Seamen Acts because he liked the city. Two free-born Bahamians likewise came to prefer life in the Civil War South to that of sleepy, but free, Nassau. Kidnapped aboard a schooner in Nassau in 1861, they were sold for eight hundred dollars each in Camden County, Georgia, and later forced to work aboard the Confederate steamer *Darlington*. To the surprise of their Union liberator, Admiral DuPont, the Bahamians felt sufficiently independent to make their way on the southern waterfront. "They never have expressed any desire to be sent to Nassau or to the North," he wrote. Despite their scare in slavery, John Stirrup and Sam Edwards preferred to navigate their own course in the lower South, a place at once terrible and attractive to free blacks. Neither desperation for work nor whites' duplicity explains entirely why free black seamen voyaged southward.[48]

Resigned to the degradation of black labor, and conscious of their own ability to endure, other northern seamen simply risked a stint in jail, accepting imprisonment as an occupational hazard. A "respectable" colored man from Boston named George Tolliver had "been incarcerated seven different times, on arriving at southern ports" by 1839. He certainly knew what loomed on a southern voyage. Twenty years later, the shipping articles of the *Moses Taylor* in Liverpool included the caveat that "should the coloured men be put in jail according to the Law at New Orleans the Captain or owners to pay all Jail fees." Under that admonition, nine black Americans signed their willingness to make the voyage. During the 1850s, jailing may have become a rite of passage in African American seafaring circles, especially among the young, who associated it with masculine bravado and contempt for "The Man."[49]

The bullwhip and the auction block worked to a degree, cowing seamen into quiescence, keeping black mariners out of the South, and nurturing seeds of betrayal within the black population. More than one colored sailor exposed a runaway slave aboard ship to protect himself. But resistance never died. Striving to forge a meaningful freedom for themselves, their families, and people of color, substantial numbers of sailors insisted on their right to work and on the righteousness of abolition. Southern legislators were right on the mark when they fulminated against "the moral contagion which the intercourse with foreign negroes will introduce."[50]

As the proprietor of one of the largest boardinghouses for black sailors in New York City, and a founder of the Manhattan Anti-Slavery Society, William P. Powell created a network of antislavery messengers. Seamen boarding at Powell's got a steady dose of his passionate Garrisonian convictions. "Slavery is the creature of sin, and not of Law!" he thundered, "and a violation of God's holy law, thou shalt not Steal." In a letter to a black abolitionist written during an extended stay in Liverpool, Powell instructed him "to send the [antislavery] books by Mr. Fisher, Steward of the ship *Saranak* or Mr. Freeman, Steward of ship *Tonawanda*, both Philadelphia packets running to L'pool, either gentleman will be glad to serve me." Powell occasionally collected money "from the Colored Sailors Home to aid the Mass. Anti Slavery Society," and requested William Lloyd Garrison to "acknowledge the same in the Liberator."[51]

Yankee seamen publicly displayed antislavery sentiments. When "the colored people of New Bedford, with numerous representatives of their friends from Boston, Providence, and elsewhere, celebrated" West Indian emancipation on July 24, 1858, black seamen formed a prominent procession "under the marshallship of Mr. Thomas Price, who was mounted for the occasion." But by no means were all sailors activists. Like the free black population as a whole, only a minority threw themselves into the struggle.[52]

Seafaring abolitionists incurred considerable personal risk by assisting fugitives like Tom Wilson, who, in his own words, still carried "14 buck shot" in his hip; was "marked with the whip from the ankle bone to the crown of my head"; and "felt safer among the alligators than among the white men" while splashing through Lake Pontchartrain in flight to New Orleans in 1858. "When I got down to the wharf," remembered Wilson, "some of the coloured crew of the American cotton ship *Metropolis* took me on board, and hid me away among the bales." Later betrayed by "one of the coloured men," Wilson nevertheless managed to avoid searchers on the *Metropolis*. He knew, however, the danger to which he had subjected his rescuers, and he remembered being "frightened too for the coloured men who had befriended me." During the passage to London they kept him "out of sight of the white men." Countless unheralded escapees were assisted to freedom in much the same way. A slave oysterman named Joshua Davis from Portsmouth, Virginia, successfully stowed away "in a schooner to N.Y. not known to any person on board, except to a colored man," according to an agent of the Boston Committee of Vigilance, and by the help of that sailor, arrived at New York in 1847. The ex-slave Solomon Northrup was exaggerating when he claimed that it would be easy for a determined slave to "escape from New Orleans on some northern vessel." But runaways in the care of sympathetic black seamen were likely to succeed.[53]

Stowaways ignorant of ships and without the help of experienced sailors could easily perish. Secreting himself aboard a turpentine-laden schooner in 1859, a fugitive from St. Mary's, Georgia, realized once the hatches were closely battened that the volatile fumes had no escape. They saturated the hold, transforming it into a gas chamber and then a coffin. A desperado named Davis secured himself to the paddlewheel guards of the steamer *Keystone State* in Savannah, spending several days with "the water frequently sweeping over him." Not until sailors heaving the lead in Delaware Bay heard cries for help was he discovered. Seamen knew firsthand what slaves would risk for freedom.[54]

Stowaways seriously compromised unwitting black sailors. Four free blacks shipped on the schooner *George Harriss* in the summer of 1859 for Wilmington, North Carolina, and cursed their bad luck shortly into the return voyage, when a slave fleeing "a minister of the Gospel" revealed himself to the captain. "The penalty for" assisting slaves to freedom "by the laws of this state," they wrote from jail, "is 'death.'" Referring to the facts of the case, they claimed, "We will be acquitted." "If without counsel, and our case is tried here," however, "with popular feeling against us, we fear the result." By the late 1850s, southern waterfronts were a minefield for seamen of color. William Brodie, "a free colored sailor of the Bark Overman, of New York," was charged in Darien, Georgia, with helping slaves to freedom in 1858, after which he was sentenced to be sold for sixty-five years. Citizens in Camden County, Georgia, demanded in 1859 "the right of search of all [northern] vessels, and the right of selling into slavery all free negroes who enter our waters."[55]

Self-confident northern seamen were by no means quiet in the South. Ashore at Charleston in 1857, after passports had been substituted for the incarceration of black sailors, G. E. Stevens wrote irately to a friend that slaves "invariably believe that white men are superior." He referred to an elderly laundress's calling little white children "Master" and "Mistress." "I could not stand this, and reprimanded her," remembered Stevens, echoing Denmark Vesey's dangerous professions of equality. "She was perfectly astonished, commenced an argument with me to prove that those children were entitled to this distinction. She told me I must not talk this way—some of the people might overhear me and tell master." Slaves did not need outsiders to remind them of their masters' whippings, family-sundering sales, constant anxiety, or the right of every worker to the proceeds of his or her own labor. Sailors nevertheless exposed individual slaves like the laundress to untold possibilities and new ways of thinking about slavery.[56]

Free dark young men from the North stood out in the lower South—not only because of their speech, but because most local free blacks were either mulattoes or older people manumitted after they became enfeebled. Embodying black freedom of movement and black-white equality in the workplace, northern sailors subverted local racial mores with their very presence. Equally paid black and white sailors emerging from the forecastle scuttle of a northern ship, for instance, mocked white pretensions of racial superiority. They subverted slavery more actively with travel stories and news of free life. Candid sailors conceded that white terror was not confined to the South, bemoaning vicious race riots in Providence, New York, and Philadelphia. Self-confident sailors probably attracted slaves' attention with accounts of the free black convention movement, blacks' demands for suffrage, northern employment prospects, and black churches independent of white oversight. Most compellingly, seamen spoke passionately on the condition of black people elsewhere—a topic of constant interest throughout the African diaspora.[57]

Ostracized by a xenophobic society that labeled alien free blacks as infectious, transient black sailors rarely had patrons in the lower South. Resident free blacks cultivated white "protectors," exchanging deference for whites' paternalistic control. But few white South Carolinians advocated the employment of blacks as mariners. Those who did were slaveholders, without regard for northern free blacks. Without services to withhold from those who directly oppressed them, and bereft of white patrons to protect them in the South, free black sailors remained inordinately vulnerable.

LEGISLATORS' ATTEMPTS to exclude free black sailors from the lower South undeniably circumscribed seamen's freedom, movement, and livelihood. But the struggle with slavery never cowed them entirely, nor did it insulate seaport slaves from their pernicious abolitionism. Like waves on a beach, black sailors kept coming—rapidly or rarely, with fury or measured determination, but always coming. Chain-gangs and prisons starkly impressed upon them the uncertainty of their personal safety. Fearful or not, African American sailors resisted the degradation of southern laws by filing lawsuits, manipulating shipmasters against the state, and spiriting fugitive slaves to freedom. But the plight of at least ten thousand free men jailed under the Negro Seamen Acts highlighted the increasing racial animosity in seafaring. Whereas black labor once had been crucial to maritime industry, and maritime labor vital to the support of northern free black communities, blacks' employment aboard ship had become less steady and less remunerative by mid-century. Although the southern states loosened some restrictions on black sailors during the 1850s, the over-all story was one of declining opportunities. Jim Crow was going to sea.

8. TOWARD
JIM CROW
AT SEA

Oh, the times was hard, an' the wages low,
Leave her, Johnny, leave her.
But now once more, ashore we'll go,
And it's time for us to leave her.

Leave her, Johnny, leave her,
Oooh! leave her Johnny, leave her!
For the voyage is done, an' the winds don't blow,
And its time for us to leave her!

NINETEENTH-CENTURY SHANTEY

B Y THE MIDDLE of the nineteenth century, changes in the maritime industries worked against African Americans' best interests. Although the shifting of blacks' roles in maritime work was neither uniform nor entirely negative, the general trend was unmistakable. Black men were finding fewer opportunities at sea.

Maritime culture, however, increasingly displayed the legacy of African Americans in the age of sail, notably in the shanteys with which sailors paced their work and expressed their sardonic worldview. Black sailors had remade Atlantic maritime culture, and in the process formed their identities through it. They had contributed substantially to the formation of black America by earning a living at sea and by spreading news to black communities. But after the general emancipation of 1863, the sailor's role as newsmonger became less significant, and seafaring became less meaningful to black America as a whole. Freedom opened black society considerably to outside influences and cross-cultural perspectives, making sailors' vantage point less distinctive. The constriction of blacks' employment during Reconstruction, however, had serious repercussions for a community always struggling to make ends meet. It foreshadowed blacks' segregation by late-nineteenth- and early-twentieth-century maritime unions, which allowed men of color to sail only as cooks and stewards or as seamen in marginal trades. Jim Crow was going to sea.

As SEAFARING became less important to black society, blacks' influence on sailors as a whole became more pronounced. Similarities had always existed between aspects of Atlantic maritime culture and the cultural predispositions of the larger black population, which helps to explain why blacks fit so comfortably within maritime culture in the age of sail, and how their presence shaped it.

Aboard ships sailors were "hands," not faces. Black seamen thus found it easy to abide by Fats Waller's timeless injunction: "Don't give your right name, no, no, no!" Cambridge Pendleton sued for wages earned on the schooner *Retrieve*, but he had signed aboard her as "Harry Cook." Thomas Benjamin Spaldwin shipped out of Boston for about six years: "some times he called his name Addams some time Morris and at other times Spaldwin."[1] Just as the first generation of freed slaves were given the power to define themselves by selecting their own first and last names, so black seamen took advantage of sailors' anonymity to name themselves at will. Although historic African American naming practices are not yet fully understood, it is clear that multiple identities and nicknames were common among slaves and free blacks before the Civil War. White Americans had multiple names less frequently. Yet a prominent whaling merchant in New Bedford noted in 1837 that it had "become very fashionable for Sailors to assume some fictitious name by which they ship and are known before they sail." With their black shipmates, white sailors shared assumptions about anonymity in an exploitative workplace.[2]

Sailors' attitudes toward authority (at once truculent and accommodating), their stylistic touches, such as earrings, and their expressive work-songs were also shared across the color line. Although blacks' contributions to sea shanteys have long been acknowledged, it has been assumed that white sailors picked up rhythmic structures and antiphonal styles from enslaved stevedores. This is only partly correct. The shanteys' late-eighteenth-century origins corresponded with rising numbers of black sailors, and the period of the shantey's greatest development after 1820 was one of black prominence at sea. One of the earliest mentions of shanteys in print was Francis Allyn Olmstead's *Incidents of a Whaling Voyage,* published in 1841, in which "Mr. Free-man," the black cook, held center stage. When the crew pulled to-gether, he "usually officiates as chorister and with many demisemi-quavers strikes up the song, while all the rest join in the chorus." "Demisemiquavers" sounds like a white man's attempt to articulate the vital melodic accents—the "yelps and hitches," as another shan-teyman called them—that punctuated the hollers of black field hands, blacks' psalmody, and sea shanteys.[3]

Interracial musical exchange was common on the waterfront long before Mr. Freeman sailed. An "impertinent" runaway "Negro woman" was described in the *Virginia Gazette* in 1774 as notoriously "fond of Liquor, and apt to sing indecent and Sailor Songs." A New England merchant who continually watched ships loading and unloading at St. Domingue in 1785 commented on the "cheerful and pleasant" "sound of the negroes' labor song while at the tackle fall."[4] White sailors listened to the singing of female slaves and black stevedores, but they also listened to black sailors. As had been the case at Dartmoor Prison in 1814, black sailors sang and played in string orchestras and military bands, fusing and reformulating many musical traditions. Clearly, the "chanter-response performance type" that characterizes the shantey is more common to African singing style than to European.[5]

By the nineteenth century, white sailors spent a significant amount of time singing in what had once been a characteristically black style. "All of this work," wrote a seasoned tar about sailors loading cotton in Gulf ports, "was accompanied by a song, often improvised, and sung by the 'chantie' man, the chorus being taken up by the rest of the gang." "When hauling taut the weather main-brace," noted an-other observer, "they sing a perversion of the old negro melody, 'Hey,

Jim along, Jim along, Josey!' but the sailors put it, "Way, haul away—
haul away, Josey—Way, haul away—haul away Joe!"[6] Yet as blacks'
influence on maritime culture grew, free blacks faced dwindling employment opportunities. At sea, they increasingly worked as transient
mariners rather than career seamen, and they found it ever more
difficult to hone skills or provide for families through maritime work.

Racial segregation came to the maritime industries during the 1850s,
resulting in short-term social gains and long-term economic costs for
men of color. "Colored men do very well for deck hands, and firemen,
and the like of that," explained a Great Lakes captain in 1864. "They
are the best men we have." But, he continued, "we have to keep them
separate from white sailors. We cannot mix them. We always carry
either a black crew or a white one."[7] That practice extended well
beyond the Great Lakes. The *W. Libby* sailed from Baltimore in 1857
with an all-white crew, and in Liverpool reshipped an all-black one.
After the Civil War a new phenomenon arose: "checkerboard" crews.
Captains on some ships filled the starboard watch with whites and the
larboard watch with blacks, hoping that racial rivalry would spur each
to outdo the other. "Checkerboard" crews competed fiercely, and
associated very differently than had the "promiscuous crowd of black
and white sailors" who spent a day in 1825 "parading through [New
Orleans's] streets bearing the National Flag" and "huzzahing" for "the
purpose of raising wages."[8]

Segregation also became more prominent in the navy. "The blacks
must . . . be used to defend the vessels," ordered Admiral David D.
Porter from his flagship *Black Hawk* in 1863, delineating a policy that
would have been familiar to naval sailors during the Revolution, the
Quasi War with France, and the War of 1812. But at the height of black
Americans' war for liberation, Porter simultaneously described a new
policy: black sailors were to "be exercised separately at great guns and
small arms," and "in all cases they must be kept distinct from the rest
of the crew." Although practice never fully conformed to policy, the
situation of black sailors in 1863 was different from that of their
counterparts in the integrated navy of 1812. Atlantic maritime culture
had always felt some influences from shore. Unfortunately for blacks
aboard ship, the new emphasis on racial segregation ashore at mid-
century eroded the protective bulwarks of nautical custom and diminished blacks in an occupation long important to them.[9]

Black sailors' worsening situation at mid-century is especially ironic in light of changes in the nature of seafaring itself. Once New England's economic mainstay, and a central aspect of the coastal economy north of Virginia, shipping declined in relative importance as industrialization caught American entrepreneurs' imaginations and their investment capital. As one successful shipmaster had put it earlier in the century, working at sea had seemed to many "the most sure and direct means of arriving at independence." Consequently, during the early national years, much of northern society, black and white, accepted it. Elmo P. Hohman exaggerated when he wrote that early-nineteenth-century crews were "drawn from the best stock of New England, and could look forward to becoming officers and owners."[10] Aristocratic Federalists would have resented the inference that they begot common sailors, and in reality most seamen came from the laboring population. Yet in the early national period seafaring clearly offered the possibility of prestige and promotion to white men who could withstand its rigors, and regular, even tolerant, employment to blacks. Northern men shipped in large numbers, including the talented and ambitious from each race.[11]

Sailors at mid-century inhabited a different world. Larger ships, lower wages, increased brutality, and a new matrix ashore of boardinghouse keepers, crimps, and outfitters accentuated the most exploitative elements of seafaring.[12] Labeling themselves as "vassals," or "slaves of the lowest cast," white seamen wailed: "And now I ask what slave at the south suffers more hardships or feels more keenly the bitterness of oppression than the poor care worne sailor."[13] Violent captains like Frank Thompson reinforced their shame:

> You see your condition! . . . I'll make you toe the mark, every soul of you, or I'll flog you all, fore and aft, from the boy up! You've got a driver over you. Yes, a *slave-driver—a nigger-driver!* I'll see who'll tell me he isn't a *nigger* slave![14]

Conditions at sea thus mocked the "liberty" and "equality" white American men had come to expect at mid-century. Given black Americans' traditional seafaring, logic would dictate that America's most degraded caste of workers—black men—would have shouldered more of the merchant fleet's burdens as they became distasteful to white Americans. Ironically they did not. With Irishmen and other white foreigners "willing to submit to oppressive and despotic treatment," blacks' sea-going tradition seemed to count for little at hiring time. Mid-century racial discrimination extended not only to new occupations in the expanding economy, but to established professions such as seafaring.[15]

Occasionally a high-profile success story drew attention away from the generalized pattern of decline. "There is little invidious discrimination against them as seamen," wrote a New York journalist. "One colored seaman, George Brooks, received his certificate as shipmaster in 1867, and sailed from this port in command of the *James F. Waterbury* for the coast of Africa." Black men in sailortown dives looking for a ship were not so sanguine.[16]

To begin with, the ranks of black seamen began to shrink east of the Hudson river. African Americans had accounted for 14 percent of New York sailors in 1835, but only 4.6 percent in 1866. During the 1830s black men filled between 20 and 30 percent of the available berths in Providence; twenty years later, they filled only 9 percent. The proportion of black Bostonians who described themselves as sailors fell from 29 percent in 1850 to 19 percent in 1860. In Boston, Providence, New Bedford, and New York black mariners were becoming less common at mid-century.[17]

Although black men would continue to work on American ships throughout the nineteenth century, the shipboard experience began to change significantly for individuals in northern ports during the 1850s. In Rhode Island, at least, fewer all-black crews existed to provide the workplace camaraderie that had been so important to the previous generation. In New Bedford, fewer black men shipped on whalers during the 1850s and 1860s than during the 1810s and 1820s—or after the discovery of petroleum reduced whaling to a marginal industry in the 1870s. The cross-racial fraternization that had once characterized the forecastle eroded as that part of the ship became increasingly the province of white men. "A negro in the forecastle of a British ship," commented an Englishman at sea in the 1870s, "is a lonely being. He has no chums." The same might be said for American ships as the century wore on.[18]

Of course we must use caution when inferring a state of mind from statistics. Individual black sailors in predominantly white forecastles may not have been completely isolated: interracial tolerance once prevailed at sea. The single black man whose presence the Kentuckian J. Ross Browne found so disconcerting in a whaleship forecastle during the 1840s apparently did not offend the other white sailors. It is safe to say, however, that after mid-century black sailors from New England seaports were generally dependent on their white shipmates for companionship, a situation that hinged on individual personalities and racist proclivities. Perhaps some blacks continued to find congenial situations in predominantly white crews, but after mid-century black Yankees could no longer create their own shipboard communities as they once had.[19]

Blacks preferred sailing in all-black crews. In 1803 more than a quarter of the black men who sailed from Providence signed aboard ships on which only the officers were white; and many other blacks made voyages from New York, Philadelphia, and Baltimore with a black majority before the mast.[20] "Our crew were all black men, the captain's peculiar choice," remembered the mate Joseph Bates of a voyage on the *Francis F. Johnson* to South America in 1817. "I often regretted that we two were the only white men on board, for we were sometimes placed in peculiar circumstances, in consequence of being the minority." Aboard the *Johnson* a black man ruled the cook's caboose; and unless the captain always headed a watch, a black man also had charge of the deck at times, an officer in fact if not in name. Black sailors on ships like the *Francis F. Johnson* found a more congenial workplace than many of their brethren ashore. Black men who signed aboard ships with an entirely black crew were conscious of the opportunity to mold their own forecastle social life from the camaraderie of an isolated, masculine, and African American world. Many probably chose seafaring precisely for this sociability in the workplace. But in New England the number of all-black crews declined at mid-century. In both New York and New England, crews with black majorities decreased as well. Individual black sailors in the North became increasingly isolated.[21]

Simultaneously, opportunities for blacks to socialize with one another at sea improved among sailors shipping at Baltimore. In 1806 only 8 percent of the African American men sailing out of Baltimore had sailed in all-black crews; in 1816, only 5 percent had. But between

1852 and 1866 no less than 33 percent of the black sailors shipping from Baltimore worked in all-black crews. Crews were increasingly supplied by shipping agents who often doubled as boardinghouse keepers, and their boarders were either all black or all white. Rising segregation signaled a change in racial attitudes among those who controlled the allocation of maritime labor on the Baltimore waterfront, a change that would squeeze black men out of seafaring jobs during Reconstruction.[22]

The overall slide in the quality of seafaring work, and blacks' declining position within the industry at mid-century, made shipping out a more casual occupation. No longer could a large number of skilled black sailors aboard Providence-based ships claim Rhode Island as their birthplace; nor would they return to Providence as their homeport. By the 1850s, black *sailors*—the real seamen who persisted in shipping out time and time again—had disappeared from the Rhode Island fleet. The black men aboard Rhode Island ships in the 1850s were all casual laborers, men who made one or two voyages at most. The prominent group of black mariners who considered themselves professionals, the "old salts" in the two generations that included Cato Burrill, Prince Brown, Daniel Watson, and David O'Kee, were gone. Although seafaring still provided casual employment to black men with limited options ashore, it was no longer a bastion of black professionalism, or a bulwark of the tiny black "middle class."[23]

Although black men were not excluded from seafaring jobs in Baltimore until the 1870s, seafaring provided less financial support for blacks in every port after mid-century. At Baltimore in 1870, black seamen aboard schooners earned $2.50 per month less than whites; black seamen aboard brigs earned $4.20 less. This represented a 10 to 20 percent differential. Northern blacks who traditionally looked to seafaring for wage parity had to swallow a bitter pill. Meanwhile, other occupations once available to black men became off-limits. "Fifteen or twenty years ago," thundered a speaker at the 1860 Crispus Attucks Meeting in Boston, "colored men had more than an even chance in menial employments; today we are crowded out of almost everything." "White men are becoming house servants," lamented Frederick Douglass in 1853, and "cooks and stewards on vessels."[24]

Career seafaring among African Americans declined in every port.

U.S. naval enlistment records for Baltimore between 1846 and 1852 reveal that the overall percentage of black men joining the navy was small, but that a substantial number of those men had prior merchant marine experience. Enlistment records for Baltimore, Philadelphia, and Norfolk from 1858 to 1859, however, show significantly fewer black *sailors* entering the navy. Black men were still signing up, but those who did were waiters, barbers, cooks, bakers, or men without occupations. Fewer black men possessed seafaring skills and experience as the decades passed, a trend that continued after the Civil War. The naval historian Frederick S. Harrod found that "the proportion of blacks who listed mariner as their previous occupation decreased from 13.1 percent in 1870 to 5.9 percent in 1890" among naval enlistees, and that "the percentage of blacks who had been cooks and waiters increased from 28.9 percent to 49.3 percent."[25]

A decline in careerism among native-born white seamen has been attributed to the industry's "degradation" and to better options ashore. But black men had no better options, and it seems unlikely that they would voluntarily forsake the sea. As W. E. B. Du Bois pointed out, "The question of economic survival [was] the most pressing of all questions" for nineteenth-century American blacks. Yet the ranks of regular seafarers in New York and New England whitened noticeably prior to the Civil War, and the relative number of black men with seafaring skills decreased in ports such as Norfolk and Baltimore.[26]

In order to understand the mid-century squeeze on black seafarers, it is necessary to examine changes in American society as a whole, in seaport economies, and in maritime hiring practices. Several social trends converged at mid-century to begin the transition from an American merchant marine manned prominently by blacks to one in which Jim Crow prevailed.

The replacement of regular black sailors with white men in New England is attributable in some degree to the influx of "downeast" ships in New England ports at mid-century. As Rhode Islanders diverted their capital into industry, they increasingly relied on out-of-state ships, particularly those from Maine, for their commerce. Not surprisingly, Maine men predominated among the ships' crews. Although crews changed after almost every voyage, Maine skippers generally hired downeasters, if they were available, before Rhode

Islanders. This put undeniable pressure on black employment prospects, though Maine captains like Edward Tilley of Eastport did occasionally hire black seamen: an all-black crew manned his brig *Nelson* to Nova Scotia for coal in 1834.[27]

The robust immigration and increasing class stratification that marked society as a whole also eroded black mariners' prospects. White foreigners undoubtedly competed with black men for seafaring jobs. In 1845 the chairman of the Committee on Naval Affairs asserted, with some exaggeration, that 90 percent of the men in the United States Navy and merchant marine were foreigners; the same year, *Hunt's Magazine* claimed that 66 percent were foreign-born. A few years before, Captain Frederick Marryat had concluded that, exclusive of masters, mates, and other specialists who were native-born, about 70 percent of the men before the mast were foreigners. Although such "statistics" are not verifiable, the overwhelming impression of every observer was that as the century progressed fewer and fewer white Yankees sailed on American ships. "What [white] American," asked the seaman Roland Gould, "would ever be content to rivet the chains of slavery upon himself?" But the mere presence of white immigrant and foreign labor does not explain why whites were hired instead of the black Americans who had traditionally manned the fleet, or why black men increasingly were shunted into marginal vessels, or relegated to cooking aboard ship.[28]

During the early nineteenth century, there were several different markets in maritime labor. In primary ports such as New York and Philadelphia, the maritime labor market was frequently impersonal, and captains' and sailors' chief relationship was that between buyer and seller of labor. But at secondary ports such as Salem and Providence, and at a host of smaller seaports central to colonial and early national commerce, relationships between masters and men frequently went beyond that of employer and employee. Many vessels were manned not through a free market in labor, but through patron-client, kin, or neighborly relationships.

Black mariners competed with one another and whites as faceless hands in a competitive maritime labor market, but they also operated in a personal patron-client system. Evidence suggests that blacks did so more than whites, and that this system of hiring persisted longer for blacks—especially cooks and stewards in "service" jobs. Some made careers sailing repeatedly with the same captain. Captains who assumed a proprietary relationship with a particular black steward benefited from a degree of stability and trust, and accrued the status that came to whites who were served by blacks. Men of color relied on this holdover from a patriarchal era to stave off unemployment and shield themselves from the abuse and servility that captains so often imposed on sailors. This is not to say that no captain ever abused his regular steward, or that no psychological costs accompanied clientage, but that patronage entailed a degree of protection. After escaping from slavery in the 1790s, Money Vose sailed out of Gloucester, Massachusetts, under Captain Fitz William Sargent, "in whose employ he had been twelve years." The free-born Charles Benson sailed for years as the steward of the bark *Glide* at mid-century. Neither man participated in an anonymous labor market, and both seemed to appreciate the personal niche they created.[29]

Patronage had social costs, however. Stewards and cabin boys, especially, knew on which side their bread was buttered. Aboard the *Tatler*, Captain Nathaniel Garland suppressed a mutiny in 1822 after sailors killed his mate. Garland would have failed but for the help of "Peter, the black boy, and his friend throughout," who fetched his gun. The black steward of the schooner *Splendid* testified for his captain in 1830, hindering the other sailors' claim that the captain had shortchanged them their share of salvaged goods. Black mariners competing with whites and other blacks in an anonymous labor market were more likely to structure shipboard social relations around class than were those hired by patrons. Most important, during the late eighteenth and early nineteenth centuries black men found shipboard jobs in several ways.[30]

When the responsibility for hiring sailors shifted from shipowners and captains to middlemen called "crimps," or shipping masters, blacks were profoundly affected. Middlemen had long been involved in the hiring of sailors in major English ports such as London and Bristol, but in the late-eighteenth and early-nineteenth-century United States, they interceded only for naval sailors.[31] As the market revolution intensified, however, and an ever-more specialized workforce became increasingly stratified, the traditional patriarchal relationship between employers and employees collapsed. Deference eroded, "masters" became "bosses," and workers—now expected to be independent and self-regulating—rarely lived under the boss's roof. Attitudes associated with this more democratic and class-based system affected even those workers, like seamen, who had never lived in the master's household ashore.

Until about 1820, captains or owners personally hired their own crews in every American port, whether through a relatively anonymous labor market or via patronage. When the *Astrea* left New York for India in 1796, the men were "shipped by William Dodge, Master." An owner of the schooner *Nancy* hired a captain and a mate in 1794, and the captain then hired an all-black crew at Baltimore. Captain Elijah Cobb noted that at Norfolk in 1812 he had "visited the Sailors' boarding houses, where I shipped my crew." A prominent Boston merchant testified in 1813 that for twenty years he had "always had the particular care of that part of our business which relates to the shipping of our seamen." Except when shipping for the navy, sailors expected a face-to-face interview with the owner or captain.[32]

Word of jobs circulated in several ways. "Able Seamen Wanted for a new ship lying at Edenton, N.C.," proclaimed the *Virginia Gazette* in 1776. Newspaper readers in New Bedford in 1796 saw the notice "A Crew Wanted for the Schooner Swain, now lying at Fairhaven, and bound on a Southern & Bahama Whale Cruise." Much more typically, however, during the eighteenth and early nineteenth centuries "when a ship required a crew, a signal to that effect was hoisted; sailors came on board and signed the articles, rating themselves according to their respective qualifications . . . They selected the ship for themselves; talked with the captain; made their own bargains; [and] brought their chests and bedding as security that they would go."[33]

Between 1820 and 1845, however, crimps gained control of the maritime labor market.[34] Promising punctual delivery of a crew on departure day for a fee, crimps freed captains from the aggravation of hiring. Once established, they worked in league with boardinghouse keepers to control the flow of sailors, holding captains hostage to their demands. This did not happen immediately. New Orleans was one of the first ports in which they organized; Boston, one of the last. Various forms of hiring persisted side-by-side for a time. Evidence from Savannah and New York suggests that during the 1830s, a transitional era, sailors might sign articles directly with the captain or a shipping master. In Baltimore in 1831, a retired captain attempted to open a "Marine Register Office" to publish the "Names, Character and Capability of the Seamen of the Port," hoping to "lessen the imposition which merchants and shipmasters are often subject to." Despite these variations, crimps ultimately prevailed as intermediaries in maritime hiring.[35]

By 1851, according to Richard Henry Dana, the hiring of crews "usually is left up to the shipping masters, who are paid so much a head for each of the crew, and are responsible for their appearance on board at the time of sailing. When this plan is adopted, neither the master nor owner, except by accident, knows anything of the crew before the vessel goes to sea." A former U.S. consul lamented that, with this system, "unless the master or owner acceded to [the crimps'] demands, his vessel might lay at the docks for days, at heavy expense." Thus well before the Civil War crimps had secured a strangle-hold on seafaring labor. Captains had to accept the men crimps provided and pay kick-backs as well. As the caliber of seafaring labor declined, sailors became pawns. "In some cases," wrote William P. Powell from the Coloured Sailors' Home in 1866, crimps "*extort* fabulous sums for the poor privilege of signing shipping articles."[36]

Reliance on crimps not only signaled rising class stratification in northern seaports, but changed the way race worked at hiring time. Often proprietors of taverns and inexpensive boardinghouses, crimps belonged to a shadowy lower-middle-class entrepreneurial group increasingly significant in the expanding commercial economy. The growth of this urban petit-bourgeoisie indicates the evolution, and increasing complexity, of antebellum social structure—a process that affected racial attitudes. Northern whites not only reacted consciously to what they perceived as a growing "race problem," but they also unconsciously developed new assumptions about blacks as class stratification shaped the nation.

Many captains and shipowners in the early republic who hired their own crews thought of themselves as the "better sort" and acted aloof and indifferent to labor in general—black or white. After revenue service officers sealed his personal chest and trunk in 1811, the captain of the modest merchant brig *Hazard* complained that the luggage contained "his Wearing Apparel," and that "he had not been able for many days . . . to make those changes in his dress . . . expected of a Gentleman." Mid-century crimps never postured as "Gentlemen," displaying instead the aggressive egalitarianism and competitiveness of white democrats. The widespread conviction of equality among white men in antebellum America rested in part on a sense of superiority to blacks. Exemplifying this mentality, white crimps became the agents through which the increased salience of race in antebellum America was translated into increasingly restricted employment options for African Americans aboard ship.[37]

Blacks ran crimping establishments as well, but they could not guarantee berths for black sailors. In 1856 there were at least six black boardinghouses in Baltimore sufficiently stable to be listed in the city directory; and black crimps such as Andrew Boston made a living procuring seamen. Black sailors' boardinghouses as a rule, however, were undercapitalized and susceptible to ready closure. Their clientele was poorer than that of white boardinghouses. One hundred and thirty-one white mariners (including officers) deposited an average of $43 each with the American Seamen's Friend Society in 1869, but the deposits of 134 black men that year averaged only $14. Black landlords were less likely than whites to own their premises, and it seems likely—given the seamy aspects of boardinghouse life—that blacks felt more police pressure in the wake of riotous assemblies, noxious sewers, and infamous prostitution. Black shipping masters faced, as one put it, "various obstacles in the way of shipping *coloured* seamen."[38]

The policy of "hiring white first" gained momentum in the maritime industry as a whole at mid-century. Attributing this change "to the prejudice of the whites," a New Bedford selectman observed in 1863 that "the proportion of colored men in the whaling business is not as great now as formerly . . . The proportion gradually diminished until in a majority of cases the cooks and stewards only were colored." By 1869 the British consul in Baltimore was writing to the Foreign Office that "the Shipping Masters and the Boardinghouse Keepers have . . . determined not to ship a white man on board the same vessel with a colored man." Evidence from crew lists in the North suggests that as early as the 1850s, black men who might have preferred the minimal occupational stability and rewards that regular seafaring once offered men of their race were being consciously edged out of the industry.[39]

It is easy to blame the decline of African American seafaring on crimps, the seedy proprietors of down-at-the-heels boardinghouses who traded in men, and who by mid-century dominated the maritime labor market. But the crimps themselves were no *deus ex machina:* no single group ever is. Crimps mediated social and cultural changes in American seaports at mid-century and, in the process, affected seaport society and culture. Crimps emerge not as the cause of black Americans' circumscribed opportunities at sea, but as the exemplar of social changes that reworked the meanings of waged work and race in the Atlantic maritime world. As black sailors' story so clearly shows, the invigorated white supremacy fundamental to the market revolution made the hard times of free blacks even harder.

F OLLOWING the American Revolution, the first generation of freed blacks turned to the sea in unprecedented numbers. Few other work-places welcomed them so readily, and northern black men routinely confronted seafaring perils as they strove to earn a livelihood. The relatively fortunate situation of black mariners came to a close as the market revolution transformed the maritime industries during the antebellum era. Heightened race-consciousness among crimps who hired antebellum sailors and an influx of white immigrants who competed with black men for fewer jobs aboard ship spelled the end of blacks' best sea years. Seafaring remained economically important to some northern blacks in 1865, and it would continue to play a role in black life. The glories of Marcus Garvey's Black Star Line were yet over the horizon, as were Langston Hughes's musings in *The Big Sea.* But within the world of the ship, the black man's position declined. More likely each year after 1830 to be harassed by his white shipmates, thwarted by northern crimps, or incarcerated by southern officials, the antebellum black seafarer lost what little maneuvering room he had. When maritime opportunities nationwide contracted at mid-century, blacks were hit particularly hard. A serious blow was dealt to antebellum African American society as the avenues to self-esteem open to black men were further restricted. In the interim, however, by tapping an international maritime culture that allowed them to "feel as men" in the presence of co-workers and to "presume upon their equality," several generations of black men partially circumvented the racist norms of American society. In the words of Ralph Ellison, a twentieth-century black mariner, they "helped create themselves out of what they found around them."[40]

Blacks' seafaring clearly had a considerable impact on the lives of innumerable black people and thousands of shipboard societies. It also touched black America as a whole. Maritime work meant the most to black America before cotton cultivation wrenched the population to the southwest, isolating more blacks from the influence of the sea; and before general emancipation redefined seafaring within black society. Freedom opened what had been a relatively closed world for slaves, ushering in new possibilities and complicating blacks' social and cultural landscapes. Prior to freedom's jubilee, black sailors were distinguished from the mass of slaves by their cosmopolitanism, and were thus revealing to them. Sailors had long emphasized the particularities, the ambiguities, the oppressions, and the extent of the black diaspora from vantage points denied to most blacks. Emancipation closed the gap.[41]

Transient black sailors in the eighteenth century were citizens of the world who kept other blacks informed of happenings abroad. Tarrying with people of color in London, with stick-fighters in Dominica, or with stevedores in Charleston, enslaved mariners forged a pan-Atlantic African identity through active encounters with other people—both black and white. Among the best traveled people of color, they were central to the process through which early black society constructed and defined itself. Whether under way by their masters' compulsion or their own volition, sailors contributed to a larger sense of black collectivity, and to the cultural hybridization so fundamental in the formation of black America.

For about eighteen thousand free blacks, sea service in the War of 1812 defined what it meant to be free and black—to be armed with and working alongside white sailors, but to remain separate from them because of cultural differences and disparities in social power. Eleven hundred black prisoners of war interacted regularly with white shipmates at Dartmoor Prison, but simultaneously built a black nation-within-a-nation in their own Prison Number Four. That memory, and other knowledge contributed by sailors, long persisted among black people in northern seaports who debated the meaning of blackness in America: sailors voyaging to revolutionary Haiti who became citizens of the nascent black republic and pressed on with a new sense of racial pride and possibilities; a handful of free black captains from the North and upper South who commanded small coasters back and forth across 39° 30' North latitude (the maritime equivalent of the Mason-Dixon line) and established ties between enslaved and free blacks; ten thousand free black northern sailors who languished in southern jails during the era of the Negro Seamen's Acts and, except for the unfortunates sold into slavery, returned to freedom to tell their tales.

These seamen cross-pollinated a host of separate black communities, revealing what separated them, and what they shared. Although most seamen of color had connections to specific communities ashore, such as those in Bermuda, Baltimore, and Boston, they clearly worked in an international world as members of the Atlantic community of color. Communities are not always bounded by locale; indeed, sailors reinforced shared understandings of black community that transcended place. But sailors of color also formed, selected among, and were excluded from a whole variety of black communities. As had been the case at Dartmoor Prison, various social interactions defined sailors' lives, both within and across the color line. Communities of the sacred and the profane existed, as did communities of the politicized and the acquiescent, the urbane and the provincial. Crimps, hustlers, and criminals made their own communities and preyed on others. Stark differences existed between financially successful captains and common black deckhands. Seafarers rarely denied these crucial distinctions, but their cosmopolitan vantage point made them particularly conscious of the fact that all blacks around the Atlantic rim shared a defining history.

Voyaging exposed sailors to a variety of styles and ways of thinking, and as they returned to communities ashore they served as windows on a wider world. Sailors such as Money Vose and John Jea constantly adapted and refashioned themselves as they traveled. These were not marginal men, but men comfortable crossing boundaries. They contributed substantially to the ongoing reformulation of what it meant to be black in America; and their lives reveal clearly how black culture evolved in contact with, yet in separation from, white culture. Like Caribbean and Carolinian market women, and black domestics everywhere who moved easily between black and white worlds, sailors were crucial cultural mediators in the formation of black America.

Sailing ships have had a bad reputation in black America. Ships were the means by which captive ancestors watched Africa recede into the mist, the haunting emblems of the unspeakable Middle Passage. That memory has shadowed the story of Black Jacks who seized liberating possibilities from the obligation and opportunity of life before the mast. The drama of their restless lives was shaped by the fury of the sea and of slaveholders—yet laced with irony. For the very vessels that carried Africans to New World slavery not infrequently became a pipeline to freedom for slaves on the lam. Black men who understood the way of a ship found a degree of protection, liberation, and worldliness at sea.

During the age of slavery, canvas sails whitened Atlantic sealanes, bowing to the breezes as they powered ships full of sugar, tobacco, and cotton that slaves produced but did not enjoy. Black Jacks hoisted and trimmed those sails, and stitched together the ports and peoples of the Atlantic world. They steered for the horizon in search of freedom and a livelihood; and they shaped themselves and black America. To tell their forgotten tale is to unbind another black Prometheus. And for those concerned with the creation of America, Black Jacks' story splices together African American and Atlantic maritime histories, fusing them in ways that storytellers worth their salt can no longer ignore.

TABLES

Note on the Tables

U.S. law required that a list identifying each crew member on every American ship departing on a foreign voyage be deposited at a U.S. customs house. Crew lists specified each sailor's name, place of birth, residence, age, height, hair type, and complexion—but not race. The crew lists I used for this study contained 50,245 names and 28 descriptions of complexion.

The number of sailors referred to as "Indian," "Chinese," "Lascar," "Kanaka," or "South Sea Islander" was very small, so I omitted them from the tables. "Copper" complexions referred to Native Americans or African Americans, but I could usually determine African descent among "copper" men by descriptions of their hair. African Americans' hair was almost always described as "wooly" or "wool."

Sailors described as "black," "African," "Negro," "colored," "sable," "sambo," "mulatto," and "yellow" I determined to be of African descent. White sailors were described as "pale," "white," "light," "fresh," "fair," "sandy," "ruddy," "florid," "sallow," "olive," "swarthy," "chestnut," and "dark." Considerable cross-referencing of hair and of the complexions of the same men on different lists revealed that "dark" and "chestnut" almost invariably referred to white men, as "yellow" did to men of African descent.

The most problematic description of complexion was "brown." Deeply tanned by years outdoors, many men who were racially "white" were described as "brown" on the crew lists. But men of African descent were also described as "brown." Given this ambivalence, I did not classify "brown" sailors by race unless corroborating data were available. My intuition is that this omission ignored more black sailors than white ones. Thus the percentage of African American sailors is probably slightly understated in Table 1.

TABLE 1. Percentages of African American and white seamen in the crews of American ships, 1803–1866

Year	Berths held by African Americans (%)	Berths held by whites (%)	All berths
	PROVIDENCE		
1803–1804	22.0	78.0	723
1807	23.0	77.0	381
1808	15.5	84.5	245
1810	21.5	78.5	683
1816	21.6	78.4	333
1818	18.7	81.3	609
1820	23.0	77.0	456
1822	19.0	81.0	788
1825	23.8	76.2	554
1829	23.3	76.7	459
1830	18.0	82.0	396
1832	22.5	77.5	517
1834	29.0	71.0	543
1836	30.5	69.5	246
1839	20.0	80.0	440
1840	16.0	84.0	361
1844	11.4	88.6	369
1846	15.0	85.0	342
1850	7.5	92.5	200
1853	11.0	89.0	277
1856	9.0	91.0	242
	NEW YORK		
1803–1806	17.1	82.9	561
1818–1819	17.4	82.6	688
1825	18.2	81.8	734
1835	13.8	86.2	523
1840	8.3	91.7	1,407
1846	6.9	93.1	686

TABLE 1 (*continued*)

Year	Berths held by African Americans (%)	Berths held by whites (%)	All berths
1856	7.6	92.4	499
1866	4.6	95.4	3,830

PHILADELPHIA

Year	Berths held by African Americans (%)	Berths held by whites (%)	All berths
1803	17.4	82.6	811
1810	22.4	77.6	1,047
1820	18.4	81.6	1,026
1825	19.5	80.5	1,083
1830	17.0	83.0	862
1838	16.6	83.3	946
1840	15.4	84.6	643
1846	18.0	82.0	1,039
1850	13.2	86.8	1,127
1853	17.0	83.0	1,029

BALTIMORE

Year	Berths held by African Americans (%)	Berths held by whites (%)	All berths
1806	14.5	85.5	1,137
1812*	17.0	83.0	4,704
1816	14.7	85.3	1,385
1835	13.0	87.0	182
1843	14.5	85.5	1,316
1852	15.0	85.0	1,312
1857	13.0	87.0	1,714
1866	12.7	87.3	1,555

SAVANNAH

Year	Berths held by African Americans (%)	Berths held by whites (%)	All berths
1803	13.0	87.0	367
1811	14.5	85.5	565
1817	15.0	85.0	693
1819	12.0	88.0	730
1821	14.0	86.0	693
1827	14.0	86.0	498

TABLE 1 (*continued*)

Year	Berths held by African Americans (%)	Berths held by whites (%)	All berths
1828	10.0	90.0	318
1829	15.0	85.0	419
1830	9.0	91.0	593
1833	4.0	96.0	245
1834	8.0	92.0	229
1835	3.0	97.0	174
1836	2.0	98.0	240
NEW ORLEANS			
1804*	16.4	83.6	585
1805*	15.8	84.2	1,916
1807*	17.0	83.0	1,802
1808*	14.1	85.9	431
1817*	22.4	77.6	2,629
1821*	14.0	86.0	3,226
1825*	15.8	84.2	4,184
1829*	11.6	88.4	5,906
1830*	10.7	89.3	6,120
1832*	9.8	90.2	5,340
1834*	10.1	89.9	7,056
1836*	9.3	90.7	9,223
1839*	7.8	92.2	10,522
1840	10.8	89.2	1,171
1843	3.0	97.0	1,339
1845	1.3	98.7	1,520
1851	1.0	99.0	1,437
1855	7.3	92.7	1,225
1860	3.0	97.0	1,482

Sources: Providence crew lists, U.S. Customs House Papers, Providence, R.I., RG 28, Manuscript collection, RIHS; New York, Philadelphia, Baltimore, Savannah, and New Orleans crew lists, Records of the U.S. Customs Service, RG 36, NA.

* Data from Martha Putney, *Black Sailors* (Westport, Conn.: Greenwood Press, 1987), table 1, p. 120, table 2, p. 121.

TABLE 2. Percentages of African American seamen working on ships with all–African American crews (except officers)

Year	Number of African American seamen sampled	African American seamen working in all–African American crews (%)
PROVIDENCE		
1803–1804	160	27.0
1820	105	9.0
1830	71	18.0
1836	75	41.0
1839	89	20.0
1840	58	7.0
1853	30	0.0
1856	22	0.0
NEW YORK		
1803–1806	96	9.3
1818–1819	120	15.8
1825	133	7.5
1835	72	22.2
1840	117	7.6
1846	47	0.0
1856	38	10.5
BALTIMORE		
1806	176	8.0
1816	204	5.4
1843	191	13.6
1852	198	32.8
1857	223	39.9
1866	198	34.3

Sources: Providence crew lists, U.S. Customs House Papers, Providence, R.I., RG 28, RIHS; New York crew lists, Records of the U.S. Customs Service, RG 36, NA; Baltimore crew lists, Records of the U.S. Customs Service, RG 36, NA.

TABLE 3. Seamen's ages

Ages	1803 Black	1803 White	1830 Black	1830 White	1850 Black	1850 White
			PHILADELPHIA			
To 19	10.8%	18.0%	8.9%	20.1%	5.7%	—
20–29	62.5	62.8	47.9	45.4	37.5	—
30–39	20.0	16.2	30.2	24.2	30.7	—
40–49	5.0	2.3	7.5	8.3	20.4	—
50+	1.7	0.7	5.5	2.0	5.7	—
	100.0%	100.0%	100.0%	100.0%	100.0%	—
N	120	513	146	566	88	—
			PROVIDENCE			
To 19	15.0%	30.0%	11.0%	22.5%	—	22.0%
20–29	62.0	54.5	41.0	55.5	60.0	53.0
30–39	17.0	12.0	35.0	16.0	33.0	19.5
40–49	6.0	3.0	11.0	5.0	7.0	5.0
50+	—	0.5	2.0	1.0	—	0.5
	100.0%	100.0%	100.0%	100.0%	100.0%	100.0%
N	48	167	46	157	15	153

Sources: Providence crew lists, U.S. Customs House Papers, Providence, R.I., RG 28, RIHS; Philadelphia crew lists, Records of the U.S. Customs Service, RG 36, NA.

NOTES

Abbreviations

AACP Afro-American Communities Project, National Museum of
American History, Smithsonian Institution

AHR *American Historical Review*

BPL Boston Public Library

FSSP Freedmen and Southern Society Project, University of Maryland,
College Park

JAH *Journal of American History*

MdHR Maryland Hall of Records, Annapolis

MdHS Maryland Historical Society, Baltimore

MHS Massachusetts Historical Society, Boston

MSA Massachusetts State Archives, Boston

MSM G. W. Blount-White Library, Mystic Seaport Museum, Mystic,
Connecticut

NA National Archives, Washington

NBFPL New Bedford Free Public Library, New Bedford, Massachusetts

ODHS Old Dartmouth Historical Society, New Bedford, Massachusetts

PEM Peabody Essex Museum, Salem, Massachusetts

RIHS Rhode Island Historical Society, Providence

SCDAH South Carolina Department of Archives and History, Columbia

USC Caroliniana Library, University of South Carolina, Columbia

WMQ *William and Mary Quarterly*

Introduction

1. Frederick Douglass, *Life and Times of Frederick Douglass, Written By Himself: His Early Life As A Slave, His Escape From Bondage, And His*

Complete History (New York, 1892; reprint, New York: Macmillan Publishing Company, 1962), pp. 125, 199.

2. Ibid., p. 199.

3. *Virginia Gazette*, June 12, 1779, in *Runaway Slave Advertisements: A Documentary History from the 1730s to 1790*, comp. Lathan A. Windley (4 vols., Westport, Conn.: Greenwood Press, 1983), vol. 2, pp. 126–127; Charles Ball, *Fifty Years in Chains: Or, The Life of an American Slave* (New York: H. Dayton, 1858), p. 418.

4. *The Black Abolitionist Papers*, ed. C. Peter Ripley (5 vols.; Chapel Hill: University of North Carolina Press, 1985), vol. 1, p. 191.

5. John Jea, *The Life, History, and Unparalleled Sufferings of John Jea, the African Preacher* in *Black Itinerants of the Gospel: The Narratives of John Jea and George White*, ed. Graham Russell Hodges (Madison, Wis.: Madison House, 1993), pp. 1, 126, 128.

6. *Maryland Gazette*, July 28, 1785, in Windley, *Runaway Slave Advertisements*, vol. 2, pp. 154–155.

7. William P. Powell to William Lloyd Garrison, Nov. 10, 1853, Garrison Papers, Rare Book Room, BPL.

8. "Negroes Protest Against Taxation Without Representation, 1780," in *A Documentary History of the Negro People in the United States*, ed. Herbert Aptheker (2 vols., New York: Citadel Press, 1951), vol. 1, p. 15; "Protest Against Kidnapping And The Slave Trade," ibid., vol. 1, p. 21.

1. The Emergence of Black Sailors in Plantation America

1. *A Narrative of the Uncommon Sufferings, and Surprising Deliverance of Briton Hammon, A Negro Man—Servant to General Winslow, Of Marshfield in New England* (Boston: Green and Russell, 1760), in *Early Negro Writing*, ed. Dorothy Porter (Boston: Beacon Press, 1971), pp. 522–528, quotations from pp. 522–523. Eighteen percent of male slaves in Suffolk County, Massachusetts, were owned by mariners; 24 percent were owned by shipwrights, merchants, or farmers who also owned small coastal vessels. N = 51 male slaves. Suffolk County Probate Records, 1740–1744, MSA.

2. Vittore Carpaccio, "Scenes from the Life of St. Ursula," in Jean Divisse and Michel Mollat, *The Image of the Black in Western Art*, vol. 2, *From the Early Christian Era to the "Age of Discovery,"* part 2, *Africans in the Christian Ordinance of the World (Fourteenth to Sixteenth Centuries)* (New York: William Morrow & Co., 1979), p. 190; J. E. Harris, "The African Diaspora in the Old and New Worlds," in *Africa from the Sixteenth to the Eighteenth Century*, vol. 5 of *General History of Africa* (Berkeley: UNESCO,

1992), pp. 113–136; J. F. Rippy, "The Negro and Spanish Pioneers in the New World," *Journal of Negro History* 6 (1921), pp. 183–189; Helen Tunnicliff Catterall, *Judicial Cases Concerning American Slavery and the Negro* (5 vols., Washington: Carnegie Institution, 1926–1937), vol. 1, p. 76; Ira Berlin, "From Creole to African: Atlantic Creoles and the Origins of African-American Society in Mainland North America," *WMQ*, 3rd series, 53 (April 1996), pp. 251–288. On slaveowning versus slave societies and the influence of race in each, see Philip D. Morgan, "British Encounters with Africans and African-Americans, circa 1600–1780," in *Strangers within the Realm: Cultural Margins of the First British Empire* (Chapel Hill: Institute of Early American History and Culture, 1991), pp. 157–219, esp. pp. 163–164.

3. Philip D. Curtin, *The Rise and Fall of the Plantation Complex: Essays in Atlantic History* (Cambridge, England: Cambridge University Press, 1990), pp. 11–13; Sidney W. Mintz, *Caribbean Transformations* (Baltimore: Johns Hopkins University Press, 1974), pp. 59–82, quotation from pp. 64–65; Charles Wilson, *England's Apprenticeship, 1603–1763* (New York: St. Martin's Press, 1965); Ralph Davis, *The Rise of the English Shipping Industry in the Seventeenth and Eighteenth Centuries* (London, 1962); John J. McCusker and Russell R. Menard, *The Economy of British America, 1607–1789* (Chapel Hill: Institute of Early American History and Culture, 1985), pp. 5–90; Barbara L. Solow, "Slavery and Colonization," in *Slavery and the Rise of the Atlantic System*, ed. Barbara L. Solow (Cambridge, England: Cambridge University Press, 1991), pp. 21–42.

4. Wilson, *England's Apprenticeship*, p. 169.

5. Mintz, *Caribbean Transformations*, p. 64; Eric Williams, *From Columbus to Castro: The History of the Caribbean, 1492–1969* (New York: Harper and Row, 1971), p. 148; Philip D. Curtin, *The Atlantic Slave Trade: A Census* (Madison: University of Wisconsin Press, 1969), table 65, p. 216. Considerable controversy exists over the total number of Africans shipped to the Americas. For refinement of Curtin's calculations of approximately 9.5 million, see Paul E. Lovejoy, "The Volume of the Atlantic Slave Trade: A Synthesis," *Journal of African History* 23 (1982). For substantially larger estimates, see *The Atlantic Slave Trade*, ed. Joseph E. Inikori and Stanley L. Engerman (Durham, N.C.: Duke University Press, 1992).

6. Curtin, *Rise and Fall of the Plantation Complex*, pp. 12–13, 47. *Sailors v. Daniel*, Jan. 25, 1726, Mass. Vice-Admiralty Court, MSA; *Sailors v. Cumberland*, Sept. 12, 1718, ibid.; *Fall v. Burt*, May 20, 1729, ibid.

7. *Massachusetts Archives*, vol. 61, doc. 357 (1690), MSA; ibid., vol. 40, doc. 309 (1694), MSA.

8. Ibid., vol. 9, doc. 151 (May 1, 1703), MSA.

9. Ibid., vol. 9, docs. 187–188 (1724), MSA.

10. The literature on piracy is vast. I have relied on John Esquemeling [Alexandre Olivier Exquemelin], *The Buccaneers of America* (London, 1684; reprint, New York: Charles Scribner's Sons, 1893); Daniel Defoe, *A General History of the Pyrates,* ed. Manuel Schonhorn (London, 1724; reprint, Columbia, S.C.: University of South Carolina Press, 1972); Hugh F. Rankin, *The Golden Age of Piracy* (Williamsburg, Va.: Colonial Williamsburg, 1969); Robert C. Ritchie, *Captain Kidd and the War against the Pirates* (Cambridge, Mass.: Harvard University Press, 1986); Marcus Rediker, *Between the Devil and the Deep Blue Sea: Merchant Seamen, Pirates, and the Anglo-American Maritime World, 1700–1750* (Cambridge, England: Cambridge University Press, 1987), pp. 254–287.

11. Rediker, *Devil and Deep Blue Sea,* pp. 254–257; Rankin, *Golden Age of Piracy,* p. 82.

12. *The Colonial Records of North Carolina,* ed. William L. Saunders (30 vols., Raleigh: P. M. Hale, State Printer, 1886–1914), vol. 2, pp. 324–327; Defoe, *General History of the Pyrates,* pp. 82, 245, 298, 593–598.

13. Defoe, *General History of the Pyrates,* pp. 211, 244, 587.

14. *Privateering and Piracy in the Colonial Period: Illustrative Documents,* ed. J. Franklin Jameson (New York: Macmillan Co., 1923), p. 222; Ritchie, *Captain Kidd,* p. 84; Defoe, *General History of the Pyrates,* pp. 213, 423; Rankin, *Golden Age of Piracy,* pp. 33–34.

15. Luce Petition, July 27, 1727, Mass. Vice-Admiralty Records, MSA; Rediker, *Devil and Deep Blue Sea,* p. 283.

16. Rediker, *Devil and Deep Blue Sea,* p. 260; Ritchie, *Captain Kidd,* p. 161; Rankin, *Golden Age of Piracy,* p. 148; Esquemeling, *Buccaneers of America,* pp. 81–82, 189, 250.

17. William Williams, *Mr. Penrose. The Journal of Penrose, Seaman,* ed. David Howard Dickason (Bloomington: University of Indiana Press, 1969), pp. 17, 79.

18. Brian S. Kerby, "The Loss and Recovery of the Schooner *Amity:* An Episode in Salem Maritime History," *New England Quarterly* 62 (Dec. 1989), pp.553–560; *Massachusetts Centinel,* Sept. 14, 1785.

19. *Antigua Act, No. 351, of 1773,* quoted in Elsa V. Goveia, *Slave Society in the British Leeward Islands at the End of the Eighteenth Century* (New Haven: Yale University Press, 1965), p. 162.

20. David Barry Gaspar, *Bondmen and Rebels: A Study of Master-Slave Relations in Antigua with Implications for Colonial British America* (Baltimore: Johns Hopkins University Press, 1985), pp. 107–108; Edward Long, *History*

of Jamaica (3 vols., London: T. Lowndes, 1774), vol. 1, pp. 380–381; Goveia, *Slave Society in the British Leeward Islands,* p. 147.

21. Long, *History of Jamaica,* vol. 1, pp. 496, 504; Richard Pares, *A West India Fortune* (London and New York: Longmans, Green, 1950), p. 354, n. 29.

22. B. W. Higman, *Slave Populations of the British Caribbean, 1807–1834* (Baltimore: Johns Hopkins University Press, 1984), table S7.1, pp. 550–551, combined with sex-ratio data, p. 116.

23. Deposition of Nathaniel Millbury (1762), Maryland Vice-Admiralty Court Minutes 1754–1773, MdHR, p. 95; *South Carolina Gazette* (July 8, 1784), in Windley, *Runaway Slave Advertisements,* vol. 3, p. 739; J. Stewart, *A View of the Past and Present State of the Island of Jamaica* (Edinburgh: Oliver and Boyd, 1823), pp. 124–125.

24. *Naval Documents of the American Revolution,* ed. William Bell Clark (9 vols., Washington: U.S. Government Printing Office, 1964–1986), vol. 6, pp. 295–296.

25. Ibid., p. 263; Gaspar, *Bondmen and Rebels,* p. 111, n. 51; Philip Morgan, "Black Life in Eighteenth-Century Charleston," *Perspectives in American History* 1 (1984), pp. 187–232, esp. p. 198; Paul Edwards and James Walvin, *Black Personalities in the Era of the Slave Trade* (Baton Rouge: Louisiana State University Press, 1983), pp. 16–19.

26. *Williams v. Brown,* 1802, in Catterall, *Judicial Cases Concerning the Negro,* vol. 1, pp. 5–6, 23–25. For a similar case in Washington, see "Simmons v. Gird," 22 *Federal Cases* 157 (1814).

27. Philip D. Morgan, "Colonial South Carolina Runaways: Their Significance for Slave Culture," *Slavery & Abolition* 6 (Dec. 1985), pp. 57–78, esp. p. 65; Converse D. Clowse, "Shipowning and Shipbuilding in Colonial South Carolina: An Overview," *American Neptune* 44 (Fall 1984), pp. 221–244, esp. p. 243; *South Carolina Gazette,* Jan. 21, 1772, in Windley, *Runaway Slave Advertisements,* vol. 3, p. 308.

28. *The Letterbook of Robert Pringle,* ed. Walter B. Edgar (Columbia: University of South Carolina Press, 1972), pp. 173, 471, 490–492, 566, 777. *Papers of Henry Laurens,* ed. Philip M. Hamer (12 vols., Columbia: University of South Carolina Press, 1968–1990), vol. 1, pp. 111, 313, 336.

29. Parry to Colonial Office, in Ruth Anna Fisher, "Manuscript Materials Bearing on the Negro in British Archives," *Journal of Negro History* 27 (Jan. 1942), pp. 83–93; quotation from p. 88.

30. Morgan, "Colonial South Carolina Runaways," *Slavery & Abolition* 6 (Dec. 1985), p. 64; *South Carolina Gazette and General Advertiser* (July 27–July 29, 1784), in Windley, *Runaway Slave Advertisements,* vol. 3, p. 741.

31. *South Carolina and American General Gazette,* Nov. 24 to Dec. 8, 1775, in

Windley, *Runaway Slave Advertisements*, vol. 3, p. 477; Sylvia R. Frey, *Water from the Rock: Black Resistance in a Revolutionary Age* (Princeton: Princeton University Press, 1991), pp. 57–58, 91; Leila Sellers, *Charleston Business on the Eve of the American Revolution* (Chapel Hill: University of North Carolina Press, 1934), p. 67.

32. Gerald W. Mullin, *Flight and Rebellion: Slave Resistance in Eighteenth-Century Virginia* (New York: Oxford University Press, 1972), pp. 94, 95, 98. Arthur Pierce Middleton, *Tobacco Coast: A Maritime History of the Chesapeake Bay in the Colonial Era* (Newport News, Va.: Mariners' Museum, 1953; reprint, Baltimore: Johns Hopkins University Press, 1984), pp. 135, 288–289; Allan Kulikoff, *Tobacco and Slaves: The Development of Southern Cultures, 1680–1800* (Chapel Hill: Institute of Early American History and Culture, 1986), pp. 96, 107.

33. Mullin, *Flight and Rebellion*, p. 87.

34. Middleton, *Tobacco Coast*, pp. 279–282; David C. Klingaman, "The Development of the Coastwise Trade of Virginia in the Late Colonial Period," *Virginia Magazine of History and Biography* 77 (1969), pp. 26–45.

35. Edward C. Papenfuse, *In Pursuit of Profit: The Annapolis Merchants in the Era of the American Revolution, 1763–1805* (Baltimore: Johns Hopkins University Press, 1975), pp. 254, 257–262; Thomas J. Wertenbaker, *Norfolk: Historic Southern Port* (Durham, N.C.: Duke University Press, 1931), p. 102; Bills of Lading, 1774, section 38, Carter Family Papers, Virginia Historical Society; *Virginia Gazette*, June 12, 1778, in Windley, *Runaway Slave Advertisements*, vol. 1, p. 271.

36. Middleton, *Tobacco Coast*, pp. 287–309, quotation from pp. 305–306; *Maryland Gazette*, April 29, 1762, in Windley, *Runaway Slave Advertisements*, vol. 2, p. 44; *Maryland Gazette*, Dec. 1, 1763, ibid., p. 52.

37. "Ship Registers for the Port of Philadelphia, 1726–1775," *Pennsylvania Magazine of History and Biography* 26 (1902), pp. 470–471; Gary Nash, "Slaves and Slaveowners in Philadelphia," *WMQ*, 3rd series, 30 (1973), pp. 223–256.

38. John Lax and William Pencak, "The Knowles Riot and the Crisis of the 1740s in Massachusetts," *Perspectives in American History* 10 (1976), pp. 163–216, quotation from p. 197.

39. "Free Negroes and Mulattos," *Massachusetts Legislative Documents, 1817–1822*, no. 46, pp. 5–16, Massachusetts State Library, Boston; Louis P. Mazur, "Slavery in Eighteenth-Century Rhode Island: Evidence from the Census of 1774," *Slavery & Abolition* 6 (Sept. 1985), pp. 140–145; Agreement between Aaron Sheffield and Nathaniel Briggs, Sept. 6, 1775, Reverend Pardon Grey Seabury Collection, Special Collections, NBFPL; Valerie Cunningham, "The First Blacks of Portsmouth," *Historical New Hampshire* 44

(Winter 1989), pp. 181–201; Ralph E. Lukar, "'Under Our Own Vine and Fig Tree': From African Unionism to Black Denominationalism in Newport, Rhode Island, 1760–1876," *Slavery & Abolition* 12 (Sept. 1991), pp. 23–48, quotation from p. 28.

40. Suffolk County Probate Inventories, boxes 78–84, 1740–1744, MSA; Fanueil, inventory no. 7877, ibid.; Daniel Vickers, "Nantucket Whalemen in the Deep-Sea Fishery: The Changing Anatomy of an Early American Labor Force," *Journal of American History* 72 (Sept. 1985), pp. 277–296; John A. Sainsbury, "Indian Labor in Early Rhode Island," *New England Quarterly* 48 (Sept. 1975), pp. 378–393.

41. Hammon, *Narrative*, in Porter, *Early Negro Writing*, p. 523.

42. Quoted by Jesse Lemisch, "Jack Tar in the Streets: Merchant Seamen in the Politics of Revolutionary America," *WMQ*, 3rd series, 25 (1968), p. 375; *Maryland Gazette*, July 28, 1785, in Windley, *Runaway Slave Advertisements*, vol. 2, pp. 154–155; *South Carolina Gazette*, April 11, 1771, ibid., vol. 3, p. 299.

43. *Daily Advertiser*, Oct. 11, 1800, quoted in Shane White, *Somewhat More Independent: The End of Slavery in New York City, 1770–1810* (Athens: University of Georgia Press, 1991), p. 127.

44. *Sailors v. Oliver*, Jan. 1, 1742, Mass. Vice-Admiralty Records, MSA; Samuel Welles to Capt. Hector McNeill, May 2, 1777, quoted in Richard E. Winslow, *"Wealth and Honour": Portsmouth during the Golden Age of Privateering, 1775–1815* (Portsmouth, N.H.: Peter Randall Publisher, 1988), p. 27.

45. J. R. Hutchinson, *The Press-Gang Afloat and Ashore* (New York: E. P. Dutton, 1914), p. 82; N. A. M. Rodger, *The Wooden World: An Anatomy of the Georgian Navy* (Annapolis: Naval Institute Press, 1986), p. 159. Richard Pares minimized blacks' presence in "The Manning of the Navy in the West Indies, 1702–1763," *Transactions of the Royal Historical Society* 20 (1937), pp. 31–33.

46. *Papers of Henry Laurens*, vol. 1, p. 336. On impressment, begin with G. J. Marcus, *Heart of Oak: A Survey of British Seapower in the Georgian Era* (London, 1975), pp. 99–114; Rediker, *Devil and Deep Blue Sea*, pp. 32–34; J. H. Parry, *Trade and Dominion: The European Overseas Empires in the Eighteenth Century* (New York: Praeger Publishers, 1971), pp. 216–217; James Fulton Zimmerman, *Impressment of American Seamen* (New York: Columbia University Press, 1925).

47. *The Colonial Records of North Carolina*, ed. William L. Saunders (Raleigh: P. M. Hale, State Printer, 1886), vol. 2, pp. 702–703; *Records of the Vice-Admiralty Court in Rhode Island, 1716–1752*, ed. Dorothy S. Towle (Washington, D.C.: American Historical Association, 1936; reprint, Millwood, N.Y., 1975), pp. 397–398.

48. Nathaniel Uring, *Voyages and Travels of Capt. Nathaniel Uring* (London,

1726), p. 165; Olaudah Equiano, *The Interesting Narrative of the Life of Olaudah Equiano*, in *The Classic Slave Narratives*, ed. Henry Louis Gates, Jr. (New York: Mentor, 1987), pp. 50, 82–83, 96–107, 149–166.

49. Rodger, *Wooden World*, pp. 113–137, 160–161.

50. Jameson, *Privateering and Piracy*, pp. 384, 418; Equiano, *Life of Olaudah Equiano*, p. 57; Rodger, *Wooden World*, pp. 27, 28, 113, 160.

51. Philadelphia crew lists, 1803, RG 36, NA; Baltimore crew lists, 1806, RG 36, NA; Salem, Massachusetts, crew lists, 1803, 1804, 1810, RG 36, NA (Boston branch); Providence crew lists, Customs House Papers, RG 28, RIHS. *N* of African American sailors each year = 100 to 105.

52. *Massachusetts Archives*, vol. 244, folio 319, doc. 444 (1732), MSA; *Gazette of the State of South Carolina*, March 3, 1779, in Windley, *Runaway Slave Advertisements*, vol. 3, p. 366; *Naval Documents of the American Revolution*, vol. 8, p. 894; Equiano, *Life of Olaudah Equiano*, p. 47; John Marrant, *A Narrative of the Lord's Wonderful Dealings With John Marrant, A Black*, in Porter, *Early Negro Writing*, pp. 430, 444; *Ramblin' Jack: The Journal of Captain John Cremer*, ed. R. Reynall Bellamy (London: J. Cape, 1936), p. 39; Harold D. Langley, "The Negro in the Navy and the Merchant Service, 1798–1860," *Journal of Negro History* 52 (Oct. 1967), p. 277.

53. Hammon, *Narrative*, in Porter, *Early Negro Writing*, p. 528.

54. *Virginia Gazette*, May 2, 1751, in Windley, *Runaway Slave Advertisements*, vol. 1, p. 20; James Clifford, *The Predicament of Culture: Twentieth-Century Ethnography, Literature, and Art* (Cambridge, Mass.: Harvard University Press, 1988), p. 344.

55. *Virginia Argus*, June 23, 1802; ibid., April 9, 1796.

56. Hammon, *Narrative* (Boston, 1760); James Albert Ukawsaw Gronniosaw, *A Narrative of the Most Remarkable Particulars in the Life of James Albert Ukawsaw Gronniosaw, an African Prince, as Related by Himself* (Bath, England, c. 1770; reprint, Nendeln: Kraus Reprints); Olaudah Equiano, *Life of Olaudah Equiano* (London, 1789); John Marrant, *Narrative of the Lord's Wonderful Dealings with John Marrant, a Black* (London, 1785); Venture Smith, *A Narrative of the Life and Adventures of Venture, a Native of Africa* (New London, Conn., 1798); Boston King, "Memoirs of the Life of Boston King, a Black Preacher," *The Methodist Magazine* (London, March, April, May, June, 1798), pp. 105–110, 157–161, 209–213, 261–265.

57. George Pinckard, *Notes on the West Indies* (London: Longman, Hurst, Rees, and Orme, 1806), vol. 2, pp. 75–76; Morgan, "Colonial South Carolina Runaways," *Slavery & Abolition* 6 (Dec. 1985), p. 71; Billy G. Smith, *"The Lower Sort": Philadelphia's Laboring People, 1750–1800* (Ithaca: Cornell University Press, 1990), p. 157.

58. Equiano, *Life of Olaudah Equiano*, pp. 1, 12, 17, 51, 182.

59. James Forten to Paul Cuffe, Jan. 25, 1817, in *Classical Black Nationalism: From the American Revolution to Marcus Garvey*, ed. Wilson Jeremiah Moses (New York: New York University Press, 1996), pp. 50–52; quotation from p. 51.

60. *South Carolina Gazette*, Nov. 10–17, 1758, in Windley, *Runaway Slave Advertisements*, vol. 3, p. 167; *The Horrors of Slavery and Other Writings by Robert Wedderburn*, ed. Iain McCalman (New York: Marcus Wiener Publishing, 1991). Blacks' communication and consciousness are treated by Julius Sherrard Scott, "The Common Wind: Currents of Afro-American Communication in the Era of the Haitian Revolution" (Ph.D. diss., Duke University, 1986); Paul Gilroy, *The Black Atlantic: Modernity and Double Consciousness* (Cambridge, Mass.: Harvard University Press, 1993), pp. 1–40.

61. Scott, "The Common Wind," p. 299.

62. *South Carolina Gazette*, June 25–July 2, 1763, in Windley, *Runaway Slave Advertisements*, vol. 3, p. 231; *South Carolina Gazette and General Advertiser*, Aug. 12–16, 1783, ibid., vol. 3, p. 719.

63. Scott, "The Common Wind," pp. 59–113, esp. p. 75; N. A. T. Hall, "Maritime Maroons: *Grand Marronage* from the Danish West Indies," *WMQ*, 3rd series, 42 (Oct. 1985), p. 489; Jane Landers, "Gracia Real de Santa Teresa de Mose: A Free Black Town in Spanish Colonial Florida," *AHR* 95 (Feb. 1990), pp. 9–30.

64. *A Black Woman's Odyssey Through Russia and Jamaica: The Narrative of Nancy Prince*, ed. Ronald G. Walters (Boston, 1850; reprint, New York: Marcus Wiener, 1990), pp. 2–3.

65. Ibid., pp. 2–3; Robert Rantoul, "Negro Slavery in Massachusetts," *Historical Collections of the Essex Institute* 24 (1887), pp. 81–108.

66. *Black Woman's Odyssey*, p. 2.

2. African Roots of Black Seafaring

1. *Maryland Gazette*, Aug. 25, 1780, in *Runaway Slave Advertisements: A Documentary History from the 1730s to 1790*, comp. Lathan A. Windley (4 vols., Westport, Conn.: Greenwood Press, 1983), vol. 2, pp. 126–127; *Virginia Gazette*, June 12, 1779, ibid., vol. 1, p. 203.

2. *South Carolina Gazette*, Jan. 12–19, 1738, in Windley, *Runaway Slave Advertisements*, vol. 3, p. 30. This interpretation of a shared African cultural orientation follows Sidney W. Mintz and Richard Price, *An Anthropological Approach to the Afro-American Past: A Caribbean Perspective* (Philadelphia: Institute for the Study of Human Issues, Occasional Paper 2, 1976).

3. Robert Farris Thompson, *Flash of the Spirit: African and Afro-American*

Art and Philosophy (New York: Random House, 1983); Wyatt MacGaffey, "The West in Congolese Experience," in *Africa and the West: Intellectual Responses to European Culture,* ed. Philip D. Curtin (Madison: University of Wisconsin Press, 1972), pp. 51–56; Wyatt MacGaffey, "Kongo and the King of the Americans," *Journal of Modern African Studies* 6 (1968), pp. 171–181; Wyatt MacGaffey, "Cultural Roots of Kongo Prophetism," *History of Religions* 17 (1977), pp. 186–187; Michael Mullin, *Africa in America: Slave Acculturation and Resistance in the American South and the British Caribbean, 1736–1831* (Urbana: University of Illinois Press, 1992).

4. Jean-Pierre Chauveau, "Une histoire maritime africaine est-elle possible? Historiographie et histoire de la navigation et de la pêche africaines à la côte occidental depuis le XVe siècle," *Cahiers d'études africaines* 26 (1986), pp. 173–235; Walter Rodney, *A History of the Upper Guinea Coast, 1545–1800* (Oxford: Clarendon Press, 1970), pp. 1–121; John Thornton, *Africa and Africans in the Making of the Atlantic World, 1400–1680* (Cambridge, England: Cambridge University Press, 1992), pp. 1–71, quotation from p. 19.

5. Stewart C. Malloy, "Traditional African Watercraft: A New Look," in *Blacks in Science, Ancient and Modern,* ed. Ivan Van Sertima (New Brunswick: Transaction Books, 1984), pp. 163–176, quotation from pp. 164–165; Robert Smith, "The Canoe in West African History," *Journal of African History* 11 (1970), p. 518; William Bosman, *A New and Accurate Description of the Coast of Guinea, Divided Into the Gold, the Slave, and the Ivory Coasts* (1705; reprint, New York: Barnes and Noble, 1967), pp. 43, 129.

6. Smith, "Canoe in West African History," pp. 515–533; Rodney, *History Upper Guinea Coast,* p. 78; Philip D. Curtin, *Economic Change in Precolonial Africa: Senegambia in the Era of the Slave Trade* (Madison: University of Wisconsin Press, 1975), p. 98.

7. Nathaniel Uring, *Voyages and Travels of Captain Nathaniel Uring* (London, 1727), pp. 137–138.

8. Smith, "Canoe in West African History," pp. 519–520.

9. Rodney, *History Upper Guinea Coast,* pp. 16–18; Charles Ball, *Fifty Years in Chains; Or, The Life of an American Slave* (New York, 1859), p. 198; Edward Long, *The History of Jamaica* (London, 1774), vol. 3, pp. 736–737; Monica Schuler, *"Alas, Alas, Kongo": A Social History of Indentured African Immigration into Jamaica, 1841–1865* (Baltimore: Johns Hopkins University Press, 1980), pp. 73–74.

10. George E. Brooks, Jr., *Yankee Traders, Old Coasters, and African Middlemen: A History of American Legitimate Trade with West Africa in the Nineteenth Century* (Boston: Boston University Press, 1970), pp. 224–225; Ronald W. Davis, "Historical Outline of the Kru Coast, Liberia, 1500 to the Present"

(Ph.D. diss., Indiana University, 1968), p. 51; Margaret Washington Creel, "Gullah Attitudes toward Life and Death," in *Africanisms in American Culture,* ed. Joseph E. Holloway (Bloomington: University of Indiana Press, 1990), pp. 69–97, esp. p. 69.

11. Smith, "Canoe in West African History," pp. 516–517; Robin Law, "Trade and Politics behind the Slave Coast: The Lagoon Traffic and the Rise of Lagos, 1500–1800," *Journal of African History* 24 (1983), pp. 321–324.

12. David Henige, "John Kabes of Komenda: An Early African Entrepreneur and State Builder," *Journal of African History* 18 (1977), pp. 1–3.

13. Curtin, *Economic Change in Precolonial Africa,* pp. 95–100.

14. Rodney, *History Upper Guinea Coast,* pp. 1–8, 77–79; John Atkins, *A Voyage to Guinea, Brasil, and the West Indies* (London, 1735), in *Documents Illustrative of the Slave Trade to America,* ed. Elizabeth Donnan (Washington: Carnegie Institution, 1930–1935), vol. 2, pp. 264–265, 277; Nicholas Owen, *Journal of a Slave-Dealer: A View of Some Remarkable Axcedents in the Life of Nics. Owen on the Coast of Africa and America From the Year 1746 to the Year 1757,* ed. Eveline Martin (Boston and New York: Houghton Mifflin, 1930), p. 39.

15. Curtin, *Economic Change in Precolonial Africa,* pp. 95–100; Rodney, *History Upper Guinea Coast,* pp. 77–79; Daniel Defoe, *A General History of the Pyrates,* ed. Manuel Schonhorn (London, 1724; reprint, Columbia: University of South Carolina Press, 1972), p. 247.

16. *Naval Documents of the American Revolution,* ed. William James Morgan (9 vols., Washington: U.S. Government Printing Office, 1964–1986), vol. 9, p. 986; Richard Rathbone, "Some Thoughts on Resistance to Enslavement in West Africa," *Slavery and Abolition* 6 (Dec. 1985), pp. 17–18, 20; Daniel P. Mannix and Malcolm Cowley, *Black Cargoes: A History of the Atlantic Slave Trade, 1518–1865* (New York: Viking, 1962), pp. 132–133.

17. Rathbone, "Resistance to Enslavement in Africa," pp. 11–22, quotation from pp. 17–18; William Piersen, "White Cannibals, Black Martyrs: Fear, Depression, and Religious Faith as Causes of Suicide among New Slaves," *Journal of Negro History* 62 (April 1977), pp. 147–159; Joseph C. Miller, *Way of Death: Merchant Capitalism and the Angolan Slave Trade, 1730–1830* (Madison: University of Wisconsin Press, 1988), pp. 3–7; Daniel McKinnen, *A Tour Through the British West Indies* (London, 1804), pp. 218–219.

18. *London Chronicle,* March 6–9, 1779, in James Oldham, "New Light on Mansfield and Slavery," *Journal of British Studies* 27 (Jan. 1988), pp. 45–68, quotation from p. 65; Curtin, *Atlantic Slave Trade,* p. 160.

19. Rathbone, "Resistance to Enslavement in Africa," pp. 18–20; *Maryland Gazette,* Oct. 23, 1760, in Windley, *Runaway Slave Advertisements,* vol. 2,

p. 39. On creolization, see Edward Brathwaite, *The Development of Creole Society in Jamaica, 1770–1820* (Oxford: Clarendon Press, 1971), pp. 296–307; Charles Joyner, *Down by the Riverside: A South Carolina Slave Community* (Urbana: University of Illinois Press, 1984), p. xxi.

20. Ray A. Kea, *Settlements, Trade, and Politics in the Seventeenth-Century Gold Coast* (Baltimore: Johns Hopkins University Press, 1982), pp. 11–12, 40–42, 105–107, 145, 216–243, 308, 321–326; Henige, "John Kabes of Komenda," pp. 1–2; Peter C. W. Gutkind, "Trade and Labor in Early Precolonial African History: The Canoemen of Southern Ghana," in *The Workers of African Trade*, ed. Catherine Coquery-Vidrovitch and Paul E. Lovejoy (Beverly Hills, Calif.: Sage, 1985), pp. 25–50.

21. Gutkind, "Canoemen of Southern Ghana," pp. 27–30, 41.

22. Ibid., pp. 36–45; quotations from pp. 36–38.

23. Kea, *Seventeenth-Century Gold Coast*, pp. 197–247.

24. Gutkind, "Canoemen of Southern Ghana," pp. 29–30; A. J. H. Latham, *Old Calabar, 1600–1891: The Impact of the International Economy upon a Traditional Society* (Oxford: Clarendon Press, 1973), pp. 31–32.

25. Martin Klein and Paul E. Lovejoy, "Slavery in West Africa," in *The Uncommon Market: Essays in the Economic History of the Atlantic Slave Trade*, ed. Henry A. Gemery and Jan S. Hogendorn (New York: Academic Press, 1979), pp. 181–212; Curtin, *Economic Change in Precolonial Africa*, pp. 34–35, 155; P. Diagne, "African Political, Economic, and Social Structures during This Period," in *Africa from the Sixteenth to the Eighteenth Century*, ed. B. A. Ogot, vol. 5 of *General History of Africa* (Berkeley: UNESCO, 1992), pp. 23–45.

26. Gutkind, "Canoemen of Southern Ghana," pp. 33–36. On cross-cultural assessment, see Greg Dening, *Islands and Beaches: Discourse on a Silent Land, Marquesas, 1774–1880* (Honolulu: University of Hawaii Press, 1980), p. 5.

27. *Virginia Gazette*, Dec. 24, 1772, in Windley, *Runaway Slave Advertisements*, vol. 1, p. 126.

28. Among thirty-three sailors and boatmen from South Carolina and Georgia (1737–1790), 15 percent were African-born. Among forty-eight sailors and boatmen working the Chesapeake (1736–1790), 22 percent were African-born. Windley, *Runaway Slave Advertisements*, vols. 1–4. Walter Nugent to Abraham Redwood, April 11, 1731, in *Commerce of Rhode Island, 1726–1800* (2 vols., Boston: Massachusetts Historical Society, 1914–1915), vol. 1, p. 15; *Virginia Gazette*, Dec. 10, 1772, in Windley, *Runaway Slave Advertisements*, vol. 1, p. 126.

29. *South Carolina Gazette*, Oct. 3–10, 1761, in Windley, *Runaway Slave Ad-*

vertisements, vol. 3, p. 202; *Virginia Gazette*, June 27, 1771, ibid., vol. 1, p. 96; Mullin, *Africa in America*, pp. 28–29; Mullin, *Flight and Rebellion*, pp. 41–42.

30. Olaudah Equiano, *The Interesting Narrative of the Life of Olaudah Equiano, or Gustavus Vassa, the African*, in *The Classic Slave Narratives*, ed. Henry Louis Gates, Jr. (1789; reprint, New York: Mentor, 1987), pp. 34–35.

31. William Smith, *A New Voyage to Guinea* (London, 1744; reprint, Frank Cass: London, 1967), pp. 10–11.

32. James F. Stanfield, *The Guinea Voyage* (Edinburgh, 1807), in George Francis Dow, *Slave Ships and Slaving* (Salem: Essex Institute, 1927), p. 166; Alexander Falconbridge, *An Account of the Slave Trade on the Coast of Africa* (London, 1788; reprint, New York: Arno Press, 1973), p. 11; Mannix and Cowley, *Black Cargoes*, pp. 137–138; Marcus Rediker, *Between the Devil and the Deep Blue Sea: Merchant Seamen, Pirates, and the Anglo-American Maritime World, 1700–1750* (Cambridge, England: Cambridge University Press, 1987), pp. 46–48; Curtin, *Atlantic Slave Trade*, pp. 275–286; Jay Coughtry, *The Notorious Triangle: Rhode Island and the African Slave Trade, 1700–1807* (Philadelphia: Temple University Press, 1981), pp. 63, 105, 154; George Pinckard, *Notes on the West Indies* (3 vols., London, 1806), vol. 1, p. 326.

33. Pinckard, *Notes on the West Indies*, vol. 1, p. 336.

34. Mannix and Cowley, *Black Cargoes*, p. 111; James A. Rawley, *The Transatlantic Slave Trade: A History* (New York: W. W. Norton, 1981), p. 299; M. Priestly, "An Early Strike in Ghana," *Ghana Notes and Queries* 7 (1965), p. 25; Rathbone, "Resistance to Enslavement in Africa," pp. 11–22.

35. John Willock, *The Voyages and Adventures of John Willock, Mariner. Interspersed With Remarks on Different Countries in Europe, Africa, and America; With the Customs and Manners of the Inhabitants; And A Number of Original Anecdotes* (Philadelphia: Hogan and M'Elroy, 1798), pp. 27–28.

36. Rusty Fleetwood, *Tidecraft: An Introductory Look at the Boats of Lower South Carolina, Georgia, and Northern Florida: 1650–1950* (Savannah, Ga.: Coastal Heritage Society, 1982), pp. v, 30–32, 62; Francis Moore, *A Voyage to Georgia Begun in the Year 1735* (London: Robinson, 1744), p. 49.

37. *Naval Chronicle* 11 (1804), p. 456; Edouard de Montule, *Travels in America, 1816–1817*, trans. Edward D. Seeber (1821; reprint, New York: Kraus, 1969), p. 54; Edward Long, *History of Jamaica* (London: T. Lowndes, 1774), vol. 3, pp. 736–737; William C. Fleetwood, Jr., *Tidecraft: The Boats of South Carolina, Georgia, and Northeastern Florida, 1550–1950* (Tybee Island, Ga.: WBG Marine Press, 1995), pp. 31–44.

38. Equiano, *Life of Equiano*, p. 71; Peter H. Wood, "'It Was a Negro Taught

Them': A New Look at African Labor in Early South Carolina," *Journal of Asian and African Studies* 9 (July and Oct. 1974), p. 167.

39. Willock, *Voyages and Adventures*, pp. 27–28; Equiano, *Life of Equiano*, p. 87.

40. Sterling Stuckey, *Slave Culture: Nationalist Theory and the Foundations of Black America* (New York: Oxford University Press, 1987), pp. 12–15; Thompson, *Flash of the Spirit*, pp. 72–83, 108–142; John S. Mbiti, *African Religions and Philosophy* (New York: Praeger, 1969), pp. 54–55, 78–91.

41. Gwendolyn Midlo Hall, *Africans in Colonial Louisiana: The Development of Afro-Creole Culture in the Eighteenth Century* (Baton Rouge: Louisiana State University Press, 1992), pp. 41–55, quotation from pp. 49–50; Piersen, "White Cannibals, Black Martyrs," p. 153; MacGaffey, "West in Congolese Experience," pp. 51–56, quotation from p. 55; MacGaffey, "Kongo and the King of the Americans," pp. 171–181; MacGaffey, "Cultural Roots of Kongo Prophetism," pp. 186–187.

42. Robert Farris Thompson, "Kongo Influences on African-American Artistic Culture," in *Africanisms in American Culture*, ed. Joseph Holloway (Bloomington: Indiana University Press, 1990), pp. 148–184, quotation from p. 152; Diary of William Chancellor, 1749–1751, E. A. Williams Papers, mss. 899, MdHS, p. 44.

43. Curtin, *The Atlantic Slave Trade: A Census* (Madison: University of Wisconsin Press, 1969), p. 157; Melville J. Herskovits, *The Myth of the Negro Past* (New York: Harper and Brothers, 1941), p. 232.

44. Pinckard, *Notes on the West Indies*, vol. 1, pp. 271–274.

45. *Maryland Gazette*, Oct. 22, 1761, in Windley, *Runaway Slave Advertisements*, vol. 2, p. 42.

46. Thompson quoted in Stuckey, *Slave Culture*, p. 12; MacGaffey, "Kongo and the King of the Americans," p. 177; Thompson, *Flash of the Spirit*, p. 135; Leland G. Ferguson, *Uncommon Ground: Archeology and Early African America, 1650–1800* (Washington: Smithsonian Institution Press, 1992), pp. 109–120.

47. Matthew Lewis, *Journal of a West Indian Proprietor* (London, 1823), p. 51. P. Amaury Talbot quoted in Stuckey, *Slave Culture*, pp. 68–69. For John Canoe, see Stuckey, *Slave Culture*, pp. 68–73, 104–106; Judith Bettelheim, "Jamaican Jonkonnu and Related Caribbean Festivals," in *Africa and the Caribbean: The Legacies of a Link*, ed. Margaret Crahan and Franklin W. Knight (Baltimore: Johns Hopkins University Press, 1979), pp. 80–100.

48. Thompson, *Flash of the Spirit*, pp. 72–81, quotation from pp. 76–77. On Yoruba slaves, see Robin Law, *The Oyo Empire, c. 1600–1800* (Oxford: Oxford University Press, 1977), pp. 217–228, 304–308; Peter Morton-Wil-

liams, "The Oyo Yoruba and the Atlantic Trade, 1670–1830," *Journal of the Historical Society of Nigeria* 3 (1964), pp. 24–45.
49. Paul Edwards and James Walvin, *Black Personalities in the Era of the Slave Trade* (Baton Rouge: Louisiana State University Press, 1983), pp. 165–166.

3. The Way of a Ship

1. Herman Melville, *Billy Budd, Sailor (An Inside Narrative)*, ed. Harrison Hayford and Merton M. Sealts, Jr. (Chicago: University of Chicago Press, 1962), p. 43.
2. William Williams, *Mr. Penrose. The Journal of Penrose, Seaman*, ed. David Howard Dickason (Bloomington: Indiana University Press, 1969), p. 74.
3. On technological and navigational changes at sea, see J. H. Parry, *Trade and Dominion: The European Overseas Empires in the Eighteenth Century* (New York: Praeger, 1971), pp. 203–234; Ralph Davis, *The Rise of the English Shipping Industry in the Seventeenth and Eighteenth Centuries* (London: Macmillan, 1962).
4. *Virginia Gazette*, July 18, 1771, in *Runaway Slave Advertisements: A Documentary History from the 1730s to 1790*, comp. Lathan A. Windley (4 vols., Westport, Conn.: Greenwood Press, 1983), vol. 1, p. 314; *North Carolina Gazette*, March 27, 1778, ibid., p. 449. Sea shanteys are treated more fully in Chapter 8.
5. William Ray, *The American Tars in Tripolitan Slavery* (Troy, New York, 1808; reprint, New York: William Abbatt, 1911), pp. 19, 301.
6. *Samuel Kelly, An Eighteenth Century Seaman, Whose days have been few and evil, to which is added remarks, etc. on places he visited during his pilgrimage in this wilderness*, ed. Crosbie Garstin (New York: Frederick A. Stokes Company, 1925), p. 232; Howard M. Chapin, *Privateering in King George's War* (Providence: Rhode Island Historical Society, 1928), pp. 131–132; Protest of Woodbridge Odlin, Jan. 24, 1797, in Patrick Keating folder, box 6, Miscellaneous Correspondence Regarding Impressed Seamen, Records on Impressed Seamen, RG 59, NA; *The Trial Record of Denmark Vesey*, ed. John Oliver Killens (Boston: Beacon Press, 1970), pp. 148–151, quotation from p. 151.
7. Parry, *Trade and Dominion*, p. 217; Jacob Israel Potter to ———, Nov. 11, 1811, in John Briggs folder, box 2, Copies of Letters from Sundry American Seamen in the British Service Impressed, Miscellaneous Correspondence Regarding Impressed Seamen, Records on Impressed Seamen, 1794–1815, RG 59, NA; G. J. Marcus, *Heart of Oak: A Survey of British Seapower in the Georgian Era* (New York: Oxford University Press, 1975), p. 121; Jesse

Lemisch, "Jack Tar in the Streets: Merchant Seamen in the Politics of Revolutionary America," *WMQ*, 3rd series, 25 (1968), pp. 381–382.

8. Letter of Jacob Israel Potter, Nov. 11, 1811, in John Briggs folder, box 2, Copies of Letters from Sundry American Seamen, Records on Impressed Seamen, 1794–1815, RG 59, NA; N. A. M. Rodger, *The Wooden World: An Anatomy of the Georgian Navy* (Annapolis, Md.: Naval Institute Press, 1986), pp. 113–137, 160–161.

9. Richard B. Morris, *Government and Labor in Early America* (New York: Columbia University Press, 1946), pp. 225–228; Frederic R. Sanborn, *Origins of the Early English Maritime and Commercial Law* (New York: Century Company, 1930), pp. 63, 64, 96; Myra C. Glenn, "The Naval Reform Campaign against Flogging: A Case Study of Changing Attitudes toward Corporal Punishment, 1830–1850," *American Quarterly* 35 (1983), pp. 408–425.

10. Stephen Reynolds, *The Voyage of the New Hazard*, ed. Judge F. W. Howay (Salem: Essex Institute, 1938), p. 37; Deposition of John Stanford, Oct. 1803, folder 27, collection 98, Marine Jurisprudence Papers, MSM. See also Greg Dening, *Mr. Bligh's Bad Language: Passion, Power and Theatre on the Bounty* (Cambridge, England: Cambridge University Press, 1992), p. 118.

11. Reynolds, *Voyage of the New Hazard*, pp. 9, 11, 13, 14, 15, 19, 20, 57, 80, 112, 135.

12. Morris, *Government and Labor in Early America*, p. 230; Lemisch, "Jack Tar in the Streets," p. 378.

13. Lemisch, "Jack Tar in the Streets," p. 378; Edward L. Cox, *Free Coloreds in the Slave Societies of St. Kitts and Grenada, 1763–1833* (Knoxville: University of Tennessee Press, 1984), pp. 94–95.

14. Gardner W. Allen, "Capt. Hector McNeill, Continental Navy," *Proceedings of the Massachusetts Historical Society* 55 (1921–1922), pp. 46–152; quotation from pp. 132–133.

15. Greg Dening, *Islands and Beaches: Discourse on a Silent Land, Marquesas, 1774–1880* (Honolulu: University of Hawaii Press, 1980), pp. 158–159.

16. Barber Badger, *The Naval Temple, Containing A Complete History of the Battles Fought By the Navy of the United States. From Its Establishment in 1794, To The Present Time.* (Boston: The Author, 1816), p. 206; Deposition of John Wilson, Sept. 16, 1820, *U.S. v. Henry H. Ford*, Criminal Case Files, U.S. Circuit Court, District of Maryland, microfilm 1010, roll 1, p. 939, RG 21, NA.

17. Providence crew lists, 1819–1821, RG 28, U.S. Customs House Papers, Providence, R.I., RIHS; Edward Carrington & Co., "Seamen's Ledgers," 1819–1821, Carrington Papers, RIHS; *The John, Abner Mosher, Master, (An*

Appeal from New Providence). 1809 (pamphlet, Manuscript Collection, RIHS); Melville, *Billy Budd,* pp. 43–44.

18. James Albert Ukawsaw Gronniosaw, *A Narrative of the Most Remarkable Particulars in the Life of James Albert Ukawsaw Gronniosaw, an African Prince, as Related by Himself* (Bath, England, c. 1770; reprint, Nendeln: Kraus Reprints), p. 15.

19. John Jea, *The Life, History, and Unparalleled Sufferings of John Jea, the African Preacher* in *Black Itinerants of the Gospel: The Narratives of John Jea and George White,* ed. Graham Russell Hodges (Madison, Wis.: Madison House, 1993), pp. 123–124.

20. Richard Henry Dana, *Two Years Before the Mast: A Personal Narrative of Life at Sea* (1840; reprint, New York: Penguin Books, 1981), p. 42.

21. For seamen's craft skill, see Eric Sager, *Seafaring Labour: The Merchant Marine of Atlantic Canada, 1820–1914* (Montreal: McGill-Queen's University Press, 1989), pp. 44, 58–66, 104, 114–117, 122–135. For the ship as factory, see Elmo Paul Hohman, *Seamen Ashore: A Study of the United Seamen's Service and of Merchant Seamen in Port* (New Haven: Yale University Press, 1952), p. 224; Peter Linebaugh, "All the Atlantic Mountains Shook," *Labour/Le Travailleur* 10 (1982), pp. 108–109.

22. *Virginia Independent Chronicle,* Jan. 2, 1788, in Windley, *Runaway Slave Advertisements,* vol. 1, pp. 392–393. For black pilots, see *The Colonial Records of North Carolina,* ed. William L. Saunders (Raleigh: P. M. Hale, State Printer, 1886), vol. 9, pp. 803–804; *The Papers of Henry Laurens* (Columbia: University of South Carolina Press, 1968–1990), vol. 10, pp. 220, 319–322; *The John Gray Blount Papers,* ed. David T. Morgan (Raleigh: North Carolina State Department of Archives and History, 1982), vol. 4, p. 136; receipt by Negro Dick for piloting, April 23, 1777, Maryland State Papers, doc. 19970–2–3–2, MdHR.

23. George Little, *Life on the Ocean* (Baltimore: Armstrong and Berry, 1843), p. 39. R. H. Dana, *The Seaman's Friend: Containing a Treatise on Practical Seamanship, With Plates; A Dictionary of Sea Terms; Customs and Usages of the Merchant Service; Laws Relating to the practical Duties of Master and Mariners* (Boston: Thomas Groom and Co., 1851; reprint, Delmar, N.Y.: Scholars' Facsimiles, 1979), p. 136.

24. Dana, *Seaman's Friend,* pp. 159–160, 169.

25. Ibid., pp. 165–167; Davis, *Rise of English Shipping,* pp. 110–113.

26. Dana, *Seaman's Friend,* pp. 158–165, quotation from p. 160; William Falconer, *An Universal Dictionary of the Marine* (London: T. Cadell, 1789), n.p. See "ordinary" and "crowning."

27. *Samuel Kelly,* pp. 225, 232; Dana, *Seaman's Friend,* p. 160.

28. Log of the *George,* Feb. 6, 1840, log 86, MSM; Dana, *Seaman's Friend,* pp. 156–157; log of the *Resource,* Dec. 29, 1803, Manuscript Collection, RIHS.

29. Dana, *Seaman's Friend,* p. 157; Francis Allyn Olmstead, *Incidents of a Whaling Voyage* (New York: D. Appleton, 1841; reprint Rutland, Vt.: C. E. Tuttle Company, 1969), p. 51; Herman Melville, *Redburn: His First Voyage, Being the Sailor-boy Confessions and Reminiscences of the Son-of-a-Gentleman, in the Merchant Service* (1849; reprint, Northwestern University Press and the Newberry Library: Evanston and Chicago, 1969), p. 81.

30. William C. Nell, *The Colored Patriots of the American Revolution* (Boston, 1855; reprint, New York: Arno Press, 1969), pp. 239–243; *Freedom's Journal* (New York), July 6, 1827, p. 65; *Thomas Saunders v. John Carman and Bartholomew Bukup,* Admiralty Case Files for the Southern District of New York, Oct. term, 1830, microfilm M-919, roll 30, case A-1–147, pp. 523–611, quotation from p. 593, RG 21, NA.

31. Dana, *Two Years,* p. 42; Falconer, *Universal Dictionary of the Marine* ("capstan"); Rediker, *Devil and Deep Blue Sea,* p. 90; Stan Hugill, *Shanties from the Seven Seas: Shipboard Work-Songs and Songs Used as Work-Songs from the Great Days of Sail* (London: Routledge & Kegan Paul, 1961; reprint, 1984), p. 7; Allen, "Captain Hector McNeill, Continental Navy," p. 89.

32. Dana, *Seaman's Friend,* p. 60; Falconer, *Universal Dictionary of the Marine* (1815 ed.), pp. 388, 530; Peter Wheeler, *Chains and Freedom: Or, The Life and Adventures of Peter Wheeler, A Colored Man Yet Living. A Slave in Chains, A Sailor on the Deep, And A Sinner At the Cross,* ed. Charles Edward Lester (New York: E. S. Arnold, 1839), pp. 202–203.

33. Dana, *Seaman's Friend,* pp. 167–168.

34. Rediker, *Devil and Deep Blue Sea,* pp. 100–106; John G. Rogers, *Origins of Sea Terms* (Mystic, Ct.: Mystic Seaport Museum, 1985), pp. 162–163; *Naval Documents of the American Revolution,* vol. 7, p. 1053.

35. Perry Green Arnold Papers, Nov. 1802, RIHS; Warrant for Aaron Gibson, Warrants for Arrest of Mariners, folder 3, box 330, Adlow Collection, Rare Book Room, BPL; James Maury to James Monroe, August 13, 1807, Despatches from U.S. Consuls in Liverpool, M-141, roll 2, Records of the Department of State, RG 59, NA.

36. James Maury to Philip Stephens, May 25, 1791, Despatches from U.S. Consuls in London, 1790–1906, T-168, roll 1, Records of the Department of State, RG 59, NA; James Maury to Thomas Pinkney, March 24, 1793, Despatches from U.S. Consuls in Liverpool, 1790–1906, M-141, roll 1, ibid.; Maury to Pinkney, April 22, 1795, ibid.

37. Gary B. Nash, *The Urban Crucible: Social Change, Political Consciousness, and the Origins of the American Revolution* (Cambridge, Mass.: Harvard

University Press, 1979), pp. 64, 167, 233, 239; Richard S. Dunn, "Servants and Slaves: The Recruitment and Employment of Labor," in *Colonial British America: Essays in the New History of the Early Modern Era*, ed. Jack P. Greene and J. R. Pole (Baltimore: Johns Hopkins University Press, 1984), pp. 157–194, quotation from pp. 182–184.

38. Equiano, *Life of Olaudah Equiano*, p. 165; *Woolford Oxford v. the Ship Henry*, June 28, 1785, Admiralty Court Papers, 1776–1812, document 7871–2–48, MdHR; *Peleg Seabury & others v. Sloop Clarissa*, June 25, 1798, Final Record Book 1, U.S. District Court at Providence, Records of the U.S District Court, RG 21, NA (Boston branch). On mariners' suits to recover wages, see Morris, *Government and Labor in Early America*, pp. 232–246.

39. Equiano, *Life of Olaudah Equiano*, pp. 84–85; Sidney W. Mintz, *Caribbean Transformations* (Baltimore: Johns Hopkins University Press, 1974), pp. 180–213.

40. Gronniosaw, *Narrative*, p. 16; Rediker, *Devil and Deep Blue Sea*, pp. 146–149; Jea, *The Life, History, and Unparalleled Sufferings of John Jea*, p. 145.

41. Paul A. Gilje, *The Road to Mobocracy: Popular Disorder in New York City, 1763–1834* (Chapel Hill: Institute of Early American History and Culture, 1987), pp. 181–182.

42. Dana, *Two Years*, p. 95; Deposition of August Lemonier, Brig Hercules, *American Insurance Company of New York v. Charles Johnson*, June 19, 1827, Admiralty Case Files of the Southern District of New York, microfilm 919, roll 26, pp. 737–985; quotation from p. 821, RG 21, Records of the District Courts of US, NA.

43. Lydia Hill Almy Diary (typescript), June 5, 1798, PEM; W. H. Bunting, *Portrait of a Port: Boston, 1852–1914* (Cambridge, Mass.: Harvard University Press, 1971), p. 250; Sager, *Seafaring Labour*, pp. 231–232; Dening, *Mr. Bligh's Bad Language*, pp. 73–75, 379–380.

44. *Hambleton et al. v. New Ceres*, June 28, 1786, Maryland Admiralty Court Papers, doc. 7871–3–33, MdHR.

45. *Maryland Journal and Baltimore Advertiser*, Aug. 10, 1779, in Windley, *Runaway Slave Advertisements*, vol. 2, p. 229; Ibid., May 14, 1782, p. 262; Ibid., Aug. 28, 1781, p. 252.

46. Deposition of August Lemonier, June 19, 1827, *The American Insurance Co. of New York v. Charles Johnson*, Admiralty Case Files for the U.S. District Court for the Southern District of New York, M 919, roll 26, pp. 737–985; quotation from p. 821, RG 21, NA.

47. Vilhelm Aubert, *The Hidden Society* (Totowa: Bedminster Press, 1965), pp. 236–258; Margaret S. Creighton, *Dogwatch and Liberty Days: Seafaring Life in the Nineteenth Century* (Salem: Peabody Museum, 1982), p. 48.

48. William Butterworth, *Three Years Adventure of a Minor in England, Africa,*

the West Indies, South Carolina and Georgia (Leeds, [1831]), pp. 205–211, quotation from p. 211; Nell, *Colored Patriots of the American Revolution*, p. 314, emphasis added.

49. Samuel Taylor Coleridge, *The Piccolomini; or, The First Part of Wallenstein*, act 1, sc. 6, epigraph in Richard Henry Dana, *Two Years before the Mast: A Personal Narrative of Life at Sea* (1840; reprint, New York: Penguin, 1981), p. 35.

50. Allen, "Captain Hector McNeill," p. 132; Edward H. Spicer, "Persistent Cultural Systems," *Science* 174 (Nov. 19, 1971), pp. 795–800; Lemisch, "Jack Tar in the Streets," p. 380; Linebaugh, "All the Atlantic Mountains Shook," p. 110; Rediker, *Devil and Deep Blue Sea*, pp. 153–169.

51. *Maryland Gazette*, March 7, 1771, in Windley, *Runaway Slave Advertisements*, vol. 2, pp. 85–86; *Maryland Journal and Baltimore Advertiser*, June 2, 1786, ibid., p. 347; *Maryland Gazette*, Nov. 15, 1759, ibid., p. 35; *Maryland Gazette*, May 18, 1775, ibid., p. 110; Wheeler, *Chains and Freedom*, pp. 143, 174.

52. *Naval Documents of the American Revolution*, vol. 7, p. 263; Shane White, "A Question of Style: Blacks in and around New York City in the Late 18th Century," *Journal of American Folklore* 102 (Jan.—March 1989), pp. 23–44, quotation from p. 33; Clifford Ashley, *The Ashley Book of Knots* (Garden City, N.Y.: Doubleday and Co., 1944), p. 565. For black sailors with earrings, see *South Carolina Gazette*, Jan. 12–19, 1738, in Windley, *Runaway Slave Advertisements*, vol. 3, p. 30; *South Carolina Gazette*, Nov. 10–17, 1758, ibid., p. 167; *South Carolina Gazette*, Feb. 9–16, 1760, ibid., p. 181; portrait of Absalom Boston, Nantucket Historical Society, Nantucket, Mass. (See ill.)

53. Ward quoted in Rediker, *Devil and Deep Blue Sea*, p. 12; Dening, *Mr. Bligh's Bad Language*, pp. 35–36; Ira Dye, "The Tattoos of Early American Seafarers, 1796–1818," *Proceedings of the American Philosophical Society* 133 (1989), pp. 520–554.

54. Ira Dye kindly made available to me descriptions of tattoos of fifty-four African American seamen. For Thomas Lane's tattoo, see Robin F. A. Fabel, "Self-Help in Dartmoor: Black and White Prisoners in the War of 1812," *Journal of the Early Republic* 9 (Summer 1989), p. 174.

55. Baltimore crew lists, 1806, Records of the U.S. Customs Service, RG 36, NA; *Maryland Gazette*, Nov. 29, 1764, in Windley, *Runaway Slave Advertisements*, vol. 2, p. 56; *Maryland Journal and Baltimore Advertiser*, Extra, May 4, 1790, ibid., pp. 406–407; Ira Dye, "Early American Merchant Seafarers," *Proceedings of the American Philosophical Society* 120 (1976), pp. 353–357; Rediker, *Devil and Deep Blue Sea*, p. 12.

56. Jameson, *Privateering and Piracy*, pp. 407–414.

57. [William Allen], *Accounts of Shipwreck and of Other Disasters at Sea* (Brunswick, Maine: Joseph Griffin, 1823), pp. 167–171.

58. *Naval Documents of the American Revolution*, vol. 9, p. 889; Criminal Actions From August 11, 1810 to July 18, 1812, Justice Stephen Gorham, July 18, 1811, Adlow Collection, Rare Book Room, BPL.

59. Jea, *The Life, History, and Unparalleled Sufferings of John Jea*, pp. 128, 125, 155, 145.

60. Ibid., p. 155; King, "Memoirs of the Life of Boston King," pp. 213, 264; Gerald W. Mullin, *Flight and Rebellion: Slave Resistance in Eighteenth-Century Virginia* (New York: Oxford University Press, 1972), pp. 98–103.

61. Wheeler, *Chains and Freedom*, pp. 49, 61, 194; Lorenzo J. Greene, *The Negro in Colonial New England* (New York: Columbia University Press, 1942), p. 161; Criminal Action Books of Justice Stephen Gorham, Jan. 9, 1807, Adlow Collection, Rare Book Room, BPL.

62. Thomas Haskell, "Capitalism and the Origins of the Humanitarian Sensibility," *AHR* 90 (April and June 1985), pp. 339–361, 547–566; Edward Braithwaite, *The Development of Creole Society in Jamaica, 1770–1820* (Oxford: Clarendon Press, 1971), p. 301; Equiano, *Life of Equiano*, p. 78; *Maryland Gazette*, Dec. 2, 1746, in Windley, *Runaway Slave Advertisements*, vol. 2, p. 4. *Maryland Gazette*, Jan. 9, 1772, ibid., p. 91.

63. Cremer, *Ramblin' Jack*, p. 144; Rediker, *Devil and Deep Blue Sea*, pp. 231–232.

64. Carl Seaburg and Stanley Patterson, *Merchant Prince of Boston: Colonel T. H. Perkins, 1764–1854* (Cambridge, Mass.: Harvard University Press, 1971), pp. 8–12.

65. Thomas Blount to John Gray Blount, Dec. 21, 1794, *Blount Papers*, vol. 2, pp. 466–470. See also pp. 452, 454.

66. Equiano, *Life of Equiano*, pp. 36, 40, 63–64.

67. Ibid., pp. 64–65.

68. Ibid., pp. 65–67; A. Leon Higgenbotham, Jr., *In the Matter of Color: Race and the American Legal Process, the Colonial Period* (New York: Oxford University Press, 1978), pp. 333–355.

69. Equiano, *Life of Equiano*, pp. 126–127, 163. See also *Naval Documents of the American Revolution*, vol. 8, p. 930.

70. James Barclay, *The Voyages and Travels of James Barclay, Containing Many Surprising Adventures, and Interesting Narratives* (Printed for the author, [Scotland], 1777), pp. 7–8; John Willock, *The Voyages and Adventures of John Willock, Mariner* (Philadelphia, 1798), p. 22.

71. Letter by "A Rambler," April 23, 1792, in Harry Miller Lydenberg, *Crossing*

the Line: Tales of the Ceremony during Four Centuries (New York: New York Public Library, 1957), pp. 59–63; quotation from p. 60. For accounts of Father Neptune ceremonies mentioning blacks, see Wheeler, *Chains and Freedom*, pp. 178–179; Olmsted, *Incidents of a Whaling Voyage*, pp. 67–71; Creighton, *Dogwatch and Liberty Days*, p. 49.

72. On sailors "Claiming a Right," see John Lax and William Pencak, "The Knowles Riot and the Crisis of the 1740s in Massachusetts," *Perspectives in American History* 10 (1976), pp. 163–216; quotation from pp. 182, 186.

73. *The Journal of Gideon Olmsted, Adventures of a Sea Captain During the American Revolution, A Facsimile*, ed. Gerard W. Gawalt (Washington: Library of Congress, 1978), pp. 53, 62–65.

74. James Kelly, *Voyage to Jamaica and Seventeen Years' Residence in That Island: Chiefly Written with a View to Exhibit Negro Life and Habits* (Belfast, 1838), pp. 29–30; Equiano, *Life of Equiano*, p. 163.

75. For an interpretation emphasizing maritime workers' multiracial "cooperation and accomplishment" instead of the ambiguities of race at sea, see Peter Linebaugh and Marcus Rediker, "The Many-Headed Hydra: Sailors, Slaves, and the Atlantic Working Class in the Eighteenth Century," *Journal of Historical Sociology* 3 (Sept. 1990), pp. 225–252.

4. The Boundaries of Race in Maritime Culture

1. Reginald Horsman, "The Paradox of Dartmoor Prison," *American Heritage* 26 (February 1975), pp. 13–17, 85; Ira Dye, "American Maritime Prisoners of War, 1812–1815," in *Ships, Seafaring, and Society: Essays in Maritime History*, ed. Timothy J. Runyan (Detroit: Wayne State University Press, 1987), pp. 293–320.

2. Horsman, "Paradox of Dartmoor," p. 14; [Josiah Cobb], *A Green Hand's First Cruise, Roughed Out From the Log-book of Memory, of Twenty-Five Years Standing: Together with a Residence of Five Months in Dartmoor* (Boston: Otis, Broaders, and Company, 1841), vol. 2, p. 44; *The Yarn of a Yankee Privateer*, ed. Nathaniel Hawthorne (New York: Funk and Wagnalls Company, 1926), p. 181. Originally published as "Papers of an Old Dartmoor Prisoner," ed. Nathaniel Hawthorne, *U.S. Democratic Review* (New York, January to September 1846), this was based on the experiences of Benjamin Brown, a pharmacist from Salem, Massachusetts, and Hawthorne's neighbor after the War of 1812.

3. Nathaniel Pierce, "Journal of Nathaniel Pierce of Newburyport, Kept at Dartmoor Prison, 1814–1815," *Essex Institute Historical Collections* 73 (January 1937), pp. 24–59, quotation from pp. 33–34.

4. See Eric Lott, "Love and Theft: The Racial Unconscious of Blackface Minstrelsy," *Representations* 39 (Summer 1992), pp. 23–50.

5. *The Chesapeake Affair of 1807,* comp. John C. Emmerson, Jr. (Portsmouth, Va.: n.p., 1954), pp. 7–8, 162–163; William/Romulus Ware folder, box 10, Miscellaneous Correspondence Regarding Impressed Seamen, Records on Impressed Seamen, 1794–1815, RG 59, NA; James Fulton Zimmerman, *Impressment of American Seamen* (New York: Columbia University Press, 1925), pp. 136–137.

6. Joseph Valpey, Jr., *Journal of Joseph Valpey, Jr. of Salem November, 1813-April, 1815, with Other Papers Relating to His Experience in Dartmoor Prison* (Michigan Society of Colonial Wars, 1922), p. 12; Adam Smith Diary, 1814–1815 (manuscript), PEM.

7. Benjamin F. Palmer, *The Diary of Benjamin F. Palmer Privateersman While A Prisoner On Board English Warships at Sea, In the Prison at Melville Island And at Dartmoor* (n.p., Acorn Club, 1914), p. 98; Joseph Bates, *The Autobiography of Elder Joseph Bates; Embracing A Long Life On Shipboard* (Battle Creek, Mich.: Seventh-Day Adventist Publishing Association, 1868), p. 72; Cobb, *Green Hand's First Cruise,* vol. 2, pp. 181–182; [Charles Andrews], *The Prisoners' Memoirs, or Dartmoor Prison* (New York, 1815; reprint, By the Author, 1852), p. 10.

8. Horsman, "Paradox of Dartmoor Prison," p. 14; George Little, *Life on the Ocean, or Twenty Years at Sea; Being the Personal Adventures of the Author* (Baltimore: Armstrong and Berry, 1843), p. 232; Andrews, *Prisoners' Memoirs,* pp. 10–12, 33; Hawthorne, *Yarn,* pp. 167–169; Cobb, *Green Hand's First Cruise,* vol. 2, pp. 181–182; Palmer, *Diary,* pp. 102–103; Bates, *Autobiography of Elder Joseph Bates,* p. 72.

9. Andrews, *Prisoners' Memoirs,* p. 11. On "keeno" see Pierce, "Journal," pp. 28–29; Cobb, *Green Hand's First Cruise,* p. 153; Adam Smith Diary, PEM.

10. Basil Thomson, *The Story of Dartmoor Prison* (London: William Heinemann, 1907), pp. 48–54, 73. I calculated blacks' numbers from *General Entry Books for American Prisoners of War,* Admiralty 103 (Adm 103/87, Adm 103/88, Adm 103/89, Adm 103/90), Public Record Office, London.

11. Andrews, *Prisoners' Memoirs,* pp. 14, 15; Little, *Life on the Ocean,* p. 233.

12. Adam Smith Diary, PEM, p. 42; Andrews, *Prisoners' Memoirs,* p. 38; Hawthorne, *Yarn,* p. 172; Valpey, *Journal of Joseph Valpey,* pp. 13, 16, 22; Pierce, "Journal," pp. 33, 39, 41, 46, 58; Palmer, *Diary of Benjamin F. Palmer,* p. 197; [Benjamin Waterhouse], *A Journal of a Young Man of Massachusetts, Late a Surgeon on Board an American Privateer* (Midgeville, Ga.: S. & F. Grantland, 1816, reprinted as Extra Number 18 of the *Magazine of History,*

New York, 1911), p. 174. Ira Dye's remarkable detective work shows that Waterhouse's informant was probably Henry Torey, a twenty-one-year-old seaman from Massachusetts. See Dye, "American Maritime Prisoners of War," p. 316.

13. Palmer, *Diary of Benjamin F. Palmer,* pp. 141, 161, 168; Little, *Life on the Ocean,* p. 234; Cobb, *Green Hand's First Cruise,* pp. 28–30, 132, 161–165; Andrews, *Prisoners' Memoirs,* pp. 39–40.

14. Cobb, *Green Hand's First Cruise,* p. 30. Whites' condescension toward and intrigue with African American expressive arts is explored in Nathaniel Mackey, "Other: From Noun to Verb," *Representations* 39 (Summer 1992), pp. 51–70.

15. Andrews, *Prisoners' Memoirs,* pp. 63, 66.

16. Palmer, *Diary,* pp. 20, 57; Robin F. A. Fabel, "Self-Help in Dartmoor: Black and White Prisoners in the War of 1812," *Journal of the Early Republic* 9 (Summer 1989), pp. 165–190, esp. pp. 176–177.

17. Shane White, "'It Was a Proud Day': African Americans, Festivals, and Parades in the North, 1741–1834," *JAH* 81 (June 1994), pp. 13–50; Joseph P. Reidy, "Negro Election Day and Black Community Life in New England, 1750–1860," *Marxist Perspectives* 1 (Fall 1978), pp. 102–117; William D. Piersen, *Black Yankees: The Development of an Afro-American Subculture in Eighteenth-Century New England* (Amherst: University of Massachusetts Press, 1988), pp. 117–128; A. J. Williams-Myers, "Pinkster Carnival: Africanisms in the Hudson River Valley," *Afro-Americans in New York Life and History* 9 (January 1985), pp. 7–17.

18. Hawthorne, *Yarn,* pp. 181–186; Waterhouse, *A Journal of a Young Man,* p. 174.

19. Ira Dye, "Physical and Social Profiles of Early American Seafarers, 1812–1815" (unpub. paper), table 17; Piersen, *Black Yankees,* pp. 124–128, 175. On Jamaican slaves' respect for headmen, see Orlando Patterson, *The Sociology of Slavery* (London: MacGibbon and Kee, 1967; reprint, London: Granada Publishing, 1973), pp. 62–64.

20. David O. White, *Connecticut's Black Soldiers, 1775–1783* (Chester, Conn.: Pequot Press, 1973), p. 11; Cobb, *Green Hand's First Cruise,* vol. 2, p. 44.

21. Shane White, *Somewhat More Independent: The End of Slavery in New York City, 1770–1810* (Athens: University of Georgia Press, 1991), p. 96; White, "It was a Proud Day," p. 18; Lorenzo Greene, *The Negro in Colonial New England* (New York: Columbia University Press, 1942), pp. 252–253; Piersen, *Black Yankees,* pp. 119–120.

22. Reidy, "Negro Election Day," pp. 110–111; Piersen, *Black Yankees,* pp. 130–131.

23. George Hugh Crichton, "Old Boston and Its Once Familiar Faces: Sketches of Some Odd Characters Who Have Flourished in Boston During the Past Fifty Years" (unpub. mss., Boston, 1881), Boston Athenaeum. On walking sticks and canes as symbols of black leadership in Africa, the West Indies, and New England, see Piersen, *Black Yankees*, p. 136; Roger D. Abrahams and John F. Szwed, eds., *After Africa* (New Haven: Yale University Press, 1983), pp. 265, 306; Alexander Barclay, *A Present View of the State of Slavery in the West Indies* (London, 1826), p. 41.

24. Cobb, *Green Hand's First Cruise*, vol. 2, p. 44.

25. Waterhouse, *Journal of a Young Man*, p. 174; Hawthorne, *Yarn*, pp. 181–183.

26. Ibid., pp. 174, 176; Valpey, "Journal of Joseph Valpey," p. 15; Cobb, *Green Hand's First Cruise*, vol. 2, p. 44; W. E. B. DuBois, *The Souls of Black Folk* (1903; reprint, New York: Penguin, 1989), p. 155.

27. Hawthorne, *Yarn*, p. 182; Cobb, *Green Hand's First Cruise*, vol. 2, p. 44; Reidy, "Negro Election Day," pp. 109–111, quotation from p. 111.

28. Piersen, *Black Yankees*, p. 134; Waterhouse, *Journal of a Young Man*, p. 174; Palmer, *Diary*, p. 20. A nautical practice brought ashore by black New-porters, cobbing was largely out of favor by 1815 as punishment aboard ship. See William Falconer, *Universal Dictionary of the Marine*, "cobbing."

29. *General Entry Books for American Prisoners of War*, Adm 103/87.

30. Dye, "American Prisoners of War at Dartmoor," p. 2; Francis G. Selman, "Extracts from the Journal of a Marblehead Privateersman Confined on Board British Prison Ships, 1813, 1814, 1815," in *The Marblehead Manual*, comp. Samuel Roads, Jr. (Marblehead, Mass.: Statesman Publishing Company, 1883), pp. 28–96.

31. Dye, "American Prisoners of War at Dartmoor," p. 2; Dye to author, March 11, 1988; ibid., June 20, 1990.

32. Dye to author, March 11, 1988, March 11, 1990, June 20, 1990, based on Adm 103 and Adm 98/121.

33. May 27, 28, 1813, Adm 103/89; White, *Somewhat More Independent*, pp. 150–151.

34. Andrews, *Prisoners' Memoirs*, p. 18.

35. Palmer, *Diary of Benjamin F. Palmer*, pp. 126–127; Adam Smith Diary, PEM, p. 22; Pierce, "Journal of Nathaniel Pierce," p. 36; Valpey, *Journal of Joseph Valpey*, p. 24.

36. Palmer, *Diary of Benjamin F. Palmer*, p. 129; *Niles Weekly Register*, Feb. 26, 1814; William C. Nell, *Colored Patriots of the American Revolution* (Boston, 1855; reprint, New York: Arno Press, 1968), pp. 190–191.

37. William Godfrey to the Congress of the United States of America, Aug. 19, 1799, William Godfrey folder, box 4, Miscellaneous Correspondence

Regarding Impressed Seamen, Records on Impressed Seamen, 1794–1815, RG 59, NA; John Backus to Abraham Bishop, Oct. 28, 1811, John Backus folder, box 1, ibid.; Jacob Israel Potter to [unknown], Nov. 11, 1811, Jacob Israel Potter folder, box 6, ibid.

38. Deposition of William West, *The American Insurance Company of N.Y. v. Charles Johnson,* May 19, 1827, Admiralty Case Files for the District Court of US for the Southern District of NY, M 919, roll 26, p. 809, RG 21, NA.

39. Franklin quoted in William H. MacLeish, *The Gulf Stream: Encounters with the Blue God* (Boston: Houghton Mifflin, 1989), p. 87; Elliott Gorn, *The Manly Art: Bare-Knuckle Prize Fighting in America* (Ithaca: Cornell University Press, 1986), pp. 22, 26–29; Waterhouse, *Journal of a Young Man,* p. 75; Palmer, *Diary,* p. 10; Cobb, *Green Hand's First Cruise,* vol. 2, p. 34.

40. Gorn, *Manly Art,* pp. 34–35. Other black sailors who were also professional boxers in England during the early nineteenth century are profiled in Peter Fryer, *Staying Power: Black People in Britain since 1504* (Atlantic Highlands, N.J.: Humanities Press, 1984), pp. 443–457.

41. Gorn, *Manly Art,* pp. 19–20.

42. Elliott J. Gorn, "'Gouge and Bite, Pull Hair and Scratch': The Social Significance of Fighting in the Southern Backcountry," *AHR* 90 (1985), p. 20.

43. William Grimes, *Life of William Grimes,* in *Five Black Lives,* ed. Arna Bontemps (Middletown: Wesleyan University Press, 1971), p. 92; Richard Henry Dana, *Two Years Before the Mast* (1840; reprint, New York: Penguin, 1981), pp. 429–430; Sidney Kaplan and Emma Nogrady Kaplan, *The Black Presence in the Era of the American Revolution* (Amherst: University of Massachusetts Press, 1989), pp. 50–51; George Hugh Crichton, "Old Boston and Its Once Familiar Faces," chap. 1, p. 7 (unpub. mss., 1881), Boston Athenaeum. See also Austin Steward, *Twenty-Two Years a Slave & Forty Years a Freeman* (1856; reprint, New York: Negro Universities Press, 1968), pp. 274–277.

44. Robert Farris Thompson, Foreword to J. Lowell Lewis, *Ring of Liberation: Deceptive Discourse in Brazilian Capoeira* (Chicago: University of Chicago Press, 1992), pp. xii–xiv.

45. William Butterworth, *Three Years Adventure of a Minor in England, Africa, the West Indies, South Carolina and Georgia* (Leeds, [1831]), pp. 301–307.

46. Hawthorne, *Yarn,* p. 239.

47. Lawrence W. Levine, *Highbrow/Lowbrow: The Emergence of Cultural Hierarchy in America* (Cambridge, Mass: Harvard University Press, 1988), pp. 16–17, 24; James H. Dormon, Jr., *Theater in the Antebellum South, 1815–1861* (Chapel Hill: University of North Carolina Press, 1967), pp. 234, 236.

48. Palmer, *Diary of Benjamin Palmer,* pp.108–109; Pierce, "Journal of Nathaniel Pierce," p. 34; Hawthorne, *Yarn,* p. 239. On whites' expectations regarding black performance, see Roger D. Abrahams, *The Man-of-Words in the West Indies: Performance and the Emergence of Creole Culture* (Baltimore: Johns Hopkins University Press, 1983), p. 48.

49. Waterhouse, *Journal of a Young Man,* p. 177; White, "It Was a Proud Day," pp. 46–47.

50. Palmer, *Diary of Benjamin Palmer,* pp. 108–109.

51. On the dynamics of stereotyping, see Roger D. Abrahams, *Singing the Master: The Emergence of African American Culture in the Plantation South* (New York: Pantheon Books, 1992), p. xxv.

52. *Maryland Gazette,* Aug. 6, 1789, in *Runaway Slave Advertisements: A Documentary History from the 1730s to 1790,* comp. Lathan A. Windley (4 vols., Westport, Conn.: Greenwood Press, 1983), vol. 2, p. 183; John Marrant, *A Narrative of the Lord's Wonderful Dealings With John Marrant, a Black* (London, 1802), in *Early Negro Writing, 1760–1837,* ed. Dorothy Porter (Boston: Beacon Press, 1971), pp. 427–447, quotation from pp. 444–445; Boston King, "Memoirs of the Life of Boston King, a Black Preacher, Written by Himself, during his Residence at Kingswood School," *The Methodist Magazine* (London, March, April, May, June 1798), pp. 105–110, 157–161, 209–213, 261–265, quotation from p. 212.

53. Marcus Rediker, *Between the Devil and the Deep Blue Sea: Merchant Seamen, Pirates, and the Anglo-American Maritime World, 1700–1750* (Cambridge, England: Cambridge University Press, 1987), pp. 170–171; Olaudah Equiano, *Life of Olaudah Equiano,* in *The Classic Slave Narratives,* ed. Henry Louis Gates, Jr. (New York: Mentor, 1987), pp. 87, 141–142.

54. "Register of Seamen's Protections," RIHS; Register of Members, First Baptist Church, Providence, R.I., RIHS; *Sailors' Magazine and Naval Journal* (April 1829), pp. 227–228; William H. Townsend, Journal, Ship *Panther,* Jan. 8, 1822, RIHS.

55. Bates, *Autobiography of Elder Joseph Bates,* p. 73; Hawthorne, *Yarn,* pp. 193–195; Palmer, *Diary of Benjamin F. Palmer,* p. 140; Pierce, "Journal of Nathaniel Pierce," p. 35.

56. Pierce, "Journal of Nathaniel Pierce," p. 34; Valpey, "Journal of Joseph Valpey," p. 23.

57. Harold D. Langley, "The Negro in the Navy and Merchant Service, 1798–1860," *Journal of Negro History* 52 (October 1967), p. 277; Bates, *Autobiography of Elder Joseph Bates,* pp. 116–117.

58. Valpey, *Journal of Joseph Valpey,* p. 19; Bates, *Autobiography of Elder Joseph Bates,* p. 73; Pierce, "Journal of Nathaniel Pierce," pp. 41, 42; Andrews, *Prisoners' Memoirs,* pp. 94, 105; Palmer, *Diary of Benjamin F. Palmer,* p. 184;

American State Papers. Foreign Relations (7 vols., Washington, 1833–1859), vol. 4, pp. 19–56.

59. Hawthorne, *Yarn,* p. 196; Waterhouse, *Journal of a Young Man,* p. 175; Pierce, "Journal of Nathaniel Pierce," pp. 37, 55.

60. Hawthorne, *Yarn,* pp. 237–238; Pierce, "Journal of Nathaniel Pierce," p. 53.

61. Hawthorne, *Yarn,* p. 193; Palmer, *Diary of Benjamin F. Palmer,* p. 176; Pierce, "Journal of Nathaniel Pierce," p. 39.

62. Pierce, "Journal of Nathaniel Pierce," pp. 28, 38, 48, 50. None of the prisoners' memoirs mention interracial fights.

63. Ibid., pp. 30–31; Valpey, *Journal of Joseph Valpey,* p. 21.

64. Valpey, *Journal of Joseph Valpey,* p. 19; Palmer, *Diary of Benjamin F. Palmer,* p. 138; Pierce, "Journal of Nathaniel Pierce," p. 27.

65. Valpey, *Journal of Joseph Valpey,* pp. 15, 16, 17, 19, 20, 21, 24.

66. Waterhouse, *Journal of a Young Man,* p. 175; Palmer, *Diary of Benjamin F. Palmer,* p. 140.

5. Possibilities for Freedom

1. Matthew Gregory Lewis, *Journal of a Residence Among the Negroes in the West Indies* (London: J. Murray, 1861), p. 23; Edward Ward, "A Trip to New England" (1699), in *Five Travel Scripts Commonly Attributed to Edward Ward,* comp. Howard William Troyer (New York: Columbia University Press, 1933), p. 4; William Nevens, *Forty Years at Sea: Or a Narrative of the Adventures of William Nevens* (Portland: Thurston, Fenely and Company, 1846), pp. 65–66.

2. On slave psychology see Bertram Wyatt-Brown, "The Mask of Obedience: Male Slave Psychology in the Old South," *AHR* 93 (December 1988), pp. 1228–1252. On elite slaves see Leslie Howard Owens, *This Species of Property: Slave Life and Culture in the Old South* (New York: Oxford University Press, 1976), pp. 121–135; Randall M. Miller, "The Man in the Middle: The Black Slave Driver," *American Heritage* 30 (1979), pp. 40–49; Eugene D. Genovese, *Roll, Jordan, Roll: The World the Slaves Made* (New York: Vintage Books, 1976), pp. 365–397.

3. Walter Clark, ed., *The State Records of North Carolina* (Goldsboro, N.C., 1905), vol. 24, p. 503; Maryland State Papers, 19970–2–3–2, MdHR; Cyril Outerbridge Packwood, *Chained on the Rock: Slavery in Bermuda* (Bermuda: Baxters Ltd., 1975), p. 22.

4. *The Destruction of Slavery,* vol. 1, *Freedom: A Documentary History of Emancipation, 1861–1867,* ed. Ira Berlin (Cambridge, England: Cambridge University Press, 1985), pp. 122–123. Lt. Penrod G. Watmough to S. F.

DuPont, April 23, 1862, Naval Records Collection of the Office of Naval Records and Library, RG 45, NA [T-611], FSSP; Cmdr. T. H. Stevens to Rear Adm. John Dahlgren, November 12, 1863, ibid. [T-640], FSSP; John W. Blassingame, *Slave Testimony* (Baton Rouge: Louisiana State University Press, 1977), p. 373.

5. Edward Long, *The History of Jamaica* (London: T. Lowndes, 1774), vol. 2, pp. 41–42; Accounts and Memoranda of Joseph Senhouse, 1772–1788, microfilmed as Material Related to the West Indies from the Senhouse Papers, 1762–1831, Carlisle Record Office, Barbados; B. W. Higman, *Slave Populations of the British Caribbean, 1807–1834* (Baltimore: Johns Hopkins University Press, 1984), p. 246; *The Weekly Register* (Antigua), May 20, 1815, quoted in Higman, ibid., p. 175.

6. Matthew Gregory Lewis, *Journal of a West Indian Proprietor* (London: John Murray, 1834; reprint, New York: Negro Universities Press, 1969), pp. 164–165.

7. James Kelly, *Jamaica in 1831: Being a Narrative of Seventeen Years' Residence in that Island* (Belfast, 1838), pp. 22, 28–29.

8. Alexander Barclay, *A Present View of the State of Slavery in the West Indies* (London, 1826), p. 273.

9. Frederick Douglass, *Life and Times of Frederick Douglass, Written By Himself: His Early Life As A Slave, His Escape From Bondage, And His Complete History* (1892; reprint, New York: Macmillan Publishing Company, 1962), pp. 73–74; George Henry, *Life of George Henry. Together With a Brief History of the Colored People in America* (1894; reprint, Freeport, N.Y.: Books for Libraries Press, 1971), pp. 15, 27.

10. *Papers Presented to Parliament by His Majesty's Command in Explanation of the Measures Adopted by His Majesty's Government for the Melioration of the Condition of the Slave Population in His Majesty's Possessions in the West Indies* (London: R. G. Clarke, 1826–1827), pp. 157–158.

11. [Louisa Susannah Wells], *The Journal Of A Voyage From Charlestown, S.C. to London Undertaken During the American Revolution By A Daughter of an Eminent American Loyalist In the Year 1778* (New York: New York Historical Society, 1968), p. 2; Testimony of Harriet Dallass, September 12, 1872, Claim of Harriet Dallass, Chatham Co., Ga., Approved Claims, Series 732, Southern Claims Commission, 3rd Auditor, RG 217, Records of the United States General Accounting Office, NA, [I-366], FSSP.

12. Okon Edet Uya, *From Slavery to Public Service: Robert Smalls, 1839–1915* (New York: Oxford University Press, 1971), pp. 6–31; Barclay, *Practical View of the Present State of Slavery*, p. 115.

13. Henry, *Life of George Henry*, pp. 30, 33.

14. Genovese, *Roll, Jordan, Roll,* pp. 443–450; Charles Joyner, *Down by The Riverside: A South Carolina Slave Community* (Urbana: University of Illinois Press, 1984), pp. 221–222.
15. Olaudah Equiano, *Life of Olaudah Equiano,* in *The Classic Slave Narratives,* ed. Henry Louis Gates, Jr. (New York: Mentor, 1987), p. 106.
16. "The Schooner Patriot," *Virginia Historical Register* 1 (1848), p. 129.
17. J. Gilpin to John Gray Blount, August 18, 1802, in *The John Gray Blount Papers* (Raleigh: North Carolina State Department of Archives and History, 1952–1982), vol. 3, pp. 532–533.
18. Nevens, *Forty Years at Sea,* pp. 65–66.
19. Moses Grandy, *Narrative of the Life of Moses Grandy, Late a Slave in the United States of America* (Boston, 1844), in William Loren Katz, ed., *Five Slave Narratives: A Compendium* (New York: Arno Press, 1968), p. 14.
20. Douglass, *Life and Times,* p. 43; Henry, *Life of George Henry,* pp. 22–23.
21. For an alternative argument, see Michael Craton, "Hobbesian or Panglossian? The Two Extremes of Slave Conditions in the British Caribbean, 1783–1834," *WMQ* 35 (April 1978), p. 356.
22. Grandy, *Narrative,* p. 9; Henry, *Life of George Henry,* p. 44. On hired slaves, see Richard C. Wade, *Slavery in the Cities* (New York: Oxford University Press, 1964), pp. 38–54; Genovese, *Roll, Jordan, Roll,* pp. 390–392.
23. For the power of the expanding market to influence "cultural metaphors" or a "cognitive style," see Rhys Isaac, *The Transformation of Virginia, 1740–1790* (Chapel Hill: Institute of Early American History and Culture, 1982), pp. 310–312; Thomas L. Haskell, "Capitalism and the Origins of the Humanitarian Sensibility," *AHR* 90, 2 parts (April 1985), pp. 339–361, and (June 1985), pp. 547–566. For an important caution about imposing the ideological presuppositions of individualistic, competitive Americans upon slaves, see Elizabeth Fox-Genovese and Eugene D. Genovese, *Fruits of Merchant Capital: Slavery and Bourgeois Property in the Rise and Expansion of Capitalism* (New York: Oxford University Press, 1983), p. 90. Quotation from ibid., p. vii.
24. Grandy, *Narrative,* pp. 12–13.
25. Henry, *Life of George Henry,* p. 38.
26. Anthony Chase to Jeremiah Hoffman, Aug. 8, 1827, in *Blacks in Bondage: Letters of American Slaves,* ed. Robert S. Starobin (New York: New Viewpoints Press, 1974), p. 120.
27. Lawrence W. Levine, *Black Culture and Black Consciousness: Afro-American Folk Thought from Slavery to Freedom* (New York: Oxford University Press, 1977), pp. 118, 121, 124–125.
28. Douglass, *Life and Times,* pp. 37–38.

29. Grandy, *Narrative*, p. 36; Henry, *Life of George Henry*, p. 37.

30. For one response by a black American to the Haitian Revolution, see "Extract from a charge delivered to the African Lodge, June 24th, 1797 . . . by the Right Worshipful Prince Hall," in William Cooper Nell, *The Colored Patriots of the American Revolution* (Boston, 1855), p. 64.

31. John W. Leonard to Commercial Agent for the United States at Cape François, April 8, 1802, Consular Despatches, Cape Haitian Series, vol. 4, M-9, roll 4, RG 59, NA. Background information on the events around Cape François can be found in Thomas O. Ott, *The Haitian Revolution, 1789–1804* (Knoxville: University of Tennessee Press, 1973), pp. 139–169; C. L. R. James, *The Black Jacobins: Toussaint L'Overture and the San Domingo Revolution* (reprint, New York: Vintage Books, 1989), pp. 269–288.

32. Benjamin Bailey to Christopher Champlin, Feb. 13, 1790, in *Commerce of Rhode Island, 1726–1800*, 2 vols. (Boston: Massachusetts Historical Society, 1915), vol. 2, pp. 409–410; Donald R. Hickey, "America's Response to the Slave Revolt in Haiti, 1791–1806," *Journal of the Early Republic* 2 (Winter 1982), pp. 362–365; Philadelphia crew lists, 1803, RG 36, NA; "Return of the American Trade at the Port of Cape Haytien" and "Statistical View of the Commerce at Port-au-Prince," Consular Despatches, Cape Haitian, microfilm M-9, roll 6, RG 59, NA.

33. Julius S. Scott, "The Common Wind: Currents of Afro-American Communication in the Era of the Haitian Revolution," (Ph.D. diss., Duke University, 1986), p. 221.

34. Paul Cuffe, *Narrative of the Life and Adventures of Paul Cuffe, a Pequot Indian* (Vernon, Conn.: Horace N. Bill, 1839), p. 5; *United States v. Jones*, 26 *Federal Cases* 644 (April 1824); Scott, "Common Wind," pp. 221, 306.

35. Scott, "Common Wind," p. 217; Petition 1797–87, South Carolina General Assembly Petitions, SCDAH; George D. Terry, "South Carolina's First Negro Seamen Acts, 1793–1803," *Proceedings of the South Carolina Historical Association* (1980), pp. 83–84.

36. Floyd J. Miller, *The Search for a Black Nationality: Black Emigration and Colonization, 1787–1863* (Urbana: University of Illinois Press, 1975), pp. 74–76; William Taylor to James Monroe, Aug. 30, 1814, Consular Despatches, Cape Haitian, microfilm M-9, roll 5, RG 59, NA.

37. William Taylor to James Monroe, Jan. 9, 1814, Consular Despatches, Cape Haitian, microfilm M-9, roll 5, RG 59, NA.

38. "Protest of the Master of the Baracoa for the forcible desertion of a slave belonging to the vesel . . . at Cape Henry," Feb. 12, 1821, Misc. Letters on Seamen From Collectors of Customs, 1817–1824 (E 145), RG 59, NA.

39. On the *Nancy*, see Scott, "The Common Wind," pp. 88–89, 108.

40. Andrew Armstrong to John Quincy Adams, Sept. 24, 1822, Consular Despatches, Cape Haitian, microfilm M-9, roll 5, RG 59, NA; Andrew Armstrong to The Honorable Fresnel, Grand Judge of Haiti [n.d.], ibid.

41. A. Armstrong to John B. Boyer, Sept. 26, 1821, Consular Despatches, Cape Haitian, series 5, microfilm M-9, roll 5, RG 59, NA; A. Armstrong to John Quincy Adams, Oct. 8, 1821, ibid.

42. Jason H. McCulloch to John Quincy Adams, Aug. 17, 1822, Misc. Letters on Seamen From Collectors of Customs, 1817–1824 (E 145), RG 59, NA; Deposition of Stephen Burgess, May 27, 1822, ibid.

43. Aaron B. Nouez to John B. Boyer, Sept. 20, 1821, Consular Despatches, Cape Haitian, microfilm M-9, roll 5, RG 59, NA; Aaron B. Nouez to A. Armstrong, Sept. 20, 1821, ibid.

44. Aaron Nouez to Andrew Armstrong, Sept. 20, 1821, Consular Despatches, Cape Haitian, microfilm M-9, roll 5, series 5, RG 59, NA; Aaron B. Nouez to John B. Boyer, Sept. 20, 1821, ibid.

45. Andrew Armstrong to Daniel Brent, July 30, 1825, Consular Despatches, Cape Haitian, microfilm M-9, roll 5, RG 59, NA; Miller, *Search for a Black Nationality,* pp. 80–81.

46. Consular Returns of American Vessels, Jan. 28, 1837, Consular Despatches, Cape Haitian, microfilm M-9, roll 7, RG 59, NA. William Dickinson, a black man from Salem, Massachusetts, became the master of a Haitian brig during the middle of the nineteenth century. See Oliver Thayer to F. H. Lee, Jan. 28, 1885, Francis Henry Lee Papers, Scrapbook Material, folder 2, box 6, PEM.

47. Tobias Lear to The Commander of This Place, Cape François, March 22, 1802, Consular Despatches, Cape Haitian, microfilm M-9, roll 4, RG 59, NA; Andrew Armstrong to John Quincy Adams, Nov. 25, 1824, roll 5, ibid.

48. F. M. Dimond to John Forsyth, May 3, 1837, Consular Despatches, Port-au-Prince, microfilm T-346, roll 1, NA; *Fueille de Commerce* (Port-au-Prince), 14 (April 2, 1837), ibid.; Thomas George Swain to Dimond, April 5, 1837, ibid.

49. Ira Berlin, "The Revolution in Black Life," in *The American Revolution: Explorations in the History of American Radicalism,* ed. Alfred F. Young (DeKalb: Northern Illinois University Press, 1976), pp. 349–382; Benjamin Quarles, *The Negro in the American Revolution* (Chapel Hill: Institute for Early American History and Culture, 1961), pp. 198–199; Thomas S. Collier, "The Revolutionary Privateers of Connecticut," in *Records and Papers of the New London County Historical Society* (New London, Conn.: The Society, 1893), part 4, vol. 1, p. 44; Barbara W. Brown, *Black Roots in Southeastern Connecticut, 1650–1900* (Detroit: Gale Research Company, 1980), p. 47.

50. Cyril Outerbridge Packwood, *Chained on the Rock: Slavery in Bermuda* (Bermuda: Baxters Ltd., 1975), p. 35. These Bermudian mariners chose to return to families, friends, and slavery in Bermuda rather than risk freedom in Massachusetts.

51. Barclay, *Practical View of the Present State of Slavery*, p. xxiv.

52. *Hay v. Conner*, Thomas Harris and Reverdy Johnson, *Reports of Cases Argued and Determined in the Court of Appeals of Maryland, In 1806, 1807, 1808, and 1809* (2 vols., Annapolis, 1826), vol. 2, p. 347; *Washington v. Wilson*, 29 *Federal Cases* 359 (1818); *Slacum v. Smith*, 22 *Federal Cases* 316 (1818); *Beverly v. Brooke*, Thomas Wheaton, *Reports of Cases Argued and Adjudged in the Supreme Court of the United States*, vol. 15, p. 100 (1817); *Emerson v. Howland*, 8 *Federal Cases* 634 (1816).

53. For the "neutral trade" practiced by American shippers during the Napoleonic Wars, see Robert G. Albion, William A. Baker, and Benjamin W. Labaree, *New England and the Sea* (Middletown: Wesleyan University Press, 1972), pp. 60–63. Of a group of 176 African American sailors shipped in Baltimore in 1806, 12 were slaves. Baltimore crew lists, 1806, Records of the U.S. Customs Service, RG 36, NA.

54. Gerald W. Mullin, *Flight and Rebellion: Slave Resistance in Eighteenth-Century Virginia* (New York: Oxford University Press, 1972), p. 94. Mullin notes on p. 94 that 24 percent of skilled fugitive slaves were mariners, but on p. 95 he notes that 14 percent "worked on the water." Professor Mullin graciously clarified this discrepancy for me in a letter of November 29, 1995, by explaining that ocean-going seamen were not included in the latter. I analyzed notices for 608 male runaways in the Norfolk area from 1815 to 1832. Of the 129 runaways with known occupations, 13 percent were maritime workers. *American Beacon and Commercial Diary* (Norfolk), Aug. 7, 1815, to July 31, 1820; *American Beacon and Norfolk and Portsmouth Daily Advertiser*, Aug. 1, 1820, to Dec. 5, 1825; *Norfolk and Portsmouth Herald*, March 4, 1818, to Jan. 16, 1832.

55. Philip D. Morgan, "Black Life in Eighteenth-Century Charleston," *Perspectives in American History* 1 (1984), p. 199. Morgan's sample was 372 male slaves. B. W. Higman, *Slave Populations of the British Caribbean, 1807–1834* (Baltimore: Johns Hopkins University Press, 1984), pp. 235–236.

56. Savannah crew lists, 1803, 1811, 1817, 1819, 1827, 1830, 1833–1836, Records of the U.S. Customs Service, RG 36, NA; Petition of the Charleston Marine Society [n.d.], c. 1825, S.C. General Assembly, Petition 2080–01, SCDAH.

57. D. Eltis, "The Traffic in Slaves between the British West Indian Colonies, 1807–1833," *Economic History Review* 25 (1972), p. 56; Higman, *Slave Populations of the British Caribbean*, p. 236; table S7.1, pp. 550–551, combined with sex-ratio data, p. 116.

6. Precarious Pillar of the Black Community

1. By 1803, blacks constituted only 10 percent of Philadelphians, but more than 17 percent of that city's sailors. In Providence, Rhode Island, black men filled approximately 20 percent of sailors' and cooks' jobs from 1800 to 1820, when blacks constituted only 8.5 percent of the city's population. Philadelphia crew lists, Records of the U.S. Customs Service, RG 36, NA; Providence crew lists, U.S. Customs House Papers, RG 28 (Manuscript collection, RIHS); U.S. Department of Commerce, Bureau of the Census, *Historical Statistics of the United States: Colonial Times to 1970* (2 vols., Washington, D.C., 1975), vol. 1, pp. 24–37. On postwar shipping, see Robert G. Albion, William A. Baker, and Benjamin W. Labaree, *New England and the Sea* (Middletown: Wesleyan University Press, 1972), pp. 52–86, 102; John G. B. Hutchins, *The American Maritime Industries and Public Policy, 1789–1914* (Cambridge, Mass.: Harvard University Press, 1941), pp. 170–324.

2. "Protest Against Kidnapping and the Slave Trade," Feb. 27, 1788, in *A Documentary History of the Negro People in the United States,* ed. Herbert Aptheker (New York: Citadel Press, 1951), vol. 1, p. 21.

3. [Anonymous], "Schooner Industry on a Whaling Cruise: A Song Composed on Board of Her," Nantucket Historical Association, ms. col. 335, folder 994 [1822]; George Moore, *Notes on the History of Slavery in Massachusetts* (New York: D. Appleton and Company, 1866), p. 117; Lorin Lee Cary and Francine C. Cary, "Absalom F. Boston, His Family, and Nantucket's Black Community," *Historic Nantucket* (Summer 1977), pp. 15–22; Barbara W. Brown, *Black Roots in Southeastern Connecticut, 1650–1900* (Detroit: Gale Research Company, 1980); James M. Rose and Barbara W. Brown, *Tapestry: A Living History of the Black Family in Southeastern Connecticut* (New London, Conn.: New London County Historical Society, 1979); Lamont D. Thomas, *Paul Cuffe: Black Entrepreneur and Pan-Africanist* (Urbana: University of Illinois Press, 1986).

4. William J. Brown, *The Life of William J. Brown, of Providence, R.I. With Personal Recollections of Incidents in Rhode Island* (Providence, 1883; reprint, Freeport, N.Y.: Books for Libraries Press, 1971), p. 6; "Return of Coloured Persons Being Housekeepers," June 24, 1822, folio 118, vol. 112, Providence Town Papers, Manuscript collection, RIHS; *The Providence Directory, Containing the Names of the Inhabitants, Their Occupations, Places of Business, and Dwelling-Houses; With Lists of the Streets, Lanes, Wharves, &c.* (Providence, 1832).

5. Jay Coughtry, *Creative Survival: The Providence Black Community in the Nineteenth Century* (Providence: Rhode Island Black Heritage Society,

[1981]), p. 52; *Early Negro Writing*, ed. Dorothy Porter (Boston: Beacon Press, 1971), pp. 42–44, 51–61.

6. Thomas, *Paul Cuffe*; James Mars, *Life of James Mars*, in *Five Black Lives*, p. 56.

7. Henry Highland Garnet to Louis Alexis Chamerovzow, Oct. 2, 1854, in *The Black Abolitionist Papers*, ed. C. Peter Ripley (Chapel Hill: University of North Carolina Press, 1985), vol. 2, p. 410; Sterling Stuckey, "A Last Stern Struggle: Henry Highland Garnet and Liberation Theory," in *Black Leaders of the Nineteenth Century*, ed. Leon F. Litwak and August Meier (Urbana: University of Illinois Press, 1988), pp. 129–149.

8. Moses Grandy, *Narrative of the Life of Moses Grandy, Late a Slave in the United States of America* (Boston, 1844), in William Loren Katz, ed., *Five Slave Narratives: A Compendium* (New York: Arno Press, 1968), p. 26; Claim of Dempsey Reid, Nansemond County, Va., April 23, 1872, Approved Claims, Series 732, Southern Claims Commission, 3rd Auditor, RG 217, Records of the United States General Accounting Office, NA, document I-170, FSSP. See also Venture Smith, "A Narrative of the Life and Adventures of Venture, a Native of Africa" (New London, Conn., 1798), in *Five Black Lives*, ed. Arna Bontemps (Middletown: Wesleyan University Press, 1971), pp. 1–34; Benjamin Rockwell's will (1777), doc. 16,434, box 180, Suffolk County Probate Records, MSA.

9. "The *Adeline*," Prize and Related Records for the War of 1812 in the U.S. District Court for the Southern District of New York, 1812–1816, microfilm M 928, roll 1, pp. 295–297, 363–369, RG 21, NA; Richard C. Wade, *Slavery in the Cities: The South, 1820–1860* (New York: Oxford University Press, 1964), p. 47; Stephen B. Chace Papers, ledger, April 4, 1810, Collection 14, MSM; Providence Town Papers, vol. 88, p. 155, RIHS; Providence crew lists, 1819–1821, 1831–1835, RG 28, U.S. Customs House Papers, RIHS; Edward Carrington & Co., "Seamen's Ledgers," 1819–1821, 1831–1835, Carrington Papers, RIHS; *The John, Abner Mosher, Master, (An Appeal from New Providence)*, appendix, 1809 (pamphlet, Manuscript Collection, RIHS); Ships' Articles, 1840s, 1850s, U.S. Customs House Papers, RIHS; articles for the ship *Samuel C. Grant*, Dec. 1856, Baltimore crew lists, inbound, Feb. 1857, RG 36, NA; articles for the ships *J. G. Richardson* and *Emily St. Pierre*, Charleston crew lists, inbound, 1859, RG 36, NA; articles for the ship *Advance*, March 24, 1857, New York crew lists, 1856 (misfiled), RG 36, NA; articles for *William Lord, Jr.*, Baltimore crew lists, Feb.–April 1857, RG 36, NA.

10. To determine pay by race, it is necessary to match vessels' crew lists and shipping articles. Vessels from New London, Connecticut—1840: *Rebecca*

Groves; 1841: *Connecticut, Palladian;* 1842: *Candace, Charles Henry, Columbus, Armata, Indian Chief, Black Warrior, Tenedos, Robert Bowne, North America, Commodore Perry, Superior, Mogul, Helvetia;* 1843: *Friends, General Williams, White Oak, Electra, Palladium, New England, Hannibal, Connecticut, Pembroke;* 1844: *Jason, Charles Carroll, Betsy.* Vessels from Fall River, Massachusetts—1841: *Rowena;* 1844, *Elizabeth;* 1846, *Leonidas;* 1852, *D. W. Hall;* 1853, *Ariel.* Crew lists and shipping articles, RG 36, NA, Boston branch. From Sag Harbor, New York—1837, *Hudson.* Log of *Hudson,* log 212, MSM. From Providence—1843, *Bowditch.* Crew list and articles of *Bowditch,* Manuscript Collection, RIHS.

11. Billy G. Smith, "Material Lives of Laboring Philadelphians," *WMQ,* 3rd ser., 38 (1981), pp. 181–201; Stanley Lebergott, *Manpower in Economic Growth: The American Record since 1800* (New York: McGraw-Hill, 1964), pp. 74, 149–150, 241–247; Donald R. Adams, Jr., "Wage Rates in the Early National Period: Philadelphia, 1785–1830," *Journal of Economic History* 28 (Sept. 1968), pp. 404–426; John J. McCusker, *How Much Is That in Real Money? A Historical Price Index for Use as a Deflator of Money Values in the Economy of the United States* (Worcester, Mass.: American Antiquarian Society, 1992), pp. 323–332.

12. *Defiance v. Young Johannes,* in *Records of the Vice-Admiralty Court of Rhode Island, 1716–1752,* ed. Dorothy S. Towle (Washington: American Historical Association, 1936; reprint, Millwood, N.Y., 1975), p. 422; *Samuel Thompson and others v. Articles From Wreck of Royal Charlotte,* 1830, Admiralty Case Files for the U.S. District Court for the Southern District of New York, M-919, roll 30, case A-1–138, p. 295, RG 21, NA; H. Lee to Mary Robie, July 26, 1779, Robie Sewall Papers, MHS.

13. Cary and Cary, "Absalom F. Boston," pp. 15–23; [Anonymous], "Schooner Industry on a Whaling Cruise."

14. "The Late Abraham Williams" (possibly from the *Essex County Mercury,* March 3, 1880), photocopy at Essex Institute. A note reads, "The following statement may be considered as substantially his autobiography. It was taken down at his dictation." Deposition of Charles Williams, *Thomas Saunders v. John Carmen and Bartholomew Bukup,* Oct. term 1830, Admiralty Case Files of the U.S. District Court for the Southern District of New York, 1790–1842, roll 30, p. 583, RG 21, NA; New Bedford Tax Book, 1838, Special Collections, NBFPL; Card File Index to Crew Lists, Special Collections, NBFPL; New Bedford City Directories, 1836, 1838, 1839, 1841, 1845, 1849, 1852.

15. Deposition of Sarah Brown, Jan. 2, 1852, Records of the Overseers of the Poor (New Bedford), 1848–1854, Special Collections, NBFPL. In 1840, 402

blacks lived in Portland. Portland City Directory, 1830, 1831, 1841, 1846; New Bedford City Directory, 1838; Henry Howland Crapo, Memorandum of Tax Delinquents [New Bedford, 1838–1840], Special Collections, NBFPL; Salem, Massachusetts, City Directory, 1837, 1846.

16. John Milton Earle, Commissioner, "Report to the Governor and Council Concerning the Indians of the Commonwealth," Senate document 96, *Massachusetts Legislative Documents* (Boston, 1861), pp. 6, 8, 34; Frederick Freeman, *The History of Cape Cod: The Annals of Barnstable County, including the District of Mashpee* (Boston, 1858), vol. 1, pp. 687, 701; Charles Edward Banks, *The History of Martha's Vineyard, Dukes County, Massachusetts* (Edgartown, 1911), vol. 1, pp. 440–441; Enumeration of the People on the Marshpee Plantation, 1832, folder 13, box 2, Guardians of Indian Plantation Records, MSA; Donald M. Nielsen, "The Mashpee Indian Revolt of 1833," *New England Quarterly* 63 (Sept. 1985), pp. 400–420.

17. Earle, "Report to the Governor and Council Concerning the Indians," pp. 17, 20; Petition of Chappequiddick Indians to Governor Caleb Strong [c. 1800–1807], folder 15, box 3, Guardians of Indian Plantation Records, MSA; Petition of Christiantown Indians, Dec. 30, 1828, folder 15, box 3, ibid.; Inventory, Dec. 16, 1828, folder 15, box 3, ibid.; "Receipts and Disbursements of the Guardians of the Indians and People of Color at Chappequiddick and Christiantown," Oct. 23, 1828, Dec. 21, 1839, Dec. 22, 1840, folder 15, box 3, ibid.

18. I selected 137 black sailors from the Philadelphia crew lists in 1850 who listed Philadelphia as their residence, and looked for them in the federal census of 1850. I chose not to pursue 27 men with names so common that they were listed more than 15 places in the census. For Baltimore I selected 223 African American sailors, all of them in the crew lists for outbound ships from Baltimore in January, February, and March 1857. Baltimore and Philadelphia crew lists, U.S. Customs Service, RG 36, NA; Matchett's City Directory, 1856–1857. See also M. Ray Della, Jr., "The Problems of Negro Labor in the 1850s," *Maryland Historical Magazine* 66 (Spring 1971), pp. 14–32.

19. John Gardner to Reubens Peale, Jan. 20, 1814, John Gardner folder, box 4, Miscellaneous Correspondence Regarding Impressed Seamen, Records on Impressed Seamen, 1794–1815, RG 59, NA; Sheppard Bourne to Major Cousins, Jan. 27, 1812, Sheppard Bourne folder, box 2, ibid. See also *Thomas Saunders v. John Carmen and Bartholomew Bukup*, Admiralty Case Files for the U.S. District Court for the Southern District of New York (Oct. term, 1830), case A-1-147, microfilm 919, roll 30, p. 561, RG 21, NA; *A Black Woman's Odyssey Through Russia and Jamaica: The Narrative of Nancy*

Prince, ed. Ronald G. Walters (Boston, 1850; reprint, New York: Marcus Wiener, 1990), p. 8.

20. Deposition of John Gardner, Sept. 30, 1831, Richard Ward Greene Papers, Manuscript collection, RIHS; Depositions of John Gardner and Mary Gardner, *State vs. Fuller and Nobles,* 1835, ibid.

21. Zora Neale Hurston, *Their Eyes Were Watching God* (J. B. Lippincott, Inc., 1937; reprint, New York: Harper and Row, 1990), p. 14.

22. Charles Benson Papers, vol. 2, 1864, PEM; George Granville Putnam, *Salem Vessels and Their Voyages* (Salem, Mass.: Essex Institute, 1925), vol 2, pp. 64–65; Linda M. Maloney, "Doxies at Dockside: Prostitution and American Maritime Society, 1800–1900," in *Ships, Seafaring, and Society: Essays in Maritime History,* ed. Timothy J. Runyan (Detroit: Wayne State University Press, 1987), pp. 217–225; A. L. Wainer to "Dear Brother," Oct. 25, 1850, folder 19, series K, Mss. 80, Cory Family Papers, Undelivered Letters, Postmaster Records, ODHS.

23. *Proceedings of the Black State Conventions, 1840–1865,* ed. Philip S. Foner and George E. Walker (Philadelphia: Temple University Press, 1980), vol. 2, pp. 207–208; William P. Powell, "Coloured Seamen—Their Character and Condition, No. I," *National Anti-Slavery Standard,* Sept. 14, 1846, in Philip S. Foner and Ronald L. Lewis, *The Black Worker to 1869,* vol. 1 of *The Black Worker: A Documentary History From Colonial Times to the Present* (Philadelphia: Temple University Press, 1978), p. 198; William P. Powell to William Lloyd Garrison, Nov. 10, 1853, Garrison Papers, Rare Book Room, BPL; David Montgomery, *Workers' Control in America: Studies in the History of Work, Technology, and Labor Struggles* (Cambridge, England: Cambridge University Press, 1979), p. 13.

24. James H. Williams, *Blow the Man Down,* ed. Warren F. Kuehl (New York: E. P. Dutton and Company, 1959), p. 178. This reference was made in 1890, but the seamanship of some black cooks was common knowledge throughout the century.

25. Philadelphia crew lists, 1803, NA; Baltimore crew lists, 1806, NA; Thomas Larkin Turner Diary, Feb. 16, 1832, Manuscript Collection 95, vol. 14, MSM; W. W. Polk to Samuel D. Ingham, June 22, 1831, in *The History of Blacks in the Coast Guard from 1790* (Washington: U.S. Coast Guard, [1977]), p. 2; David Roediger, "Race and the Working-Class Past in the United States: Multiple Identities and the Future of Labor History," *International Review of Social History* 38, supplement (1993), pp. 127–143.

26. Charles A. Benson Papers, vol. 1, May 14, 1862, PEM; John Thompson, *The Life of John Thompson, A Fugitive Slave Containing His History of 25 Years in Bondage, And His Providential Escape* (Worcester, Mass.: The Author, 1856), pp. 107–108.

27. In 1810, 51 percent of the black mariners in Providence sailed as cooks or stewards, as did 24 percent of the black seamen in Philadelphia in 1803. For evidence of cooks' being paid less than sailors from 1790 to 1820, see Jonathan Colesworthy, Log of ship *Mercury,* 1800, log 835, MSM; *Henry Seton et. al. v. Ship Astrea* (Jan. 1796), Admiralty Case Files for the U.S. District Court for the Southern District of New York, M-919, roll 2, pp. 810–814, RG 21, NA; *Flood et. al. v. Ship Phillips* (May 26, 1813), ibid., roll 20, p. 55; *Anderson et. al. v. Ship Ontario* (June 23, 1813), ibid., roll 20, p. 67. For the change by the 1830s, see Deposition of John Carson, *Henry Williams v. John Moore,* 1835, ibid., roll 40, case A-1A-131, RG 21, NA. See also New London, Connecticut, and Fall River, Massachusetts, ships' articles, RG 36, Records of the U.S. Customs Service, NA (Boston branch).

28. Thompson, *Life of John Thompson,* p. 110; William C. Nell, *The Colored Patriots of the American Revolution* (Boston, 1855), pp. 244, 255; Henry Highland Crapo, Memorandum of Tax Delinquents [New Bedford, 1838–1840], Special Collections, NBFPL; J. H. Strong to S. F. DuPont, July 24, 1862, Squadron Letters, South Atlantic Squadron, July–Sept. 1862, RG 45, Naval Records Collection of the Office of Naval Records and Library, NA, document T-550, FSSP; S. F. DuPont to Gideon Welles, Aug. 15, 1862, ibid.

29. Charles A. Benson Papers, vol. 1, May 13, 1862; vol. 3, July 2, 1878, PEM. The relationship of gender and seafaring is explored in *Iron Men, Wooden Women: Gender and Seafaring in the Atlantic World, 1700–1920,* ed. Margaret S. Creighton and Lisa Norling (Baltimore: Johns Hopkins University Press, 1996).

30. Charles A. Benson Papers, vol. 4, Aug. 11, 1880, PEM; Registers of Signatures of Depositors in Branches of the Freedman's Savings and Trust Company, 1865–1874, Records of the Office of the Comptroller of the Currency, microfilm 816, roll 13, p. 158, RG 101, NA.

31. Charles A. Benson Papers, vol. 2, Nov. 21, 1864, PEM. For Susan Rex, see Registers of Signatures of Depositors in Branches of the Freedman's Savings and Trust Company, 1865–1874, microfilm 816, roll 17, pp. 12, 642, NA. For Andrew Laurey, see Records of the Overseers of the Poor, 1864–1866, March 17, 1864, Special Collections, NBFPL.

32. Nathaniel Ames, *Nautical Reminiscences* (Providence: William Marshall, 1832), p. 38; Coughtry, *Creative Survival,* p. 39.

33. George Edward Clark, *Seven Years of a Sailor's Life* (Boston: Adams and Company, 1867), p. 12; Jesse Lemisch, "Jack Tar in the Streets: Merchant Seamen in the Politics of Revolutionary America," *WMQ* 25 (July 1968), p. 377.

34. "Report and Bill Relating to the Coal Mines of the State," House Document 33, *Massachusetts Legislative Documents* (Boston, 1839), p. 40; Diane

Lindstrom, *Economic Development in the Philadelphia Region, 1810–1850* (New York: Columbia University Press, 1978), pp. 3, 119, 187–192; Robert Greenhalgh Albion, *The Rise of New York Port, 1815–1860* (New York: Charles Scribner's Sons, 1939), pp. 97, 123, 128–129, 136, 397; Wm. Jeffrey Bolster, "The Impact of Jefferson's Embargo on Coastal Commerce," *The Log of Mystic Seaport* (Spring 1980), pp. 14–21.

35. Brown, *Life of Brown*, pp. 26, 29; Coroner's Records (Boston), folder C 290, Adlow Collection, Rare Book Room, BPL; John Codman, *A Letter to the Honorable Charles Sumner, of the U.S. Senate, on the Conditions and Requirements of the American Mercantile Marine* (Washington: G. S. Gideon Printer, 1860), p. 12; Records of the Overseers of the Poor, 1848–1854 (New Bedford), Jan. 20, 1853, March 4, 1853, Special Collections, NBFPL.

36. Juliet E. K. Walker, "Racism, Slavery, and Free Enterprise: Black Entrepreneurship in the United States before the Civil War," *Business History Review* 60 (Autumn 1986), pp. 343–382; Henry J. Cadbury, "Negro Membership in the Society of Friends," *Journal of Negro History* 21 (April 1936), pp. 151–213; Ruth Cuffe to Cyrus Treadwell, Jan. 27, 1819, Cuffe Collection, Special Collections, NBFPL.

37. Enrollment of the Schooner *Resolution*, MdHS; *Norfolk Herald*, Sept. 17, 1819.

38. *Official Opinions of The Attorneys General of the United States, Advising the President and Heads of Departments, In Relation to Their Official Duties*, comp. Benjamin F. Hall (Washington, 1852), vol. 1, pp. 506–509.

39. *Davis v. Marshall*, 4 Harrington 64 (Fall 1843), in Helen Tunnicliff Catterall, *Judicial Cases Concerning American Slavery and the American Negro* (Washington: Carnegie Institution, 1926–1937), vol. 4, p. 230; Records of the Overseers of the Poor, Nov. 3, 1864, NBFPL; Daniel Drayton, "Personal Memoir of Daniel Drayton" (Boston, 1855), in *Slave Rebels, Abolitionists, and Southern Courts*, series 4 of *Slavery, Race, and the American Legal System*, ed. Paul Finkelman (New York: Garland Press, 1988), vol. 2, p. 10.

40. Maryland General Assembly House of Delegates (Journal), 1833, pp. 10–11, 35, 60–61, 257 [MdHR 821056]; Maryland General Assembly Senate (Journal), 1833, pp. 27, 44, 48, 79, 86, 94–95, 115, 146–151 [MdHR 821202]; Maryland General Assembly House of Delegates (Journal), 1836, pp. 119, 179, 194, 196, 482, 570 [MdHR 821058]; Maryland General Assembly Senate (Journal), 1836, pp. 114, 204–205, 216, 238, 259 [MdHR 821205]; *Maryland General Assembly Printed Laws* (Annapolis, 1836–1837), Chapter 150 [MdHR 820918]; Maryland General Assembly House of Delegates (Journal), 1838, pp. 35, 196 [MdHR 821060]; E. A. Andrews, *Slavery and the Domestic Slave Trade* (Boston: Light and Stearns, 1836), p. 51.

41. Testimony of Silas Moore, May 6, 1873, Claim of Silas Moore and William Martin, Craven County, N.C., Case Files, Approved Claims, Series 732, Southern Claims Commission, 3rd Auditor, RG 217, Records of the United States General Accounting Office, NA, FSSP [I-90]; Summary Report, Dec. 14, 1874, Claim of William Martin, ibid., document [I-140], FSSP.

42. Registers of Signatures of Depositors in Branches of the Freedman's Savings and Trust Company, 1865–1874, Norfolk, Va., Feb. 1, 1873, microfilm 816, roll 26, p. 130, RG 101, NA.

43. Charles H. Wesley, *Negro Labor in the United States, 1850–1925* (New York, 1927; reprint, New York: Russell & Russell, 1967), p. 46; Benjamin J. Willard, *Captain Ben's Book: A Record of the Things Which Happened to Capt. Benjamin J. Willard, Pilot and Stevedore, During Some Sixty Years on Land and Sea* (Portland, Maine: Lakeside Press, 1895), pp. 44–45; *New York Times*, Dec. 16, 1862, p. 5.

44. *New York Times*, Dec. 16, 1862, p. 5; William P. Powell, "Coloured Seamen—Their Character and Condition, No. V," *National Anti-Slavery Standard*, Nov. 12, 1846, in Foner and Lewis, *The Black Worker to 1869*, p. 209; William P. Powell, "Coloured Seamen—Their Character and Condition, No. IV," *National Anti-Slavery Standard*, Oct. 29, 1846, ibid., p. 208.

45. *Black Woman's Odyssey*, pp. 5–21; Records of the Overseers of the Poor (New Bedford), Oct. 1, 1864, Special Collections, NBFPL.

46. See Table 1. Jay Coughtry, *The Notorious Triangle: Rhode Island and the African Slave Trade, 1700–1807* (Philadelphia: Temple University Press, 1981), p. 60; Martha S. Putney, *Black Sailors: Afro-American Merchant Seamen and Whalemen Prior to the Civil War* (Westport, Conn.: Greenwood Press, 1987), p. 13; Quarterly Report, January 1858, Coloured Sailors' Home, American Seamen's Friend Society Papers, folder 2, box 2, collection 158, MSM.

47. See Table 1. Thomas, *Paul Cuffe*; Putney, *Black Sailors*, pp. 49–78; George Henry, *Life of George Henry. Together With a Brief History of the Colored People in America* (Providence, 1894; reprint, New York, 1971), p. 62.

48. Brown, *Life of Brown*, pp. 49, 103; Charles C. Andrews, *The History of the New York African Free-Schools, From Their Establishment in 1787, to the Present Time; Embracing A Period of More than Forty Years; Also A Brief Account of the Successful Labors of the New-York Manumission Society: With An Appendix* (New York, 1830; reprint, New York: Negro Universities Press, 1969), pp. 85–96. See also Aptheker, *Documentary History of the Negro People*, vol. 1, pp. 40–41.

49. J. Ross Browne, *Etchings of a Whaling Cruise: With Notes of a Sojourn on the Island of Zanzibar* (New York, 1846; reprint, Cambridge, Mass.: Har-

vard University Press, 1968), p. 108; Powell, "Coloured Seamen, No. I," p. 198; Powell, "Coloured Seamen, No. IV," p. 207.

50. William H. Wilson, logbook of the *Cavalier,* 1848–1850, log 18, MSM; Powell, "Coloured Seamen, No. I," p. 199; Powell, "Coloured Seamen, No. IV," p. 207; Frank T. Bullen, *The Cruise of the Cachelot* (1898; reprint, New Haven, 1980), p. 4.

51. *Journals of Addison Pratt,* ed. S. George Ellsworth (Salt Lake City: University of Utah Press, 1990), pp. 14–15.

52. "Report on Gaols and Houses of Correction in The Commonwealth of Massachusetts Made By A Committee Appointed By the House of Representatives, 1833," *Massachusetts Legislative Documents, House, 1834* (Boston, 1834), doc. 36, p. 35; Putney, *Black Sailors,* p. 45.

53. I traced 167 white sailors and 48 black sailors through all the Providence crew lists from 1803 to 1810, noting all the voyages they made from that port. I repeated this for 156 white sailors and 45 black sailors in the Providence crew lists from 1830 to 1837, and 153 white sailors and 15 black sailors through those lists from 1850 to 1856. Twenty-six percent of the white sailors made at least three voyages in seven years during the 1800s; 17 percent during the 1830s; and 12 percent during the 1850s. Customs House Papers, RG 28, RIHS.

54. Providence crew lists, 1803–1810, Customs House Papers, RG 28, RIHS; Records of the Overseers of the Poor, New Bedford, Massachusetts, 1864–1866, July 25, 1864, Special Collections, NBFPL; Charles Nordhoff, *Whaling and Fishing,* part 2 of Charles Nordhoff, *Life on the Ocean* (Cincinnati: Moore, Wilstarch, Keys and Company, 1874; reprint, New York: Library Editions, 1970), p. 234.

55. "Third Annual Report of the Coloured Sailors' Home," *Sailors' Magazine* 15 (Jan. 1843), p. 157. "Colored Sailors' Home, N.Y.," *Sailors' Magazine* 20 (June 1848), p. 313. William P. Powell to American Seamen's Friend Society, April 15, 1862, folder 2, box 2, collection 158, ASFS Papers, MSM; Coloured Sailors' Home, Quarterly Reports, May 1, Aug. 1, Nov. 1, 1855, Feb. 1, 1856, May 1, 1857, ibid.

56. Powell, "Coloured Seamen, No. I," p. 199; Thompson, *Life of John Thompson,* p. 107. In 1846 Powell estimated that 2,900 blacks sailed in whalers and about 6,000 in merchant ships—even though almost four times as much merchant ship tonnage existed as whaleship tonnage. See *Whalemen's Shipping List and Merchants' Transcript* 4 (Jan. 12, 1847), p. 176; "Statement Exhibiting a Condensed View of the Tonnage of the Several Districts of the United States on the 30th day of June, 1846," in Report of the Secretary of Treasury, Report No. 7, Senate, 29th Congress, 2nd session, pp. 252–254; Elmo Paul Hohman, *The American Whaleman, A Study of*

Life and Labor in the Whaling Industry (New York: Longmans, Green, 1928).

57. New Bedford City Watch Reports, May 18, 1849, Special Collections, NBFPL; New Bedford Records of the Overseers of the Poor, 1864–1866, May 5, 27, 1864, ibid.

58. Thomas V. Sullivan, *Scarcity of Seamen* (pamphlet, Boston: J. Howe, 1854), p. 3; Mariners Home Books, 1845, New Bedford Port Society, ODHS; William D. Huntington, journal kept aboard the *Contest*, May 21, 1863, PEM.

59. *Henry Williams v. John Moore*, Admiralty Case Files for the U.S. District Court for the Southern District of New York, M-919, roll 40, p. 4, RG 21, NA; Deposition of William McCourtland, U.S. Circuit Court, District of Maryland, 1820, microfilm 1010, roll 1, p. 711, RG 21, NA; *US v. Hardwick*, Record of Joseph A. Pitman, Commissioner of Circuit Court, R.I. District, 1853, misc. vol. 149, MSM.

60. Powell, "Coloured Seamen, No. V," p. 208; *U.S. v. Abel Dungan*, Criminal Case Files, U.S. Circuit Court, Maryland District (May term 1829), microfilm 1010, roll 2, pp. 429–533, RG 21, NA; E. N. Sawtell, *Treasured Moments: Being a Compilation of Letters on Various Topics* (London: Robert K. Burt, 1860), pp. 112–113.

61. *New Hampshire Gazette*, April 9, 1800; *Judicial Cases Concerning American Slavery and The Negro*, ed. Catterall, vol. 2, p. 376; *Clayton et. al. v. The Harmony*, 5 Federal Cases 994 (1807); Richard Henry Dana, *Two Years Before the Mast* (Boston, 1840; reprint, New York: Penguin, 1981), p. 330.

62. *U.S. v. Lewis Willett*, U.S. Circuit Court, Maryland District (April 1837), microfilm 1010, roll 3, pp. 218, 231, RG 21, NA; log of the ship *Chelsea*, Jan. 18, 1841, oversize log 9, MSM; Jacob Hazen, *Five Years Before the Mast* (Philadelphia: W. P. Hazard, 1854), pp. 61, 110–120.

63. Dana, *Two Years Before the Mast*, pp. 120–121; "Capt. Peabody and the Ship Neptune," *New York Times*, Jan. 24, 1866, p. 2.

64. Sidney Kaplan, "The American Seamen's Protective Union Association of 1863: A Pioneer Organization of Negro Seamen in the Port of New York," *Science & Society* 21 (Spring 1957), pp. 154–159, quotation from p. 155; *The Colored American*, May 2, 1840.

65. Providence crew lists, 1803–1807, RIHS; William Thornpoint, 1850 Philadelphia census; Inventory of Henry Robinson, May 7, 1849, No. 36092, Suffolk County Probate Records, transcription 16.3, AACP.

66. *Sailors' Magazine* 15 (June 1843), p. 293; *Sailors' Magazine* 18 (August 1846), p. 382; James Oliver Horton and Lois E. Horton, *Black Bostonians: Family Life and Community Struggle in the Antebellum North* (New York: Holmes and Meier, 1979), pp. 23–24. For dock regulations see "Substance

of the Memorial of the West India Dock Company (London, 1822), pp. 14–18.

67. Elizabeth Blackmar, *Manhattan for Rent, 1785–1850* (Ithaca: Cornell University Press, 1989), pp. 109–149. This process is charted clearly in Paul E. Johnson, *A Shopkeeper's Millennium: Society and Revivals in Rochester, New York, 1815–1837* (New York: Hill and Wang, 1978), pp. 37–63. For the impact on blacks, see Theodore Hershberg, "Free Blacks in Antebellum Philadelphia: A Study of Ex-Slaves, Freeborn, and Socioeconomic Decline," in *Philadelphia: Work, Space, Family, and Group Experience in the Nineteenth Century,* ed. Theodore Hershberg (New York: Oxford University Press, 1981), pp. 368–391.

68. Brown, *Life of Brown,* p. 35. "Home For Colored Seamen," *Sailors' Magazine* 35 (March 1863), p. 201; [Nathaniel Spooner], *The Toilers of the Sea* (pamphlet, Boston, 1875), p. 10. On New York's state law of March 1866 for the repression of dishonest boardinghouse keepers, see "Licenses for Sailors' Boardinghouses," *New York Times,* April 22, 1866, p. 5. On the federal Shipping Commissioners' Act of June 7, 1872, see Donald R. Herzog, "A Study of Labor Relations Relating to American Seamen in the Maritime Industry" (Ph.D. diss., University of Iowa, 1955), pp. 63, 91.

69. "Boarding Houses for Colored Seamen in New York," *Sailors' Magazine* 41 (1869), p. 250; James B. Congdon, Memorandum Book on Cholera in New Bedford, Aug. 31, 1834, Special Collections, NBFPL; *The Colored American* (Oct. 20, 1838), p. 3; New Bedford City Directory, 1838; "A Model Boarding House," *Sailors' Magazine* 40 (1868), pp. 214–215; Brown, *Life,* p. 33.

70. "Return of Coloured Persons Being Housekeepers"; Brown, *Life of Brown,* pp. 92–93.

71. William P. Powell, Annual Report, April 1864, American Seamen's Friend Society Papers, MSM; Philip S. Foner, "William P. Powell: Militant Champion of Black Seamen," in *Essays in Afro-American History,* ed. Philip S. Foner (Philadelphia: Temple University Press, 1978), pp. 88–111; New Bedford City Directory, 1836, 1838; "The Colored Sailors' Home," *Sailors' Magazine* 36 (Nov. 1863), p. 83; "Boarding Houses for Colored Seamen in New York," *Sailors' Magazine* 41 (1869), p. 250. "Report of the Colored Sailors' Home for the Month of January," *Sailors' Magazine* 37 (March 1865), p. 202.

72. *Sailors' Magazine* 18 (Aug. 1846), p. 382. On the Five Points district, see "Midnight Domiciliary Visits," *New York Times,* Jan. 21, 1866, p. 6; "Boarding Houses for Colored Seamen in New York," *Sailors' Magazine* 41 (1869), p. 250.

73. See note 18 of this chapter.

74. New Bedford City Watch Reports, June 1, 1848–March 24, 1850, NBFPL; Brown, *Life of Brown,* pp. 35, 90.

75. George Lightcraft, *Scraps from the Logbook of George Lightcraft* (Detroit: F. P. Markham and Brothers, 1850), p. 45; Brown, *Black Roots in Southeastern Connecticut*, pp. xiv, 95; Mrs. Hiram Bingham, "Abominable Transactions at the Sandwich Islands," March 1, 1826, John Percival Papers, folder 6, MHS.

76. Deposition of William Jordan, Sept. 30, 1831, Greene Legal Papers, RIHS; Deposition of Richard Johnson, Sept. 30, 1831, ibid.

77. Sheriff's Record Book, Feb. 2, 1829, and Aug. 16, 1830, RIHS; Providence Town Papers, vol. 144, p. 47, RIHS; Records of the Overseers of the Poor, Aug. 27, 1864, NBFPL.

78. "The Nation's Wards," *Sailors' Magazine* 45 (March 1873), pp. 65–72, quotation from p. 68; "Colored Sailors' Home," ibid., 35 (June 1863), p. 312; Seamen's Register (1832–1843), New Bedford Port Society, ODHS. Chapter 8 treats changes in maritime hiring more fully.

7. Free Sailors and the Struggle with Slavery

1. Quotation from Georgia's Senator John M. Berrien, *The Liberator*, Oct. 25, 1850. Ira Berlin, *Slaves without Masters: The Free Negro in the Antebellum South* (New York: Pantheon, 1974).

2. William Grimes, *Life of Grimes*, in *Five Black Lives: The Autobiographies of Venture Smith, James Mars, William Grimes, The Rev. G. W. Offley, James L. Smith*, ed. Arna Bontemps (Middletown: Wesleyan University Press, 1971), pp. 104–106. Most histories of the "underground railroad" argue that white captains arranged slaves' maritime escapes. See Wilbur H. Siebert, *The Underground Railroad From Slavery to Freedom* (New York: MacMillan Company, 1898; reprint, New York: Arno Press, 1968), pp. 81, 144. An important corrective is David S. Cecelski, "The Shores of Freedom: The Maritime Underground Railroad in North Carolina, 1800–1861," *North Carolina Historical Review* 71 (April 1994), pp. 174–206.

3. Robert Greenhalgh Albion, *The Rise of New York Port, 1815–1860* (New York: Scribners, 1939), pp. 95–121; South Carolina General Assembly Petition ND-1415 [1823], SCDAH.

4. My calculation that approximately 2,500 black seamen sailed out of New York in 1825 is based on the total tonnage in the New York Customs District for 1825, divided by a ratio of twenty tons per man, multiplied by the percentage of blacks then in New York's maritime labor pool, and reduced by 10 percent because some men made repeat voyages: 304,000 tons divided by 20 sailors/ton = 15,200 sailors, multiplied by 18 percent blacks = 2,736 black sailors, minus 10 percent. Tonnage statistics in Albion, *Rise of New York Port*, pp. 393, 402.

5. *C. Perry,* Savannah crew lists, 1821, RG 36, NA; Deposition of August Lemonier, Brig *Hercules, The American Insurance Co. of New York v. Charles Johnson,* June 1827, Admiralty Case Files of the Southern District of New York, microfilm M 919, roll 26, pp. 737–985, quotation from pp. 814, 815, RG 21, NA.

6. William W. Freehling, *The Road to Disunion,* vol. 1 of *Secessionists at Bay, 1776–1854* (New York: Oxford University Press, 1990), p. 79; William W. Freehling, *The Reintegration of American History: Slavery and the Civil War* (New York: Oxford University Press, 1994), pp. 34–58.

7. Freehling, *Reintegration of American History,* pp. 40–41; *The Trial Record of Denmark Vesey,* ed. John Oliver Killens (Boston: Beacon Press, 1970), p. 11.

8. *Trial Record of Denmark Vesey,* pp. 28, 59, 70–72, 117.

9. Ibid., pp. 11, 12, 159, 160; Governor John Wilson to South Carolina Senate, Nov. 25, 1824, Governor's Message 1362, Records of the General Assembly, SCDAH; "Memorial of the South Carolina Association," South Carolina General Assembly Petition ND-1415 [1823], SCDAH.

10. "Free Colored Seamen," Report of the Minority of the Committee, Jan. 20, 1843, Report No. 80, House of Representatives, 27th Congress, 3rd session, p. 37.

11. The act is conveniently reprinted in *Denmark Vesey: The Slave Conspiracy of 1822,* ed. Robert S. Starobin (Englewood Cliffs, N.J.: Prentice-Hall, Inc., 1970), pp. 149–151. Quotation from South Carolina General Assembly, Committee Report 1854–68, SCDAH.

12. [Caroliniensis], "On the Arrest of a British Seaman" (Charleston, 1823; Caroliniana Library, University of South Carolina); Berlin, *Slaves without Masters,* pp. 327–329.

13. "Free Colored Seamen," Report 80, House of Representatives, 27th Congress, 3rd session (1843), pp. 19–20.

14. Memorial of the South Carolina Association, Petition ND-1415 [1823], South Carolina General Assembly Legislative Petitions, SCDAH; Bill for Expenses for Bringing Colored Man into Charleston, May 3, 1824, Thomas Lamb Papers, MHS; "Report on the Deliverance of Citizens Liable to be Sold as Slaves," *Massachusetts Legislative Documents,* House doc. 38 (Boston, 1839), p. 27.

15. Robert Harrison to Humphrey Peake, Feb. 19, 1824, Letters Received, Alexandria, Va., box 2, E-1251, Records of the Bureau of Customs, RG 36, NA.

16. Clement Eaton, "A Dangerous Pamphlet in the Old South," *Journal of Southern History* 2 (Aug. 1936), pp. 323–334, quotation from p. 323; Herbert Aptheker, *"One Continual Cry": David Walker's Appeal to the Colored*

Citizens of the World (1829–1830): Its Setting and Its Meaning (New York: Humanities Press, 1965), pp. 63, 83, 89; Sterling Stuckey, *Slave Culture: Nationalist Theory and the Foundations of Black America* (New York: Oxford University Press, 1987), pp. 98–137.

17. *Freedom's Journal*, Dec. 19, 1828; Stuckey, *Slave Culture*, pp. 98–137; Aptheker, *"One Continual Cry,"* pp. 42–46.

18. Eaton, "A Dangerous Pamphlet," p. 323; Ralph B. Flanders, "The Free Negro in Antebellum Georgia," *North Carolina Historical Review* 9 (July 1932), p. 263. For the case of John Glasgow, arrested in Savannah under the act in 1830 and sold into slavery, see *Black Abolitionist Papers*, vol. 1, *The British Isles, 1830–1865*, ed. C. Peter Ripley (Chapel Hill: University of North Carolina Press, 1985), pp. 261, 266, n. 6.

19. John Hope Franklin, *The Free Negro in North Carolina, 1790–1860* (Chapel Hill: University of North Carolina Press, 1943), pp. 69–70; Philip M. Hamer, "Great Britain, the United States, and the Negro Seamen Acts, 1822–1848," *Journal of Southern History* 1 (Feb. 1935), pp. 16–19.

20. Berlin, *Slaves without Masters*, pp. 108–132, quotation from pp. 130, 172; Martha S. Putney, *Black Sailors: Afro-American Merchant Seamen and Whalemen Prior to the Civil War* (Westport: Greenwood Press, 1987), p. 130; New Orleans and Savannah crew lists, RG 36, NA. See Table 1.

21. Stan Hugill, *Shanties from the Seven Seas: Shipboard Work-Songs and Songs Used as Work-Songs From the Great Days of Sail* (London: Routledge and Kegan Paul, 1984), p. 128.

22. Franklin W. Knight, *Slave Society in Cuba during the Nineteenth Century* (Madison: University of Wisconsin Press, 1970), p. 96; Gwendolyn Midlo Hall, *Social Control in Slave Plantation Societies: A Comparison of St. Domingue and Cuba* (Baltimore: Johns Hopkins University Press, 1971), p. 128; Powell in Philip S. Foner and Ronald L. Lewis, *The Black Worker to 1869*, vol. 1 of *The Black Worker: A Documentary History from Colonial Times to the Present* (Philadelphia: Temple University Press, 1978), p. 206; Albion, *Rise of New York Port*, p. 395; *The Colored American*, Oct. 21, 1837, p. 3. For passage and amendments of these laws, the best sources remain Hamer's fine essays in the *Journal of Southern History*.

23. Eighty-nine percent of the black sailors shipping from Savannah in 1811 and 91 percent in 1819 were born outside the South. Savannah crew lists, 1811, 1819, RG 36, NA; Charles Ball, *Fifty Years in Chains: Or, The Life of an American Slave* (New York, 1858), p. 418.

24. New Orleans crew lists, RG 36, NA; Richard Tansey, "Out-of-State Free Blacks in Late Antebellum New Orleans," *Louisiana History* 22 (Fall 1981), p. 370.

25. William C. Nell, *The Colored Patriots of the American Revolution* (Boston,

1855), p. 119; *The Liberator,* June 7, 1834, in Herbert Aptheker, *A Documentary History of the Negro People in the United States* (New York: Citadel Press, 1951), vol. 1, p. 153.

26. William P. Powell, "Coloured Seamen—Their Character and Condition, No. II," *National Anti-Slavery Standard,* Oct. 8, 1846, in Foner and Lewis, *Black Worker to 1869,* pp. 201–202.

27. William P. Powell, "Coloured Seamen—Their Character and Condition, No. III," *National Anti-Slavery Standard,* Oct. 15, 1846, in Foner and Lewis, *Black Worker to 1869,* p. 202.

28. "Report of the Deliverance of Citizens Liable to be Sold as Slaves," p. 21; Moses Grandy, *Narrative of the Life of Moses Grandy,* in *Five Slave Narratives,* ed. William Loren Katz (New York: Arno Press, 1968), p. 28; John W. Blassingame, *Slave Testimony: Two Centuries of Letters, Speeches, Interviews, and Autobiographies* (Baton Rouge: Louisiana State University Press, 1977), pp. 284–286; 690–695.

29. Laura A. White, "The South in the 1850s as Seen by British Consuls," *Journal of Southern History* 1 (Feb. 1935), p. 32.

30. South Carolina General Assembly, Legislative Papers, "In the Matter of John Jones, a British Colored Seaman," Message 3 of Governor J. H. Hammond, 1843, SCDAH; South Carolina General Assembly, Committee Report, 1845–66, SCDAH; South Carolina General Assembly, Resolution 1854–14, SCDAH.

31. South Carolina General Assembly, Petition ND-2916, circa 1859, SCDAH.

32. Jonathan Walker, *A Brief View of American Chattelized Humanity and Its Supports* (Boston, 1846), p. 8; Berlin, *Slaves without Masters,* pp. 225–227, 323–324; "Report on the Deliverance of Citizens Liable to be Sold as Slaves," pp. 15–17; Powell, "Coloured Seamen," no. II, pp. 200–201.

33. Andrew Dunlap Papers, Marine and Shipping Cases, 1826–1828, folder 3, box 1, PEM; "Report on the Deliverance of Citizens Liable to Be Sold As Slaves," pp. 12–13; Aptheker, *Documentary History of the Negro People,* vol. 1, pp. 152–153.

34. George Turner to Richard Ward Greene, Aug. 8, 1834, Richard Ward Greene Papers, Manuscript Collection, RIHS; *Massachusetts Legislative Documents* (Boston, 1845), Senate doc. 4, p. 1, House doc. 14, pp. 6, 13, 14, House doc. 60, pp. 1–2; *The Liberator,* Jan. 17, 1845, p. 1.

35. *The Liberator,* Nov. 4, 1842, Feb. 7, 1845; Philip M. Hamer, "British Consuls and the Negro Seamen Acts, 1850–1860," *Journal of Southern History* 1 (May 1935), p. 139.

36. Charles Barron to John Barron, Nov. 30, 1839, in Alan F. January, "The First Nullification: The Negro Seamen Acts Controversy in South Carolina,

1822–1860" (Ph.D. diss., University of Iowa, 1976), p. 278; Powell, "Coloured Seamen," no. III, p. 206; *The Liberator,* Oct. 4, 1850, p. 1; Captain Oliver Smith to Daniel W. Lord, May 2, 1826, folder 1, box 8, Daniel W. Lord Papers, Baker Library, Harvard University.

37. Tansey, "Out-of-State Free Blacks in Late Antebellum New Orleans," pp. 372–373.

38. Powell, "Coloured Seamen," no. III, p. 206. The British consul in Savannah claimed that, on average, only about 28 black sailors arrived there each year between 1848 and 1850. This seems unlikely, given that for the year ending April 1, 1848, 4,687 seamen sailed into Savannah. The actual number of black sailors was probably exaggerated by Powell and underreported by the consul. See Hamer, "British Consuls and the Negro Seamen Acts," p. 167; *Census of the City of Savannah,* ed. Joseph Bancroft (Savannah, 1848), p. 40.

39. My estimate of at least 10,000 black sailors incarcerated under the Negro Seamen Acts was calculated as follows: New Orleans: according to police records of the Third District, 88 percent of the alien free blacks arrested in New Orleans between 1859 and 1862 were seamen. Based on ship arrivals and crew lists, I estimate that at least 2,800 black sailors arrived in New Orleans between 1842 and 1852. Most were jailed. This suggests that at least 4,000 black sailors were imprisoned in New Orleans between 1842 and 1862. In addition, before 1842, when 1,500 to 1,700 black sailors arrived annually, many were jailed. South Carolina: during a nine-week period in 1823, 154 blacks were jailed in Charleston; tonnage figures and crew lists suggest that at least 700 black sailors entered Charleston that year. "Registers of Colored Seamen" maintained by the mayor and the harbor master record 220 black seamen arriving in Charleston from the "First Monday in December, 1856 to the First Monday in December, 1857." Other observations from 1837, 1839, 1842, 1844, and 1846 suggest that 20 to 50 black sailors entered Charleston each month during the 34 years these acts were enforced. At a minimum of 20 per month, or 240 per year, 8,160 would have been jailed. Tansey, "Out-of-State Free Blacks in Late Antebellum New Orleans," pp. 369–386, esp. pp. 376–379; Albion, *Rise of New York Port,* pp. 392–393; New Orleans crew lists, RG 36, NA; *Congressional Globe,* 31st Congress, 1st session (1850), appendix, part 2, pp. 1,674–1,678; South Carolina General Assembly, Miscellaneous Communications, 1857–1, SCDAH; Hamer, "British Consuls and the Negro Seamen Acts," n. 111, p. 167; *The Liberator,* Jan. 17, 1845, Oct. 4, 1850; January, "The First Nullification," p. 278.

40. Powell, "Coloured Seamen," no. II, pp. 200–201; Receipt for Incarceration

of Black Seamen, Message 3 of Governor J. H. Hammond, 1843, South Carolina General Assembly Legislative Papers, SCDAH; "Ship Medford," Bills Paid, Sept. 26, 1844, case 4, Thatcher Magoun Papers, Baker Library, Harvard University; Hugill, *Shanties From the Seven Seas,* p. 128.

41. George Henry, *The Life of George Henry. Together with a Brief History of the Colored People in America* (Providence, 1894; reprint, Freeport, N.Y.: Books for Libraries Press, 1971), p. 52.

42. J. C. Flagg to "Dear Brother," April 2, 1854, William Flagg Papers, Ms. 48, Portsmouth Athenaeum, Portsmouth, N.H.; 6 *Federal Cases* 1102, The *Cynosure* (July 1844).

43. Savannah crew lists, 1836, RG 36, NA.

44. 4 *Federal Cases* 383, *Brown v. Hartley* (Aug. 5, 1851).

45. "Report on the Deliverance of Citizens Liable to be Sold as Slaves," p. 25.

46. 23 *Federal Cases* 225, *Stratton et. al v. Babbage* (1855).

47. *New Orleans Daily Orleanian,* July 9, 1857, quoted in Tansey, "Out-of-State Free Blacks in Late Antebellum New Orleans," pp. 371, 374; 23 *Federal Cases* 225, *Stratton et. al. v. Babbage* (1855).

48. "The Autobiography of James P. Thomas: A Slave and Free Negro in the Antebellum South," quoted in Loren Schweninger, "A Negro Sojourner in Antebellum New Orleans," *Louisiana History* 20 (Summer 1979), pp. 310–312. DuPont to Gideon Welles, Nov. 14, 1862, Squadron Letters, South Atlantic Squadron, Oct.–Dec. 1862, vol. 5, pp. 148–149, Naval Records Collection of the Office of Naval Records and Library, RG 45, NA, document [T-556], FSSP.

49. "Report on the Deliverance of Citizens Liable to be Sold as Slaves," p. 26; the ship *Moses Taylor,* New Orleans crew lists, Feb. 1860, NA.

50. Report of the Committee on Federal Relations, South Carolina General Assembly, Committee Report 1843–77, SCDAH.

51. William P. Powell to William Lloyd Garrison, May 18, 1840, Garrison Papers, Rare Book Room, BPL; William P. Powell to Samuel May, Jr., Dec. 31, 1859, *Black Abolitionist Papers,* vol. 1, *The British Isles, 1830–1865,* p. 474.

52. *Proceedings of the Black State Conventions, 1840–1865,* ed. Philip S. Foner and George E. Walker (Philadelphia: Temple University Press, 1980), vol. 2, p. 96.

53. *Black Abolitionist Papers,* vol. 1, *The British Isles, 1830–1861,* pp. 430–431; *The Liberator,* Jan. 24, 1845, p. 2; Irving H. Bartlett, "Abolitionists, Fugitives, and Imposters in Boston, 1846–1847," *New England Quarterly* 55 (March 1982), p. 101; Aptheker, *Documentary History of the Negro People,* vol. 1, p. 207.

54. "Miscellany," *Afro-Anglo Magazine,* Sept. 1859, vol. 1, no. 9, p. 301; "The Fu-

gitive Slave Law and Its Victims," *Anti-Slavery Tracts* (New York, 1861; reprint, Westport, Conn.: Greenwood Press, 1970), series 1, no. 18, pp. 24–25.

55. "Abolitionists Dealt With in Camden County," in "A Fresh Catalog of Southern Outrages Upon Northern Citizens," *Anti-Slavery Tracts*, series 2, no. 14, pp. 23–24; *Douglass' Monthly*, Oct. 1859, in Foner and Lewis, *Black Worker to 1869*, pp. 235–236; "The Fugitive Slave Law and Its Victims," p. 107.

56. G. E. Stevens to ——, Jan. 8, 1858, in Foner and Lewis, *Black Worker to 1869*, pp. 234–235.

57. Berlin, *Slaves without Masters*, p. 181. For the inquisitiveness with which blacks regarded the condition of black people elsewhere, see "Free People of Color in the Island of St. Thomas, West Indies," *The Colored American*, Mar. 11, 1837, p. 4.

8. Toward Jim Crow at Sea

1. Fats Waller quoted by John Langston Gwaltney, *Drylongso: A Self-Portrait of Black America* (New York: Random House, 1980), p. xxv; Final Record Book 6, U.S. District Court at Providence, Records of the U.S. District Court, 1822, p. 146, RG 21, NA (Boston branch); Boston Coroner's Records, C 292, Adlow Collection, Rare Book Room, BPL.

2. Elmo Paul Hohman, *The American Whaleman* (New York: Longmans, Green, 1928), p. 55.

3. Francis Allyn Olmstead, *Incidents of a Whaling Voyage (1839–40); Scenery, Manners and Customs and Missionary Stations of the Sandwich and Society Islands* (New York: D. Appleton, 1841), p. 115.

4. *Virginia Gazette* (Jan. 20, 1774), in *Runaway Slave Advertisements: A Documentary History from the 1730s to 1790*, comp. Lathan A. Windley (Westport, Conn.: Greenwood Press, 1983), vol. 1, pp. 142–143; Samuel G. Perkins, "Sketches of St. Domingo from January, 1785 to December, 1794," *Proceedings of the Massachusetts Historical Society*, 2nd series, vol. 2 (Boston: Massachusetts Historical Society, 1886), p. 308.

5. Stan Hugill, *Shanties from the Seven Seas: Shipboard Work-Songs and Songs Used as Work-Songs from the Great Days of Sail* (London: Routledge and Kegan Paul, 1984), pp. 1–41; quotation from Roger Abrahams, *Deep the Water, Shallow the Shore: Three Essays on Shantying in the West Indies* (Austin: University of Texas Press, 1974), p. xiii.

6. John D. Whidden, *Ocean Life in the Old Sailing Ship Days* (Boston: Little, Brown and Company, 1908), p. 97; J. G. Jewell, *Among Our Sailors* (New York: Harper and Brothers, 1874), p. 188.

7. S. G. Howe, *Report to the Freedmen's Inquiry Commission 1864: The Refugees from Slavery in Canada West* (Boston, 1864; reprint, New York: Arno Press, 1969), p. 76.

8. Baltimore crew lists, 1857, Records of the U.S. Customs Service, RG 36, NA; Samuel Samuels, *From the Forecastle to the Cabin* (Boston: C. E. Lauriat Company, 1924), p. 292; *Democratic Press* (Philadelphia), June 17, 1825, quoted in Susan G. Davis, *Parades and Power: Street Theatre in Nineteenth-Century Philadelphia* (Berkeley: University of California Press, 1988), p. 133. On "checkerboard crews," see Robert Carse, *The Twilight of Sailing Ships* (New York: Grosset and Dunlap, 1965), pp. 103–104; Alfred John Green, *Jottings from a Cruise* (Seattle: Kelly Printing Company, 1944), p. v; William S. Swift, *The Negro in the Offshore Maritime Industry,* part 3 in *Negro Employment in the Maritime Industries: A Study of Racial Policies in the Shipbuilding, Longshore, and Offshore Maritime Industries,* ed. Lester Rubin, William S. Swift, and Herbert R. Northrup (Philadelphia: Wharton School, University of Pennsylvania, 1974), p. 66.

9. Acting Rear Admiral David D. Porter, July 26, 1863, General Order 76, area 5, box 5, Naval Records Collection of the Office of Naval Records and Library, RG 45, NA, document [T-6], FSSP.

10. Richard J. Cleveland, *Voyages and Commercial Enterprises of the Sons of New England* (New York: Leavitt and Allen, 1855), p. 26; Elmo P. Hohman, *Seamen Ashore: A Study of the United States' Seamen's Service and of Merchant Seamen in Port* (New Haven: Yale University Press, 1952), p. 3.

11. My work on occupational mobility among Providence's white seamen, 1803–1856, indicates that virtually any white man making multiple voyages through the 1830s would be promoted. See also David Montgomery, "The Working Classes of the Pre-Industrial American City, 1780–1830," *Labor History* 9 (1968), p. 16; *A Black Woman's Odyssey Through Russia and Jamaica: The Narrative of Nancy Prince,* ed. Ronald G. Walters (New York: Markus Wiener Publishing, 1990), pp. 11, 13.

12. John G. B. Hutchins, *The American Maritime Industries and Public Policy, 1789–1914: An Economic History* (Cambridge, Mass.: Harvard University Press, 1941; reprint, New York: Russell and Russell, 1969), pp. 426–427; "Unpunished Cruelties on the High Seas, A Letter to Samuel Whitbread, Esq., M.P., by a Liverpool Merchant" (pamphlet, London, 1859).

13. Jacob A. Hazen, *Five Years Before the Mast; Or, Life in the Forecastle, Aboard of A Whaler and Man-of-War* (Philadelphia: W. P. Hazard, 1854), p. 184; J. Ross Browne, *Etchings Of A Whaling Cruise: With Notes of a Sojourn on the Island of Zanzibar* (New York, 1846; reprint, Cambridge, Mass.: Harvard University Press, 1968), p. 23; Christopher Slocum, journal kept on

board the *Obed Mitchell,* quoted by Gaddis Smith, "Black Seamen and the Federal Courts, 1789–1860," in *Ships, Seafaring, and Society: Essays in Maritime History* (Detroit: Wayne State University Press, 1987), p. 321.

14. Richard Henry Dana, *Two Years Before the Mast* (Boston, 1840; reprint, Boston: Houghton Mifflin, 1869), pp. 116–117.

15. Browne, *Etchings Of A Whaling Cruise,* p. 495; Robert J. Cottrol, *The Afro-Yankees: Providence's Black Community in the Antebellum Era* (Westport, Conn.: Greenwood Press, 1982), pp. 120–121, 151–52; Charles Nordhoff, *Whaling and Fishing,* part 2 of Charles Nordhoff, *Life on the Ocean* (Cincinnati: Moore, Wilstarch, Keys and Company, 1874; reprint, New York: Library Editions, 1970), pp. 52–53.

16. "Colored Citizens: Their Condition in This City," *New York Daily Tribune,* Aug. 25, 1871, p. 2.

17. Federal census for Boston, 1850 and 1860; Providence crew lists, U.S. Customs House Papers, RG 28, RIHS; New York crew lists, Records of the U.S. Customs Service, RG 36, NA.

18. Margaret S. Creighton, *Rites and Passages: The Experience of American Whaling, 1830–1870* (Cambridge, England: Cambridge University Press, 1995), p. 214; Joseph Conrad, *The Nigger of the "Narcissus"* (New York, 1908), p. ix. For the historical roots of Conrad's fiction, including experiences with black shipmates, see Jerry Allen, *The Sea Years of Joseph Conrad* (New York: Doubleday and Company, 1965).

19. Browne, *Etchings Of a Whaling Cruise,* p. 108.

20. Providence crew lists, 1803–1856, U.S. Customs House Papers, RIHS; New York, Philadelphia, and Baltimore crew lists, Records of the U.S. Customs Service, RG 36, NA.

21. Crew list for the brig *John Josiah Arnold,* outbound, 1803, Providence crew lists, Customs House Papers, RIHS; Joseph Bates, *The Autobiography of Elder Joseph Bates* (Battle Creek: Seventh Day Adventist Publishing Association, 1868), p. 106.

22. Baltimore crew lists, 1806, 1816, 1852, 1857, 1866, Records of the U.S. Customs Service, RG 36, NA. Many community studies indicate that members of similar ethnic and occupational groups rarely had identical experiences. The checkered fortunes of many black American sailors at mid-century bear this out.

23. Providence crew lists, U.S. Customs House Papers, RG 28, RIHS.

24. Shipping articles and crew lists from twenty-four vessels, Baltimore, 1870, RG 36, NA; John S. Rock, *The Liberator,* March 16, 1860, in Philip S. Foner and Ronald L. Lewis, *The Black Worker to 1869,* vol. 1 of *The Black Worker: A Documentary History from Colonial Times to the Present* (Philadelphia:

Temple University Press, 1978), p. 164; *Frederick Douglass's Paper,* March 4, 1853, ibid., p. 255.

25. "Descriptive Lists of Men Entered at the Naval Rendezvous at Baltimore, 1846–1852," and "Enlistment Rendezvous" Records, vols. 3, 4, 5, 6, 7, 8, 10, Records of the Bureau of Naval Personnel, RG 24, NA; Frederick S. Harrod, *Manning the New Navy: The Development of a Modern Naval Enlisted Force, 1899–1940* (Westport, Conn.: Greenwood Press, 1978), p. 11.

26. Hutchins, *American Maritime Industries,* pp. 426–432; W. E. B. DuBois, *The Philadelphia Negro* (Philadelphia: University of Pennsylvania, 1899), p. 97.

27. Brig *Nelson* crew list, Providence crew lists, 1834, U.S. Customs House Papers, RG 28, RIHS.

28. Stanley Lebergott, *Manpower in Economic Growth: The American Record since 1800* (New York: McGraw-Hill, 1964), pp. 26–27; Roland Freeman Gould, *The Life of Gould, An Ex-Man-of-War's-Man; With Incidents on Sea and Shore, Including the Three-Year's Cruise on the Line of Battle Ship Ohio, on the Mediterranean Station, Under the Veteran Commodore Hall* (Claremont, N.H.: Claremont Manufacturing Company, 1867), p. 191. Richard Henry Dana, J. Ross Browne, James Fenimore Cooper, and others also claimed that foreigners were manning American ships.

29. Whidden, *Ocean Life in the Old Sailing Ship Days,* p. 172; *A Black Woman's Odyssey Through Russia and Jamaica,* p. 3; Charles A. Benson Papers, PEM.

30. *Samuel Thompson and others v. Articles from Wreck of Royal Charlotte* (1830), Admiralty Case Files for the U.S. District Court for the Southern District of New York, microfilm M-919, roll 30, case A-1–138, RG 21, NA; *Thomas Saunders v. John Carman and Bartholomew Bukup,* ibid., microfilm M-919, roll 30, case A-1–147, pp. 582–586, RG 21, NA; 26 *Federal Cases* 207, *U.S. v. Haskell* (1823).

31. Alexander Falconbridge, *An Account of the Slave Trade on the Coast of Africa* (London, 1788; reprint, New York: Arno Press, 1973), p. 49; J. Stevenson, "The London 'Crimp' Riots of 1794," *International Review of Social History* 16 (1971), pp. 41–42; Captain Thomas Truxtun to Lieutenant John Rodgers, April 1798, in *Naval Documents Related to the Quasi-War between the United States and France* (Washington: Government Printing Office, 1935), vol. 1, pp. 49–51.

32. Carl Seaburg and Stanley Patterson, *Merchant Prince of Boston: Col. T. H. Perkins, 1764–1854* (Cambridge, Mass.: Harvard University Press, 1971), pp. 146–147; *U.S. v. Brig Enterprise* (1794), Admiralty Case Files for the U.S. District Court for the Southern District of New York, microfilm M-919, roll 2, p. 290, RG 21, NA; *Henry Seton et. al. v. Ship Astrea* (Jan. 1796), ibid.,

microfilm M-919, roll 2, pp. 810–814, RG 21, NA. On *Nancy*, see depositions in the Bermuda Court of Vice-Admiralty, Jan. 17, 1795, in Donaldson Protest Book, Mss. 1160, pp. 35–44, Manuscripts Collection, MdHS; Elijah Cobb, *Elijah Cobb, 1768–1848: A Cape Cod Skipper* (New Haven: Yale University Press, 1925), pp. 21–26, 66; Depositions of Thomas H. Perkins and Benjamin T. Reed, in "Report of the Committee of the House on Impressed Seamen," *Massachusetts Legislative Documents* (Boston, 1813), pp. 39–40, 45–46; Richard Peters, *Admiralty Decisions in the District Court of the United States for the Pennsylvania District* (Philadelphia, 1807), vol. 2, p. 412.

33. *Virginia Gazette*, July 29, 1776, p. 6; *The Medley, or New Bedford Marine Journal*, May 25, 1796; John Codman, *A Letter to the Honorable Charles Sumner, of the United States Senate, on the Condition and Requirements of the American Mercantile Marine* (pamphlet, Washington, 1860), pp. 6–7; "Mode of Shipping Seamen, Now and Formerly," *Sailors' Magazine* 23 (March 1851), p. 204.

34. The following illuminate multiple ways seamen found jobs from the 1820s to the 1850s. Edward Carrington to Capt. Lloyd Bowers, April 15, 1822, William R. Bowers Papers, collection 24, MSM; Papers of the Brig *Agenora*, 1832, ibid.; bills for shipping men for the Brig *Diamond*, 1836, ibid.; receipt from Charles Fitzsimmons for shipping men on the Brig *Smyrna*, 1836, folder 5, ibid.; *Sailors' Magazine and Naval Journal* (Dec. 1829), pp. 111–112; Deposition of Daniel James, *U.S. v. Abel Dungan*, Criminal Cases Files, U.S. Circuit Court, Maryland District (May 1829), microfilm M-1010, roll 2, p. 525, RG 21, NA; Hazen, *Five Years Before the Mast*, pp. 15–26; Deposition of Capt. James Mahan, *William G. Boardman et. al. v. Peter Jansen* (1835), Admiralty Case Files for the U.S. District Court for the Southern District of New York, microfilm M-919, roll 40, p. 210, RG 21, NA; *Thomas Goin et. al. v. Brig Maria* (1835), ibid., microfilm M-919, roll 40, p. 154; *Hallett and Goin v. Ship Mt. Vernon* (1829), ibid., microfilm M-919, roll 30, pp. 866–870, 882, 899.

35. *Michael Farrell and John Campbell v. Francis M. French* (1830), Admiralty Case Files for the U.S. District Court for the Southern District of New York, microfilm M-919, roll 30, case A-1–157, pp. 774, 779, 807, RG 21, NA; William McNally, *Evils and Abuses in the Naval and Merchant Service Exposed* (Boston, 1839), pp. 46–47; *Matchett's Baltimore Director[y]* (Baltimore: Richard J. Matchett, 1831); Whidden, *Ocean Life in the Old Sailing Ship Days*, pp. 172, 240–242.

36. R. H. Dana, *The Seaman's Friend* (Boston: Thomas Groom and Co., 1851; reprint, Delmar, N.Y.: Scholars' Facsimiles, 1979), p. 132; Jewell, *Among Our*

Sailors, p. 67; McNally, *Evils and Abuses in the Naval and Merchant Service*, pp. 18–22, 194; Paul S. Taylor, *The Sailors' Union of the Pacific* (New York: Ronald Press Company, 1923), pp. 26–30; Annual Report of the Coloured Sailors' Home, April 25, 1866, American Seamen's Friend Society Papers, folder 2, box 2, collection 158, MSM.

37. Samuel and Charles Howard to A. S. Bullock, March 4, 1811, Letters Received, Savannah Collector of Customs, box 2, E 1466, Records of the U.S. Customs Service, RG 36, NA.

38. *Matchett's Baltimore City Director[y]* (Baltimore: Richard J. Matchett, 1856); *Sailors' Magazine* 41 (1869), pp. 250, 345, 346; ibid., 15 (1843), p. 157.

39. James Bunker Congdon to American Freedmen's Inquiry Commission, Sept. 19, 1863, James Bunker Congdon Collection, NBFPL; Herbert G. Gutman, "Documents on Negro Seamen during the Reconstruction Period," *Labor History* 7 (1966), pp. 307–311, quotation from p. 308.

40. Ralph Ellison, *Shadow and Act* (New York, 1953; reprint, New York: Vintage Books, 1972), p. 315.

41. For a perceptive account of the impact of freedom, see Lawrence W. Levine, *Black Culture and Black Consciousness: Afro-American Folk Thought from Slavery to Freedom* (New York: Oxford University Press, 1977), pp. 138–155.

ACKNOWLEDGMENTS

Sailors traditionally received an "advance," and fortunate scholars still do. I sincerely appreciated graduate stipends from the History Department of the Johns Hopkins University; a semester of funded research from Mystic Seaport Museum's Paul Cuffe Fellowship for the Study of Minorities in Maritime History; a predoctoral fellowship from the Smithsonian Institution, specifically the National Museum of American History's Afro-American Communities Project; a University of New Hampshire Faculty Summer Research Stipend; a National Endowment for the Humanities Fellowship for University Teachers; and the University of New Hampshire's Hortense Cavis Shepherd Professorship. These institutions matched faith with generosity.

This book has been in the making for a long time, and its final shape owes a great deal to the labor and inspiration of others. I thank the archivists who steered me through the shoals of their collections, especially Harold Kemble, at the Rhode Island Historical Society; Walter Hill, John Vandereedt, and Aloha South at the National Archives; Paul O'Pecko at Mystic Seaport Museum; Paul Cyr at the New Bedford Free Public Library; Virginia Adams at the Old Dartmouth Historical Society; and helpful staffers at the Maryland Hall of Records and the South Carolina Department of Archives and History. Interlibrary loan and reference librarians at the Johns Hopkins University and the University of New Hampshire provided yeoman service. Computing assistance came from the staff at Johns Hopkins's Homewood Academic Computing Center, and from Computing and Information

Services at the University of New Hampshire. Four excellent research assistants from Howard University and the University of New Hampshire plugged holes during the homestretch: Roger A. Davidson, Jr., Lisa Y. King, Jason Swinbourne, and Pamela Hopkins. Friends in the profession who pushed miscellaneous but important data my way include Christopher McKee, Peter Leavenworth, Graham Hodges, Robert Olwell, Daniel Vickers, Margaret Footner, Julie Winch, Judith Luckett, and Ira Dye—who graciously made available his impressive computerized research on sailors in the War of 1812. Richard Stinely drew the marvelous maps.

Black Jacks began as a doctoral dissertation under the direction of Ronald G. Walters, mentor nonpareil. Ron's sharp eye made this a better book; his sense of humor saved me from myself. In his inestimable fashion, Ron helped me cross my own River Jordan. Other members of my committee provided valuable encouragement, notably Jack P. Greene. During the early stages of the project I profited immensely from the critical reading and encouragement of Naomi Lamoreaux, Rhett Jones, David W. Cohen, Louis Galambos, Toby Ditz, and John Higham. Long before that, Edward W. Sloan and Benjamin W. Labaree introduced me to the serious study of maritime history. A paper on black sailors published in the *Journal of American History* elicited expert criticism from editors and readers, including Gary Nash, David Thelen, and Susan Armeny. At the manuscript stage I benefited from the commitment and wise counsel of Laurel T. Ulrich, James Sidbury, Ira Berlin, and James O. Horton, who carefully read the entire manuscript; and from J. William Harris, Margaret Creighton, Lisa Norling, and members of the University of New Hampshire's History Department faculty seminar, who read sections of it. My old shipmates Captain Daniel D. Moreland (master mariner) and Carlyle Brown (master playwright) not only read it but exhorted me in ways others could not. A hard taskmaster with heart, Joyce Seltzer has been an exemplary editor. She and my copyeditor, Christine Thorsteinsson, smoothed many a rough passage. As these friends well know, their assistance does not relieve me of full responsibility for what follows.

Folks closer to home have also earned a place on this page. My parents deserve considerable thanks. Years ago, Sally and Bill Bolster instilled in me both the desire to write and the conviction to fulfill long-term goals. My children, Ellie and Carl, deserve more of my time. Although six-year-old Ellie has been inspired to make many "books" as I have struggled to finish this one, she and her brother have eaten too many dinners without me. My wife, Molly, deserves more time too, and thanks for her equanimity and forbearance. She did not type or proofread, but she has been listening to tales of black sailors for a decade. Sometimes I think that shamans inspired this book, but I know that Molly anchored it.

INDEX

Able seamen, 78, 79, 80, 81, 83, 182
Abolitionism, 2, 4, 36, 41, 154, 173, 191,
   204, 205; organized, 199;
   enslavement of abolitionists, 202;
   seafaring, 211–212, 214. *See also*
   Antislavery movement
Acculturation of blacks, 38–39, 51, 53,
   55, 62
Admiralty Court, 154
Admiralty laws, 29, 32, 72, 73–74, 75, 151
Africa: deportation to, 2, 39;
   immigration from, 11; influence on
   black seamen, 44–45, 64; black
   perspective on, 45; boatmen, 47–50;
   trading, 54
African Marine Fund, 160
Ages of seamen, 170, 189
Alabama, 199
American Revolution, 6, 23, 71, 153;
   freedom/amnesty for slaves and, 3,
   4, 94, 153–154, 157; runaway slaves
   during, 28
American Seamen's Friend Society, 228
American Seamen's Protective Union
   Association, 181–182
Angola, 45, 49, 50, 64
Antigua, 17, 20, 109, 196
Antislavery movement, 20, 37, 149, 185,
   211–212. *See also* Abolitionism;
   Freedom
Argentina, 109

Atlantic maritime system, 9, 100, 215, 232
Attucks, Crispus, 96, 185, 222
Authority, 11, 74, 88, 127; of black
   seamen, 14–15, 54, 131–132, 138–139,
   221; discipline and, 72; attitudes
   and resistance to, 75, 96, 102, 145,
   216–217; of blacks, 112, 129;
   religious, 124. *See also* Captains,
   black
Autobiographies of black seamen, 4, 6,
   9, 16, 37, 38
Autonomy: of black seamen, 50, 128,
   138; of blacks, 103, 113; of slave
   captains and pilots, 140, 143–144.
   See also Mobility of blacks

Bahama Islands, 13, 18, 19, 204–205
Baltimore, 33, 223, 231; black sailors
   shipping out of, 155, 165, 221–222;
   seafaring wages, 161, 222; hiring
   practices, 228
Barbados, 9, 12, 37, 38, 52, 109; slavery
   and slave trade, 10, 18, 32, 58, 72, 133
Bay of Campeche, 7, 14
Benevolent societies, 4, 27, 124, 160,
   181–182, 184, 197, 228
Bermuda, 19, 153–154, 231
Bight of Benin, 58, 63
Black communities, 37, 38, 145, 167;
   free, promise of freedom and, 4,
   157, 158, 161, 166, 189, 214; identity

Black communities *(continued)*
with, 38, 231; religion in, 122–124;
fragmentation of, 188; outside
influences on, 216; on board ship,
221. *See also* Creation of black
America
Boardinghouses, 165, 166–167, 182–189,
207; striking seamen and, 87; as
clearinghouses for seafaring
employment, 188, 189, 222, 226, 227,
228, 229
Boatmen, slave, 18, 23, 54, 133–134;
communication with seamen, 17,
62; number of, 19, 26, 27; fugitive
slaves and, 21; mobility, 23–24, 134,
135; African, 47–50; identity among,
135. *See also* Canoe(s) and
canoemen
Boston: black population, 26, 111, 231;
riots, 27, 96; slavery and, 72, 149,
204; black sailors shipping out of,
220; crimps' organized labor
hiring, 226
Bounty and prize money, 71, 86–87,
98, 117
Boxing, 103, 111, 113, 117–119
Boy (position on ships), 77, 79, 80, 81,
83, 135
Brazil, 119
Brothels and bawdy houses, 160,
186–187, 198–199. *See also*
Prostitution
Brotherly Union Society, 160
Brown, William Wells, 2, 3, 166
Buccaneering, 13–14, 51
Bum boats, 17

Caesar (slave), 30, 44, 45, 83
Cannibalism, 94
Canoe(s) and canoemen, 19, 45, 56;
African, 47–48, 54, 55, 61; skill in
handling, 48–49, 50, 60; trade, 48,
50, 52, 55; spiritual connections to,
49, 50, 61; sailing, 51, 60; desertion
among, 54–55; strike by, 59;
Jamaican, 61, 131

Cape François, 144, 145, 152. *See also*
Haiti; St. Domingue
Cape Verde Islands, 51
Capitalism, 3, 10, 11, 28, 48, 54, 86;
ethos of trust and, 141–142
Capstans, 82–83
Captains (general discussion), 79, 85, 88
Captains, black: slave (patroons),
23–25, 28, 133, 135, 136, 139, 140, 142,
143, 157; outlawed from command,
174–175; free, 158–159, 160, 162–163,
164, 172, 173, 174–175, 176, 231
Captains, white, 15, 26; slaves owned
and sold by, 4, 18, 25, 27, 34, 194;
resistance to, 5, 85; abuse of sailors
by, 11, 29, 72–73, 85, 123, 180, 219,
225; sale of black seamen by, 52–53,
70–71; responsibility for runaways
and jailed sailors, 154–155, 211; legal
actions against, 204, 207–208;
alliances with black sailors, 208,
225; black sailors as prisoners of,
208–209; patriarchal relations with
sailors, 225–226. *See also* Hiring
practices
Career seamen, 178, 188, 222–223, 225
Caribbean, 13, 21, 41, 99, 199;
plantation system, 4; slavery in, 17,
18–19, 31, 155, 156; slave boatmen
and captains, 54, 133–134, 136; slave
rebellion in, 144–146. *See also*
specific islands
Carolina low country, 21, 22, 23, 54
Cato (slave), 23, 83, 222
Cesar (slave), 25
Charleston, 22, 23, 30, 84, 191;
maritime slavery in, 155, 156, 192;
seafaring wages, 161; slave
rebellions in, 193–194, 196, 198;
jailing of blacks, 203, 204, 205, 206,
208
Chesapeake Bay: slavery in, 1, 24–26,
28, 94, 154, 155; slave-managed
vessels, 23, 24–25, 132
Christianity, 37, 39, 87, 95, 124
Churches, 4. *See also* Religion

Citizenship: status of blacks, 5, 72, 115, 117; of seamen, 85–86; during rebellions, 147–148; protection of, 150–152; restrictions, 172, 174

Civil War, 2

Class stratification, 208, 224, 225–226, 227

Coastal shipping, 17, 18, 55, 170–171; slave seamen in, 21, 22, 23, 133–135, 154, 176; black captains, 140, 174–175, 231; free blacks in, 154, 165, 172, 174–175, 188. *See also* Boatmen, slave; Canoe(s) and canoemen

Colonization movement, 39

Coloured Sailors' Home, New York City, 178, 183, 199, 206, 227

Communication among blacks, 24, 203; by sailors, 3, 5, 6, 19–20, 40–41, 52, 134, 138, 144–145, 192, 199, 215–216, 230, 231; by slaves with black and white seamen, 17, 18, 21, 173, 202–203; by slave seamen with land-based slaves, 23, 30, 36, 39–40, 135; regarding rebellions and the struggle for freedom, 144–145, 146, 149, 181, 193–194, 196, 197–198, 199–200, 205, 211–212, 213

Communities. *See* Black communities

Competition, 140, 175; blacks and whites for seafaring jobs, 5, 17–18, 224, 229; labor force, 224–225

Confinement on board ship, 29–30. *See also* Jailing of black sailors

Congo. *See* Kongo

Connecticut, 27, 73, 153

"Contrabands," 133

Convict-lease system, 203

Cooks, 168–169, 176; black, 3, 30, 32, 33, 35, 77, 81–82, 167–168, 188–189, 216, 224, 225, 228; wages of, 76, 161, 168; white, 167, 222

Courts. *See* Legal actions

Crafus, Richard (King Dick), 102–103, 107, 108, 109, 110–111, 112, 118

Creation of black America, 36, 215, 230, 232. *See also* Black communities

Creoles/creolization, 9–10, 12, 38, 53, 66, 67

Crews: all-black, 19, 143, 146, 162, 209, 218, 220, 221–222, 224; all-white, 218

Crimps, 219, 225, 226–229, 231. *See also* Hiring practices

Crossing the line ceremony, 99–100

Cuba, 199, 205, 206

Cuffe, Paul, 2, 36, 39, 160, 164, 171, 172, 173, 176

Culture and customs, 34, 64, 66; maritime, 4, 5, 45–47, 80, 91, 100, 215, 218; African American, 17, 35, 37, 45, 49, 108, 126, 230; black hybrid, 21, 39, 42, 52, 232; African, 37, 39, 45, 58–59, 62–67; slave, 39, 65; black/white differences, 62, 66, 90–91, 130. *See also* Acculturation of blacks; Seafaring tradition and culture

Dangers at sea, 3, 43, 94, 179, 189, 229; weather 3, 5, 29, 61, 79, 83, 84, 179; disease, 26, 29, 58, 69, 85, 179; failure of equipment, 29, 94, 181; navigational errors, 29, 132. *See also* Death at sea

Dartmoor Prison: black prisoners in, 102, 105, 107, 110, 112, 113, 114; racial dynamics in, 102–103, 105–106, 109, 112, 113–114, 116, 122, 127, 128–130, 230–231; black autonomy in, 103, 130; black culture in, 103, 104, 127; boxing and sports, 103, 111, 113, 118–119, 122, 129; music and dancing, 103, 113, 121–122, 126, 217; fights and riots, 104, 111, 115–116, 126, 127–128, 130; deaths, 105, 126, 127; market, 105, 106–107, 127, 128, 130; government and discipline among prisoners, 107–112, 128, 130; white prisoners in, 109, 113; theater, 113, 120–121, 122, 126, 127; patriotism in, 115–116, 127; religion in, 122, 123–126, 127, 129; gambling, 126–127

Death at sea: of pirates, 15, 16; of

Death at sea *(continued)*
sailors, 29, 60, 61, 104; symbolic, 43; murder, 146, 180, 225; effect on communities and families, 170, 175
Deep-sea work and sailors, 16, 18, 19, 47–48, 70, 170; black seamen, 23, 25, 26, 47, 74, 188
Deficiency Laws, 17–18
Defoe, Daniel, 14
Desertion of black and slave seamen, 3, 23–24, 29, 30, 75, 85; canoemen, 54–55; from Royal Navy, 71; laws regarding, 73, 209; during rebellions, 144–145; to Haiti, 147–150, 151; captain's responsibility for, 154–155; imprisonment, 196. *See also* Freedom
Desertion of white seamen, 25, 58, 75, 85
Diaspora, black, 3, 21, 36, 37, 39, 43, 152, 214; identity and, 38, 41, 230; martial arts and, 119–120
Discipline: aboard ship, 11, 72–73, 114; floggings, 71, 72, 73, 112–114, 179–180; group, 112–113. *See also* Dartmoor Prison: government and discipline among prisoners
Douglass, Frederick, 1–2, 135, 139, 142, 185, 222
Dred Scott Decision, 166
Dress and style of sailors, 68, 70, 91–92, 111, 138–139, 146, 217
Drinking, 73, 160, 184
Droghers, 19, 134
Du Bois, W. E. B., 111–112, 223
Dunmore, Lord/Dunmore Proclamation, 3, 94

Economic condition of blacks, 2, 4, 6, 9, 74, 175–176. *See also* Occupations; Wages, black
Education, 39, 89, 176. *See also* Skills, seafaring
Egalitarianism, 3, 13, 91, 100, 127, 167, 228
Elites: white, 39, 73; black maritime slaves, 132, 133, 140, 141, 142, 143, 144, 157; black, 202

Ellison, Ralph, 230
Emancipation, 6, 36, 215–216, 230. *See also* Abolitionism; Antislavery movement; Freedom
Employment. *See* Hiring practices; Occupations
England, 7, 10, 22–23, 115; promise of freedom in, 3, 19, 20. *See also* Dartmoor Prison; London; Royal Navy
Entrepreneurship, 10, 19, 159, 162, 173, 175; of slave captains and pilots, 143–144; black maritime, 171–175; of free blacks, 207
Equiano, Olaudah, 31–40, 57, 86, 123; shiphandling skills, 61, 137; interaction with whites, 62, 97–99; purchase of freedom, 143
Exploitation of black seamen, 34, 54, 96, 101, 181, 182, 219; coping strategies, 89, 208; economic, 113, 189, 209; in boardinghouses, 183, 219

Family life of sailors, 2, 5, 13, 72, 115, 117, 171, 188; dependency on seafaring wages, 4, 159, 161, 165, 166, 169, 175, 188, 189, 218; land ownership, 158, 162, 163–165, 166, 189; working wives, 164, 165–166; stability in, 165, 173, 178; irregular work schedules, 169–170
Flogging. *See* Discipline
Folk tales, slave, 142. *See also* Storytelling
Food, 58, 59, 85. *See also* Cooks
Forecastle life, 2, 29, 81, 88–91, 102, 110, 176, 177, 220–221
Forten, James, 36, 39, 160
Free African Union Society, 27
Free black convention movement, 214
Freedom, 31, 153; runaway slaves, 1–4, 7, 12, 15, 18, 20, 21, 24–25, 28, 32, 36, 73, 74, 94, 137–138, 148–149, 185, 191, 211, 232; yearnings and struggle for, 1, 2, 6, 7, 12–13, 21, 132, 133, 151, 153, 212–213; of slave seamen compared with land-based slaves, 12, 20, 133,

142–143; through piracy, 14; negotiation and purchase of, 20–21, 141, 143, 161, 210; through seafaring, 25, 29, 137–138, 144, 219; through naval service, 32, 72; individual, 143, 144, 145, 153; through rebellion, 144–145; through privateering, 153–154; aid or betrayal of runaways by black seamen, 211, 212–213. *See also* Emancipation; Manumission

French Revolution, 157

Fugitive Slave Law, 166

Funerary practices, 39, 64, 65

Gambia, 48, 50, 51

Gambling, 74, 160, 185

Garvey, Marcus, 6, 229

General Colored Association of Massachusetts, 197

Georgia, 153, 156, 198, 200, 208

Gloucester, 41, 42

Government, black: in New England, 108, 111–112; self-rule, 109, 110, 112, 113, 130. *See also* Dartmoor Prison: government and discipline among prisoners

Grenada, 19, 20–21, 74, 156

Grumetes, 47, 49, 50, 51, 53, 54, 60

Guinea marks. *See* Scarification, ritualized

Haiti, 109, 145; revolution and independence, 36, 40, 134, 144, 145, 147, 157, 231; freedom and citizenship offered to blacks, 147–149, 150–152, 157, 231; laws, 148, 149–150, 152–153. *See also* St. Domingue

Hall, Prince, 36

Hammon, Briton, 7–9, 26, 28, 35, 36

Hazing, 77, 80

Head-butting contests, 119–120

Henson, Matthew, 6

Hierarchy, 27, 31; on board ship, 74, 76, 78, 100; social, 74, 137; of skill, 79; race-blind, 80–81; of race, 101, 113, 137; of boardinghouses, 183–184

Hiring practices, 6, 22, 26, 159, 224–229; slaves hired out as seamen, 4, 22, 133, 134, 154–156; of captains, 26, 154, 224, 225, 226–229; of slaveowners, 28; recruitment by force, 71; of boardinghouse middlemen, 188, 189; racist, 209, 220, 227, 228; social trends and, 223, 224. *See also* Impressment and press gangs

History, maritime, 2, 232

Hughes, Langston, 6, 229

Hybridity, cultural, 21, 39, 42, 52, 232

Identity/sense of self: African American, 2, 42, 117; of free blacks, 5, 188; collective, 6, 35, 51; of white men, 15, 70; of black seamen, 28, 117, 135, 143, 144, 169, 170, 215; racial, 35–36, 93, 101; as seamen, 37, 56, 187–188; self-definition, 37, 38, 39, 62, 63; African, 38–39, 41; with black community/black pride, 38, 141–142, 169, 182; occupational, 54, 92, 101, 132, 137, 139, 182; through tattoos, 92–93; through naming practices, 216. *See also* Masculinity/manliness

Impressment and press gangs, 30–31, 85, 93, 117; by Royal Navy, 26, 30, 31, 42, 58, 70, 71, 103, 113; preference for imprisonment over, 113, 114, 115

Incarceration. *See* Jailing of black sailors

Indians. *See* Native Americans

Individualism, 41, 143

Jailing of black sailors, 85, 96, 202, 203, 211, 229; in southern ports, 190–191, 195, 196, 198, 199, 200, 205, 206, 210–211, 213, 231; chain-gangs, 202, 204, 214; as exploitation, 203–204; protest against, 204–205; cost of imprisonment paid by prisoners, 206–208

Jamaica, 4, 31, 49, 109, 134, 147; as destination, 7, 52–53, 131; slavery in,

Jamaica *(continued)*
18, 136; black population, 37, 39;
canoemen, 61, 131
Jea, John, 38, 40, 77, 78, 87, 88, 95, 100,
231
"John Canoe" spiritual representation,
65
Jones, John Paul, 92

Kalunga line, 63, 64, 65
Kidd, William, 15, 16
Kidnapping, 5. *See also* Impressment
and press gangs; Man-stealing
King, Boston, 95, 100, 123
King Charles (elected black leader), 108
Knowles riot, 27
Kongo, 49, 63–64, 65, 119
Kru, 49–50

Labor market, maritime, 26, 28, 45,
224–225, 226. *See also* Hiring
practices; Shortages of seamen
Labor organization, 34–35
Labor unions, 181, 216
Land and property of blacks, 158, 162,
163–165, 166, 189
Laws, 24, 69, 73, 75; slave, 11, 98;
seafaring, 25, 69, 73–74, 132, 193,
205; citizenship, 85–86; restricting
free blacks, 194–196, 198, 199, 200,
205–206; racist, 200, 214; restricting
black wages, 206, 209. *See also*
Legal actions; Negro Seamen Acts;
specific states
Leadership, black, 2, 5, 36, 56, 108, 143;
in maritime culture, 96–97, 110,
143; religious, 124–126, 129. *See also*
Authority; Captains, black
Legal actions, 82, 108, 155, 209–210,
214, 216; suing for wages, 86;
against white captains, 204, 207–208
Liberia, 49
Lighters/lightering, 19, 60
Liverpool, 68, 161, 205
London, 149, 205, 225; black
population, 19, 20–21, 66–67
Louisiana, 198, 199, 200, 204, 208–210

Manhattan Anti-Slavery Society, 211
Man-stealing, 149, 184, 185, 200–201,
202. *See also* Impressment and
press gangs; Kidnapping
Manumission, 20, 132, 137, 200, 213
Maritime slavery, 10, 12, 16–28, 47,
51–52, 134, 154–157; plantation
system and, 15–16; in British Navy,
23; as institution, 24–25; decline
and extinction of, 35, 154–157. *See
also* Seamen, slave; Slavery
Market: values, 39, 144, 157;
involvement of slaves in, 140, 141,
142, 143; maritime labor, 154, 175,
178. *See also* Dartmoor Prison:
market
Markets, slave/slave trade, 3, 10, 11
Marlinspike seamanship, 80
Marriage of sailors, 41, 42. *See also*
Family life of sailors
Martial arts, 113, 119–120
Maryland, 24, 25, 53, 135, 155
Masculinity/manliness, 4, 76, 119, 181,
182, 211; patriotism and, 104;
authority and, 110; race and, 117;
providership and, 166, 167, 169, 170,
218; identity through, 167, 188; skill
and, 167
Massachusetts, 7, 17, 204; slave seamen
in, 5, 11–12, 27–28, 33, 164; abolition
of slavery, 41, 154; navy, 153; laws,
154; black population, 171, 172
Melville, Herman, 68, 76
Middle-class blacks and seafaring, 160,
222
Minstrelsy. *See* Music and musicians
Mississippi, 201, 202
Mobility of blacks, 20, 21–24, 134, 135,
172, 213–214; skill and, 24, 40; as
threat to whites, 40; social, 54; of
free and slave seamen, 75–76, 85,
134, 176, 192, 198; laws restricting,
199
Mortality rates. *See* Death at sea
Mulattoes, 16, 76, 121, 167, 168; as ship
masters, 25, 146; sailors, 26, 81; in
slave revolts, 199; as free blacks, 213

Multigenerational black seafaring, 43
Multilingual blacks (linguists, interpreters), 4, 9, 40–41, 50, 52, 54
Music and musicians, 32, 33–34, 70; laboring songs, 59; shanteys, 83, 93, 199, 207, 215, 217; folk songs, 90; African, 120, 121–122; interracial exchange through, 217–218
Mutiny, 2, 53, 57, 70–71, 94, 116, 132, 148, 181, 225

Naming practices, 136–137, 216
Napoleonic Wars, 114, 155, 158
Nationalism, 3, 37–38, 94, 150–151. *See also* Patriotism
Native Americans, 28, 42, 60–61, 164, 165, 195
Navy. *See* Royal Navy; U.S. Navy
Negro Election Day, 108, 109–110, 111, 121
Negrophobia, 163
Negro Seamen Acts, 172, 199, 200, 202–203, 205, 208, 210, 214, 231
Nell, William C., 82, 168
Neutral trade, 155, 158, 161
Nevis, 18–19
New England, 219, 221; slavery in, 12, 27, 61; black elections in, 108, 109–110, 112; hiring practices, 223–224. *See also specific states*
New Hampshire, 27, 73
New Jersey, 108
New Orleans, 109, 191; black seamen in, 175, 198–199, 200, 210; jailing of black sailors, 203, 204, 205–206, 207; crimps' organized labor hiring, 226
New York, 73, 74, 108
New York City, 115, 121, 160, 178; seafaring wages in, 161; black sailors shipping out of, 176, 191, 220, 221; boardinghouses, 183, 185–186, 211; maritime labor market, 224
New York Committee of Vigilance, 184
North Carolina, 31, 132, 155, 198

Oars/oarsmen, 59, 61
Occam, Samson, 164

Occupations: seafaring opportunities for blacks, 3, 4, 5, 6, 76–77, 82, 136, 158, 200, 216, 224, 228, 229; seafaring opportunities for whites, 4, 77; black/white competition for jobs, 5, 17–18, 224, 229; of slaves, 17, 18, 19, 21–22, 136; on board ship, 69, 75–76, 79; stability in, 163–164; decline of seafaring opportunities, 215–216, 218–219, 220, 222. *See also specific jobs on ships*; Work/workplace, maritime
Order, concept of, 74–75, 100
Ordinary seamen, 76, 77, 79, 80, 81, 83, 161
Organizations, black, 159, 160, 176. *See also* Benevolent societies

Passports, 213
Patriotism, 104, 114, 115–117. *See also* Nationalism
Patronage, 41, 224–225, 226
Patroons. *See* Captains, black: slave
Pay. *See* Wages
Pennsylvania, 26
Perquisites, 31, 32, 59, 136, 199; of black seamen, 36–37, 75, 135
Persistence at sea, 177–178, 222–223
Pettiaugers, 4, 14, 45, 60–61, 133
Philadelphia, 26, 160; as destination for runaway slaves, 2, 149; slavery and black population, 3, 26, 115; black sailors shipping out of, 38, 165, 176, 221; coastal trade, 170–171; riots in, 214; maritime labor market, 224
Pilots: slaves as, 23, 79, 131–133, 137–139, 140, 143; African seamen as, 50, 96, 110; as slave owners, 201. *See also* Captains
Pinks, 14, 42
Pinkster holiday, 108, 109
Piracy, 9, 13–15, 51, 152
Plantation system, 6, 9, 10–11, 13, 45; Caribbean, 4; Atlantic, 10, 11, 32; maritime slavery and, 16–17, 25, 142; outside influences on, 26;

Plantation system *(continued)*
  compared with seafaring, 37, 41,
  135; isolation of slaves in, 142
Political economy, Atlantic, 26, 30, 101
Politics/political structure, 30, 39,
  108–109, 110; on board ship, 89; of
  class, 90; of race, 90, 150
Portugal, 50, 51, 54
Poverty and homelessness, 178, 179,
  182, 183, 188
Powell, William P., 185, 186, 188, 199,
  206, 211, 227
Press gangs. *See* Impressment and
  press gangs
Prison. *See* Dartmoor Prison; Jailing
  of black sailors
Privateering, 12, 31, 33, 52, 71, 77; by
  black freemen and slaves, 32, 34,
  86–87, 153–154.
Prostitution, 166, 186–187, 228
Providence African Union Society, 160
Providership, 166, 167, 169, 170, 175
Psychology: of seamen, 4, 29, 62, 67,
  95, 101, 182; of dependency, 74; of
  slave captains, 140–141, 143; of
  freedom, 157
Puerto Rico, 199, 205

Quartermasters, 14–15, 16

Race and racism, 3, 10, 178, 180, 196,
  230; on board ship, 5, 34–35, 61, 69,
  75, 77, 80, 93–97, 100–101, 214–216,
  218, 220, 221; in slave societies, 10,
  14, 56; piracy and, 15–16; stereotypes,
  32, 34, 69, 82, 103, 110, 111, 112, 122,
  128, 129; black authors' perspectives
  on, 37; relations, 74; boundaries, 75;
  vs. skill, 82; attitudes, 176, 177, 227;
  segregation, 216, 218
Rebellion and conspiracies of blacks,
  2, 3, 4, 23, 27, 40, 157; subversion,
  21, 23, 26; rioting in Africa, 55;
  insurrection, 96; black seamen as
  agents of, 146, 181, 193–194, 196, 197,
  199, 211–213; whites' fear of, 146–147,
  199; racial violence, 180, 214, 219

Recruitment. *See* Hiring practices;
  Impressment and press gangs; Ship's
  articles
Religion: evangelical, 3, 111–112,
  124–125, 129; Christianity, 37, 39, 87,
  95, 124; Catholicism, 51, 151;
  African, 64, 65; South American,
  66; Protestantism, 94; black, in
  white communities, 123; in
  maritime culture, 123–124, 125;
  slave, 124; antislavery movement
  and, 214. *See also* Spirituality
Reputations, 1–4, 162, 180–181
Residential patterns. *See* Family life of
  sailors
Rhode Island, 27, 31, 33, 159, 161; black
  sailors shipping out of, 220, 222, 223
Rigging. *See* Sails and rigging
Roles on ship board. *See* Occupations
Rope work, 80
Royal Navy, 9, 51, 71, 113–114; blacks in,
  30–32, 70–72, 96, 117; whites in,
  30–31; conditions on board ships,
  31; black withdrawal from, 114, 115.
  See also Impressment and press
  gangs: by Royal Navy
Runaway slaves. *See* Desertion of
  black and slave seamen; Freedom

Sailors' Bethel Movement, 124
Sails and rigging, 51, 69, 80, 81, 83, 160
St. Domingue, 40, 144, 145, 146, 154,
  193. *See also* Haiti
Savannah, 23, 191, 198, 200, 206
Scarification, ritualized ("Guinea
  marks"), 2, 44, 45, 57, 62, 93
Seafaring technology, 57
Seafaring tradition and culture, 84, 90;
  Atlantic maritime, 30, 45, 56–57, 62,
  66, 69–70, 75; African, 50;
  black/white differences in, 66
Seaman's Protection Certificates, 1–2,
  5, 93, 124, 151
Seamen, free black, 2, 4, 6, 157,
  159–160; influence on black society,
  27, 162, 191; fear of impressment,
  30–31; status of, 36–37; African, 50;

exploitation of, 54; number of, 69–70, 178; materialism and, 86–87; Haitian Revolution and, 145–146; employment opportunities, 159, 214, 219; irregular work schedules, 163, 165, 218, 222; deep-sea vs. coastal, 165, 171–172; ages of, 170, 189; equality with white seamen, 176; racism and, 190; dangers and incarceration in ports, 190–191, 195, 196, 198, 199, 200, 207–209, 214; slavery and, 191–192, 194, 198; aid to runaway slaves, 199, 214; isolation of, 221; career seafaring, 222–223, 225; patronage system and, 224–225. *See also* Captains, black; Desertion of black and slave seamen

Seamen, slave, 4, 6, 22–23, 27; African descent and identity, 3, 4, 11, 56–57, 62, 147, 230; isolation of, 30, 33, 62, 91, 159; roles on board ship, 32–33; interaction with white seamen, 62, 68–69, 93–96; number of, 70; black sailors' opinions of, 100; Haitian Revolution and, 145–146. *See also* Captains, black; Desertion of black and slave seamen; Hiring practices

Seamen, white, 6, 19; cooperation and amicable relations with black sailors, 4–5, 13, 69, 70, 71, 82–84, 87–88, 90–91, 93, 99, 100, 101, 130, 230; status of, 37–38, 70; death rates, 58; on slave ships, 58–59; number of, 69–70; situational slavery of, 70; hostile relations with black sailors, 93–95, 97–98, 139, 229; aid to runaway slaves, 96; employment opportunities, 219, 223

Segregation, 105, 216, 218

Sex. *See* Prostitution

Shanteys. *See* Music and musicians

Ship construction and ownership, 22, 25

Ship's articles, 33, 75, 79, 207, 210–211, 226, 227

Shortages of seamen, 22–23, 25, 26, 30, 58, 71, 73–74, 155. *See also* Hiring practices

Sierra Leone (Upper Guinea), 50, 51–52, 61

Skills, seafaring, 1, 7, 32, 78; of black sailors, 12, 13, 14, 15, 18, 52, 60, 61, 77, 78, 97, 131, 137, 143, 218, 223; of runaway slaves, 24, 28, 40, 155; African, 45–51, 52, 58–59; shiphandling, 45, 48–49, 58, 61, 78–79, 97, 132–133, 135–136, 137, 139; European, 50, 58; protection of knowledge, 57–58; status defined by, 75, 78, 80–81; inexperience and, 77–78, 80; navigation and ship maintenance, 78–79; race and, 82, 110

Slave codes, 64, 113, 142, 148

Slave insurrections. *See* Rebellion and conspiracies of blacks

Slaveowners and masters, 26, 28, 30, 51, 61–62

Slavery, 3, 37, 45, 61, 202; as metaphor, 1, 101, 219; capitalism and, 10–11; benevolent, 35, 192; black perspective on, 37, 213; independence within bounds of, 133, 137–138, 192; effect of market economy on, 141; runaway slaves and, 148–149; war against, 195; free blacks sold into, 213. *See also* Maritime slavery

Slaves (general discussion): contact with free blacks, 3–4; registration of, 18; societies, 24, 91, 143; view of whites, 38; status of, 55–56; transportation needs, 60; as prizes, 154

Slave ships/slavers, 2–3, 53, 55, 58–59, 160

Slave trade, 51–52, 55, 115

Smuggling, 11

Society/social structure, 4, 13, 27, 35, 42, 55; slave, 24, 91, 143; race in, 34, 35; American, 45; African, 54, 64; on board ship, 68–69, 74, 75, 78, 97, 100, 221, 225, 230; antebellum, 227, 229; African American, 229

Somersett, James/Somersett case, 20, 98

South Carolina, 57; slave rebellions, 2, 147–148; maritime slavery, 21–22, 23, 62, 155, 156, 214; black population, 37, 38; slave imports, 49–50; laws, 73, 74, 147, 156, 172–173, 194, 203, 205; navy, 153; jailing of blacks, 206, 208

South Carolina Association, 196

Spirituality, 39, 41, 42, 45, 49, 58, 62. *See also* Religion; Water

Stevedores, 27, 134, 217

Steward and Cooks' Marine Benevolent Society, 182

Stewards, 176, 225; black, 32, 33, 35, 81–82, 167–168, 169, 188–189, 216, 225, 228; wages of, 166, 168; white, 167, 222; jailing of, 207

Storytelling (yarning), 1, 36, 40–41, 42, 88–90; of African roots, 42–43; of freedom, 43; by white sailors, 52; of resistance, 59

Strikes, 59, 87–88

Tattoos, 92–93

Taverns, 17, 33, 86, 227

Teach, Edward (Blackbeard), 14

Tobacco, 24, 25, 26

Trials and courts. *See* Legal actions

Upper Guinea. *See Grumetes;* Sierra Leone

U.S. Navy, 223, 224

Venezuela, 109, 119

Vesey, Denmark, 2, 36, 40, 192–194, 196–199, 213

Virginia, 3, 10, 14, 24, 25, 74, 153, 155

Wages (general discussion), 28, 74, 85, 86–87, 155; inadequacy of, 86–87, 157, 159, 161–162, 165, 218; equality of, 161, 178

Wages, black, 23, 24, 113, 189, 209; slave seamen, 4, 5, 20, 138, 159; withholding of, 9, 24, 54, 71, 86, 98, 117, 206–208; compared with white wages, 28, 76, 161, 213, 222

Wages, white, 28, 70, 76, 161, 213, 222

Walker, David, 197–198, 199, 200

War at sea, 30, 32

War of 1812, 103–104, 230

Watches, 79, 84

Water: African spirits in, 29, 45–47, 62–66; death by, 60, 61; power of, 62; Kalunga line, 63, 64, 65

West Indies, 3, 15, 17, 37–38, 97, 119, 152; slavery, 18, 31, 62, 94, 202; black seafaring, 19, 20, 132; white sailors in, 31, 99; slave rebellion, 144; emancipation, 202, 211

Whaling, 28, 162, 163, 177; slaves in, 28, 168; wages, 161, 165, 177, 178–179; manliness of, 176–177; black seamen in, 177–179, 220, 228; share system, 179

Whites: attitude toward blacks, 2, 12, 13, 32, 56. *See also* Captains, white; Race and racism; Wages, white

Widows. *See* Death at sea: effect on communities and families

Windlasses, 82–83

Women, 5; pirates, 15–16; rape of, 93; market, 106; working sailors' wives, 164, 165–166; prostitutes, 166, 186–187, 228; singers, 217. *See also* Family life of sailors

Work/workplace, maritime, 6, 68; allocation of labor, 22, 79–80, 82, 222; variances in nature of, 54, 69, 222; working conditions, 69, 180–181; collective, 82–84; black/white equality of, 213; anonymity in, 216; specialized workforce, 225–226. *See also* Occupations

Worldliness through travel, 2, 9, 19–20, 28, 36, 42, 187–188, 231, 232; mobility of blacks, 21, 22, 23–24, 134, 135, 138; spread of revolutionary ideas, 40–41, 213. *See also* Communication among blacks

Yarning. *See* Storytelling